FROM TA'IZZ TO TYNESIDE

An Arab Community in the North-East of England
during the Early Twentieth Century

Richard Lawless is a former Director of the Centre for Middle Eastern and Islamic Studies in the University of Durham and is now Emeritus Reader in Middle Eastern Studies. His main fields of research are state and society in contemporary North Africa, international migration in the Middle East, and Muslim communities in Europe. He has published extensively on these subjects. Among his many books and articles are: "The Changing Middle Eastern City" Croom Helm, London and Barnes and Noble Books, New York, 1980: "North Africa: contemporary politics and economic development", Croom Helm, London and St Martin's Press, New York, 1984: "War and refugees—the Western Sahara conflict" Pinter, London and New York, 1987, and "The Middle Eastern village: changing economic and social relations", Croom Helm, London and New York, 1987.

The background illustration on the cover shows Ta'izz, the major town in the southern highlands of the Yemen (the region from which most of the Arab seamen on Tyneside originated).

The inset is Salem Abuzed's seamen's boarding-house in East Holborn, South Shields (Courtesy of South Tyneside Libraries). Until the 1930s most Arab seamen in South Shields lived in the riverside district of Holborn, where the Arab boarding-houses were located. During the First World War, Abuzed, a seaman, had been interned for almost three years in the German prisoner-of-war camp at Ruhleben. He went into business as a boarding-house keeper after his release at the end of the war.

FROM TA'IZZ TO TYNESIDE

*An Arab Community in the North-East of
England during the Early Twentieth Century*

Richard I. Lawless

UNIVERSITY
of
EXETER
PRESS

First published in 1995
University of Exeter Press
Reed Hall, Streatham Drive
Exeter, Devon EX4 4QR
UK

British Library Cataloguing in Publication Data
A catalogue record of this book is
available from the British Library

Hardback ISBN 0 85989 447 9
Paperback ISBN 0 85989 460 6

Typeset in 10/12pt Monotype Plantin by
Kestrel Data, Exeter
Printed and bound in Great Britain
by Short Run Press Ltd, Exeter

Contents

Acknowledgements

The initial research for this book was carried out with the assistance of grants from the World of Islam Festival Trust and the Government of the former Yemen Arab Republic. I am particularly indebted to Alistair Duncan, the Director of the World of Islam Festival Trust, and to H.E. Dr Hussain al-Amri for their encouragement and assistance in this project.

Additional funding from the British Council enabled me to travel to Yemen during 1986 and to visit some of the villages of origin of the Arab community in South Shields. The British Council in London and Sanaa and the Centre for Yemeni Studies and Research, University of Sanaa, were most helpful in making the arrangements for this visit. The Arab–British Chamber of Commerce, the British–Yemeni Society, the Seven Pillars of Wisdom Trust and the World of Islam Festival Trust generously contributed to the cost of publication of the book.

I should like to record a special debt of gratitude to Brigid O'Connor who undertook most of the research into local newspapers and also provided invaluable help during interviews in the Arab community in South Shields. Doris Johnson and Keith Bardwell of the Local Studies Library, South Tyneside Libraries, South Shields introduced me to local documentary sources and provided much help, assistance and advice throughout the project.

Penelope Tuson, Curator of Middle East Archives at the Oriental and India Office Collections of the British Library, gave me valuable advice on relevant material held in the extensive archives of the Aden Residency and Colony. The late Professor R.B. Serjeant generously shared with me his experiences of the Yemeni communities on Tyneside and in Cardiff during the early 1940s and provided much valuable background information on Yemen.

Heather Bleaney edited the manuscript with meticulous care and attention to detail and helped to sort out the numerous inconsistencies in the transliteration of Arab names.

Above all I must thank those members of the Arab community in South Shields who welcomed me into their homes with great courtesy and unfailing hospitality and gave up their time to answer my questions. It was always a great pleasure to visit them. Mr and Mrs Hussein and Mr Mohamed Hussein were my first contacts in the community, and it was with their assistance that I was able to meet other members of the community. There was always a friendly welcome at the Hussein's boarding-house in Brunswick Street. Other members of the community who were especially helpful were Mr Norman Hassan, the late Mrs Anne Saleh and the late Mr Michael Muckble. I hope that the many people who assisted me in this project and shared with me their information and insights into the history of the Arab community on Tyneside will not be disappointed by the results.

A note on the transliteration of Arab names
The names of Arab tribes have been transliterated according to the system adoped in *Transliteration of Arabic Proper Names in Common Use in Al Yemen and the Aden Protectorate* (PRO CO 725/34/10). In many cases the rendering of Arab names in the local Tyneside press was a travesty of the original or simply idiosyncratic. As it is sometimes impossible to reconstruct the Arabic form, I have retained the spellings given in the original source.

List of Illustrations

Photographs: plates 1 to 11 are between pages 86 and 87; plates 12 to 24 between pages 182 and 183
  1. The Post Office Pier, Aden in the 1890s
  2. The Mill Dam, South Shields
  3. Muhammad Muckble's seamen's boarding-house in
       East Holborn, South Shields
  4. The *zawiya* established by Sheikh Abdullah Ali al-Hakimi
       in the former Hilda Arms on the corner of Cuthbert Street
       and Smith Street, South Shields
  5. Arab and British supporters of the Seamen's Minority
       Movement
  6. Arab and British seamen at one of the meetings of the
       Seamen's Minority Movement in South Shields
  7. The police keep a watchful eye on the situation as seamen
       cluster in the narrow confines of the Mill Dam on Saturday
       2 August 1930

Introduction

The years leading up to and including the First World War saw the arrival of several thousand Arab seamen at a number of British ports. The major concentrations were found in the Bristol Channel ports, principally Cardiff, and on Tyneside in South Shields. Smaller communities were established in Liverpool and Hull. Most of these seamen came from the Yemen and neighbouring parts of Britain's Aden Protectorate. Together with Somali seamen, they represent the first significant Muslim communities to settle in Britain. Until recently these early Muslim communities have been neglected by researchers, with attention focussing on the later and more numerous Muslim communities from South Asia.

To a certain extent the early twentieth century remains the pre-history of race relations in Britain but one that is now attracting more attention. Much of the existing research on this subject has considered the Arabs to be one component of the black community in Britain along with the West African and West Indian seamen who also settled in some of these ports at this time. Perhaps inevitably, the Arabs' relations with the host community have been given priority. In contrast, the internal dynamics of these Arab communities and their relations with their country of origin and with the wider Muslim world have been neglected. Yet most of the Arab seamen who established themselves at British ports during the early twentieth century were temporary migrants and after a few years working on British ships they returned to their home villages. Most Arab seafarers were therefore temporary sojourners rather than permanent settlers. The vast majority had little contact with British society.

This study examines the economic, social, religious and political life of Arab seamen in South Shields on Tyneside in the first half of the twentieth century. It is the first in-depth study of any of the early Arab seafaring communities in Britain.[1] The Arab community in Cardiff was more important but the local documentary sources are far richer for South Shields. They provide a unique insight into the everyday lives of Arab seamen in Britain and complement information from national archives. By focussing on the relations between the Arab seamen and the host society, on the internal organization and dynamics of this seafaring community, and on the links with their country of origin, the study attempts to cover important aspects of the lives of Arab seamen in Britain that have so far been neglected. Events in South Shields are set in their national and international contexts. The research draws on information from local newspapers and archives in South Shields and Tyneside, from documents held in the Oriental and India Office Collections and Public Record Office, and extensive interviews with Arab seamen and their families, some of whom very kindly allowed me to copy photographs and documents in their possession. In 1986 a short visit was made to some of the villages of origin of the seamen in what is now the Republic of Yemen.

The first chapter looks at the earliest Arab seamen to arrive and establish themselves in South Shields—the 'pioneers' of the Arab community—and at the emergence of an 'Arab colony' there. Most of the Arab seamen who came to South Shields before the First World War had originally been engaged as firemen on steamers calling at the British port of Aden in south-west Arabia. Contrary to popular belief, many of the Arab seamen engaged at Aden served first on foreign ships and only transferred to British ships later after being discharged at European ports. During the First World War the number of Arab seamen living in South Shields and shipping out from north-east ports increased rapidly. The Arab seamen invariably claimed to have been born in Aden but few were actually British subjects. Nevertheless the British authorities upheld their claims to British nationality during the First World War when they formed a useful reserve army of labour.

The port of Aden was occupied by the British in 1839 and developed as an important coaling station on the route from Suez to India and the Far East. This affected Britain's relations with the tribal rulers of the Aden hinterland and the political and economic conditions in the Yemen during the late nineteenth and early twentieth centuries. The British occupation of Aden introduced a new phase of migration from the southern highlands of the Yemen and seafaring was one of the new employment opportunities that opened up as the port of Aden expanded. The tribal origins of the

Arab seamen engaged at Aden, the characteristics of the village societies from which the seamen were drawn and the influence of the tribal sheikhs all played their role in the temporary migration of seamen.

The Arab boarding-house masters in South Shields were the 'big men' of the community. In South Shields, as in other British ports, seamen's boarding-houses were run on ethnic lines. For Arab seamen arriving in a strange land with little knowledge of its language and customs, the Arab boarding-house was virtually essential for their survival. It offered not only accommodation and food that was lawful according to their religion, but its master provided essential assistance to Arab seamen in securing another ship, credit if their resources ran out before they signed on for the next voyage, and help and advice if they were in trouble. The boarding-house masters made strenuous efforts to secure employment for their boarders, but there were bitter rivalries between them over the shipping of men, and they played a role in the illegal entry of Arab seamen into Britain after the First World War. They also acted as local agents in the highly organized networks established by seamen's agents in Aden to assist Arabs eager to travel to Britain in search of employment.

Dramatic changes took place in the lives of Arab seamen in South Shields after the First World War. When the exceptional demands of the war years were over, Arab seamen at British ports found themselves unwanted guests. The demobilization of white British seamen from the armed forces and the onset of the economic depression of the inter-war period, which was particularly marked in the shipping industry, resulted in declining employment opportunities for seamen and intense competition for jobs. Of all the coloured seamen established at British ports, the Arabs became the main target of a rising tide of racial hysteria.

Chapter four describes the serious street violence that erupted in South Shields in 1919 when white crowds attacked Arab boarding-houses and cafes and examines how a number of government and non-government agencies responded to popular demands to regulate and control the Arab community. Restrictive legislation introduced in 1920 and 1925 and its forceful implementation effectively reclassified most Arab seamen as 'coloured aliens' and gave the authorities much greater control over them. Few agencies came to their defence. The Arab seamen themselves failed to organize effectively at the national level, and at the local level their leadership remained faction-torn and divided. Examples of letters written to the local newspaper about the employment of Arabs on

3

British ships are included to illustrate the strength of popular hostility and racial prejudice towards the Arabs in South Shields at this time.

South Shields gained national notoriety at the time of the so-called 'Arab riot' at the Mill Dam on the 2 August 1930 when a crowd of mainly Arab seamen was involved in violent clashes with the local police. Chapter five examines events leading up to these violent clashes and focusses attention on the role of the National Union of Seamen (NUS). During the inter-war period the NUS had become one of the most vocal opponents of the employment of Arab seamen on British ships. In 1929 the NUS had renewed its campaign against the Arabs accusing them of obtaining employment through corrupt methods and demanding their deportation. But the NUS leadership itself was challenged at this time by the rise of the Seamen's Minority Movement. This radical movement denounced the close co-operation between the NUS leadership and the shipowners and called for a new union that would fight for an increase in wages, shorter hours and better working conditions for the ordinary seaman whatever his colour. In May 1930 the South Shields branch of the Seamen's Minority Movement took up the cause of the Arab seamen. In July, when the NUS and shipowners announced the introduction of a rota system of registration for Arab seamen with effect from 1 August, they denounced the new scheme as a new form of control over the Arabs.

Contrary to existing opinion, this research reveals that the Arabs of South Shields were divided on the question of the rota system. Some Arabs opposed it and joined the communist-led Seamen's Minority Movement. Those who were willing to accept the new scheme were led by local officials of the Western Islamic Association and had the support of the association's national leadership. Tensions at the Mill Dam rose dramatically at the end of July as the Seamen's Minority Movement and their Arab supporters picketed the NUS and Board of Trade Offices. The violent disturbances which took place on 2 August 1930 are analysed using original transcripts from the subsequent trial of the Arabs and Minority Movement members arrested for their part in the riot. On the basis of these documents, which other researchers have failed to utilize, existing interpretations of these events are challenged.

After the Arab riot, the Western Islamic Association played a role in the eventual acceptance of the rota system by the Arab seamen of South Shields and the collapse of resistance to the new scheme. Despite their acceptance of the rota system, unemployment among Arab seamen in the town remained high, yet unemployed and destitute Arabs were denied outdoor relief by the South Shields Public Assistance Committee. When a hundred Arab seamen applied for indoor relief at the Poor Law Institution, commonly known as the South Shields workhouse, angry rate-payers demanded their repatriation. The event hit the national headlines. In January 1931 thirty-eight of the Arab seamen who had accepted indoor relief were deported to Aden. The threat of further deportations forced the Arab boarding-house masters to resume responsibility for those Arab seamen who were unable to find work.

The passing of the British Shipping (Assistance) Act in 1935 further reduced the number of jobs available for Arab seamen and at the same time harsh new restrictions were imposed at Aden on Arab seamen wishing to travel to Britain in search of employment. These restrictions were only relaxed somewhat in the months leading up to the outbreak of the Second World War. Whereas imperial interests had been overruled after the First World War and stringent controls imposed on the entry of Arab seamen into Britain, by 1939, as the war clouds gathered once more over Europe, political considerations came to the fore again and secured a small concession for Arab seamen wishing to enter Britain to seek employment.

The arrival of the Arabs in South Shields generated 'moral panics' and in particular popular resentment at the association of Arabs with white women. The voices of moral outrage were loud and clear and are illustrated by examples of letters written to the local newspaper on the subject. It shows how local officials exploited widespread popular fears of moral danger from 'the Arab menace' and reveals that in the years following the First World War allegations of immorality, feelings of sexual competition and jealousy, fears of miscegenation and the need to defend the purity of the white race, the problem of a growing number of half-caste children and the dangers of disease were all used by the authorities to justify tougher restrictions and controls over the Arab population. Moral dangers were also evoked by some councillors in debates in the Town Council to support demands to limit the number of Arabs in South Shields and to confine them to one part of the town. Not content with segregating the Arabs in one of the most overcrowded parts of the town, they then accused them of being responsible for the slum conditions prevailing there. When a major slum clearance pro-gramme was announced in 1935 affecting large parts of Holborn where most of the Arab community lived, fears were expressed that the Arabs might penetrate into 'good class residential areas'. The Town Council was opposed to the Arabs moving with displaced white slum dwellers to new housing estates and an attempt was made to segregate them by rehousing Arab families in a block of tenement flats. Throughout the long debate over the rehousing of the Arab community, little or no consideration was given to the views of the Arabs themselves.

A number of international Islamic organizations were active in the town during the first half of the twentieth century. The Islamic Society became involved with the Arab seamen in South Shields in 1919 after racial tensions erupted in violent street demonstrations. In 1930 the Western Islamic Association urged acceptance of the government-backed rota system for Arab seamen and its officials sought to counter the activities of those Arabs who chose resistance and solidarity with the radical alternative provided by the communist-led Seamen's Minority Movement. Both of these organizations were led by London-based professionals whose social class gave them access to senior officials in the British Government. The third organization, the 'Alawi religious brotherhood, was more firmly rooted in the Arab community and its leaders were drawn from the same tribal background as the seamen and lived among them. The arrival of the charismatic Sheikh Abdullah Ali al-Hakimi in South Shields in 1936 brought about a dramatic religious revival among the town's Arab community. New rituals and practices were introduced, special attention was given to the religious education of the children of the community and new efforts were made to secure funds for a mosque. At a time of continuing high unemployment when many Arabs were destitute and unrest was always a possibility, the strengthening of the religious organization of the community provided a useful mechanism to control the behaviour of its members. Sheikh Abdullah's activities did not threaten the status quo and appear to have been welcomed and supported by the authorities. But Sheikh Abdullah developed political ambitions and during the 1940s and early 1950s he became an outspoken critic of the Imam's regime in the Yemen and one of the leaders of the Free Yemeni Movement. His political campaign divided the community between supporters of the Free Yemenis and those loyal to the Imam, but these political rivalries went largely unnoticed by non-Yemenis and remain part of the hidden history of the community.

The final chapter, by way of a postscript, briefly traces developments in the community since the end of the Second World War. It shows that the post-war years have seen the Arab community gradually 'dissolving' into the general population of South Shields. With the decline of the British shipping industry and with it the port of South Shields, there was little new immigration into the town from Yemen and the continued absence of immigrant women encouraged marriage outside the community. A new urban re-development programme beginning in the 1950s resulted in the demolition of much of the Laygate area where most of the Arab community lived and the dispersal of Arab families across the town.

Soon after the Second World War it was observed that the second generation were abandoning the customs and values of the community on reaching adolescence and were increasingly adopting the ways and values of British society. Despite the opening of a new mosque in 1972, it is mainly the older generation who have retained their Arab and Islamic identity. The racial hostility and prejudice experienced by the Arab community during the inter-war years has declined. But it is argued that this is largely because integration has been accompanied by the assimilation of most of those of Arab descent into the larger society of South Tyneside and the loss of their Arab and Islamic identity.

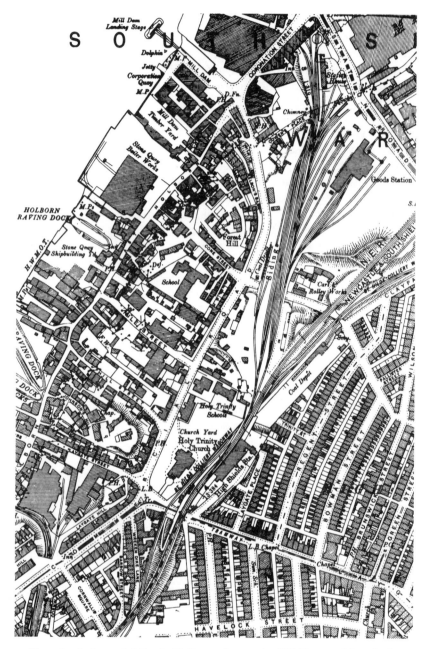

Figure 1. Arabs settled first in Holborn, close to the Mill Dam, and later in the streets on either side of Laygate Lane. *Source:* An extract from the Old Ordnance Survey Map of South Shields 1895 as published by Alan Godfrey Maps, 1982. The scale is approximately 1:4340 or about fifteen inches to a mile.

8

One

The Earliest Arab Immigrants: The Pioneers

I South Shields at the turn of the century

At the beginning of the twentieth century, the estuary of the River Tyne was Britain's fourth largest shipping centre after London, Cardiff and Liverpool. As in Cardiff, exports from the Tyne ports, principally coal and coke from the nearby coalfields, exceeded imports. Exports from the Tyne ports in 1909 for example exceeded those of Liverpool, the country's third largest port.[1] After discharging their cargoes at other British ports, many ships proceeded to Cardiff or the Tyne to take on a cargo of coal for the outward journey and to engage a new crew. Trade and commerce on the Tyne had expanded rapidly after 1850 when a vast scheme of river improvement was inaugurated by the newly-established Tyne Improvement Commissioners. South Shields, at the southern entrance of the Tyne, had become a separate port in 1848 and Tyne Dock, covering an area of some fifty acres, the property of the North-Eastern Railway Company, was opened there in 1859. By the end of the nineteenth century, most of the coal-carrying vessels clearing from the Tyne shipped their cargoes at Tyne Dock which handled upwards of six million tons of coal and coke a year, the largest quantity shipped from any single dock in the world. It made South Shields the most important port on the north-east coast. Ships from many countries in the world traded in and out of Tyne Dock and South Shields became home to seamen of many different nationalities.

9

II The origins of the Arab community

Arab seamen appear to have started visiting the north-east coast of England at the end of the nineteenth century and in the early years of the twentieth century. Ali Said, the first Arab to establish a seaman's boarding-house in South Shields and a former seaman, claimed to have settled in the town in 1894[2] and in an interview with the local newspaper referred to other Arab seaman who had lived there since 1906.[3] We know that Ali Hassan, a seaman who opened the second Arab boarding-house in South Shields, shipped out from north-east ports as early as 1908.[4] By 1909[5] Ali Said was running a licensed seamen's boarding-house for Arab seamen in Nile Street, Holborn (see Figure 1, p.8) and in September 1911 he was fined for having too many lodgers and for accommodating them in unlicensed parts of the house; at that time the boarding-house was licensed for fifteen seamen.[6] As the only Arab seamen's boarding-house in the town, all the Arab seamen who came to South Shields stayed there giving Ali Said a monopoly of the trade. The establishment of an Arab boarding-house suggests that by this time Arab seamen were being discharged and were shipping out of ports in the north-east on a regular basis. Along with other coloured seamen they were probably not welcome in those boarding-houses catering for white seamen.

In August 1912 a quarrel broke out between Ali Said, his English wife, Mary Ellen Said, and Ali Hassan, a young Arab seaman who had recently married a local girl, Maud Deans, and wished to settle down in the town and open a seamen's boarding- house. To get a licence to start a seamen's boarding-house, an applicant had to have a good character. Ali Hassan stated that he had not been in trouble before and accused Mary Ellen Said of starting the quarrel to prevent him from getting the licence because she and her husband did not want a rival establishment in the town. Mary Ellen Said, who accused Ali Hassan of assaulting her during the quarrel, denied that she wished to get a conviction against him to prevent him from getting a licence.[7] The incident does not appear to have prevented Ali Hassan from opening an Arab boarding-house at 93 and 95 East Holborn in 1913. By that time there were already between twenty and thirty Arabs living in East Holborn[8] and numbers were clearly increasing even before the outbreak of the First World War. Nevertheless before 1914 Arab seamen were greatly outnumbered at the port by North European seamen from Scandinavia, the Baltic, Germany and the Low Countries. The census returns for 1911 show only a handful of Arabs in the town, but over a thousand men from continental northern Europe. Byrne estimates that North European seamen formed some thirty per cent of the seagoing labour force at the port at this time.[9]

The emergence of an Arab colony in Holborn provoked a hostile reaction from at least some of the residents as this report in the local newspaper for April 1913 illustrates:

> The suggestion which has come from more than one prose-cution recently heard by the South Shields magistrates that an Arab colony is materialising in our midst—in Holborn to be precise—is exciting some attention, and not undeservedly so. In degree and extent I cannot speak as to the character of the Arab settlers here, excepting that they have obtained a footing and that they are a growing quantity. It is for the authorities to say how far this development may go on without detriment to ourselves as a community. Sufficient has transpired, I believe, to show that the residents in the neighbourhood where these Orientals have established themselves, very strongly for some reason resent their presence. The reason and the results, therefore, are subjects for investigation other than through the channels of the police court, if the peace of the neighbourhood is to be restored, and the rest I am content to leave to the powers that be.[10]

The number of Arab seamen living in South Shields and shipping out from north-east ports increased rapidly during the First World War. With so many British seamen serving in the Royal Navy and other branches of the Armed Forces, and with the departure of many North European seamen now classified as enemy aliens or German-inclined neutrals, there was no shortage of jobs for Arab firemen and at substantially higher wages than before the war. The monthly rate for seamen on vessels employed in the foreign trade rose from £5.10s. in 1914 to £9 in 1916 and peaked at £14.10s. in 1918.[11] This encouraged a flow of new migrants, with South Shields establishing itself during these years as the second largest centre of Arab seamen in Britain after Cardiff.[12] A number of new Arab boarding-houses opened to accommodate the new arrivals including by 1916 that of Muhammad Muckble (Muqbil) at 5 East Holborn[13] and Abdul Rahman Zaid at 63 Thrift Street.[14]

Muhammad Muckble was born in the village of Sulwi in the Maqbana district north-west of Ta'izz in Yemen and began his journey to South Shields in 1911 when he joined a ship at Aden in south-west Arabia bound for Trieste. There he signed on another

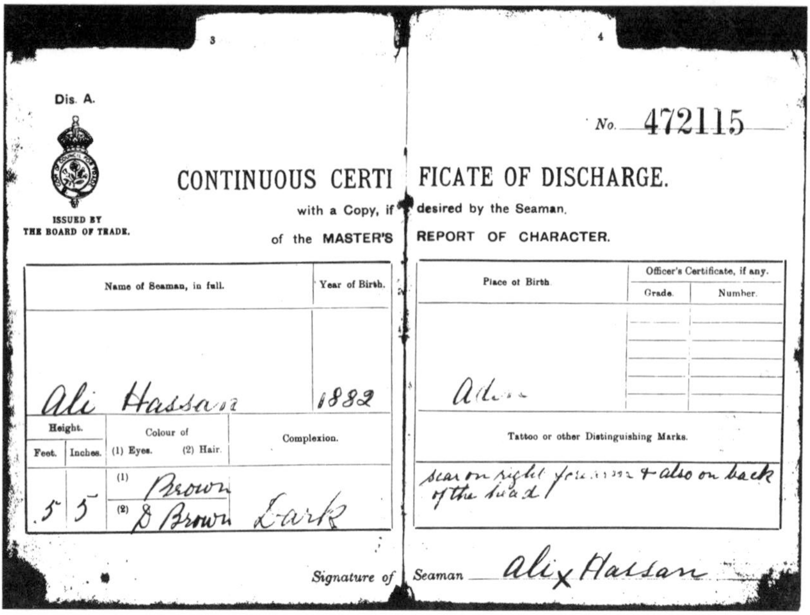

3 4

Dis. A.

No. 472115

ISSUED BY THE BOARD OF TRADE.

CONTINUOUS CERTIFICATE OF DISCHARGE.

with a Copy, if desired by the Seaman,

of the MASTER'S REPORT OF CHARACTER.

Name of Seaman, in full.	Year of Birth.	Place of Birth	Officer's Certificate, if any. Grade.	Number.
Ali Hassan	1882	Aden		

Height. Feet.	Inches.	Colour of (1) Eyes.	(2) Hair.	Complexion.	Tattoo or other Distinguishing Marks.
5	5	Brown	D Brown	Dark	scar on right forearm & also on back of the head

Signature of Seaman Ali x Hassan

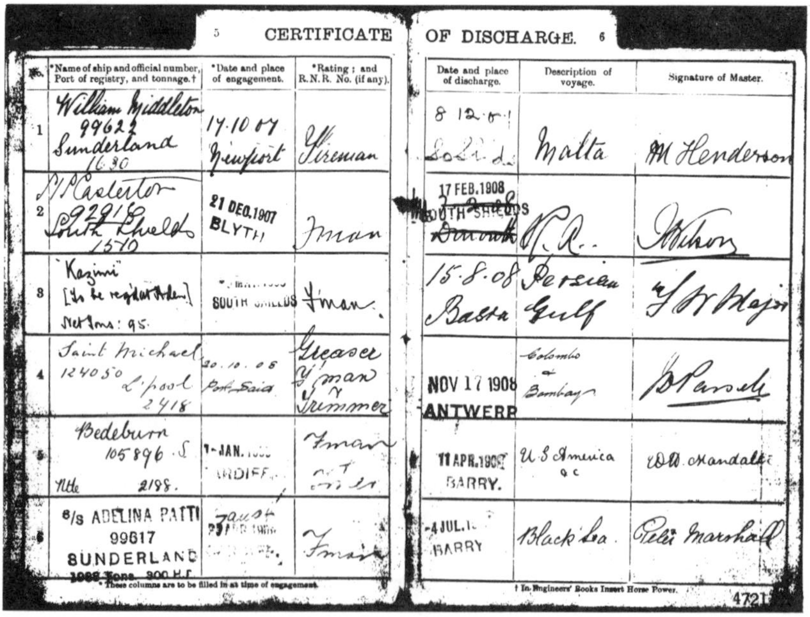

5 CERTIFICATE OF DISCHARGE. 6

No.	*Name of ship and official number, Port of registry, and tonnage.†	*Date and place of engagement.	*Rating; and R.N.R. No. (if any).	Date and place of discharge.	Description of voyage.	Signature of Master.
1	William Middleton 99622 Sunderland 1630	17.10.07 Newport	Fireman	8.12.07 [illegible]	Malta	M Henderson
2	N. Casterton 92918 South Shields 1570	21 DEC.1907 BLYTH	Fman	17 FEB.1908 SOUTH SHIELDS	N.R.	Wilson
3	"Kazimi" [to be regd at Aden] Net Tons: 95	[illegible] SOUTH SHIELDS	Fman	15.8.08 Basra	Persian Gulf	[illegible] Major
4	Saint Michael 124050 L'pool 2418	20.10.08 Port Said	Greaser Fman & Trimmer	NOV 17 1908 ANTWERP	Colombo & Bombay	[illegible]
5	Bedeburn 105896 S Ntle 2198	1 JAN. [illegible] CARDIFF	Fman	11 APR.1909 BARRY	U.S. America Q C	[illegible] Mandal[illegible]
6	S/S ADELINA PATTI 99617 SUNDERLAND 1968 Tons 900 H.P.	7 Aug [illegible]	Fman	4 JUL. [illegible] BARRY	Black Sea	Peter Marshall

* These columns are to be filled in at time of engagement. † In Engineers' Books Insert Horse Power.

4721

Figure 2. Pages from Ali Hassan's Continuous Certificate of Discharge. He began shipping out from North-East ports in 1907. (Courtesy of Mr Norman Hassan) ship again as a fireman and eventually docked in the Tyne. Settling in South Shields, he married a Scottish girl from Newcastle, Rosetta, and was probably the first Muslim in the town to marry in a Roman Catholic Church. His children, five daughters and two sons, were brought up as Roman Catholics.[15]

In May 1916 the local newspaper reported in more positive, if somewhat patronizing, terms about the Arab community, emphasizing the contribution they were making to the war effort:

> In one part of the town there has come together during recent years a foreign element who now form quite a colony. I refer to the Arabs who have gravitated chiefly to the East and West Holborn district. They used to be, until very recent times, a somewhat turbulent lot, but latterly one has heard much less of those disturbances which used to occur so frequently in times past. Indeed if one may accept the statement of one who made a personal tour of that vicinity a week or so ago they have become quite tolerable neighbours to the rest of the community. Originally sons of the desert, they have become seafarers of no mean account and in these days when there is such a dearth of labour in connection with the manning of British vessels, they have been in great demand by shipmasters, especially as firemen, in which particular class of work they are said to give an excellent account of themselves. The Arabs of Holborn have also seen something of modern maritime warfare, but of that one cannot speak without special authority from the powers that be.[16]

But if the war brought prosperity for some in the growing Arab community, for other Arabs it brought death and suffering. Many Arab seamen from South Shields were killed when their ships were torpedoed and others were interned in German prisoner-of-war camps. One report states that during the war years as many as 700 Arab seamen sailing from the Tyne lost their lives through enemy action.[17] Said Saleh Hassan of 2 Lytton Street, who had married the widow of Ali Hassan, one of the first Arab boarding-house keepers in the town, died when his ship, the SS *Zillah*, was torpedoed and sunk off Murmansk in Russia in October 1917 with the loss of all its crew. Three months before his death, his wife had given birth to a son, Norman, one of the first children to be born into the Arab community in South Shields. Salem Abuzed of 17 East Holborn was serving as a fireman on the Sunderland steamer *May Scott* when war broke out in August 1914. He was interned

13

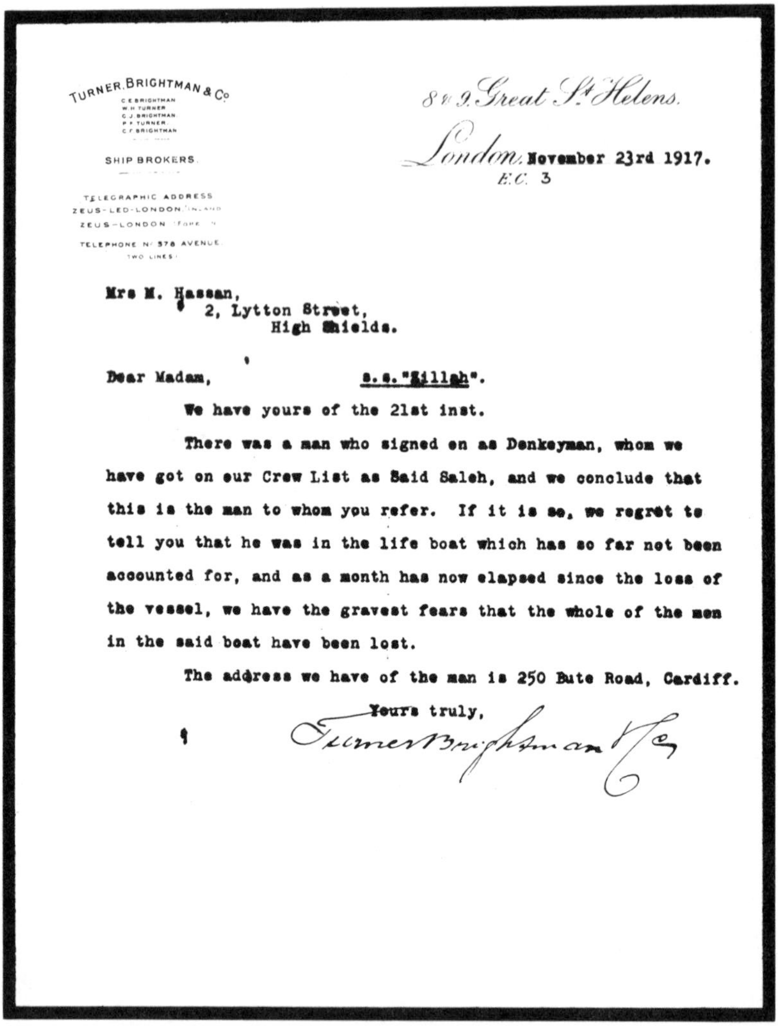

TURNER, BRIGHTMAN & Co

C E BRIGHTMAN
M H TURNER
G J BRIGHTMAN
P F TURNER
C F BRIGHTMAN

SHIP BROKERS

TELEGRAPHIC ADDRESS
ZEUS-LED-LONDON
ZEUS-LONDON

TELEPHONE N° 578 AVENUE
TWO LINES

8 & 9 Great S.t Helens.

London, November 23rd 1917.
E.C. 3

Mrs M. Hassan,
   2, Lytton Street,
    High Shields.

Dear Madam,   s.s. "Zillah".

   We have yours of the 21st inst.

   There was a man who signed on as Donkeyman, whom we have got on our Crew List as Said Saleh, and we conclude that this is the man to whom you refer. If it is so, we regret to tell you that he was in the life boat which has so far not been accounted for, and as a month has now elapsed since the loss of the vessel, we have the gravest fears that the whole of the men in the said boat have been lost.

   The address we have of the man is 250 Bute Road, Cardiff.

         Yours truly,

Turner Brightman & Co

Figure 3. The letter to Mrs Maud Hassan informing her that her husband, Said Saleh Hassan, a donkeyman on the *SS Zillah*, owned by Turner, Brightman & Co., has been lost at sea. The *SS Zillah* was torpedoed off Murmansk, Russia in October 1917 with the loss of all the crew. (Courtesy of Mr Norman Hassan)

along with the rest of the crew in a German prisoner-of-war camp at Ruhleben. Released due to ill health, he returned to South Shields in May 1917 and spoke of the hardships he had suffered during almost three years of imprisonment. The German authorities at the camp, he explained, had marked out coloured men for special ill-treatment. When he refused to carry out a task assigned to him because it was forbidden by his religion he was thrown into a prison cage in which he could only stand upright and could not even turn round. He was left there for seventy-two hours and given only one slice of black bread a day. On his release he was often subjected to personal violence and was on the verge of starvation when food parcels started to come from England. He became very ill and after spending three months in hospital he was included in a group of prisoners, most of them old and weak, who were sent back to England.[18]

The Arab community continued to grow in the years immediately following the end of the First World War and Arabs progressively replaced Scandinavians and Germans as the 'alien' element in the seagoing labour force of South Shields.[19] In January 1920 the Immigration Office in Newcastle reported to the Home Office in London that there were eight Arab boarding-houses in South Shields and that the number of Arab seamen in the town at any one time varied from 300 to 600.[20] In addition to the boarding-houses, there were several refreshment houses and shops run by Arabs who had retired from seafaring and set up in business. By this time a number of Arabs had settled down in the town, marrying local girls and starting families. But the majority of Arab seamen visiting the town were temporary sojourners not permanent settlers. After a few years, when they had earned a certain amount of money, they would return to their home villages in Yemen. Some tried to come back to Britain in order to look for work when their savings were exhausted but many were replaced by others, often by members of their own family, village or tribe. Those who did not marry and settle in the town must have been relatively insulated from British society. On board ship they worked mainly with other Arabs as the stokehold crew was normally made up of men of the same nationality and on shore they lived in one of the Arab boarding-houses run by a fellow countryman. Consequently, they probably gained no more than a superficial understanding of British society and culture.

III Steamships and stokers: origins of the recruitment of Arab seamen at Aden

The first Arab seamen who came to South Shields had originally been engaged as firemen and trimmers at the port of Aden in south-west Arabia which had been a British colony since 1839. Most claimed to have been born in Aden and therefore claimed to be British subjects. There is some evidence to suggest that Arabs together with some Somalis were being engaged as firemen and stokers on board foreign steamers calling at Aden as early as the 1850s and by 1874 the practice was certainly well established. During the second half of the nineteenth century a structural and technological transformation of the merchant shipping industry was taking place. The introduction of the steamship

> ... involved the creation of a new rating with no sea-going tradition, whose job was shovelling coal into a furnace. As an occupation, the new rating—that of fireman—was 'arduous, dirty and hot'; and it eventually came to account for nearly half the total number of seamen employed afloat.[21]

The speed and reliability of the steamer together with the improvement in communications brought about by the telegraph resulted in the appearance of a new type of vessel, the Tramp Steamer:

> This category of ship did not ply regular routes, but went instead from port to port depending on the availability of cargo. Employment aboard such ships generally meant longer periods away from home and tended to be insecure and discontinuous, since it might begin and end at any port. Both the new rating of fireman and the Tramp Steamer were shunned by white European labour, and it was with these that colonial labour quickly became identified.[22]

Frank Bullen has left us a vivid description of the harsh working conditions of the stokehold crew at the turn of the century:

> It must, however, be remembered that pitching coal into the furnace, though it is the principal work of the fireman, does not by any means complete his work. After he has been 'firing' for a certain length of time he perceives the necessity for 'cleaning fires'. He has been carefully raking and poking his fires at intervals so that no clogging of the bars shall hinder the free

upward draught, and this operation, performed with long tools called a slice, a rake and a devil, is very severe. The operator must stand very close to the furnace mouth and peer within at the ferment glow, while he searches the vitals of his fire as quickly and deftly as may be, lest the tell-tale gauge shall reveal to the watchful engineer that the pressure of steam is lessening, bringing him into the stokehold on the run to know what the all-sorts of-unprintable-words that particular fireman is doing. But this is only the merest child's play to cleaning fires. When the time comes the other furnace or furnaces (each fireman has two or three under his charge) must be at the top of their blast, doing their very utmost. Then the fireman flings wide the door of the furnace to be cleaned, plunges his tools into the heart of the fire, and thrusts, rakes and slices until he presently, half-roasted, drags out on to the stokehold floor a mass of clinker. This sends out such a fierce upward heat that it must needs be damped down, the process being accompanied by clouds of suffocating steam-smoke. But there is no time to be lost. Again and again he dives into the heart of the furnace, each time purging it of some of the deadening clinker, until, at last with smarting eyeballs, half-choked, half-roasted, and wholly ex-hausted for the time, he flings a shovelful or so of coal upon the now comparatively feeble fire, and returns to call up his reserve of strength.

The providing of coal for the use of the fireman is the duty of the 'trimmer', the nature of whose work is so terrible that he should receive the sympathy of every kindly man and woman whom he serves. The coal is kept in vast magazines called bunkers, giving on to the stokeholds by means of watertight doors. In merchant ships these bunkers are placed so as to be most convenient for the transmission of coal to the stokehold, and are as little subdivided as possible. What their capacity is may be imagined from the fact that some ships require three thousand tons of coal for a single passage, it being consumed at the rate of between twenty and thirty tons per hour! At the commencement of the passage the trimmer's work is com-paratively easy. The coal lies near the outlet, and by a little skilful manipulation it is made to run out upon the stokehold floor handy for the fireman's shovelling. But as the consumption goes on, and the 'face' of the coal recedes from the bulkhead, the trimmer's work grows rapidly more heavy. His labour knows no respite as he struggles to keep the fireman's needs supplied. And there is no ventilator pouring down fresh air into the bunker. In darkness, only punctuated by the dim light of a safety-lamp, in an atmosphere composed of the exhalations from the coal and a modicum of dust-laden air, liable at any moment to be overwhelmed by the down-rushing masses of coal as the ship's motion displaces it, the grimy, sweat-soaked man works on.[23]

The number of Arabs and Somalis, together with West Indians, West Africans, Indians and Chinese, employed in the merchant shipping industry began to increase during the second half of the nineteenth century to satisfy a rapidly expanding industry's demand for labour. Documentary evidence suggests that Arabs and Somalis were engaged on foreign steamers calling at Aden before they were employed on British ships. The first company to engage Arabs and Somalis as firemen and stokers at the port of Aden was the Messageries Maritimes Steam Navigation Company of France which was under contract to the French Government to convey mail between Marseilles and Shanghai.[24] Messageries Maritimes, which had its headquarters at Marseilles, was the largest shipping company in the world at that time and a fierce rival of the British P & O Company on many eastern routes. Arab seamen were recruited at Aden to serve on the company's steamers operating between Marseilles and Shanghai. Correspondence between the Shipping Master and the Political Resident, Aden in 1874[25] indicates that the system of hiring native firemen for the Messageries Maritimes steamers calling at the port had existed 'for many years' and that the arrangement was already in force in the 1850s. Certainly by 1869 there is firm evidence that Arab seamen were being engaged by the Compagnie des Services Maritimes des Messageries Impériales (the predecessor of the Messageries Maritimes Company) at Aden. In March of that year the French Agent complained to the First Assistant Resident, Aden that two Arab seamen had deserted after receiving an advance on their wages and had taken with them clothes belonging to the company. He requested that they be apprehended and imprisoned. The men were eventually arrested and admitted to being absent without leave but claimed that they had arranged to substitute other Arabs to do their work. In October the French Agent again wrote to the First Assistant Resident drawing his attention to the case of an Arab serang (the native foreman in charge of the stokehold crew) employed by the company who had lent money to an Arab fireman which the seaman now refused to repay.[26]

By 1874 it is possible that Dutch, Italian, Austro-Hungarian, and

German companies were also engaging Arabs and Somalis at Aden as firemen on their steamers[27] but this practice does not appear to have been employed by British companies until the 1880s.[28] During the First World War Arabs and Somalis were also engaged at Aden as firemen on ships of the Royal Navy.[29] Few statistics are available as to the number of Arabs and Somalis engaged as firemen at Aden during this period but we do have the following figures for Arab seamen engaged in foreign vessels provided by the Shipping Master, Aden in 1906: 1902/3—1,357 seamen, 1903/4—1,506 seamen, 1904/5—1,018 seamen and 1905/6—1,364 seamen.[30] Recruitment appears to have been at its height in the years before the First World War and to have declined substantially after the war ended.

Probably the majority of Arab seamen who came to north-east England had engaged first on foreign vessels and transferred later to British ships, often after their discharge at European ports such as Marseilles; others joined British ships directly at Aden. Said Saleh Hassan, one of the first Arab seaman to settle in South Shields, had served as a fireman on the German steamer *Elita Nossack* and was discharged in Hong Kong in October 1900. From 1908, he worked on British ships sailing from ports in the north-east and the Bristol Channel.[31] Ibrahim Ismaa'il, a young Somali fireman who shipped out from South Shields in the early 1920s, worked his passage to Marseilles on a French steamer at the end of the First World War. At Marseilles he joined the crew of a British ship bound for London because the pay was higher than on the French steamers and from London made his way in 1919 to Cardiff where there were many Somalis.[32]

Ismaa'il's first experiences of Europe at the end of the First World War are described in his autobiography and must have been very similar to those of other Arab and Somali seamen arriving for the first time at a European port:

> While in Basra I had heard of a place called Europe, which was the other side of Djibouti, and where life was easier, wages being higher. I decided to try my luck there ... The ship stopped opposite Port Said. We Somalis decided to land, as we thought we were practically in Europe ... At last we came to Marseilles, and here we all went ashore. On landing in Marseilles, I found there other Somalis who gave me European clothes and boots. I noticed that all had their hair trimmed in European fashion, being cut at the back of the head, so I thought I would also in this conform to the custom of the country. I went into a barber's shop, and, not knowing a word of the

language, I explained by signs what I wanted. The barber beckoned me to sit in an armchair and started to cut my hair. Then he pointed out to me a number of flasks and I agreed to all his suggestions. By the time he had finished I was scented all over, and felt very satisfied with myself. I put one franc in his hand—then the equivalent of tenpence—and waited for my change. It was some time before I understood that my bill amounted to five times the sum I was giving him. But five francs was all the money I possessed, and I determined not to part with it. A customer, seeing I was a stranger and did not understand what I had done, interfered in my favour, and finally, it was decided that I should be let off after giving another franc to the barber. Since that day I never ask for anything until I have enquired about the price.

My Warsangeli countrymen did everything they could for me: it is their custom to do the same for any new-comer from home, until he gets to know the place and can look after himself. The shops in Marseilles were a continual surprise to me. I was glad when the sun rose on another day so that I could get out and see more of these wonders. I spent day after day just staring about me and looking in at the shop windows. The overhead bridge was an amazing structure, the like of which I had seen no where else. One night I was taken to a cinema and enjoyed it so much that I went almost every night afterwards. Though it was summer I felt the cold very much. . . .

Eventually we arrived at Sancerre . . . Here I made my first real acquaintance with the cold. We were at the beginning of November 1918. I had no underwear, and only a flannel on my chest, a coat and a pair of trousers. On my feet I had only old boots but no socks. I shall never forget how much I suffered: my fingers were paralysed; the whole of my body was numbed.

. . . The first thing we did when we got back to Marseilles was to go and buy second-hand clothes and mufflers; an Arab explained to me the use of underwear, for which I became very grateful. So now, I covered myself thoroughly well. I stayed sometime in Marseilles looking for work as a fireman on a ship, for I was now feeling much stronger. The pay on French ships being low, some friends and I decided to look for an English ship. Since it is by his papers that a man is judged, and I had lost mine in Djibouti, a Somali friend gave me his own. A few days later we heard that an English ship was looking for a crew 'by the round'. Several of us jumped at this opportunity; we had to give a commision to the man who found us the job.[33]

IV Brokers and bribery

From the outset the system of hiring Arabs and Somalis as firemen and stokers at Aden was open to abuse. The brokers who brought these men to the port for employment were in the habit of making considerable deductions from their wages before they were allowed to board ship. The supply of men always exceeded demand, placing the broker in a strong position. In 1874 the Shipping Master, Aden wrote to the Political Resident drawing his attention to these abuses. He stated that the Parsi Dubash entrusted with the shipping of these men readily admitted that each man was milked of three to four rupees, a practice dating back to the 1850s. The broker justified his actions on the grounds that the men who brought seamen for employment had to be paid and that these deductions took place to make good any loss sustained by him from seamen deserting after receiving one month's advance on their wages.[34] The number of desertions, however, appears to have been very small. The sum deducted from a seaman's wages could amount to over one half. The Shipping Master quotes the case of a fireman engaged on a steamer of the Messageries Maritimes Steam Navigation Company at seventeen rupees a month who was paid six rupees but debited as receiving a month's pay. He was actually cheated out of ten and a half rupees; half a rupee being the standard shipping fee.[35]

A memorandum by the Shipping Master, Aden dated 1907 suggests that some seamen had to pay a commission to the broker (often referred to as the *guard* or *ghat* serang) on a monthly basis and that payment was made to the broker's agent on board ship, usually the serang (often referred to as the ship's serang).[36] The serang himself, usually an Arab or Somali, had to pay a substantial fee to the broker in order to secure his position. To cover these expenses he in turn extracted a further commission from the ordinary seamen. On board ship the serang could exert considerable control over the men in his charge and if they did not fee him he would give them a bad character and have them charged and punished by the engineers. Some ship's engineers made the serangs pay for their positions, and there is some evidence that clerks in the Shipping Office at Aden, certain ranks in the Aden police and the local agents of the shipping companies may also have been part of a complex network of bribery and corruption. The result of this being the serious exploitation of the ordinary Arab and Somali seamen engaged at Aden port.[37]

A report by the Deputy Superintendent of Police, Aden in 1910 describes how part of this network operated:

Some engineers it is said will not employ serangs without receiving 'douceurs'; in other cases engineers practically delegate their powers of selecting serangs to the seamen serangs who then virtually sell serangs' appointments. In the same way serangs who pay for their appointments levy blackmail from the crews they select and as long as all goes well there are no complaints. I hear that sums of 300, 400 and 500 rupees are paid by serangs for engagements of a year and as a salary of a serang is not more than 60 rupees per month such payments seem incredible. But it appears serangs in addition to recouping themselves by levying blackmail on their crews do a large retail trade from port to port which more than pays them and it follows that in a vessel where everyone has paid for his appointment that the standard of honesty is not high and that cargoes are frequently turned to avert loss. Direct evidence to prove this is not forthcoming but the above indicates the internal state of affairs. I understand the difficulties experienced here are common to all ports where crews are signed on and off. The remedy is not easy.[38]

In the same year, the port authorities at Aden admitted that bribery in connection with the shipping of men was and always had been rife there but that it was impossible to check it and action taken in the past had failed.[39] These abuses were particularly acute in connection with the engagement of seamen for foreign steamers calling at Aden, because it was not compulsory for their masters to engage and sign off their crews at the Shipping Office.[40] At first the Political Resident was reluctant to intervene pointing out that the prosperity of Aden depended on the amount of shipping attracted to it and any changes in the existing system might deter foreign ships from using the port.[41]

In 1889, however, an official broker was licensed by the Resident to procure firemen, but the new system does not appear to have eliminated abuses and in 1891 the broker's licence was revoked.[42] The shipping company agents at Aden then appear to have appointed their own serangs to engage firemen, as they were legally entitled to do, but these serangs were not officially licensed by the Political Resident. A Somali, Adan Ali, acted for the Messageries Maritimes Steam Navigation Company, P & O, Luke Thomas and Cowasjee Dinshaw Bros; an Arab, Mohamed Nassir, for the Aden Coal Company. In 1904 the British authorities at Aden resolved that no seaman was to be made to pay for obtaining employment and that he was to be protected by the Shipping Master, Aden from all exactions. The broker's fees were to be paid by the master or owner of the ship. But corrupt practices continued in spite of the fact that the two serangs, Adan Ali and Mohamed Nassir, were officially licensed by the Residency in 1907 in an attempt to regulate the engagement of seamen. The serangs were accused of demanding bribes of fifteen, twenty and even thirty rupees from each man engaged.[43] Even though there was no doubt that seamen were being subjected to unlawful exactions by the serangs, most men, fearing certain retribution if they complained to the authorities, simply paid up and kept quiet. When charges were made it proved almost impossible to obtain a conviction because the seamen could provide no corroborative evidence, payments often being made at sea without witnesses. The licensing of brokers continued until the early 1930s but from 1918 the number of seamen engaged at Aden declined dramatically. In January 1918 a restriction was placed on Arab firemen leaving Aden. This was a wartime measure introduced because of the great demand for labour at Aden at that time. After the war the restrictions remained in force because of the depressed condition in shipping and severe unemployment at the British ports where Arab seamen went to seek work.[44]

V Turks or Arabs?

When questioned by immigration officials almost all the Arab seamen who arrived in South Shields, like those at other ports in Britain, invariably claimed that they were born in Aden and were therefore British subjects. Few, however could produce documentary evidence to prove their claim, except the entry of nationality in their seamen's continuous discharge books. They explained that they could not produce a birth certificate because there was no registration in Aden. Their status as British subjects does not appear to have been challenged locally until March 1917 when three boarding-house keepers, Ali Said, Muhammad Muckble and Abdul Rahman Zaid, were charged with failure to register as aliens. The case came before the South Shields magistrates. The Chief Constable of South Shields, William Scott, argued that in the opinion of the people living in the district half of the Arabs were in fact Turks. He therefore thought it prudent to instigate enquiries starting with the boarding-house keepers because of the great influence they exerted over their boarders. The Ottoman or Turkish Empire, it should be remembered, had entered the First World War on the side of Germany. Mr Ruddock, the solicitor acting for the three boarding-house keepers, stated that the three men were not

Turks but useful and loyal British subjects who keenly resented being treated as aliens. There were no restrictions placed on Arab seamen who enrolled for the Navy and were liable to be called up. Many were serving with British forces both on sea and land and others were interned prisoners at Ruhleben because they were British subjects. An official of the Shipping Federation, Wm Albert Stephenson of Gateshead, appeared for the defence and stated that he had shipped numbers of men from the defendants' boarding-houses and that they had been accepted for government service. Joseph Harrison Surtees, manager of Cook's Tourist Agency at Sunderland, stated that he had sent many men from the three defendants' boarding-houses to Aden since the war began and had had no difficulty in getting passports for them. The authorities[45] accepted the nationality stated on their seamen's discharge books. The case against the three men was dismissed[46] and the Home Office instructed the Chief Constable to take no further action:

> . . . the Secretary of State does not think that Arab seamen can be expected to produce strict documentary evidence of their nationality and unless in any particular case, you have good ground for suspecting a claim to British nationality, the entries in their discharge books may be accepted as sufficient proof. If any particular case of difficulty arises, it should be reported to the Secretary of State, so that if necessary such enquiries as are possible may be made.[47]

On the basis of interviews and documentary evidence it is clear that while some of the Arab seamen in South Shields came from the Aden Protectorate and therefore had the status of British Protected Persons, the majority, as in other British ports, came from the southern highlands of the Yemen, notably the provinces of Ibb and Ta'izz, which from 1872 to 1918 were occupied by the Ottoman Turks (see Chapter Two p.35). Until 1918 these seamen were technically Turkish subjects and this may explain the confusion locally as to whether they were Arabs or Turks. The Chief Constable of South Shields admitted in 1917 that he did not know the difference between a Turk and an Arab![48] This confusion continued well after the end of the First World War with one local resident even attempting to rewrite history to explain their origins. In a letter to the *Shields Daily Gazette* in February 1925, 'Disgusted' wrote:

> Sir, I have been greatly interested in reading the letters in your paper on the above subject especially that of Ali Said, in which

he says he is as British as any white man. According to the great majority of Arabs' discharge books, they claim Aden as their birthplace. Now, sir, there are almost as many Arabs sailing out of Great Britain as there are male Arabs in Aden. Perhaps Ali Said is not aware that about 130 years ago, Aden was called Mocha, and that a king ruled there. At that time the Turks made a raid, captured the town and beheaded the king. They retained possession until 1839 when our troops took it from them. When our officers entered the town, they exclaimed 'What a den of filth, squalor and thieves'. Hence the name—Aden.

Now as the Turks were in possession of Mocha or Aden for over 40 years, it's a moral certainty that those so-called Britishers must have had Turkish fore-parents.—Yours etc.[49]

From the outset it would appear that Arab seamen engaged at Aden were hardly ever British subjects or even permanent residents of Aden and were usually termed 'foreigners' by the British authorities at Aden. The First Assistant Resident reported in 1874:

I believe it is actually the case that the firemen engaged by M & M in Aden are in nearly every case Arabs or Somalis who merely come to Aden temporarily for their own convenience and cannot be said to owe allegiance to the British Crown. While they reside at Aden they are of course amenable to our laws and entitled to our protection, but I do not think that we owe them the same obligation as due to our fellow subjects in India.[50]

Such men, it was assumed, would not think of claiming the privileges of British subjects. Later there may have been some competition for work on board steamers between Arabs living in Aden and 'foreigners' from the Yemen. In August 1908 for example a number of Arab residents from Sheikh Othman, Aden, submitted a petition to Captain Meek, the Superintendent, stating:

We are poor people of S. Othman and your humble British subjects. We are strong seedies and hardworking men and are unable to get our work on board steamers as firemen, unless we give to the serangs bribes of Rs20 or 30 before being employed. We are entitled to the rights and privileges of being engaged first as firemen etc on board steamers than foreigners (who are Zaidies and Jublies) come down from 'Yemen' and are soon engaged by serangs for the sake of bribes.[51]

In forwarding the petition to the First Assistant Resident, Captain Meek observed:

> They complain that they cannot obtain work without paying heavy bribes. Men from the interior come down and appoint one of their number mucaddum. He goes to the serang and finds out what number of men he requires and what bribe he will accept, Rs15/ Rs20/ or what it be. This applies to all boats. A former port-officer on being informed of this practice forbade it, according to the petitioners' statement, whereas they are now told the matter rests entirely with the serangs.[52]

Following the outbreak of the First World War, the British authorities in Aden advised that Arabs from parts of Arabia outside British jurisdiction engaged as seamen at Aden should be treated as British Protected Persons to facilitate their departure from European ports such as Marseilles. In reply to some opposition from British consular officials in Europe, the Political Resident, Aden stressed that this recommendation was dictated by political and diplomatic expediency:

> I may, however, bring to your notice that the majority of Arabs engaged as seamen in Aden come from beyond our legitimate sphere and these usually go to Djibouti (French Somaliland) where they sign on as firemen in French steamers. It will be impolitic at this time when the whole of Yemen is in a state of flux and Turkish territories and ours are no longer, by reason of the war, clearly defined, to dismiss all trans-border Arabs as beyond the pale of our consideration and to treat them as enemy subjects. Most of them bear little love for the Turks and Aden is the natural outlet for their activities. In such cases I am proposing to the India Office to treat all such Arabs as British Protected Persons. If these Arabs come to Marseilles and wish to go away I would suggest you place them in this category, even if without certificates.[53]

In Britain, Arab labour was needed for the war effort, especially in the critically important shipping industry, and the Board of Trade suggested to the Home Office that the claims of Arab seamen to British nationality should not be challenged:

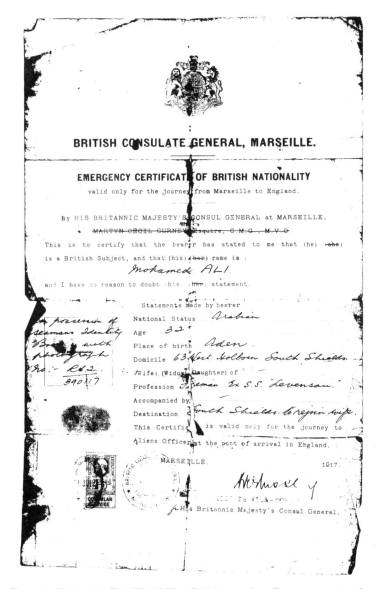

Figure 4. During the First World War, British consuls at European ports such as Marseilles were advised to treat Arab seamen from the Yemen as British subjects and to provide them with travel documents to England. After the war ended the Board of Trade and the National Sailors' and Firemen's Union campaigned to restrict entry to Britain of Arab seamen unless they could prove they were born in Aden and were therefore British subjects. (Courtesy of Mr Norman Hassan)

I am, however, to state that it appears to the Board to be improbable that Arab seamen even if nominally Turkish subjects, would have enemy sympathies. The Board consider it undesirable that action should be taken which might result in strikes or other labour troubles among these men; I am therefore to suggest that Aliens' Officers should exercise a certain amount of discretion in administering the Aliens' Restriction Order, where Arab seamen are concerned, in cases in which the men do not seem to have enemy affiliations or sympathies.[54]

The First World War therefore saw a rapid growth in the number of Arab seamen settling in South Shields and certain other British ports such as Cardiff, Hull and Liverpool. They formed a useful reserve army of labour during these critical years and although the majority were nominally Turkish subjects and therefore technically enemy aliens, their claims to British nationality were supported and upheld.

Two

Aden and the Yemen: Emigration and Society

I The port of Aden[1]

On the 19 January 1839 a small British naval force and several hundred British and Indian troops attacked and occupied the port and town of Aden in south-west Arabia (see Figure 5, p.30). As a result Aden became the first colonial territory acquired during the reign of Queen Victoria. With one of the few natural harbours on the south Arabian coast and an easily defensible site, the town had enjoyed great prosperity in the fourteenth and fifteenth centuries when it was the principal emporium of Arabia. But in the early seventeeth century Aden was eclipsed by the port of Mocha on the Red Sea coast and its commercial importance declined so that by the time of the British occupation the town had less than two thousand inhabitants.

The growth of British power in India during the second half of the eighteenth century and the establishment of a regular steamer service to carry mails from Bombay to Suez early in the nineteenth century set the stage for the decision by Britain to occupy Aden. By the late 1830s a suitable coaling station between Bombay and Suez where steamers could refuel was urgently needed. But the port was not occupied only for the establishment of a coal depot. Britain was deeply concerned about the rapid advance of Muhammad Ali of Egypt into Arabia and the threat that this might pose for the defence of India. The powerful vassal of the Ottoman Sultan was believed to have designs on Aden, then ruled by the Sultan of Lahej, and to be intent on conquering the whole of the Arabian peninsula. Political and strategic factors therefore dictated that Aden should be made

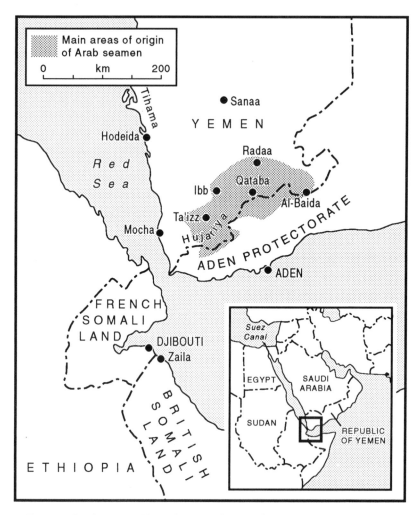

Figure 5. South-west Arabia: main areas of origin of the Arab seamen engaged at Aden. Inset location map shows present-day boundaries of the Middle East. The Republic of Yemen includes the former Crown Colony of Aden, the former Aden Protectorate and the former Imamate of the Yemen.

a British possession. The plunder of a British-protected vessel which had run aground at Aden in 1837 provided the British authorities with a convenient pretext to seize the port. For a long time, Aden was administered from Bombay in India and only became a Crown Colony in 1937.

The Peninsular and Oriental Steamship Company (P & O) was the first to establish a coal depot at Tawahi (also known as Steamer Point) on the other side of the peninsula from Aden town in 1842. P & O had pioneered a monthly mail steamer link between Suez and Calcutta via Aden in 1842 and a few years later had extended their service to Australia. By the late 1860s two P & O steamers were calling at Aden each week for coal and other services. In 1856 a French agent opened a coal depot next to that of P & O to service the French steamers operating on the Anglo-French service to the island of Mauritius in the Indian Ocean. From 1860 the monthly French Government steamers which carried troops between France and Indo-China refuelled at Aden and in 1869 the troopships were replaced by a fortnightly service of regular mail steamers of the Service Maritimes des Messageries Impériales, laying the foundations of the future Messageries Maritimes Company. The coal bunkering business brought a new prosperity to Aden. The volume of shipping using the port increased rapidly after the opening of the Suez Canal in 1869 and again in the 1870s and 1880s as freighters began to switch from sail to steam after substantial improvements in engines and boilers finally sealed the fate of the sailing ship.[2] From the middle of the nineteenth century Aden occupied a key position on sea routes from the Red Sea to India and the Far East, Australia and East Africa.

The expansion of the port and its associated activities attracted migrants to Aden in search of employment. They came from India, Somalia and in particular from the highlands of the Yemen to the north beyond the less populous areas of Aden's hinterland that fell within the sphere of British influence. During the second half of the nineteenth century Aden's population more than doubled in size to between 40,000 and 50,000 inhabitants by 1900. Whereas Indians outnumbered Arabs in the 1850s, by the 1890s almost half the population was Arab, the vast majority being migrant labourers from the Yemen highlands. These hillmen from the north, often referred to as *jabalis*, formed a shifting population staying on average for no more than three or four months before returning to their villages in the interior. Many had no permanent homes in the settlement but occupied temporary mat and reed huts which mushroomed up around the coaling depots at Tawahi and Ma'alla. Others lived in caves in the hills behind Tawahi. Living and working conditions for this floating population of coolie labour were appalling.

The supply of labour was controlled and organized by a system of brokers or labour contractors. Each major employer at Aden had his chief broker, often referred to as *muqaddam* or serang, who in turn employed several sub-*muqaddams* who recruited the men and were responsible for paying their wages, finding accommodation for them and making sure that they were fed. For example each coaling agent had from three to eight sub-*muqaddams* according to his labour requirements and each sub-*muqaddam* recruited some thirty to fifty coolies from his own tribe.[3] Various deductions were made from the labourers' wages by the brokers for their services. To ensure a ready supply of labourers for his employer, the *muqaddam* sometimes had to give advances to his coolies. He was particularly vulnerable at harvest time when many labourers returned to their villages and this was a time when the coolies were in a better bargaining position. But on the whole the coolies' bargaining power was weak because the supply of labour almost always exceeded demand. The Yemen highlands appear to have provided an inexhaustible reservoir of labour. It was this abundance of labour employed at low wages that enabled Aden to compete effectively with other bunkering ports.

The coaling companies and other commercial firms found that the *muqaddam* system worked to their advantage. Brokers had been established in the Red Sea ports for years and the first labour contractors to set up business in Aden came from Mocha. But it was at Aden that the system became particularly well-developed. Government officials were less enthusiastic and some saw the *muqaddam* as a parasite who bled the labourers dry. Various attempts were made by the British authorities during the late nineteenth century to break the *muqaddam* system in certain sectors of the labour market but almost all of these efforts met with failure.

II The Aden Protectorate

After the occupation of the port of Aden, the British authorities were faced with the problem of safeguarding the landward approaches to the port and protecting and developing trade routes from the interior. Inevitably the trade and security of the port involved the Aden authorities in the tangled and complex web of inter-tribal politics in the hinterland. From the outset contacts were made with the tribal rulers controlling the principal trade routes, the chiefs of the 'Abdali, Fadhli, Haushabi and Amiri tribes, who were offered British stipends and gifts. Considerable efforts were made by the

British authorities at Aden to divert trade routes away from rival ports. Economic relations between the British-held port and its immediate hinterland expanded steadily and extended northwards to the richer centres of agricultural production in the highlands of the Yemen beyond. Caravans carried the produce of the interior down to Aden; coffee from the Hujariya district south of Ta'izz, grain from the regions beyond Qataba and saffron, madder and beeswax from the central highlands south of Sanaa. Through growing economic links the tribal populations occupying Aden's hinterland were drawn into closer relations with the port.

Until 1872 the British authorities were able to pursue their policies in Aden's hinterland without any organized political opposition from the north. Yemen was in the throes of political dis-integration. But the political vacuum created there invited the intervention of outside forces and in 1872 Turkish troops marched into the Yemen highlands and declared Yemen a province of the Ottoman Empire. Almost immediately the Turkish Governor-General of Yemen demanded that the tribal leaders of the Aden hinterland accept Ottoman suzerainty. With Turkish garrisons now established at Ta'izz and Qataba, the British Government responded by requesting that the Turks respect the independence of what became known as 'the nine tribes', the 'Abdali, Fadhli, 'Aulaqi, Yafa'i, Haushabi, Amiri, 'Alawi, 'Aqrabi and Subeihi. By this action a British sphere of influence essential for the proper functioning of the port and base at Aden was defined, though it stopped short of declaring a protectorate over the nine listed tribes. The Ottomans continued to regard the entire Arabian Peninsula as part of the Sultan's historic possessions, but in practice after 1875 the Governor-Generals of Yemen showed little interest in the barren, inhospitable and sparsely populated territories of the nine tribes.

It was the threat of French and German encroachment in the region in the 1880s that induced the British to put forward a scheme for securing South Arabia by a series of Protectorate Treaties. As the scramble to lay claim to colonial territories intensified, an informal sphere of influence in the Aden hinterland was regarded as too vulnerable to the ambitions of other European powers. Consequently between 1888 and 1903 a series of Protectorate Treaties were signed with tribal rulers in the Aden hinterland and further east in the politically sensitive Hadramaut. The Protectorate Treaties were almost all drafted in much the same form. In each case the tribal ruler was granted British protection and in return for a stipend he agreed to have no relations with any foreign power without the permission of the British Government and to inform the British Government immediately if there was any attempt at interference by any other power. In some cases the treaties were supplemented by agreements about the security of roads or other matters of common interest. Britain always maintained that it had no wish to interfere in the internal affairs of the tribes. But in practice the British became heavily involved in tribal politics, supporting certain rulers or factions and deposing others as a system of British-imposed order was slowly established in the protectorate after the First World War. While working within the existing political framework, attempts were made by British officials to improve administration, and to develop agriculture, health and education services in tribal areas. The protectorate was ruled from India through the Government of Bombay until control was transferred to the Colonial Office after the First World War.

III Yemen

The people of the northern and central highlands of Yemen belong predominantly to the Zaidi sect of Islam, a Shi'a sect closer to orthodox or Sunni Islam in belief and practice than other Shi'a sects.[4] From the ninth century AD the Zaidi were ruled by their own Imams who were selected from among the sayyids, descendants of the Prophet Muhammad through his daughter Fatima, and son-in-law, Ali, and his grandsons, Hussein and Hasan. The Imams were both spiritual and temporal rulers of the Zaidi sect. Only occasionally, however, did they successfully extend their control over the Shafi'i or Sunni population[5] who occupy the southern highlands and coastal plains of the Yemen together with Aden and the Aden hinterland. Doctrinally there is little difference between the Shafi'i and the Zaidi sects. The main differences relate to the call to prayer and the act of praying. According to Wenner:

> Zaydis say their prayers without ever moving their hands, which are kept rigidly at the sides of their bodies, and at the close of prayers they do not say 'amen'. Shafi'is begin praying with their hands at their sides, but they then raise them to their heads and place them in front of their bodies with the hands crossed right over left.[6]

Nevertheless the difference between Zaidis and Shafi'is is significant. Leigh Douglas argues that:

> . . . the distinction between the two sects owes much more to

34

geo-political and economic factors (such as the tribal base and essentially conservative nature of the Zaydis, as compared to the village orientation and more progressive nature of the Shafi'is) than to their religious identifications, which have become convenient descriptive labels for essentially different people living in the same country.[7]

For much of the eighteenth and nineteenth centuries the Yemen was plagued by disputes between rival Imams and by tribal disorder. By the middle of the nineteenth century the whole country was suffering a serious economic decline. Coffee, which had been the country's major source of wealth for many years, now had to compete with a cheaper product from the plantations of Ceylon, the West Indies, Java and later Brazil, and major markets were lost to these new rival producers. These problems intensified when the country was also affected by drought, famine and disease in the 1860s. Indeed, the 1850s and 1860s have been described as the worst years of Yemen's recent history. Major Merewether, the Political Resident, Aden (1863–7) reported in 1863 that Yemen had become a barren wilderness. Economic decline was accompanied by political disintegration and for much of this period the country was ruled by one or other of the great tribal confederations.

Turkish forces had occupied the port of Hodeida and parts of the coastal plain in 1849 and in 1872 they advanced into the highlands and occupied the capital Sanaa. They were welcomed by some of the population who had become weary of years of chaos and misery. Within a few months most of the country had been brought under Turkish control. The Governor-General of the new Ottoman province of Yemen proclaimed a policy of economic development and social improvement under the Sultan. At first the Turks succeeded in imposing peace over much of the country. Roads were constructed, trade was developed and a few modern schools and hospitals were built. But the Turks were foreigners, the country was garrisoned with foreign troops who brought with them strange habits and customs, and Ottoman administrators interfered with traditional political structures.

In 1891 the Imam Muhammad ibn Hamad al-Din led a revolt against the Turkish occupation which was only suppressed with difficulty and much of northern Yemen rose in revolt again in 1899. Yahya ibn Muhammad, who became Imam on the death of his father in 1904, immediately called for a new revolt against the Turks. Massive reinforcements were needed for the Turks to reconquer the country and though the capital Sanaa was reoccupied, Turkish forces failed to capture the Imam's headquarters at Shahara. The 1904–05 revolt had disastrous economic effects and widespread famine left the country exhausted. In 1911 Imam Yahya once again beseiged Sanaa and after the city had been relieved the new Turkish military governor entered into negotiations with the Imam. A treaty signed at Da'an in October 1911 and ratified by imperial firman two years later virtually ceded control over Zaidi districts to the Imam. He was recognized as the spiritual and temporal head of the Zaidi community, the Islamic Shari'a, rather than the Qanun or Ottoman civil code, became the official legal code for the Zaidi districts and the Imam was granted power to appoint all governors and judges there. The Imam achieved most of his demands, and became a Turkish ally receiving an annual subsidy of 2,500 Turkish gold pounds. The capital Sanaa and the Shafi'i districts in the south and west of the province, including the town of Ta'izz, remained under direct Turkish rule.

The First World War brought important changes to the map of south-west Arabia. When the Ottoman Empire entered the war on the side of Germany, the Imam remained loyal to his Turkish ally and the British failed to win him over to the Allied cause. The Turks called on tribal chiefs in the Aden Protectorate to join the Ottoman camp and in June 1915 a Turkish force crossed the border, attacked and occupied Lahej, the capital of the 'Abdali sultan, and advanced to Sheikh Othman close to Aden. A British force drove them back towards Lahej. Aden was secured and there were no further military advances for the remainder of the war.[8]

At the end of the First World War the defeated Ottomans withdrew their military forces from Yemen and in November 1918 the Imam entered Sanaa where he was recognized by the Turkish Governor-General as his successor.[9] In addition to establishing his authority over the territories of the former Ottoman province, Imam Yahya had ambitions to recapture those lands which his ancestors had once ruled as part of a Greater Yemen. His claims included the British port of Aden, often described by Yemenis as 'the eye of Yemen', and the hinterland tribes who had been brought under British protection during the late nineteenth century and the early years of the twentieth century. In 1919 the Imam's forces invaded and occupied parts of the western protectorate. Prolonged negotiations failed to secure a solution to the dispute between the Imam and the British over the future of the Aden Protectorate and in 1928 the Royal Air Force attacked targets across the Yemen border and restored most of the former boundary agreed with the Turks in 1905. The conflicting claims of the Imam and the British were not reconciled, but in 1934 both parties agreed to maintain the existing frontier situation. The Imam withdrew his remaining forces from the protectorate and the Anglo-Yemeni Treaty of 1934 was signed. The British Government formally recognized the independence of Yemen. Frontier incidents continued to sour relations between the two countries and after Imam Yahya's death in 1948 his successor, Imam Ahmad, vigorously renewed his father's campaign to regain control of the Aden Protectorate.[10]

The internal policies of Imams Yahya and Ahmad have been the subject of much controversy. Large scale, independent actions by the northern Zaidi tribes were certainly almost entirely suppressed[11] and a high level of internal security enforced after years of endemic anarchy, though the methods used by the Imams were often harsh. In the northern part of the country the Zaidi tribes were governed by indirect rule with subsidies provided for the chiefs. The Shafi'i populations of the south and west were less fortunate and were brought under direct rule by the Imam's officials. The Imams appointed Zaidi governors and soldiers from the north to collect taxes from the richer agricultural districts of the south. These officials were often corrupt and together with the local headmen, who received a cut of the tax they assisted in collecting, they oppressed the Shafi'i peasantry. The harsh taxation system that resulted was a real and well-justified grievance of the southern villagers.[12] Another form of petty corruption grew up in the south through the practice of 'selling orders' to the many northern tribesmen who were stationed in small groups with the local *amil* or district governor.

> When these tribesmen were sent out on tanafidh (executive duties), to bring someone to court or to the presence of the Imam's officials, they would charge their prisoner a riyal a head for their trouble. The practice of 'selling orders' (mabi al-awamir) became widespread. The official would sell to the tribesman the job of bringing someone in, and the tribesman would turn a profit by charging the prisoner. Northern tribesmen began to attach themselves to officials in the west and south without any appointment by the state but as khabitis, freelance policemen and bailiffs. Numerous men from the north drifted to the south and west in this way and stayed there permanently.[13]

In addition, conscription was sometimes imposed on the Shafi'i areas if a particular district failed to provide the number of volunteers for the regular army that was required by the Imam.

Under the Turks the Imam had been personally responsible for governing the Zaidi districts and after independence the Imams continued to control almost all aspects of government themselves. Few decisions, even on small, local matters, were delegated to officials which led to criticism that their rule was absolute and tyrannical. Opposition groups emerged during the reign of Imam Yahya and grew in strength under his successor. Imam Yahya had followed a policy of isolationism to keep Yemen free from European colonial ambitions and Yemenis free from foreign influences and ideas. He is alleged to have remarked to a visitor:

> Don't you know, my son ... that the colonisation of India, China and other weak oriental countries came about because the governments of those countries gave foreigners concessions for the extraction of salt, petroleum and other resources? I would rather that my people and I remain poor and eat straw than let foreigners in, or give them concessions, no matter what advantage or wealth might result from their presence.[14]

But with large numbers of Shafi'is emigrating from the southern highlands to Aden and beyond and returning regularly to their villages, such a policy was doomed to failure. Yemeni emigrants to Aden and those who found employment in Europe and America, could not fail to compare conditions there with the backward state of their own country and the lack of almost all modern amenities. The country lacked surfaced roads and motorized transport was virtually non-existent. Medical services were rudimentary and there were no modern schools. Foreign newspapers and, until the late 1930s, also radios were banned. The vast majority of Yemenis were engaged in subsistence agriculture.

Shafi'i merchants, who travelled widely to conduct their business, became the main channel for importing new ideas into the Yemen. Other critical voices were found among the prominent sayyid families of Yemen who had become alienated by the Imam's policy of concentrating economic and political power in the hands of members of his own family. The relative political freedom of Aden made the British-held port the obvious focus for the various groups opposed to the Imam. After coming to power, Imam Ahmad attempted to placate the opposition by promising reforms but few were ever carried out. Sir Reginald Champion, the Governor of

Aden, who visited Imam Ahmad at his capital, Taʿizz, in November 1948 commented:

> He is eager to raise the prosperity and the reputation of the Yemen from its present situation of reproach. His motive herein is not the betterment or happiness of the people for themselves, but the justification of his Kingship and the position of Yemen among nations and the enrichment of the Treasury. His mentality has not developed beyond the point of the divine right of Kings and the conception of the people as providers of the King's resources.[15]

Many more foreigners were invited to Yemen by Imam Ahmad than by his father, and their influence, especially on the army, did assist the opposition which eventually succeeded in sweeping away the Imamate in 1962.

IV The 'seafaring tribes' of south-west Arabia

There is little doubt that emigration has been a key characteristic of south-west Arabia from ancient times. Indeed the Yemen highlands have been described as an 'ethnic reservoir' from which migration movements extended far beyond its borders. In the modern period a new phase of migration began in the second half of the nineteenth century, and was initiated by the intrusion of Western colonial powers into the region, in particular the British occupation of Aden in 1839. As the port of Aden expanded, the demand for unskilled coolie labour was increasingly met by migration from the southern highlands of the Yemen. But, as an international port, Aden became more than just the final destination for tribesmen who journeyed along the river valleys from the mountains down to the sea: for some it became a stage in their migration overseas.[16] French steamers were the first ships to engage Arab seamen at Aden, probably as early as the late 1850s. By the end of the nineteenth century the recruitment of Arab seamen at Aden for service on steamers of many nations was already well established and resulted in the creation of Yemeni communities at ports in Europe, America, East Africa, South East Asia and the Far East. For many Yemeni seamen, the French port of Djibouti at the entrance to the Red Sea, occupied by France in 1884, became an important staging post in their search for employment overseas. This helps to explain the presence of Yemeni communities in many French, as well as British, colonies.

Seafaring was only one of the new employment opportunities opening up at this time. By the early years of the twentieth century Yemeni labourers were being recruited for work in the Rhodesian mines, on plantations in Britain's East African Protectorate, at Messageries Maritimes' coaling station at Diego Suarez in Madagascar and as askaris (native troops) in Italian Somaliland. By the beginning of the First World War, a shortage of labourers was reported at Aden and the British authorities prohibited coolie emigration.[17] It is possible that the flow of new migrants from the southern highlands of the Yemen was interrupted by the advance of Turkish forces towards Aden in 1915 and the ensuing military hostilities.

It is commonly held that the Arab seamen who engaged at Aden came principally from the Hujariya district of Yemen[18] which lies south of the provincial capital, Ta'izz, on the border of the West Aden Protectorate and therefore in close proximity to the British-held port. Evidence from documentary sources in particular, together with information from interviews with Arab seamen, however, does not support this view and strongly suggests that Arab seamen came from many parts of the southern highlands of the Yemen and in some cases beyond, and that large numbers of seamen were recruited from certain tribes.[19] Seamen are recorded from the following tribes: Amiri, Haushabi,[20] Shamiri, Audi, Dalali, Badani, Jubani, Dhubhani, Mureisi, Riashi, Areiqi, Sha'ibi, Khubani, Maqtari, Shari, Shargabi and Sharabi. The majority of these tribes (Dalali, Badani, Jubani, Riashi, Mureisi, Audi, Shari, Sha'ibi[21] and Amiri) live in that part of the southern highlands of Yemen lying between the towns of Ibb, Radaa and al-Baida known as the Central Region (al-Mintaqa al-Wusta) and its extension southwards into the West Aden Protectorate (see Figure 5, p.30). Most of the others (Shamiri, Areiqi, Dhubhani, Maqtari and Sharabi) live in the highland areas around Ta'izz to the south-west. Only the Dhubhani, Areiqi and Maqtari are tribes of the Hujariya.

Seamen are also recorded from tribes in the south-west of the Aden Protectorate (e.g. Dubeini) and the northern part of the coastal plain of Yemen, the Tihama (e.g. Mori). The Shamiri, together with the Dalali and Jubani appear to have been particularly important seafaring tribes. The specialization by migrants from a certain tribe or tribes in a particular type of employment, though difficult to explain, is a common feature of emigration from peasant societies in the Arab world. All the districts from which seamen were recruited are predominantly Shafi'i, although around al-Baida and in parts of Ibb Province, Zaidis are found and in some

40

cases the two religious groups live side by side. The vast majority of seamen, like other migrants at this time, were Shafi'is. Indeed there was little emigration from Zaidi districts until more recent times.

Among the seamen who settled in South Shields, the following Yemeni tribes were represented; from the Central Region, the Audi, Dalali, Jubani, Badani, and Shari and from the Ta'izz region, the Shamiri, Areiqi, Dhubhani and Sharabi. There were also seamen from tribes in the protectorate notably from the Amiri and Haushabi. Shamiris certainly played an active and important part in the political life of the community and may well have been the largest group. Shamiris appear to have formed the most numerous tribe among the Arab seamen at Cardiff.[22] As we have already noted, the vast majority of Arab seamen at South Shields claimed to have been born at Aden and therefore to be British subjects. Others stated that they belonged to tribes within the Aden Protectorate. One South Shields' boarding-house keeper, Ali Hamed Dheli of 95 and 103 West Holborn, even went to the trouble of producing a printed list of the tribes in the Aden Protectorate to which Arab seamen lodging with him belonged.[23] In fact very few Arab seamen were born in Aden, and while some were certainly from tribes in the protectorate, there is evidence that seamen from Yemen may have bribed chiefs of tribes in the protectorate to acknowledge them as their subjects.[24] After the First World War an Arab seaman's status as either a British subject, British Protected Person or an alien became increasingly important as the authorities in Britain sought to deny Arabs access to employment and to enforce repatriation.

Most Arab seamen who were engaged at Aden were peasant farmers or the sons of peasant farmers. They came from small villages of a hundred inhabitants or less where the families gained a living by cultivating the terraced fields cut into the steep mountain slopes and by herding animals. Many were independent tribesmen who owned and worked their own land. Disputes among them would have been settled by their own sheikhs according to customary law. Some may have been sharecroppers farming land owned by their chiefs. Unlike the Somalis, some of whom already had experience of seafaring on native dhows before they went to work on the steamers,[25] most of the Arabs who engaged as firemen at Aden had not previously worked as seamen; the majority would not even have seen the sea before they arrived at Aden. Of course as firemen they did not really need seafaring experience when their job was merely to shovel coal and maintain a good head of steam for the engineers.

41

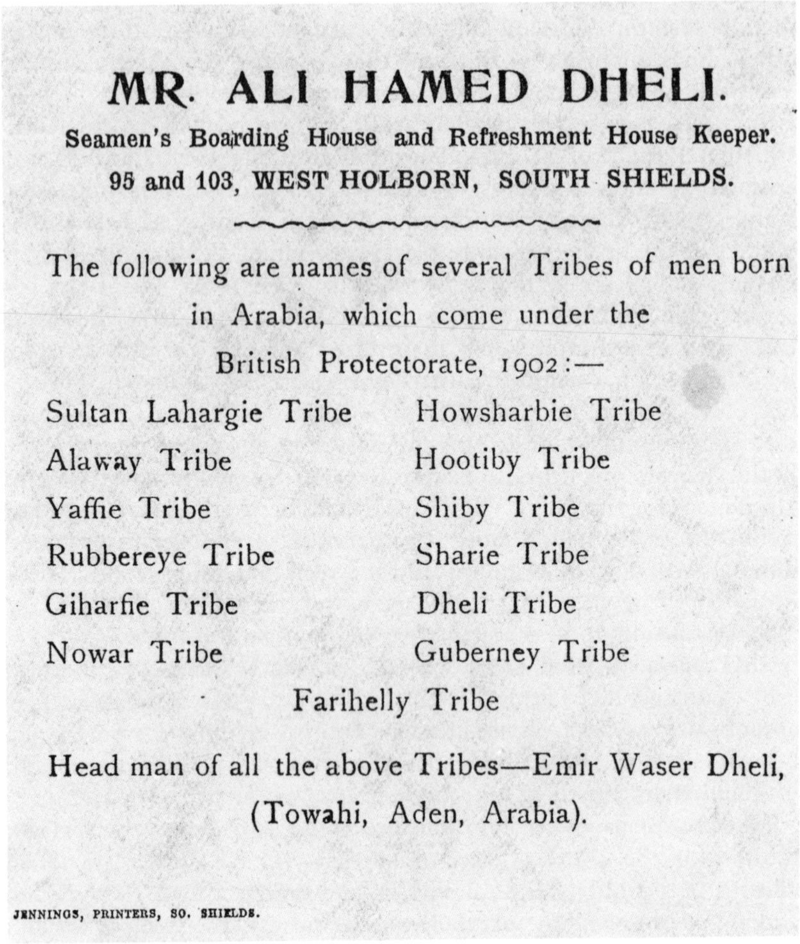

MR. ALI HAMED DHELI.

Seamen's Boarding House and Refreshment House Keeper.

95 and 103, WEST HOLBORN, SOUTH SHIELDS.

The following are names of several Tribes of men born
in Arabia, which come under the
British Protectorate, 1902 :—

Sultan Lahargie Tribe	Howsharbie Tribe
Alaway Tribe	Hootiby Tribe
Yaffie Tribe	Shiby Tribe
Rubbereye Tribe	Sharie Tribe
Giharfie Tribe	Dheli Tribe
Nowar Tribe	Guberney Tribe
Farihelly Tribe	

Head man of all the above Tribes—Emir Waser Dheli,
(Towahi, Aden, Arabia).

JENNINGS, PRINTERS, SO. SHIELDS.

Figure 6. Mr Ali Hamed Dheli, one of the Arab boarding-house masters in
South Shields, prepared this printed list of the tribes in Britain's Aden Protectorate
to which he claimed seamen lodging with him belonged. He sent it to the
Under-Secretary of State for India in London as part of his campaign to oppose
the introduction of the rota system in South Shields. (PRO CO 725/21/9 Letter
from Mr Dheli to the Under-Secretary of State for India dated 4 December 1930)

Some writers have argued that Yemenis left their villages and migrated to Aden and overseas because of the Imam's oppressive taxation system.[26] Indeed this is a standard explanation given by Arab seamen themselves. But now that we know that Arab seamen were engaged on steamers at Aden from the middle of the nineteenth century and that recruitment appears to have peaked in the years immediately before the First World War, this explanation is unsatisfactory. After the First World War, when Imami rule was established in Yemen, recruitment of Arab seamen at Aden had declined dramatically and countries like Britain were imposing tough restrictions on the employment of Arab seamen and the entry of new arrivals. By this time Yemeni communities had already become established at a number of British ports. There were new arrivals from the Yemen, but on the whole these men replaced others who had returned home.

The southern highlands of Yemen receive abundant rainfall and are the richest agricultural region in the country. Walter Harris, who travelled across the eastern part of the southern highlands of Yemen in 1892 on his journey from Aden to Sanaa has left us this discription of the al-Aud district along the Wadi Banna north of Qataba:

> On all sides of us were tiny streams, splashing and tumbling through fern-covered banks over pebbles and stones. Everywhere were green fields in which young barley showed promise of rich crops, everywhere great shady trees and jungle covered the slopes ... The land, carefully terraced to allow more cultivation, presented from a distance an appearance of a great flight of steps, so evenly was this immense work carried out.[27]

Neverthless, droughts are a regular occurrence[28] and during the second half of the nineteenth century and the early years of the twentieth century natural disasters such as drought and famine were aggravated by political instability as the country rose in successive revolts against the Turks. These misfortunes may well have forced some villagers to migrate in search of employment in order to support their families. The port of Aden, where a range of new employment opportunities were opening up at this time offering the prospect of cash wages, must have exerted a powerful attraction. After the First World War the oppressive taxation system imposed on the Shafi'i districts by the Imami Government may well have been a factor encouraging continued emigration. Seamen who had returned to their villages and had exhausted their savings may have been forced to seek employment again at British ports or to nominate another member of the family to replace them. But as the restrictions imposed on the entry of Arab seamen to Britain became more stringent in the years following the First World War, the movement became increasingly difficult and often clandestine.

Although the evidence is fragmentary, it does indicate that at least some tribal chiefs took an active interest in the recruitment of their tribesmen as seamen. A petition from some fifty-five Arab seamen to the First Assistant Resident, Aden dated 8 May 1919 in defence of one of the licensed brokers, Mahamed Nasir Ali (also known as Mohamed Nassir), states:

> We respectfully inform you that Mahamed Nasir Ali is a man known by our Arab sheikhs and chiefs to be of an excellent character and good standing. If the statement of his enemies was at all true we are quite sure that our Arab sheikhs would have communicated with you on this subject.[29]

Some tribal chiefs may have gained financially from the employment of their tribesmen as seamen. In 1904 Sheikh Ali Abdul Karim, the chief Sheikh of Juban (an important seafaring tribe) whose territory was within the Turkish sphere of influence, sought permission from the British authorities to enter Aden in order to recover certain amounts due to him from Jubanis employed as seamen on Messageries Maritimes steamers.[30] It is possible that the Sheikh was exploiting a new source of tribute or that he had advanced them money to secure their employment and was seeking repayment, presumably with interest. It is perhaps significant that the Sheikh's representative at Aden was a ship's serang, presumably a Jubani. Serangs played an important role as intermediaries in the recruitment of seamen. In 1948 the Saqladi Sheikh Muhammad Muqbil, who had invaded and occupied Sha'ib territory in the Aden Protectorate in the previous year, was criticized by the British authorities for the severity of his rule because he was reported to have imposed a levy of two and a half per cent on remittances sent home by Sha'ibi seamen.[31]

In 1934 the Amir of Dhala, one of the senior chiefs of the Aden Protectorate, wrote to the Resident, Aden requesting that certificates of nationality and identity be given to two of his tribesmen (Amiris) so that they could proceed to Britain to seek employment as seamen and offering personally to guarantee all expenses incurred in the event of their repatriation. The certificates were granted but when the two men arrived in Cardiff they were immediately arrested and deported back to Aden. In 1935 when a further five applications for certificates were received from Amiris, again with a guarantee from the Amir, the Resident was instructed by the Home Office to refuse them permission to travel to Britain. The Amir protested to the Resident at the refusal to accept his guarantee and against the barring of employment abroad to the individuals concerned. The case is an interesting one because the Resident pointed out to the Colonial Office and Home Office that

> ... this new restriction has the effect of throwing permanently out of employment British Protected persons who have been seamen and who have been visiting their native country or have been out of employment. It also completely debars young men from adopting the occupation of seamen although this is a profession that has been followed by people from these parts of the Protectorate for generations. I realise the necessity of preventing Arabs from Aden and the Aden Protectorate becoming stranded in the United Kingdom or elsewhere, but the restrictions now imposed appear to me to be unduly harsh and I suggest that they be modified in a manner that will leave an opening for employment to former seamen and to young men who wish to adopt this profession.[32]

The Home Office refused to modify their restrictions and stated that their decision in no way reflected on the guarantee of the Amir but was based solely on the chronic unemployment among coloured seamen in Britain.[33]

There are also examples of seamen looking to their tribal sheikhs for assistance when they were in trouble overseas. One such case came to light in 1914 when a number of Arab seamen were arrested in France on suspicion of being Turks. One of the seamen, Said Salim al-Khaishani al-Shabi, wrote the following letter to his tribal chief, Sheikh Haza Kasim of the Dubeini (a sub-tribe of the Subeihi):

> We have absented ourselves from you for a long time. We do not know who of you is alive and who is dead. We are now in the prison of the French Government. They (French Govt) thought us to be a Turk. On hearing this from them we gave them an excuse that we were (of the residents) of Djibouti and so they asked us to bring them a register sheet. We remained at Djibouti for sometime but did not take out a register sheet. Meanwhile kindly make some arrangement for our release and return to Aden. We do not want to remain in this country any

longer. Please do not treat the matter with slackness. Your father is the English Government and you will be able to arrange for our release in case you possess influence with your Government otherwise we will not be released. After leaving the prison we will come to you by the first steamer. Please do not think that we have done any crime (but simply accused of being a Turk). Whatever disgrace we will be put is attached to all of you. May you be preserved.[34]

Sheikh Haza Kasim asked the Political Resident, Aden to secure his release pointing out that Said Salim and his clan were his subjects and paid him annual tribute. In January 1915 the Political Resident informed the sheikh that the British Government had contacted the French Government and that Salim and the other Arabs detained would be released very soon.[35]

The majority of Arabs who engaged as seamen at Aden were temporary migrants and after a few years working on the steamers they returned to their villages.[36] A few, often those men who had held the more lucrative position of ship's serang, opened a shop or other small business at Aden. But for most seamen the bulk of their earnings was used to support their families at home. Though they were living and working far from home and contact was often irregular and intermittent, the seamen remained a part of village society and most of them took a keen interest in the social, economic and religious life of their own community. Letters exchanged between seamen in South Shields and their families in Yemen discuss how remittances should be distributed, marriage alliances, the construction of new houses, the state of the harvest, the sale of land and animals, and donations for the upkeep of and repairs to the village mosque. For those seamen who married and settled down in South Shields, the links with village and family in rural Yemen sometimes became weaker but they were rarely broken.

Three

The 'Big Men' of the Community: the Arab Boarding-house Masters

I The importance of the Arab boarding-house and its master

The majority of Arab seamen in South Shields lived in boarding-houses run by Arabs. These boarding-houses catered not only for Arab seamen who shipped out regularly from north-east ports but also for Arabs from other ports who came to South Shields in search of a ship. As a coal port and, above all, an export port, South Shields, together with the other north-east ports, was an important centre for signing on men. Seamen who had been paid off at other ports proceeded to South Shields to join a new ship. South Shields was described as a centre of supply of Arab seamen 'not only for the north-east district, but all over the country', and 'to have become more or less the clearing house for Arab and Somali seamen over the whole of the North of England.'[1] There were no Arab boarding-houses in any of the other north-east ports. The other major centre where Arab seamen congregated was Cardiff, which was also a coal port and one of the most important ports in Britain for signing on men. Strong links existed between the Arab communities in South Shields and Cardiff with seamen moving from one port to the other in search of employment. The occupants of the Arab boarding-houses in South Shields therefore experienced a substantial turnover and would have been constantly changing as ships and their crews came and went.

Since the late nineteenth century, legislation had made it an offence against the law for any private person or householder to accommodate a seaman.[2] In an attempt to protect seamen against exploitation, they were required to stay in licensed seamen's lodging-houses. In order to secure a licence, the keeper of an authorized seamen's lodging-house was required to observe a number of regulations relating to the number of lodgers accommodated, to health and general hygiene, and to allow right of access and inspection to the premises by the Medical Officer of Health, officers of the Board of Trade and the police. Before a house could be licenced as a seamen's lodging-house, the premises had to be inspected and approved for the purpose by the Medical Officer of Health and the keeper had to produce a certificate from the Chief Constable that he was a fit and proper person to have charge of such a house and that no conviction had been made against him in any police court during the three years preceding his application.

In South Shields as in other British ports, boarding-houses were run on ethnic lines. For Arab seamen arriving in a strange land with little knowledge of its language and customs, the Arab boarding-house was virtually essential for their survival. The Arab boarding-house and its keeper or master, as he was often referred to, was a vitally important institution for the Arab seafaring community. It provided not only accommodation and food that was lawful according to their religion, but essential assistance in securing another ship, and credit if their resources ran out before they signed on for the next voyage. In some boarding-houses in South Shields a place was set aside where the men could pray and carry out other religious observances (see Chapter Eight, p.207). The Arab boarding-house master provided a vital link between the seamen and the outside world. He could advise them if they were in difficulty, stand surety for them if they got into trouble with the police, and if they did not return from their next voyage, dispose of any money or belongings they had left in his safekeeping and return their effects to their relatives. Some boarding-house masters acted as local representatives of seamen's agents based in Aden, recovering debts, delivering letters for their customers, sending money to the families of seamen in Yemen and arranging passages for seamen wishing to return home. Even Arab seamen living outside the boarding-houses sometimes looked to the boarding-house masters for assistance in time of trouble. For example, when Hassan Abdullah and his wife Isabella of Portberry Way in South Shields needed money to bring a young boy they had looked after as child from Aden in 1938, Mohamed Dowah, a boarding-house keeper of 40 Portberry Street, agreed to pay for the boy's passage to Britain.[3]

It was the same Mohamed Dowah who organized a collection among the Arab community to pay for the funeral of Ali Nagi, an Arab seaman who committed suicide in Durham Prison in 1935 while awaiting deportation to Aden.[4]

Most Arab boarding-house masters were former seamen who had chosen to settle in South Shields and go into business there. The majority were from Yemen or adjacent parts of the Aden Protectorate but at least one of the boarding-houses was kept by an Egyptian. Abdul Hamid, who kept a boarding-house at 2 East Holborn, was from Port Said. Where possible Arab seamen preferred to go to a boarding-house run by an Arab of their own tribe. In the absence of close relatives, or even men from the same village, seamen sought the company of members of their own tribe. A Shamiri tribesman, for example, was a Shamiri before he was a Yemeni. There was little sense of unity in those times. Most of the Arab boarding-houses appear to have catered exclusively for Arabs but a few took seamen of other nationalities. For example, Indian and Malay seamen stayed at Muhammad Muckble's boarding-house in East Holborn and Somali seamen at Hassan Mohamed's boarding-house at 10 Chapter Row.

Until the late 1930s, all the Arab boarding-houses were located in East and West Holborn and adjacent streets close to the Shipping Federation Offices on the Mill Dam. Some had already been licensed seamen's lodging-houses run mainly by local people before they were purchased by Arabs; others had been private houses. Some Arab boarding-houses changed hands several times but the new owner was normally another Arab. They varied greatly in size, in terms of the number of lodgers who could be accommodated. In 1911 Ali Said's boarding-house in Nile Street was registered for fifteen seamen; in 1917 when Ahmed Nogen obtained a licence for 25 East Holborn it had only two rooms, one licensed for eight men and the other for four; in contrast, in 1919 some sixty or seventy boarders were reported to be living at Faid Abdulla's boarding-house which consisted of two premises opposite one another on either side of the street at 4 and 63 Thrift Street. Some masters ran more than one boarding-house. Some lived on the premises where they had a private set of rooms for their families; others lived with their families in a separate house close by in Holborn. In many of the boarding-houses the ground floor rooms were where the seamen congregated to have their meals, to talk and to meet their friends. To amuse themselves, some of the men would play the flute and sing; others, as in Yemen, would recite poetry they had composed themselves. Dominoes were a popular pastime among the seamen and many liked to put a bet on the horses. A seaman who could read English would often read out stories of interest from the local newspaper to the other lodgers. Hassan Mohamed even installed a slot machine in his boarding-house to amuse his lodgers. Not all boarding-houses provided meals for their lodgers and seamen from these houses frequented a number of Arab refreshment houses in the neighbourhood where a range of traditional dishes were served, together with fruit and Arab coffee.

Some boarding-house masters became wealthy men. Said Hassan, who kept a boarding-house at 25 East Holborn, branched out into the garage and transport business, setting up a coach service from South Shields to London.[5] During the 1920s his varied business activities also included a tobacco and grocery shop, a shipping butcher's business at Tyne Dock, a temperance hotel at Dunston and a sheep farm at Hedworth. He also owned three motor launches, which he used for his varied business activities,[6] and moved his family into Simonside House, a large house in its own grounds on the outskirts of the town. Unfortunately he overextended himself and in 1930 was declared bankrupt with debts of over £5,000.[7] Running a boarding-house also brought dangers as violence was never far below the surface on the South Shields waterfront. Some boarding-house masters were bitter rivals and their rivalry sometimes led to violent confrontations, even death. During outbreaks of racial violence, the Arab boarding-houses and refreshment houses were the first targets for attack and on occasions considerable damage was done to their properties.

There were also frequent disputes between the boarding-house masters and their boarders, normally over money. For example in May 1916 an Arab firemen, Salah Sirvie, was charged with attacking Ali Said, a boarding-house keeper of 72a East Holborn, and wounding him with a knife. Salah had been a boarder at Ali Said's house for three weeks and had then been put out. Ali Said claimed that Salah owed him money. Salah alleged that Ali Said had a large sum of money belonging to him and refused to return it. A fight had broken out when Ali Said and two other men attacked him.[8]

In another case during June 1921 an Arab fireman, Abbas Heider, was charged with attempting to murder Ali Hassan, a refreshment house keeper of 75 East Holborn. Heider, who boarded with Hassan, claimed that he had handed over money totalling £100 to Hassan who was supposed to send it to Heider's relatives in Aden but that none of the money had been received. When the case came to the Durham Assizes, Mr C.B. Fenwick defending Heider stated that it was customary for Arab seamen to hand over money to boarding-house and refreshment house keepers who acted in the capacity of honorary bankers and transmitted money to their relatives. But instead of sending the money to Aden, Hassan had used most of it to support unemployed Arab seamen who were in distress and that this was the root of the trouble. Heider was sentenced to six months' imprisonment.[9]

When such disputes over money arose there is evidence that efforts were made to reach an amicable settlement within the Arab community itself through the appointment of an arbitrator. This was common practice in Yemen and the Aden Protectorate at this time and avoided recourse to the courts. Such a case occurred in August 1921 when five seamen boarding with Said Hassan at 25 East Holborn began to owe a considerable amount of money for board and lodgings. Hassan insisted on having receipts to show how much money was owing to him and when the men refused to sign the receipts they were told to leave. A cousin of one of the seamen was appointed arbitrator and Hassan agreed to abide by his decision and pay expenses. After listening to the case the arbitrator declared that the men should pay Hassan all the money that was due to him, a total of £93, but as Hassan had insulted the men by putting them out he would be fined £75.[10]

But many other cases did come before the courts. For example in May 1914 Ali Said sued one of his boarders, Abdul Said, a seaman, because the man had not paid for his board and lodgings. Ali Said claimed that Abdul Said had stayed at his boarding-house for three weeks and four days. As the charge for board and lodgings was 16s. per week, he owed £2 17s. 6d. and he had also borrowed £2 15s. Abdul Said had not paid for his board and lodgings nor repaid the loan. In reply Abdul Said stated that he had stayed only two days at the boarding-house, had paid 9s. 6d. and denied borrowing any money. The court ruled in favour of Ali Said with respect to the sum owing for board and lodgings, but not for the money lent.[11]

In January 1919 an Arab seaman, named as Said Abdul, accused Hassan Ahamed, a refreshment house keeper of 63 East Holborn, of refusing to repay money which Said Abdul had sent to Ahamed to keep for him. Ahamed claimed that Said Abdul's money, together with other money deposited with him by seamen totalling between £500 and £1000, had been stolen. The police had investigated the theft but found no trace of the money. They had doubts that the money had in fact been stolen. Ahamed was fined £5 and ordered to repay the missing money.[12] In November 1931 Said Mabrouk, a boarding-house keeper of Laygate Street, claimed £282 from seven boarders for their board and lodgings. The seven Arab seamen made a counter claim in respect of money they alleged they had paid to Mabrouk. When the case came before the South Shields' County Court, the judge declared in favour of Mabrouk but reduced the amount that was due to him to £248. Mabrouk's claim had been based on 30s. a week for board and lodgings but the judge ruled that £1 was a reasonable amount.[13]

Boarding-house keepers handled large amounts of money in their role as bankers for the seamen lodging with them and although many had bank accounts, the nature of their business meant that it was necessary to keep large amounts of cash on the premises. The fear of robbery must have always been present. On 18 February 1919 Faid Abdulla, a boarding-house keeper of 4 and 63 Thrift Street was found beaten to death in front of an open safe in his private room at the boarding-house. The case was reported in great detail in the local press and these accounts provide a fascinating insight into the life and work of an Arab boarding-house master.

Faid Abdulla came to South Shields in 1913 and established a boarding-house and refreshment house for Arab seamen. He was joined shortly after by his brother Nasser who assisted him in the running of the business. Faid's English wife, Margaret, also helped her husband in the boarding-house which accommodated between sixty and seventy boarders. They had a young baby who was sleeping in their private room when Faid was murdered. At the time of the murder the business was prospering and Faid had £1,340 in his bank account and several hundred pounds in cash in the safe at the boarding-house. In 1918 the two brothers had made out wills in each other's favour with a local solicitor. During the investigation, the police found a box in Nasser's room containing £1,234 in notes, cheques and money orders. Much of the money had been deposited with Nasser by seamen staying at the boarding-house. The trunk also contained certain items belonging to his murdered brother and on this evidence Nasser was arrested and brought to trial for Faid's murder. But Nasser was later acquitted. He was able to prove that he had not left the refreshment room at the time of the murder. He also maintained that he had taken certain items belonging to his brother into safekeeping only after his brother's murder had been discovered. It emerged from the trial that a fierce argument had broken out between Faid and a number of Arabs on the day of the murder when they were returning by train from visiting a ship at Sunderland. The murder also occurred at a time of serious racial tensions in the town resulting in a number of clashes between Arabs and white crowds including recently demobilized soldiers (see

Chapter Four, p.79). Faid was murdered only a few days after the Mill Dam riot when violence erupted between white seamen and Arab seamen. The murderer appears to have escaped justice.[14]

Several boarding-house keepers carried loaded revolvers for their own protection. Some of the Arab seamen lodging with them also had revolvers and the police instructed the boarding-house keepers to confiscate them and to report the matter to the authorities. For example in December 1924 Ahmed Alwin, a refreshment house keeper of 42 and 43 Commercial Road, and his wife Kate Amelia, were jointly charged with possessing four revolvers and 179 rounds of ammunition without certificates. In their defence they claimed that they had confiscated them from seamen but had forgotten to report this to the police. One of the seamen whose revolver had been confiscated had threatened Mrs Alwin and it was this man who had reported Alwin and his wife to the police to get his own back. The two defendants were fined £10 each.[15] Serious accidents with revolvers were not unknown in the boarding-houses when these weapons were not confiscated. For example, in December 1921 a revolver went off by accident at 63 Thrift Street seriously injuring one of the lodgers, Abdul Ramen. A certain Ahmed Hassan was sentenced to two months' imprisonment for causing the injury and fined £2 for possession of a firearm without a certificate.[16]

The Arab boarding-house master was a man of substance who wielded considerable influence over the seamen lodging with him and indeed within the wider Arab community in the town. He represented a key intermediary between the Arab seamen and the host society and was often well known in the town. Ali Said, who opened the first Arab boarding-house in South Shields, in a letter to the *Shields Daily Gazette*, emphasized that licences to Arab boarding-house masters were essential as only Arabs could manage Arab seamen and English people would not give them rooms because of their religion and customs.[17]

When the British and Foreign Sailors' Society agreed to offer temporary financial assistance to unemployed Arab seamen in the town during the depression in 1921, an agreement was made between the society and the boarding-house masters to pay a weekly allowance for the men's maintenance directly to the boarding-house masters. On this occasion the Mayor of South Shields, Councillor A.D. Johnston, paid tribute to the boarding-house keepers for the way they had carried on during the recent lean months, and 'the excellent influence they had exercised over the men living in their houses'.[18]

Later that year the mayor, the boarding-house masters and the

British and Foreign Sailors' Society co-operated in identifying those Arab seamen who were prepared to accept repatriation. The *Shields Daily Gazette* reported:

> The Mayor, in harmonious negotiation with the Boarding House Masters and the men in South Shields, and with the assistance of a representative of the Society, has for some time past been collating the names and particulars of the Arab seamen at our doors who have expressed their willingness to be sent home to Aden.[19]

But more often than not the Arab boarding-house master was the target of adverse criticism, even abuse, especially by union officials, the police and some local councillors, particularly with regard to allegations of bribery in the shipping of men and the illegal entry of Arab seamen into the country.

II The role of the Arab boarding-house masters in the shipping of men

An important, if not the most important, task of the Arab boarding-house master at this time was to secure employment for seamen lodging with him. Until the rota system was introduced in August 1930 (see Chapter Five, p.126), most Arab crews were recruited through the Arab boarding-house masters. Some of these masters had regular contracts to supply Arab firemen for steamers of a particular shipping company. Others appear to have had a regular arrangement with the chief engineer of a ship for the engagement of Arab crew. As early as 1913, Ali Hassan, who kept a boarding-house in East Holborn, was corresponding with the Trechmann Streamship Company in West Hartlepool about the supply of Arab firemen for their steamers.[20]

The letters of one boarding-house master, Muhammad Muckble, written during the 1920s, reveal the strenuous efforts that he made to get work for his boarders. Muckble corresponded directly with a number of shipping companies and agents, including Andrew Weir & Co. of London, Kaye Son & Co. of London and Liverpool, Watts, Watts & Co. of London, and Wait & Dodds of Newcastle, to supply crews for their steamers at ports in the north-east of England but also as far away as Glasgow, Belfast and Bordeaux. He received regular information from James Maxton & Co, Naval Architects, Consulting Engineers and Surveyors of Belfast about steamers under construction there and therefore likely to require crews and with

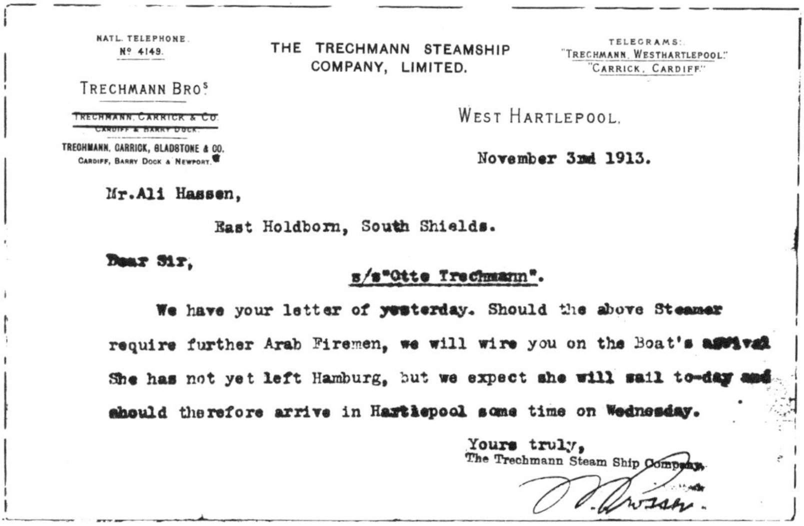

NATL. TELEPHONE.
Nº 4149.

TRECHMANN BROS

TRECHMANN, CARRICK & CO.
CARDIFF & BARRY DOCK

TRECHMANN, CARRICK, GLADSTONE & CO.
CARDIFF, BARRY DOCK & NEWPORT.

THE TRECHMANN STEAMSHIP
COMPANY, LIMITED.

TELEGRAMS:
"TRECHMANN, WESTHARTLEPOOL."
"CARRICK, CARDIFF."

WEST HARTLEPOOL.

November 3rd 1913.

Mr. Ali Hassen,

East Holdborn, South Shields.

Dear Sir,

s/s "Otto Trechmann".

We have your letter of yesterday. Should the above Steamer require further Arab Firemen, we will wire you on the Boat's arrival. She has not yet left Hamburg, but we expect she will sail to-day and should therefore arrive in Hartlepool some time on Wednesday.

Yours truly,
The Trechmann Steam Ship Company.

Figure 7. Copy of a letter dated 3 November 1913 from the Trechmann Steamship Company of West Hartlepool to Ali Hassan, one of the two Arab boarding-house masters in South Shields at that time, about the supply of Arab firemen for one of their ships. (Courtesy of Mr Norman Hassan)

Maxton's help supplied crews to a number of steamers of the Standard Fruit Co. of New Orleans. Muckble was required to supply men with experience of oil-fired boilers for the steamers of the Standard Fruit Co. He also corresponded with, and met the captains of steamers requiring crews. In this work he was assisted by a Mr L.B. Johnston, an employee or former employee of Wait and Dodds, Steamship Owners and Brokers of Newcastle, who drafted and typed letters for him, negotiated with the owners on his behalf and advised him on procedures.[21]

The efforts of the Arab boarding-house masters to secure employment for their boarders was strongly criticized especially by union officials. They were accused of gaining an unfair advantage over British firemen because they resorted to giving bribes to ships' engineers in order to persuade them to engage an Arab stokehold crew from their boarding-house and because the boarding-house master then charged each seaman a commission for finding him a job. An article in *The Seaman*, the official organ of the National Union of Seamen, in December 1929 declared that 'bribery was rampant in connection with the employment of Arabs' and that the methods of the Arab boarding-house masters were 'akin to the crimps of other days.'[22] In 1923 when taking part in a deputation to the Board of Trade, J. Henson of the National Sailors' and Firemen's Union stated:

> He [the Arab seaman] is competing in our opinion by what we call unfair methods. There are two standards of morality, the morality of the East and the morality of the West. The Eastern never seems to recognise the Western so far as morality is concerned. Men of the Western nations compete in the open market on equal terms without paying for the privilege of getting employment. Men of the Eastern nations, especially the Arabs, are always prepared to bribe the employer for the purpose of giving them employment. That, in our opinion, is unfair competition.[23]

His colleague from South Shields, a Mr Walsh, agreed:

> These men [the Arab boarding-house masters] were open to bribe anybody, either Union officials or any other officials, and I dare say that Union officials who would like to make a small fortune quickly, could do it if they fell in with the views of the Arab Boarding Masters.[24]

In 1930 the Assistant General Secretary of the National Union of Seaman, G. Gunning, wrote:

> It is very well known that Arab Boarding Masters have pro-
> ceeded to British ships in England, and after interviewing the
> Engineers have handed them a list of names. The Engineer has
> made out the Provisional Engagement slips, the Boarding
> Master takes them to his Board House and issues them to the
> men, whom he is desirous of getting off his hands as early as
> possible. It is very hard, in circumstances of this kind, to obtain
> evidence of bribery. It is very natural that no Engineer would
> admit having received payment, neither would any Boarding
> Master admit giving payment, but it is a well known fact that
> the Arabs who are employed, have to pay large sums for the
> purpose of obtaining these Provisional Engagement slips from
> the Boarding Masters.[25]

This issue provoked a lively debate in the local press. According to 'Ashes':

> It would be interesting to learn why engineers prefer Arabs,
> as I have been told on several occasions by white mem-
> bers of the crews where Arabs are carried, that they are
> not near as efficient as white men. I have also heard it said
> that an Arab pays so much for a job, and a little every week
> to keep it. I am loth to believe that British engineers would
> consent to such an arrangement, but there is surely
> something wrong somewhere, and I hope engineers will
> take notice and give a chance to the men who carried on
> during the war, and let them earn a living for their wives and
> children.[26]

'Justice' wrote:

> ... the only way I can account for the Arabs having a ship
> before a Britisher is because some of our British shipowners
> leave some of the chief engineers to pick the firemen themselves.
> I have been on board of ships and seen the Arab boardinghouse
> keepers come and have an interview with the chief engineer,
> and within a day or two after on marched a crowd of Arab
> firemen.[27]

In defence of the engagement of Arab firemen, G.B. Wilson, an ex-naval man who wrote letters for Arab boarding-house masters, argued as early as 1916 that:

> The reason engineers prefer Arabs in some cases which are far the minority is not far to seek. It is because of the good books they possess, and also the fact that they are life abstainers, as well as God-fearing men so far as their particular religion is concerned.[28]

Ali Said, one of the Arab boarding-house masters, maintained that: 'The reason why Arabs are accepted in preference to Englishmen is simply for their ability to work and for discipline given while carrying out their duty.'[29] These views were supported by 'Engineer' who wrote:

> These coloured men are engaged as firemen for their great reliability as steam raisers on time, their reliability as workers during working hours, and best of all, their sober habits when joining ship or when in foreign ports. I have given white men many chances myself of employment thinking it was a shame to see them out of work. But a few times bitten a few times shy is my motto in the future. I have sailed with all nationalities down below, so I am writing from experience.[30]

There is little doubt that the Arab seamen were good and reliable workers. Their discharge books provide ample proof of this, and cases of drunkenness when in port were very rare. According to one report they were frequently preferred by the masters of steamers on account of their better discipline and greater energy, especially important on voyages to the Tropics.[31] Arab seamen may also have been preferred by engineers because they were willing to carry out extra duties or put in overtime without pay. In spite of the lack of direct evidence, it seems highly probable that bribes or *douceurs* were paid by the Arab boarding-house masters to ships' engineers to ensure that men from their boarding-house were engaged as stokehold crew and that the men hired in this way were required to pay the boarding-house master a commission for finding them a ship. After all, the boarding-house master could claim that he provided a service and was merely charging a fee for that service. After the First World War, the practice of offering bribes for places on ships by the boarding-house masters may well have intensified as a result of competition for jobs and constant agitation against the employment of Arab seamen by the National Sailors' and Firemen's Union. However, such practices were rife throughout the entire system of recruitment of Arab seamen (see Chapter One, p.21).[32]

A small but unique insight into the complexities of this system is provided by a case which came before the police court in South Shields in July 1929. Several charges were made against a boarding-house master, known as Mohamed Abdul of 87 West Holborn, for having received payments from a number of Arab seamen for securing them engagement on the steamer *Anglo-Columbian* at Blyth contrary to the Merchant Shipping Act of 1894. The crew of the *Anglo-Columbian* had been paid off at Barry and the Arab firemen were informed that if they wished to be re-engaged they would have to join the ship at Blyth and sign on again. According to the Arab firemen, when they reported to the ship at Blyth the chief engineer sent them to Mohamed Abdul in South Shields who told them that if they wanted to be re-engaged they would have to pay him £2 each. They maintained that they paid the money and the boarding-house master took their discharge books. The donkeyman, Abdul Said, stated that the defendant demanded £40 from him so that he (the donkeyman) could pick the crew from seamen of his own tribe. Under cross-examination by the defence, the donkeyman admitted that he offered the boarding-house master money to allow him to select the crew. The boarding-house master stated that he was instructed by the chief engineer to find a crew but was given a list of eight men who had served on the ship before and were therefore to be re-engaged. A further nine men were required and these were to be supplied from men living in his boarding-house who had been ashore for a long time. He had been maintaining these men during a long period of unemployment and they could only repay him when he got them a ship. For this reason he refused to agree to the donkeyman's request to be allowed to supply the extra nine men, even though he was offered as much as £60 by the donkeyman and the donkeyman's messengers. The boarding-house master strongly denied demanding money from any of the Arab seamen who had brought charges against him because, he argued, the chief engineer had specified that these men had to be re-engaged.

It is interesting to note that two out of the eight men who made charges against the boarding-house master did not appear in court and a third withdrew the charges, presumably because they feared that proceeding with legal action might jeopardize their chances of securing employment in the future. The chief engineer of the ship was never called to give evidence, and the Chairman of the Court stated pointedly that engineers were not always very anxious to come. Yet his role was crucial. Why did he send the eight men to the boarding-house master in South Shields when he intended to re-engage them unless there was some form of financial arrangement between him and the boarding-house master whereby the boarding-house master charged the men a fee for signing on and then paid a *douceur* to the engineer for the privilege of supplying the crew? On a number of occasions during the hearing, the Chairman of the Court and the prosecutor stated that the practice of Arab seamen being forced to pay the boarding-house masters in order to sign on was widespread. In the words of the prosecutor:

> ... these coloured seamen came into this country to serve on British ships, and were very much in the hands of 'coffee house' proprietors and it was a disgraceful thing that they should be held up to ransom before they could secure a ship ... There was a well-founded suspicion abroad that this kind of thing was not an uncommon way of doing business, and it was essential that it should be known that these men ought to be able to obtain engagements without these sums being demanded of them.[33]

He called for some substantial penalty if the cases were proven. After a long hearing the boarding-house master was fined £5, the maximum penalty, on each of five charges and three charges were dismissed.

Of course, the seamen's boarding-house keepers as a class, whether British or foreign, had a bad reputation for exploiting seamen. Melville, for example, describes the waterfront inhabited by a

> ... variety of land-sharks, land-rats, and other vermin, which make the hapless mariner their prey. In the shape of landlords, barkeepers, clothiers, crimps and boardinghouse loungers, the land-sharks devour him limb from limb; while the land-rats and mice nibble at his purse.[34]

The Arab boarding-house masters may have been no better or worse than the others.[35]

III Rivalries between the Arab boarding-house masters

From the outset there was strong rivalry between at least some of the Arab boarding-house masters and also between the seamen lodging in different establishments. As early as June 1913 a fight broke out between a seaman, Mohamed Abdu, who was lodging at Ali Hassan's boarding-house, and Ahmed Ali and Salem Ahmed, two seamen staying at Ali Said's boarding-house, following a quarrel which had taken place earlier at the Mill Dam. When the case came before the South Shields magistrates, Abdu maintained that the two men from Ali Said's boarding-house had been put up to assault him and that he had merely defended himself.[36] In May 1916 fighting broke out between two different groups of Arab seamen at the Mill Dam who were armed with sticks, bottles and bricks. Five seamen from Muhammad Muckble's boarding-house were arrested and charged with committing a breach of the peace. At the hearing the Chief Constable reported that no fewer than seven outbreaks of this kind had occurred recently.[37]

A much more serious incident occurred in 1919 when two men were killed during violent clashes between seamen from Ali Said's boarding-house in East Holborn and others from a neighbouring establishment run by Abdul Rahman Zaid. The two seamen from Abdul Rahman Zaid's boarding-house, Mohamed Farah and Ahmed Ahmet together with Farah's cousin Nagi Nagi, had been to the Shipping Office at the Mill Dam. On their way home they were attacked in front of Abdul Rahman Zaid's boarding-house by some twenty men who rushed out from Ali Said's boarding-house armed with sticks, stones and bottles. During the fight that ensued, Farah and Ahmet were stabbed to death and police later arrested four men who were found hiding in Ali Said's boarding-house. Two of the men were concealed in his private quarters there. One of the men arrested had a bloodstained knife in his possession. Trouble had evidently broken out between the two boarding-houses the day before and a number of other boarding-house keepers, Said Hassan, Muhammad Muckble and Saleh Hobshibi, together with Mohamet Salie, a coffee shop keeper, had tried to mediate but had failed. Ali Said claimed that his house had been attacked by men from Abdul Rahman Zaid's house and several witnesses stated that Ali Said had incited men from his house to seek revenge by attacking Abdul Rahman Zaid's house, promising them that he would defend them if the matter came to court. Saleh Hobshibi stated that he had actually seen Ali Said give the murder weapon, a knife with a silver and ivory handle, to one of the prisoners. Ali Said denied this.

Summing up the evidence at the inquest the Deputy Coroner stated that Ali Said as a boarding-house keeper had great influence over his men and that it was he who was responsible for urging them to go out and kill men from Abdul Rahman Zaid's house:

> It seems to me that Ali Said is the man at the bottom of the whole of the trouble. I don't think there would have been any blood shed if Ali Said had cared to have said something to the men which would have stopped this fight on the Thursday morning.[38]

The jury found Hassan Hamed and Farra Allap guilty of the murders, aided and abetted by the other two prisoners; Ali Said was charged with being an accessory after the fact. The five men accused were commited to trial on the charge of wilful murder. No details of the subsequent trial are available, but surprisingly Ali Said and one of the accused men, Hassan Mohamad, were found not guilty and discharged. Hassan Hamed, Farra Allap and the fourth prisoner, Abdulla Said, were found guilty of manslaughter and sentenced to between five and six years' penal servitude. At the conclusion of the trial, Mr Justice Rowlatt delivered a stern warning as to the future conduct of the Arabs in the town:

> ... here we have an affray in the streets of South Shields which has led to the loss of two lives. This has got to be stopped. The Arab community in South Shields had better mend their ways because if we are going to have faction fights between various boarding houses in South Shields there will be people hanged for it and if they are not hanged they will be very severely punished if found guilty of manslaughter as in this case. No doubt there are many sensible men among the Arabs in South Shields. We have seen some in court in connection with this case. I recommend them to use their influence with their fellow countrymen and have the laws of this country obeyed.[39]

Quarrels between seamen belonging to different tribes may have contributed to the trouble which erupted between the boarding-houses[40] but the key factor appears to have been rivalry between the boarding-house masters over who should have the right to ship men. According to an official of the National Sailors' and Firemen's Union, after the violent clashes which took place between seamen from the two boarding-houses in 1919, the Board of Trade, the Chief Constable and the union met and formed a plan which involved setting up a rota, with all the Arab boarding-house masters taking it in turn to ship men. In his opinion this arrangement made large concessions to the Arab seamen. No details were given about the scheme, but it appears to have been effective certainly until 1923 when one of the principal boarding-house masters, speaking on behalf of all the others, demanded that the rota be scrapped and they revert to the system they had before.[41]

It is clear from other reports that some form of rota system was in place during the 1920s whereby the boarding-house masters took it in turn to ship men from South Shields when an Arab crew was required.[42] The system appears to have been unique to South Shields and does not seem to have been in place at Cardiff. It is equally clear that this system broke down regularly as some boarding-house masters sought to circumvent these restrictions by shipping men from other north-east ports. When they were caught they were penalized and forced to miss their next turn in the rota. For example, in February 1923 Said Mabrouk, who kept the Point Ferry boarding-house, was refused permission to ship men because he had just shipped men at Newcastle. Muhammad Muckble was allowed to ship men in his place. Instead of accepting this, Mabrouk instructed the men he had taken to the Shipping Office to sign on to attack Muckble who was severely beaten and stabbed in the mouth. Mabrouk was fined £5 and bound over for six months. When the case came to the South Shields police court, Mr Grunhut, acting for Muckble, stated that: 'It was very unfortunate that both parties in the case were boarding house masters, and the trouble was the old one of the scheme whereby the masters shipped the men when their turn came round.'[43]

Some time before, Muhammad Muckble had been refused permission to ship men when his turn came because he had shipped seamen from Middlesbrough.[44] Another incident occurred in March 1927 at the Shipping Federation Offices at the Mill Dam when rival boarding-house masters and their men clashed over the signing on of a donkeyman for the steamer *Maid of Andros*. It appears that a boarding-house keeper of 4 Thrift Street known as Abdul Sophie, accompanied one of his men, Monsoor Farah, to the Shipping Federation Offices where Farah was to sign on as donkeyman on the ship, having been interviewed earlier by the chief engineer. When they arrived, two other boarding-house masters, Ali Said and Said Mabrouk, were there with a large number of their own men, and they set upon Abdul Sophie, Farah and another man, Ali Hassan, who was with them, stabbing them with knives.[45]

Despite the fact that the National Sailors' and Firemen's Union were a party to the arrangement whereby the boarding-house masters took it in turn to ship men, a case which came before the South Shields police court in December 1924 indicates that union officials tried to interfere with the scheme and to replace Arab crews with white seamen. Said Mabrouk, who kept a boarding-house at Point Ferry Approach, was instructed by the Shipping Federation to contact the chief engineer of the steamer *Sandgate* which required nine Arab firemen and one donkeyman. The chief engineer signed the necessary requisition forms and Mabrouk took the names of the seamen who were to be signed on to the Shipping Office where the forms were endorsed. The men had been unemployed for some months and their union subscriptions were in arrears amounting to £60. After their subscriptions had been paid up to date the union official refused to give them the PC5 forms which were necessary before they could sign on (see Chapter Five, p.122), and informed the chief engineer that he had to sign on a white crew. Mabrouk summoned the union official, George Grey, with conduct likely to cause a breach of the peace. Mr J. Muir Smith, acting for Mabrouk, reminded the court that:

> . . . we do know what has happened in the past, and it was to avoid this that proper steps were taken and proper arrangements made with the boarding house keepers. If this sort of thing is allowed to go on the consequences might be of a disastrous nature.[46]

Grey denied the offence and the case was dismissed. One of the magistrates, Alderman Wylie, commented, 'I know how I would get over the trouble. I would dispense with the Arabs'.[47]

In an effort to find ships for their men, some boarding-house masters from South Shields looked to ports outside the north-east. For example a group of Arabs from South Shields arrived at the Merchant Shipping Office at Hull in April 1928 and it appears that some previous agreement had been made for them to sign on as firemen aboard the steamer *Portishead*, presumably through the efforts of one of the South Shields boarding-house masters. A rival group of Arabs from Hull, who had been waiting for a ship for several months, got wind of this and went to the Shipping Office to stop them. Police reinforcements were called in to separate the rival groups and after consultations between the Board of Trade, the Seamen's Union and the captain of the steamer, the Arabs from Hull were finally signed on.[48] There were also clashes between Arabs and Somalis in South Shields over the signing on of Arab seamen. For example in October 1928 Said Mabrouk took two Arab seamen from his boarding-house to sign on a ship lying in the Middle Docks where a quarrel broke out because the Somali crew did not want the Arabs on board. Mabrouk stated that he and his men only tried to protect themselves and did not start the disturbance. He was nevertheless fined and bound over for twelve months.[49] In February 1929 a dispute over the signing on of an Indian crew instead of an Arab crew for the steamer *Kinross* at Sunderland resulted in the murder of a boarding-house runner, Benjamin George Franklin, a Maori from New Zealand. Franklin was accused of inducing the owners of the *Kinross* to sign on an Indian rather than an Arab crew. He was set upon by a group of Arab seamen in South Shields and during the struggle Franklin was stabbed to death.[50]

IV   The boarding-house masters and the illegal entry of Arab seamen into Britain

In addition to accusations of bribery in connection with the shipping of men, the Arab boarding-house masters were accused of instigating the illegal entry of Arab seamen into Britain. During the First World War Arab seamen had entered Britain and taken up employment at British ports with few restrictions or controls. After the war the severe depression in shipping resulted in pressure to exclude any further influx of Arabs. In 1920 the Home Office therefore instructed immigration officers to refuse Arab seamen permission to land unless they could prove that they were British subjects (see Chapter Four, p.100). These actions proved ineffective and Arab seamen were successfully smuggled in.

The Arab boarding-house masters in South Shields were accused of being actively engaged in inducing Arabs to come from Aden to Britain for employment[51] and 'not overscrupulous in their methods of assistance'.[52] The smuggling in of Arab stowaways, it was argued, was a highly organized business in which boarding-house and cafe keepers co-operated.[53] One report suggests that boarding-house masters at South Shields may have paid the fares of men who landed irregularly as a 'speculation' with the intention of keeping them as boarders until they could find employment.[54] Even when further restrictions were introduced in 1925, concern was expressed that Arab seamen still slipped through the net and managed to land irregularly. It was alleged that they were assisted by the boarding-house masters who hoped eventually to obtain employment for them which would more than pay for their keep.

The route followed by most Arabs who sought to enter Britain illegally began at the French-held port of Djibouti. Some men travelled on from there to Suez and Port Said in Egypt, presumably in the hope of obtaining work on British ships calling at these ports. But the majority took one of the regular Messageries Maritimes steamers calling at Djibouti and travelled to Marseilles either as members of the crew, passage workers or deck passengers. The French steamship company did not insist on the men holding passports. The men appear to have encountered no restrictions on landing at Marseilles and proceeded by train to Rouen or Le Havre in northern France and remained there until arrangements could be made to get them on board a ship sailing for Britain with an Arab crew. There were numerous British weekly cargo vessels trading between northern France and the north-east coast and Bristol Channel ports. The men were either smuggled across as stowaways with the help of the Arab crew or with the knowledge of the ship's officers who received a monetary consideration. On landing they were taken in by one of the Arab boarding-house masters at South Shields or Cardiff which became the two major centres where illegally-landed Arab seamen gathered. A man landing at South Shields might go to Cardiff to evade detection and there was a similar movement from Cardiff to South Shields. If a seamen who had landed illegally was found and questioned by the immigration authorities, he refused to divulge the name of the ship or port at which he had landed. Even when the name of the ship was discovered, the master of the vessel normally denied all knowledge of the stowaway and it was impossible to hold him responsible for the man's repatriation.

The police also complained that when cases of illegal entry were brought before the courts, it proved difficult to obtain a conviction. The man charged insisted that he was a British subject and magistrates upheld the view that it was up to the prosecution to prove that he was not. The police felt that the onus of proof should be on the accused. In such cases the man's legal expenses were probably defrayed by one of the boarding-house masters.[55]

During the First World War Arab seamen employed on British ships had earned high wages and those who returned home after a few years with their savings probably encouraged other Arabs from the same village or tribe to follow their example. Having exhausted their savings, some seamen undoubtedly wished to return to Britain in order to look for work. Even when unemployment among Arab seamen at British ports became acute in the late 1920s, there appears to have been no shortage of Arabs trying to reach Britain to seek employment on British ships. The conditions for chain migration had been firmly established. When the authorities at Aden tried to stem this movement by refusing permission for seamen to travel to Djibouti, there is evidence that very large numbers of men travelled to Zaila in Somaliland, as there were no passport restrictions between Aden and Somaliland, and then walked the sixty kilometres to Djibouti to sign on one of the Messageries Maritimes steamers.[56] In 1920 the Aden police reported that 204 Arabs had left Aden for Zaila in the last four voyages, at an average rate of fifty per week. Enquiries from seamen's agents revealed that most of them were seamen going to Djibouti to sign on Messageries Maritimes steamers.[57]

Some of the Arab boarding-house masters at South Shields and Cardiff were part of a network of sub-agents established by seamen's agents in Aden and used to assist Arabs seeking to travel to Britain in search of employment as seamen. Seamen's agents had been active at Aden for a long time. They advanced money to seamen and through a network of local agents in European ports, normally Arab boarding-house masters, recovered debts, and arranged to deliver letters and remittances from seamen to their families in Yemen on a commission basis. As restrictions were imposed on Arab firemen leaving Aden and entering Britain, the seamen's agents became involved in assisting seamen who had returned home and wanted to resume their employment in Europe and also new customers who wished to follow their example. They employed local agents in the tribal homelands of the seamen in Yemen and at the main transit points along the route to Britain. All the seamen's agents appointed local agents at Djibouti who were able to arrange passages for seamen who did not possess passports on one of the Messageries Maritimes' steamers to Marseilles, thus evading passport regulations at Aden. On arriving at Marseilles they would be assisted by the local agent there to make the next part of their journey. Good profits could be made from this business which resulted in strong competition between the agents for customers.[58]

Seamen's agents in Aden also assisted Arab seamen who had entered Britain illegally and tried to regularize their position by obtaining special certificates of nationality and identity for them. There is no doubt that they handled spurious claims and that false witnesses and referees could be obtained for a small remuneration to testify to a seaman's claim to British nationality. The usual procedure was for the applicant to send his photograph to Aden in advance, together with a certain sum of money, via the local agent so that the witnessess would be able to recognize him when subsequently shown the photograph which accompanied the application. Fraudulent applications were helped by the fact that complete records of births had not been maintained at Aden and some of the records had been destroyed during the First World War.[59] Some Arab boarding-house masters from Britain returned to Aden where they established themselves as seamen's agents. For example Abdul Rahman Shadli, who bought Hassan Mohamed's boarding-house at 132 Commercial Road, South Shields in 1932, later became a seamen's agent in Aden, though his business does not appear to have prospered.[60] In 1927 Mohamed Ahmed Dalali, a boarding-house keeper in Cardiff, who had been the local agent there for Awad Ahmed al-Hadrami, one of the most prosperous seamen's agents in Aden, set up a rival agency in Aden with the help of his two brothers and tried to put his former employer out of business.[61]

There is some evidence that Arab boarding-house masters were engaged in trafficking in seamen's discharge papers which could be used by newcomers to establish their claim to previous service on British ships. In 1928 the Chief Constable of South Shields cited the example of a case where a large number of discharges belonging to Arab seamen who had died were found in the possession of a boarding-house master.[62] Reference was also made to the traffic in discharge books in October 1929 during the trial of the boarding-house keeper Ali Said on a charge of receiving stolen goods, which included a seaman's discharge book, identity book and wage book. During the trial the prosecution stated that this was the most serious aspect of the case: 'The police have reason to believe that among Arab lodging house keepers at British ports there is a traffic in these books. The photographs can be removed and others put in their place.'[63]

Other sources point to the widespread trading in documents of nationality and identity.[64] Certain boarding-house masters also tried to regularize the status of boarders who had landed irregularly by making strenuous efforts to obtain certificates of nationality and identity for them from the Office of the High Commissioner of India in London.[65] For example, Ali Hamed Dheli who kept a boarding-house at 95 and 103 West Holborn, obtained certificates of nationality and identity for several Arabs boarding with him and was well known at the Office of the High Commissioner for India.[66]

During the First World War the Arab boarding-house masters had made good profits. But immediately after the war their livelihood was threatened as many Arab seamen were repatriated and others, having worked for a number of years and accumulated savings, decided to return home. The restrictions imposed on the entry of Arab seamen into Britain unless they could prove conclusively that they were British subjects no doubt forced the boarding-house masters to encourage and support the illegal entry of Arabs into the country to replenish their stock of customers in a highly segregated market. The precise numbers involved are impossible to determine. It was in the interests of the National Sailors' and Firemen's Union to exaggerate the magnitude of the influx, while the Board of Trade and Home Office maintained that the terms of the Aliens Act were being strictly enforced.[67] There seems little doubt that the number of Arabs who entered irregularly certainly equalled the number of those departing and enabled the boarding-house keepers to maintain their supply of customers.[68] In July 1930 the Chief Superintendent of the Mercantile Marine Office, North Shields estimated that there were approximately 600 Arab seamen ashore in South Shields and commented:

> The large total of Arabs at South Shields may be due, to a large extent to the depression, but I fear these men continue to land in the country surreptitiously. A prominent Arab at South Shields, (who by the way is alleged to be a Turk) told me only yesterday that a considerable number of new Arabs had reached South Shields recently, having entered through Southampton. I can well believe it; for whereas in 1922 when I took a census of the Arab population there, I found a total of 630. As the Board will remember, 100 of these accepted repatriation, and I found that within six months another 300 disappeared; and in spite of deaths, and the restrictive operation of the Aliens Immigration Orders, the total stands at, or near the original figure ... The figures are of course approximate as the numbers vary from day to day, but they may be accepted as reliable.[69]

Significantly, the number of Arab boarding-houses increased from six in 1919 to fourteen in 1929. In that year there were forty seamen's lodging-houses in South Shields licensed to accommodate 541 seamen; the fourteen Arab boarding-houses were licensed to accommodate 268 Arab lodgers representing about half of the licensed seamen's accommodation in the town. Given the large number of Arab seamen in South Shields, licensed accommodation was insufficient and those who could not find lodgings in one of the Arab boarding-houses were accommodated in common lodging-houses and in temperance hotels. The usual practice was for the men to sleep out but obtain their meals at one of the Arab refreshment houses.[70]

At first the boarding-house masters were able to find work on weekly boats sailing from the Tyne to northern France and the Low Countries, the so-called Home and Coasting Trades, for those Arabs who had landed irregularly. Unlike steamers engaged on foreign trade, the weekly boats were not required to engage or discharge their crew at the Board of Trade Offices[71] as they were in the Home Trade Limits and simply furnished a return to the Board of Trade every six months. The large number of these boats made strict regulation of their crews difficult. As early as November 1920 it was claimed that seventy per cent of British steamers from the north-east coast employed in the Home and Coasting Trades were manned by Arabs in the stokehold, many of whom had entered the country illegally.[72] A memorandum from the Aliens Department of the Home Office in 1924 confirmed that Arab seamen who had landed illegally found 'an easy place of refuge on ships in the Home and Coasting Trades.'[73]

When these men had served for some time on a Home Trade or Coasting vessel, they returned to Yemen with their savings, handing over their sea papers to some newcomer who used them as proof of previous employment so that the business continued. Even when the restrictions governing the engagement of Arab seamen were tightened in 1925,[74] the new rules did not apply to vessels engaged in the Home Trade so that men who had been recently smuggled into the country could still get a footing in sea service.[75] But as pressure was brought to bear on ships' masters to engage only seamen who possessed certificates of registration and as immigration officials increased the checks made on weekly boats, it certainly became more difficult to find employment in Home Trade vessels for Arabs who had landed illegally. In December 1930 Ahmed Alwin, who kept a boarding-house at 43 Commercial Road, South Shields, complained to the Home Office that two of his boarders employed for the last sixteen months on one of the weekly boats sailing from the Tyne, had been removed from the ship by an NUS official. The Immigration Office, Newcastle commented:

> For some time past it has been the practice on the Tyne to discourage Masters of Home Trade vessels from signing on coloured seamen without papers and there is reason to believe that our efforts are meeting with success. This channel of sea employment has in the past been largely exploited by Coloured Boarding House Keepers to 'place' coloured seamen without

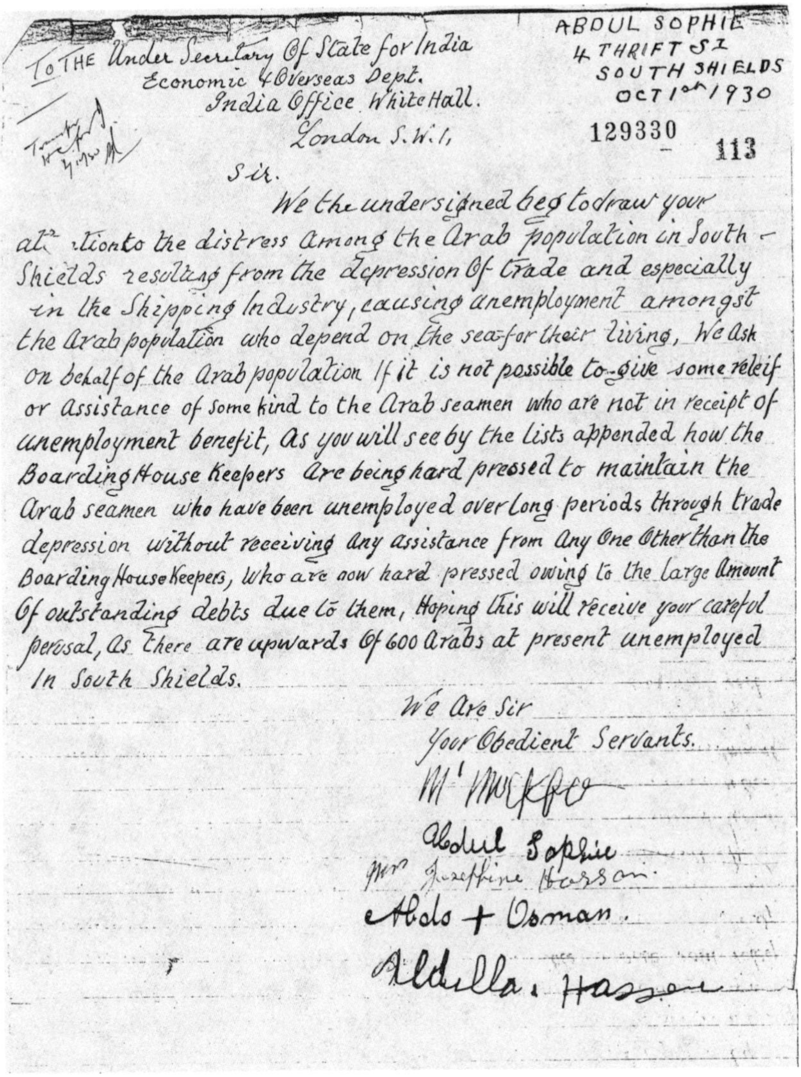

To THE Under Secretary Of State for India
Economic & Overseas Dept.
India Office White Hall.
London S.W.1,

ABDUL SOPHIE
4 THRIFT ST
SOUTH SHIELDS
OCT 1st 1930

129330
—
113

Sir.

We the undersigned beg to draw your attention to the distress among the Arab population in South Shields resulting from the depression Of trade and especially in the Shipping Industry, causing unemployment amongst the Arab population who depend on the sea for their living, We Ask on behalf of the Arab population If it is not possible to give some relief or assistance of some kind to the Arab seamen who are not in receipt of unemployment benefit, As you will see by the lists appended how the Boarding House Keepers are being hard pressed to maintain the Arab seamen who have been unemployed over long periods through trade depression without receiving any assistance from Any One Other than the Boarding House Keepers, Who are now hard pressed owing to the large Amount Of outstanding debts due to them, Hoping this will receive your careful perusal, As there are upwards Of 600 Arabs at present unemployed In South Shields.

We Are Sir
Your Obedient Servants.

Mᴿ Muckpo
Abdul Sophie
Mʳˢ Josephine Hassan.
Abdo + Osman.
Aldilla. Hassen

Figure 8. Copy of a letter dated 1 October 1930 from Abdul Sophie of 4 Thrift Street and other Arab boarding-house masters in South Shields to the Under-Secretary of State for India drawing attention to their financial plight because of the large number of outstanding debts due to them from unemployed Arab seamen. (PRO CO 725/21/9 Letter from Abdul Sophie *et al* to the Under-Secretary of State for India dated October 1, 1930)

Police registration certificates, and now that the requirements, as to registration etc. of the Rota System are being rigidly enforced it is becoming increasingly difficult for coloured seamen without certificates (who no doubt have entered the country surreptitiously) to find employment on Home Trade vessels.[76]

By the late 1920s and the onset of the depression boarding-house masters found themselves maintaining more and more seamen who could not find employment. Newcomers continued to arrive and the boarding-house masters felt obliged to take them in. A Home Office memorandum in May 1928 reported that:

It is known that boarding-house keepers are now beginning to feel the pinch of having to keep in idleness seamen whose irregular landing they have encouraged or connived at; and that this indirect financial pressure on the boarding-house keeper is one of the means of checking irregular landing.[77]

By 1930 many boarding-house masters were on the verge of bankruptcy. In October 1930 six boarding-house keepers wrote to the Under Secretary of State for India drawing his attention to their plight and requesting some kind of assistance for those Arab seamen who were not receiving unemployment benefit. They enclosed details of the debts owed to them by their boarders. Abdu Osman of 50 Commercial Road claimed outstanding debts of £1,626; Mrs Said Hassan of 10 Chapter Row, £672; Ali Said of 77 and 81 East Holborn £1,952; Muhammad Muckble of 11 East Holborn £629; Abdulla bin Hassen £265; and Abdul Sophie of 4 Thrift Street, £522. Some of the seamen boarding with them had not worked since 1927.[78] Muhammad Muckble claimed to hold promissory notes dating back to 1920 from seamen who still owed him money for food, board and lodgings.[79] Other boarding-house keepers wrote to the High Commissioner for India complaining that they had been practically ruined by providing food and accommodation to Arab seamen who could not find employment and were therefore destitute. Dr Khalid Sheldrake of the Western Islamic Association, who visited South Shields in September 1930, stated in an interview that:

The position of the boarding masters is, I am well aware, desperate. As a matter of fact, I know one whose mortgages on his property are taken up. The reason the boarding house keepers have continued to maintain these men is that there is an unwritten Mohammedan law that whatever you have you share it with a destitute brother. Therefore, these men have been maintaining the Arabs all along, and have ruined themselves by their kindness.[80]

One of the main aims of the rota system introduced in August 1930 by agreement between the Shipping Federation and the National Union of Seamen (see Chapter Five, p.126) was to put an end to the boarding-house master's role as a vital intermediary in the shipping of Arab firemen and in this way to provide more opportunities for the engagement of white crews. Under the new rota system when an Arab crew was required priority was to be given to men with the lowest number on the register, that is those who had been unemployed for the longest time. Unfair competition through the use of bribery by the boarding-house masters, it was claimed, would therefore be eliminated and this would ensure more jobs for white crews. The rota system was clearly intended to break the power of the boarding-house masters once and for all. A Home Office minute dated 3 October 1930 concluded:

> The rota system was a private invention, brought off by the collaboration of the Seamen's Union and the employers in certain ports. No Government Department could have managed it with existing powers, but it looks like being a success; and if it is, it will deal with the boarding house keeper, indirectly if not directly, touching him hard in his pocket.[81]

Four

Unwelcome Guests: Competition for Jobs[1]

I   Early prejudice and hostility towards Arabs

Examples of hostility from the local community towards Arab seamen settling in the town can be found from the outset. On 5 April 1913 a crowd of local men gathered outside Ali Hassan's boarding-house and refreshment rooms in East Holborn shouting abuse at the inmates. A disturbance broke out during which the crowd smashed the shop windows of the refreshment rooms and caused a great deal of damage. Several Arabs living close by came to the assistance of the boarding-house master and his family and during the fighting that ensued a number of people were injured. The police intervened and eventually dispersed the crowd. Five Englishmen and two Arabs later appeared before the South Shields police court and after a lengthy hearing the chairman of the magistrates stated that a very serious disturbance had taken place. He advised Englishmen to remember that 'Arabs were very excitable and it was a dangerous thing to irritate them.'[2] A week later there was a further disturbance in East Holborn when a boatman, John Raine, together with a dozen other local men, was arrested by the police outside an Arab boarding-house for being drunk and disorderly and using foul language.[3]

In September 1914 a dispute occured at the Mill Dam between an Arab seaman, named as Mahamed Abdulla, and an official of the Seamen's Union, John Barnes Fye. It appears that Fye had brought a number of seamen, including Abdulla, to a ship's engineer who wanted two firemen. The engineer took Abdulla's discharge book but told him that he preferred to employ 'Britishers', i.e. white

74

men, but that if he could not get Britishers he would sign him on. The engineer evidently obtained two white firemen and a violent quarrel then broke out between Abdulla and Fye which quickly involved other white men and Arabs who had also been waiting at the Mill Dam for ships. Fye claimed that Abdulla had accused him of bribing the engineer to choose white firemen and had assaulted him with a stick. A large number of Arabs also armed with sticks joined in and this led to a confrontation between the white men and the Arabs. Abdulla, on the other hand, stated that the quarrel began because he had difficulty getting his discharge book back from the engineer and that Fye had struck him first. The magistrates found Abdulla guilty of the assault charge and fined him 20s. and costs.[4]

In May 1916 in a letter to the editor of the *Shields Daily Gazette*, 'True Briton' requested an opportunity

> ... to ventilate a long-standing grievance in reference to the engaging of Arabs at our local shipping office.
>
> I noticed a week or two ago that Chief Constable Scott praised them up as a quiet class of people and that they had been of great service to our mercantile marine as it was impossible to supply Britishers for our vessels. Now, sir, I think it is about time our merchant seamen and firemen were waking up, otherwise they will be completely ousted by these men. I know several Britishers who have good books and have been ashore for several weeks and cannot get a ship, and yet those Arabs are being signed on every day to the disadvantage of Britishers.
>
> It seems rather strange that whenever a set of Arabs sign on a particular ship, they are all from the same boarding-house. Of course I am aware that they are all members of the Seamen's Union, but still some of those men's relatives may be conspiring against our own lads in the desert at the present time. Even the C.T. boats are engaging Arabs in preference to Britishers. I was under the impression that vessels under Admiralty orders were not allowed to ship aliens. Now I would like to see all our shipowners give orders to their captains and engineers not to engage an Arab whilst there was a Britisher wanting a job. Talk about patriotism, why, it makes me sick when I see the way our men are being treated.[5]

Ali Said, an Arab boarding-house master of 79a East Holborn, replied in a letter to the *Shields Daily Gazette* published three days later:

It is so easy to slander a quiet, decent class of people and at the same time it is mean, cowardly and certainly un-English to hide behind a nom de plume. I should think that 'True Briton' must be a disguised foreigner. The Chief Constable is not likely to praise a class of men who do not merit that praise and I would rather have the opinion of the Chief of Police on a matter of this kind than any person who is so afraid of his identity that he has to sling mud under an assumed name.

The Arabs for whom he has such a contempt, I would point out are all British subjects and it is surely to their credit that they are preferred by shipmasters to the alleged Britishers whom 'True Briton' is trying to champion and a serious reflection upon the ability and character of these said Britishers. Of course there are Britishers and Britishers. He admits that the Arabs are all Union men, the shipmasters evidently appreciate them; and now 'True Briton' endeavours to prejudice them by saying that some of the Arabs' relatives 'may be conspiring against our own lads in the desert at the present time.' 'True Briton' must be one of the 'Weary Willie' and 'Tired Tim' brigade, who do not care for work themselves and seem to take a dislike to anyone willing to work honestly for their living. Let 'True Briton' try to sail under true colours, make his complaint in his own name in an honest way, and be sure of his facts before he dubs British subjects aliens.[6]

Ali Said's defence of the Arabs was supported by G.B. Wilson, an ex-naval man, who described 'True Briton's' letter as 'nothing but a fabrication of untruths from beginning to end'. Wilson strongly denied that there were British seamen with good discharge books who were unable to get ships because of the Arabs and challenged 'True Briton' to name one Britisher with a record equal to that of the Arabs who was ashore and unemployed. Every day Arab seamen were playing a vitally important role in ensuring that Britain was supplied with food. If 'True Briton' was prejudiced against the Arabs because of their colour, Wilson reminded him that 'their blood is every bit the same colour as his'. Furthermore, far from conspiring against British soldiers, the Arabs were fighting on our side in the desert. Arab seamen were British subjects not aliens and were noted for their loyalty. Some of them were prisoners of war at Ruhleben in Germany along with British soldiers. Indeed he knew of one Arab firemen who had been a prisoner in Ruhleben for fifteen months and had returned to South Shields a physical wreck. Nevertheless, as soon as he recovered, this man wanted to go back to work in order to help Britain defeat Germany.[7]

Even before there was competition for jobs, it is clear that some white seamen were prejudiced against Arabs. For example, on 20 April 1918 a vessel engaged in the Admiralty coasting trade was due to sail from South Shields, but when two of the firemen failed to report for duty the captain went ashore and engaged two Arabs to take their places. When one of the white stokehold crew, Arthur Goodwin of South Shields, learned that two Arabs had been shipped he refused to sail because he objected to having Arabs as shipmates. As a result of Goodwin's refusal to go to sea the ship was delayed and was unable to sail until the next morning. Goodwin was fined £10 by the magistrates or two months' imprisonment.[8]

II Economic depression and declining employment opportunities in shipping

Once the exceptional demands of the First World War were over, the Arab seamen in South Shields found themselves unwelcome guests and discrimination, abuse, regulation and control intensified. During the war Arab seamen had contributed significantly to the war effort, filling vacancies, especially in the Merchant Marine, created when British seamen were called up for service in the Royal Navy. When the war ended there was strong competition for jobs as white seamen were discharged from the Royal Navy and demanded their old jobs in the Merchant Marine. But the war had dislocated the vitally important coal trade of the north-east ports (Table 1, p.78) and the onset of the economic depression of the inter-war period seriously affected the shipping industry which now faced intense international competition. Economic depression and declining employment opportunities in shipping brought intense competition for jobs which became the major source of tensions between white seamen and the Arabs. Sexual jealousy and moral outrage at the marriage of Arabs to white women and the appearance of half-caste children also contributed to the tensions (see Chapter Seven, p.174), and together with the demobilization of large numbers of disgruntled soldiers and sailors produced a potentially explosive situation.

Table 1 Coal and coke shipments from Tyne Dock illustrate the dramatic fluctuations in the coal trade and in the prosperity of South Shields:

Year	Coal/tons	Coke/tons	Total/tons
1913	7,054,176	94,939	7,149,115
1914	6,505,514	63,474	6,568,988
1915	5,026,389	141,379	5,187,768
1916	5,146,136	336,826	5,482,962
1917	4,512,113	308,269	4,820,382
1918	3,711,813	152,214	3,864,027
1919	4,409,620	162,477	4,572,097
1920	2,048,087	186,283	3,134,370
1921	2,748,291	57,476	2,805,767
1922	6,019,173	228,983	6,248,156
1923	6,080,022	501,489	6,581,511
1924	3,550,386	193,115	3,743,501
1925	2,471,593	112,619	2,584,212
1926	1,125,822	26,277	1,152,099
1927	2,182,821	42,689	2,225,510
1928	2,485,430	77,517	2,562,947
1929	4,183,391	121,589	4,304,980

Source: SG 30.12.1927 p. 5

Before the First World War, Chinese seamen had been the main focus of hostility but after the war it was the Arabs who became the target of a rising tide of racial hysteria. There were calls for the repatriation of Arab seamen and tough measures to prevent new arrivals. The authorities had no wish to see the free and easy recruitment policies of the war years continue and a number of government and non-government agencies—the police, immigration officers, Board of Trade officials, the National Sailors' and Firemen's Union and the Shipping Federation representing the shipowners—responded to popular demands to control and regulate the Arab community. Of all these agencies, the National Sailors' and Firemen's Union was the most vocal and aggressive in its attack on the Arabs. During the inter-war years its officials carried out a virulent campaign against Arab seamen to ensure that white seamen were given preference for jobs on British ships. After the war Arab seamen found their claims to be British subjects, claims which had been upheld during the war years when their labour was urgently needed, now consistently challenged. Restrictive legislation and its forceful implementation effectively reclassified most Arab seamen as 'coloured aliens' giving the authorities greater control over them, more extensive powers to restrict new arrivals and eventually the power to deny them employment.

Against such an onslaught, resistance was weak and divided. The Governor of Aden, the India Office, the Office of the High Commissioner for India and the Colonial Office, conscious of the political implications in south-west Arabia and among Muslims in the empire of the restrictive measures imposed on Arab seamen in Britain, occasionally expressed their concern but with little effect. They certainly proved unable to act together on this issue. There is no record that the Imam of the Yemen intervened to protest against the treatment of Arabs in Britain, although the majority were his subjects.[9] The Arab seamen themselves failed to organize effectively at the national level, and at the local level their leadership appears to have been faction-torn and divided. Even efforts at self-help among the Arab community were organized at the level of the individual boarding-houses. In South Shields the Western Islamic Association, through its President, Dr Khalid Sheldrake, together with Mr Muir Smith, the Arabs' local legal adviser, appealed for united action but failed to achieve it. Certain Arab boarding-house masters appear to have acted on their own initiative and although they made vigorous if poorly articulated attempts to take their case to the Colonial Office, the India Office and the Office of the High Commissioner for India the response was less than helpful. Sheldrake and a number of influential Arabs in the South Shields branch of the Western Islamic Association were strongly opposed to the activities of those Arab boarding-house masters in the town who supported the breakaway Seamen's Minority Movement whose principal leaders were members of the Communist Party.

III The 1919 Arab 'riot' in South Shields

The racial tensions that had been simmering at a number of British ports at the end of the First World War erupted first in South Shields, although the clashes were on a much smaller scale than at Liverpool or the South Wales ports where the most violent racial disturbances occured at Cardiff.[10] In January 1919 a large crowd of white men, including ex-soldiers and sailors, attacked an Arab shop in Waterloo Vale in South Shields smashing all the windows, pulling out the gas fittings and causing a tremendous amount of damage. The attack appears to have been part of a pre-arranged plan. There were further clashes the next day as a white mob pursued and assaulted a number of Arab seamen who defended themselves with sticks and other weapons. When the police intervened and attempted to separate the protagonists and disperse the crowd, which numbered over 200 people, one of the white mob shouted, 'We are White people; stay where you are'. Two white men and two Arabs were arrested and charged. A few days later a white mob attacked an Arab boarding-house belonging to Abdul Magi, breaking the shop windows and smashing the furniture.[11] In a separate incident, a soldier home on leave, John William Jones, was charged with attacking an Arab seaman, named as Mague Cassim, and seriously wounding him. Jones denied the charge and claimed that he had been attacked by three Arabs branishing loaded sticks and had merely defended himself. He had succeeded in disarming Cassim and with the help of a sailor took him to the police station. The magistrates dismissed the charge.[12] It is interesting to note that later that month there were violent clashes between gangs of ex-soldiers and the police in South Shields. The white crowd which gathered was hostile to the police, incited the soldiers to resist and obstructed the police when they attempted to arrest the soldiers.

A more serious outbreak of street violence occurred at the beginning of February 1919. On the afternoon of 4 February a group of nine Arab firemen arrived at the Shipping Office on the Mill Dam to sign on the crew of the SS *Trowalland*. It appears that the ship's engineer had seen the Arabs at one of their boarding-houses and had made arrangements with them to sign on. The Arabs went first to the offices of the Seamen's Union and paid £18 arrears on their subscriptions in order to keep their books clear and then presented themselves at the Shipping Office where the master and officers of the *Trowalland* were signing on the crew. When the Arabs arrived Mr J. Gilroy, an official of the Union, told the chief engineer it would have been better if he had picked his men outside and had given every man a chance. The engineer stated that he had been given to understand that he could not get a white crew but given the circumstances agreed to pick white men. He then went outside where a large crowd, including many white seamen, were assembled and selected nine white men. When he brought them into the office the Arabs, who were still in the pen, walked quietly out of the yard onto the quay. Outside the Shipping Office, Mr J.B. Fye, an official of the Cooks' and Stewards' Union, was addressing the crowd and urging them to stop any Arabs signing on. He is reported to have shouted to the crowd, 'Don't let these Arabs sign on the ship' and 'Come out you black —— You are not going to join the ship'. At a time when large numbers of white seamen were waiting for employment, the practice whereby engineers selected firemen at the Arab boarding-houses was a source of serious friction between the Arabs and the white population. One of the Arabs asked Fye why they could not join the ship when they had paid their union subscription and he is reported to have replied, 'You black —— this ship is not for you'. The Arab seaman was so provoked that he struck Fye with his hand. Fye retaliated by knocking him down and other Arabs came to his assistance. The white seamen, who outnumbered the Arabs, rushed to Fye's defence and from this incident a fierce conflict developed between white men and Arabs. A number of reports suggest that the white crowd was not composed entirely of 'Britishers'.

The white crowd pursued the Arabs back to their boarding-houses in Holborn pelting them with stones. The Arabs, who were outnumbered, armed themselves with knives, sticks and revolvers and drove the white crowd back in an effort to defend their own quarters. The Arabs fired their revolvers into the air to show the white mob that if they were attacked they were prepared to defend themselves. Feelings no doubt ran high on both sides. The police intervened and a group of Royal Navy bluejackets and a detachment of Durham Light Infantry were called in to help restore order.[13] No one was killed in the affray but a dozen people, Arabs and whites, were injured. The authorities claimed that a riot had taken place and that the Arabs started it. The first press reports, headlined 'Arab Riot: revolvers fired on Shields crowd', told of

Tumultuous scenes the like of which have never before been seen in South Shields . . . The disturbance apparently originated amongst a number of Arab seamen who were seeking employment at the South Shields Shipping Office, and in an incredibly short space of time hundreds of people became involved in a fierce conflict which assumed alarming proportions, and necessitated the calling out of naval and military detachments. Numerous gangs of Arabs, armed with revolvers, knives, sticks and bottles, attacked the crowd indiscriminately and as far as can be ascertained more than a dozen persons sustained injuries, though fortunately the revolver shots all went astray. Had it not been for the fact that in their state of frenzied excitement the Arabs discharged their weapons wildly and at random, very serious consequences would have resulted.[14]

The report included eyewitness descriptions of the conflict and fulsome praise for the police and the brave and decisive personal intervention of the Chief Constable himself. The number of Arabs involved in the incident was greatly exaggerated by the press. Fifteen Arabs, mainly seamen but including two refreshment house keepers, were arrested and charged that

> ... together with divers other evil disposed persons to the number of ten or more unlawfully, riotously and routously did assemble and gather together to disturb the public peace, and there unlawfully, riotously, routously and tumultuously did make a great noise, riot, tumult and disturbance to the great terror and disturbance of His Majesty's subjects there being and residing, passing and repairing against the peace and contrary to the statute therein made and provided.[15]

Later reports from the trials of the Arabs at the South Shields' magistrates court and then at the Durham Assizes permit a more accurate reconstruction of events on the 4 February. There is little doubt that it was the actions of the union official, Fye, in inciting the crowd that triggered off the violence. In the first press reports Fye is described as a gallant and disabled ex-soldier who sustained serious injuries during the Arabs' assault. However a week later, Fye was charged at the magistrates' court with assaulting one Abdul Zaid[16] at the Mill Dam on the 4 February and having used language likely to cause a breach of the peace. At the trial the prosecution argued that Fye's language to a crowd anxious for employment was like 'the dropping of a match into a keg of gunpowder'. Had it not been for his remarks to the crowd, there would have been no incident. Fye claimed that he had not used any bad language and that when the Arabs spoke to him about signing on he told them that it was nothing to do with him. One of the Arabs then struck him in the face with what appeared to be a knuckle-duster. Several other Arabs then rushed up and attacked him and he was knocked down before he had a chance to defend himself. In spite of the fact that several witnesses gave evidence in support of Fye's version of the events, the magistrates were satisfied that he had used language that was likely to cause a breach of the peace and ordered him to be bound over for twelve months. However the charge of assault was dismissed. Fye, it will be recalled, had been at the centre of a dispute between white seamen and Arabs at the Mill Dam in September 1914.

No other white men were arrested or charged. Mr J.M. Smith,

defending the Arabs, admitted that a number of his clients had been mixed up in the fighting but argued that the incident could not be described as a riot only a street disturbance. Eventually twelve Arabs were commited to Durham Assizes for trial. Three Arab seamen were found not guilty and were discharged. The rest were sentenced to imprisonment for between one and three months. At the trial the police, naval and military forces were complimented by His Lordship 'for their prompt and judicious handling of a very difficult situation'.[17]

Only a few days after the trial at Durham Assizes ended there was a further outbreak of violence in Holborn this time between a group of soldiers and a number of Arab seamen. According to the two Arab seamen, Abdulla Hassan and Ahmed Ali, who were staying at an Arab boarding-house at 10 Chapter Row, they were walking down Coronation Street on Saturday night when they met several soldiers. As they passed, one of the soldiers struck Hassan on the back of the neck and then kicked him to the ground. The soldier produced a knife and attempted to steal Hassan's watch and chain. Hassan took out his razor to defend himself. Another soldier attacked Ahmed Ali with a stick. The two soldiers, Percy Victor Lenimell, a corporal in the Durham Light Infantry, and one Micke Wolk, a private in the DLI, denied that they had provoked the Arabs and claimed that it was the Arabs who attacked them. Wolk, who is described in the press reports as a Syrian who understood Arabic, is alleged to have heard one of the Arabs say, 'I'll kill all the soldiers'. A struggle followed during which Hassan took out a razor and cut Lenimell on the arm. Both soldiers denied possessing any weapons or striking one of the Arabs and attempting to rob him. Hassan was charged before the South Shields police court with assaulting Lenimell and there were counter charges by Hassan against Lenimell. Wolk was charged with assaulting Ali. Although both the police and Mr Muir Smith, the solicitor defending Hassan, pointed to certain discrepancies in the evidence given by the two soldiers, the charges against them were dismissed whereas Hassan was charged with common assault and fined forty shillings. In his address to the court, Muir Smith made an impassioned plea on behalf of Arab seamen in the town:

> The life of these Arab seamen is becoming intolerable. There is a prejudice against them in the town—a prejudice born of ignorance, and since the last riots it appears that there has been an absolute set-back against them. The behaviour of people down at the Mill Dam, unfortunately soldiers amongst

them, whose uniform we are bound to respect, although there
is no telling what type of individual is beneath it, is such that
an Arab is now afraid to walk along the street.[18]

These sentiments were repeated by Dr Abdul Majid, an Indian
barrister based in London, who held a watching brief for the Islamic
Society at the trial of the Arab seamen at Durham Assizes. According to a report in the *Shields Daily Gazette* which carried an interview
with Dr Abdul Majid, the Islamic Society had been founded in 1886
to look after the interests of Muslim peoples throughout the world
and had branches in several countries (see Chapter Eight, p.215).
Dr Abdul Majid, the society's president, had been educated at
Cambridge University and was called to the bar in 1906. He
practised chiefly before the Privy Council in Indian and Colonial
appeals and was the first Indian lecturer in Islamic law at the
Colonial Office. He appears therefore to have been very much an
'establishment' figure though there is some evidence that both the
India Office and the Home Office were critical of his efforts to take
up the cause of coloured seamen.[19]

    After the trial ended Dr Abdul Majid visited South Shields for a
few days and held talks with the mayor and other local government
officials. Local officials were clearly impressed by his delightful
manners and bearing, 'inseparably associated with our English
public school "boys" and pleasantly accentuated by that peculiar
refinement typical of the educated classes of the East'. During the
interview with the *Shields Daily Gazette*, Dr Abdul Majid stated that
the main object of his visit was to create a better feeling in the town
towards the Arabs. Above all people must understand that the Arabs
were British subjects and most loyal. Although they came from Aden
they were under the jurisdiction of Bombay in India. They had made
great sacrifices during the war and many hundreds of Arabs who
sailed from the Tyne had lost their lives during the First World War
through enemy action.[20] Indeed he claimed that when there was a
shortage of firemen in this country several Arabs in the town had
spent thousands of pounds to bring their fellow countrymen from
Aden to serve in British ships. Now these men were unable to find
jobs. The Arabs did not want to take jobs away from British seamen
but asked for fair competition as British subjects. After all, the Arabs
were British subjects on British soil. The British Empire should be
run for the benefit of everybody, regardless of their colour. He went
on to stress the contribution the British Empire, and especially India,
made to England's prosperity:

If you do not afford these people protection, what of the future? Trade, commerce, everything that goes to make up a great Empire is based on the goodwill of the people. What is colour? You should forget that there is such a thing as white people, as such. What would the British Empire be without India? It would lose half its overseas trade—five hundred millions. If India went out of the British Empire it would lose its trade with China, with Africa and many other countries. England would again become a very small Empire. These Arabs belong to Indian soil, and must be counted with India.[21]

He argued that the Arabs, as British subjects, should be given preference in employment over foreigners:

They [the Arabs] have adopted European life and customs to a large extent and in sympathy and in their domestic life they are English. Look at it from any point of view you like—loyalty or citizenship—economically it is a very short sighted policy to endeavour to cut these men out. You should follow a higher policy in the interests of all. The country would not lose by it, I am sure. It is better for British subjects to be employed than foreigners, for all the wealth acquired by British subjects is under our control and we tax them, with income tax and so on. If you employ foreigners you lose their wealth; investments are transferred to other countries, as with the Germans before the war.[22]

To deal with the problem of the employment of Arabs and other Indian subjects, Dr Abdul Majid stated that he was making arrangements with the Government of India for these men to be selected from a 'waiting list': 'In future we shall know how many men there are to dispose of, and they will be engaged according to the time they have been ashore. That is the best way to solve the problem.'[23]

He stated that he had already taken up the claims of Arab seamen serving on British and foreign ships who had been interned by the Germans because they were British subjects. The India Office was appointing officials to look into this matter and it had already been agreed that these men should get their old wages, plus twenty-five per cent. If Arab seamen could prove loss of property through the war they would get compensation from the shipping companies, the German Government or the India Office. There is no record, however, that these promises were fulfilled. The proposal for a waiting list to ensure that Arabs were engaged according to the length of time they had been ashore, appears to have been replaced by a scheme whereby the Arab boarding-house masters took it in turn to ship men when Arab crews were required (see Chapter Three, p.63). In order to bring about a better understanding between the Arabs and other sections of the community, Dr Abdul Majid indicated that he had already established a committee of Arab boarding-house keepers and representatives of seamen from different parts of the world to be known as the South Shields branch of the Islamic Society. The committee would seek to protect the interests of Muslims in the town and look after their economic, moral and religious welfare. He hoped to obtain the support of prominent local citizens.[24]

IV   Popular hostility and racial prejudice

Dr Abdul Majid's efforts at reconciliation appear to have done little to change popular feeling in the town against the Arabs. A constant stream of letters to the editor of the *Shields Daily Gazette* throughout the 1920s and early 1930s on the subject of Arab seamen in the town vividly illustrates the strength of popular hostility and racial prejudice. Many more letters were received than were published. Indeed on several occasions the editor remarked that as no new arguments were raised and too much bitter feeling was being expressed, the paper declined to publish any more letters on this subject.

Certain views are constantly repeated in the correspondence. The majority of Arabs had been engaged during the war to fill the places of British seamen who left the merchant service to join the army or navy. Now that the war was over, it was only right that the Arabs should be made to relinquish their jobs and be sent back to their own countries so as to give the men whose jobs they had filled a better chance of getting employment. British seamen had risked their lives to defend their country but now found themselves unemployed in favour of Arabs. Unlike white British seamen, the Arabs had shown cowardice when under fire during the war. White men should be given preference in British ships. Arabs had received good wages during the war while white seamen were serving their country for sixpence a day. Let the Arabs use some of the money they had accumulated during the war to pay for the cost of their repatriation. Other writers criticized the Arabs for taking their money out of the country. Because Arabs sent the money they earned back to Aden, Britain gained nothing from their presence

Plate 1. The Post Office Pier, Aden in the 1890s. (Reproduced by permission of the Oriental and India Office Collections, British Library)

Plate 2. The Mill Dam, South Shields. Arab and British seamen 'walk the stones' waiting for a ship. (Courtesy of the *Shields Gazette*)

Plate 3. Muhammad Muckble's seamen's boarding-house in East Holborn, South Shields. (Courtesy of South Tyneside Libraries)

Plate 4. The *zawiya* established by Sheikh Abdullah Ali al-Hakimi in the former Hilda Arms on the corner of Cuthbert Street and Smith Street, South Shields. (Courtesy of South Tyneside Libraries)

Plate 5. Arab and British supporters of the Seamen's Minority Movement outside the Movement's office in Brewery Lane, South Shields. (Courtesy of the Bede Gallery, Jarrow)

Plate 6. Arab and British seamen at one of the meetings of the Seamen's Minority Movement in South Shields. (Courtesy of the *Shields Gazette*)

Plate 7. The police keep a watchful eye on the situation as seamen cluster in the narrow confines of the Mill Dam on Saturday 2 August 1930. (Courtesy of the *Shields Gazette*)

Plate 8. Police with batons drawn during the fighting which erupted at the Mill Dam on Saturday 2 August 1930. (Courtesy of the *Shields Gazette*)

Plate 9. Arab seamen arrested by the police during the so-called 'Arab riot' at the Mill Dam on Saturday 2 August 1930. (Courtesy of the *Shields Gazette*)

Plate 10. Arabs being removed by the South Shields police during the disturbances on Saturday 2 August 1930. (Courtesy of the *Shields Gazette*)

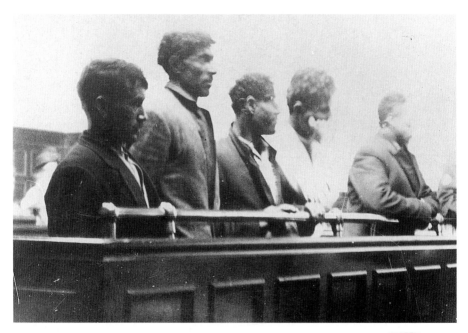

Plate 11. Five of the Arabs charged with rioting on Saturday 2 August 1930, photographed secretly in the dock during their trial. (Courtesy of the *Shields Gazette*)

here. Indeed they were a burden because Britain was having to keep unemployed white seamen and their families.

Strong feelings were expressed that Arabs were not 'Britishers' and never would be. Those people who held that the Arabs were part of the empire and that the Union Jack was for Black as well as white were reminded that the Arabs, along with other coloured people, were subjects of the flag and all it represented, not those who made the flag. One writer pointed to the example of the United States where Arabs like all coloured people were segregated and did not get the same treatment as white men.

The National Sailors' and Firemen's Union (later the National Union of Seamen) was vigorously attacked and held responsible for unemployment among white seamen because the union accepted Arabs as members and took their contributions. The union should not have allowed Arabs to join. It was the British seamen who had made the union long before the Arabs came to South Shields. The Arabs should be expelled and the union made a white man's union as it was when it was founded. Why was the union not looking after the welfare of British seamen? Why should white seamen pay their contributions when the union allowed Arabs to sign on ships? One writer hinted that some union officials took bribes from Arab boarding-house keepers and advised British seamen to join a union where there were no Arabs.

Other writers held the shipowners responsible for the 'Arab menace'. British shipowners were blamed for allowing engineers to pick the crews and for employing Arabs because they were cheap. Arabs would work overtime for nothing and were not being true to their union principles. Arabs were willing to put up with poor conditions aboard ship without complaining whereas British seamen would not. Why did shipowners prefer Arabs when during the war Arabs had to be forced to do their duty at gun point? When accidents happened at sea the Arabs were the first into the lifeboats with bag and baggage. Arabs could not stand the heat of the stokehold like a white man. It took two Arabs to do the work of one British seaman. Many writers urged British seamen to refuse to sail on ships carrying Arabs as firemen.

Some writers argued that of all the British ports, only South Shields allowed Arabs to settle in the town. South Shields was referred to as 'a dumping ground for Arabs' who took jobs from white firemen. There were calls for the Arab problem to be made an issue at both local and national elections. Demands were made for changes in the law to prevent the employment of foreigners while a British person was available. Some examples of the letters published in the *Shields Daily Gazette* during this period are presented in full below.

> While walking through the Mill Dam this morning my attention was attracted to an unusual crowd round the Shipping Office entrance. Being curious, I walked across to find out what the commotion was about. I was soon to be made wise. A British ship signing on, and to my disgust engaging Arabs whilst hundreds of white men were walking the stones outside, many of whom, I daresay, had never tasted breakfast that morning. How such a state of things is allowed puzzles me. Our noble Prime Minister during the war boasted about making the country a fit place for heroes to live in. I and many others, I daresay, think a man is a hero who can live in it.
>
> During the time these men were being engaged I heard expressions of disgust on all sides, and thoroughly agreed with them. Why are these men, or the greater part of them, not sent back to the country they belong to? People may say, 'They did their bit during the war'. Granted, but so did our own men but when anything happened such as the ship being mined or torpedoed, they were the first to rush for boats or rafts. I hold no brief for anyone, but when you see a state of things such I had the "pleasure" of witnessing this morning, you begin to think seriously and wonder whether, after all, the country you belong to was worth fighting for.
>
> Signed ONE WHO ALSO DID HIS BIT[25]

> Is it not time the Labour Bureau, the Board of Trade and the men's unions were tackling the question of aliens getting employment on British ships in preference to British sailors and firemen who are quite willing and eager to fill such posts, but instead are shouldered aside and cast on the dole? Is this the reward they receive for services rendered, to be replaced by crowds of Arabs etc? Who is to blame for such a state of things?
>
> Surely the shipowners cannot truly say there is no preference shown towards the coloured section who during the war had to be forced to do their duty at the revolver's point, as the seafaring fraternity are well aware.
>
> It was only on Monday of this week, I was passing the New Quay where there was a dispute about Arabs vs white men which resulted in the business of signing on being held up for two or three hours. Another ship paid off the same day with

the same class of men, a Cornish company this time. Whatever are the captains and officers thinking of to prefer such men instead of their own nationals? Let us raise the cry, 'British men for British ships'.

Signed A WHITE MAN[26]

The time is a long way overdue for our Union officials to tackle the job of having Britishers in British ships. If you remember when some Arabs were before the police court at South Shields, the solicitor who appeared for them told our officials that as these men paid their contributions the same as a white man, they had the same right to have work in our ships. Now, what had our officials to say to that? Nothing; they did not answer; they simply had not a leg to stand on because the solicitor was right.

I have my union card in front of me now, and on the front of it in big type is printed 'The National Sailors' and Firemen's Union of Great Britain and Ireland'. Now, were these Arabs born in Great Britain or Ireland? I say no; a few of them are British subjects, and very few at that. The majority are Turkish Arabs that walk into Aden, and then reckon they were born there. Now was it the intention of the white men who paid the first contributions and joined the Sailors' and Firemen's Union to allow Arabs to take the bread out of our white children's mouths? I say no, emphatically no.

Therefore it is the fault of the present-day officials of the union that is the cause of all this trouble of keeping the white man on the unemployed list while taking contributions from the Arabs. I say chuck them out and make it a white man's union, the same as it was when it was started.

Signed A MILL DAM WHITE MAN[27]

I am a seaman myself and I find it most degrading after I have signed on a British ship to find that our sleeping berth is only separated from the Arabs by a narrow alleyway and all other accommodation had to be shared with the Arabs. The only reason I can see for it, is that Arabs will accept food at less than the rations which regulations of the Board of Trade allows every seaman and also to work overtime without demanding money in return, which a British seaman would justly claim and stand out for.

I agree that British seamen that are a credit to the world should refuse to sail with Arabs, but I cannot see that the responsibility lies with us as much as it does with our union, whom we pay to look after our interests.

I only ask, sir, that your readers will imagine that they were being replaced at their different trades by Arabs, then they will know how every British seaman standing on the Mill Dam feels, if they broach the subject to him.

Signed A.B.[28]

To say that an Arab is the equal of a Britisher—I don't know whether to laugh or get mad when I think of it. Why not ten per cent of them are British subjects even although they claim to be. As for their bravery during the war the less said about that the better; from my own experiences, and those of my friends, half the Arabs lost during the war died of fright before the sea got them.

The Union was built up by white sailors and firemen and a going concern long before Arabs came here to deprive white men of work, and gain for South Shields the name of Cardiff the second. I am sure it would not go bankrupt now if all the Arabs were out of it. My advice to these gentlemen as they are too thick-skinned to see they are not wanted, is to get while the going is good. Furthermore, I don't merely dislike Arabs, I hate them.

Signed 'BURGOO'[29]

A very big reduction would be made in the number of un-employed if white men were given preference in British ships. At the present time there must be thousands of Arabs, Lascars and Chinamen etc., doing work in British vessels that could be done by our own unemployed. There must be hundreds of Arabs sailing out of our town alone. What makes matters worse, is the fact that the majority of these men send every halfpenny that they possibly can back to Aden, or wherever they hail from, so that the town and country at large gain nothing from their presence but on the contrary lose to the extent of having to keep the unemployed and their families, and the money which would be spent in the town by white firemen and their dependants.

Signed COLLIER[30]

Would you spare me a little space regarding the unem-ployment among seagoing firemen of South Shields? Surely something can be done, seeing two thirds of the ships that are signing on here at present are taking Arabs, while so many of our own townsmen are walking about practically starving.

Where are the Labour Exchange officials, whose duties, I understand, include that of trying to find work for the unemployed? Can they not help to put a stop to this? And what about the Union and Federation Officials, can they do something to discourage the signing on of these men who are taking the bread out of the mouths of our own men?

I think it is about time we got on to the same footing as our North Shields friends, who prefer to give their own a chance.

Signed SUFFERER[31]

We live in a country that sincerely believes in fiction invented by priests and as a result have been blinded to greater things that pertain to our own general welfare. Darwin and others have taught us that the human race and apes have descended from a common stock so there can be no harm in the admission that the Arab is a distant relation. Theology is of very little use to the seamen standing day after day looking for employment, afraid to go home for an hour lest some ship should sign on in his absence, only to find out that white men were not wanted as Arabs were engaged. Mr Bergman blames the shipowner and looks for the remedy there, mindful of the fact that they have exploited every race from Norway to China. We have the remedy in our own hands and must use it by making it a test at every election, municipal and national, until the law of the land is no foreigner shall be engaged while a Briton is available.

Signed FREEDOM[32]

We are told the Arabs served the country well. Yes and were well paid for it. It wasn't for love of the country; it was the big money. See how many would serve the country for the tanner a day as our lads had to do. What a rush? But it would be to their own country. Yet still they come, can get work while the white man is left out, simply because he was away fighting for the glorious sum of 6d and hasn't got a book; he hasn't a chance now. Yet the Arab must have the run of the town because he served the country well. I wish we had a few more men like Councillors Smith and Watson who dare speak their mind and stick to what they say, to limit them and give our own men the chance they were promised and have waited for since the war. All they ask is work, yet 33,000 alien firemen are in British

91

ships, while we have six to seven hundred unemployed seamen. Now where is the justice there? Certainly there isn't any for the Britisher. It almost makes one feel ashamed to think they belong to this land fit for heroes to live in.

Signed 'MAXWELLITE'[33]

Admitted they [the Arabs] are British subjects, and they were wounded and half-drowned during the war. What about the thousands of white British firemen who can prove they took part in the war and are out of jobs through the Arabs? Does 'Fair' know that 40,000 British merchant seamen lost their lives during the war, while poor Mohamed was receiving £14 a month regular, and bringing more of his countrymen over to England. I have been told by the Arabs themselves that they have never seen Aden, but say they come from there so that they will be regarded as British subjects. No matter how bad conditions are aboard ship, Mohamed (who can live on the smell of an oily rag or a stick of incense for a week) will not complain, but a Britisher will and does. This is why poor, puzzled, ostracized, uncomplaining Mohamed is given preference to Britishers. And what do they do with the money? Send it or take it out of the country, and when they have funds they clear off back to Arabia to live in comfort for the rest of their lives. But if for some unforseen reason Mohamed is unable to get back, he doesn't worry. Our kindhearted ratepayers will keep him.

Signed SEAMAN[34]

From within the Arab community, one of the boarding-house masters, Ali Said, put up a particularly spirited defence of the rights of Arab seamen and attempted to counter the attacks made in the press against the employment of Arabs in British ships. A number of white women married to Arabs also spoke out on this issue and translated into English letters written in Arabic by their husbands. Not surprisingly given the strength of racial prejudice, there were very few voices of support for the Arabs from the white community. Most Arab writers placed great emphasis on the fact that Arab seamen were loyal British subjects. Many Arabs had lost their lives during the First World War and were ready to do so again. They claimed the same right as Englishmen to sail on British ships. Arabs had settled in South Shields long before the union was founded and many Arab seamen were among its first members. Indeed Arabs had no alternative but to join the union in order to sign on British

92

ships. Arab seamen were employed because of their ability to work and their good discipline in carrying out their duties. Very few Arabs served as deck crew, so that even on ships where Arabs were engaged for the stokehold, three quarters of the crew were white seamen. Arabs did not waste their money on drink. They paid rates and taxes and spent money in England. They asked for British justice for British subjects whatever their colour. One writer, however, argued that the Arabs had been forced to seek work in Britain because the white man had occupied their country; if the white man left their country, the Arabs would leave Britain. Another was of the opinion that religious and racial prejudice against Arabs grew out of 'an old Christian dogma for self-aggrandisment' and accused Christian capitalist shipowners of growing rich exploiting Arab labour.

Supporters among the white community argued that as Christians it was the duty of Englishmen to treat Arabs fairly. Christians should speak out against prejudice on the basis of colour. The Arabs' war service should not be forgotten. They had responded to the call of the flag and many white people owed their lives to black seamen who manned the ships that brought food to this country. Arab seamen also suffered during the war and some were held as prisoners of war. The Arabs were British subjects, born under the Union Jack and should have preference for jobs over foreigners. Many Arabs had settled permanently in the town and were good and peaceful citizens. It was not just white seamen who could not get ships; there were many Arabs ashore who had been unemployed for long periods. Some examples of letters written to the *Shields Daily Gazette* by Arab writers and by those members of the white community who spoke out in defence of the Arabs are presented in full below.

> Please allow me to reply to the 'One Who Did His Bit'. Well, I daresay he and many more have done their bit. But it does not follow they have the right to say, send Arabs from this country. Because Arabs are British subjects and born under the Union Jack. As for saying that when the war was on and ships were torpedoed or mined, the Arabs were the first to run, well everybody for themselves, not only Arabs. I don't know why they want Arabs from this country. What about foreigners? They are never spoken about. When the Arabs walk through the streets they never insult anybody if they are left alone, but maybe if they send all the foreigners from this country an Englishman might get a better chance to sign. I know plenty of Arabs who

have been ashore now eight months and can't get a chance, and best part of them are married men.

Signed LIVE AND LET LIVE[35]

In answer to 'A MILL DAM WHITE MAN', I ask him why is he so down on the Arabs, as it isn't many of our men who get the chance of a job nowadays. If a ship signs on a crew it stands ten to one that three parts English men are taken to one part Arabs. Suppose two ships of the same company go away the same day, say one ship thirteen white men and the other ship six Arab men, we make one meal every day enough to do our work on while the other ship has three or four meals every day. Now which ship is the best, Mr 'Mill Dam White Man'? As for taking the bread out of the white children's mouths, well we do our best as we can't see our own children at home suffer.

Signed ALWAYS DOWN[36]

Allow me to answer 'A.B.' on the subject of British and Arab firemen. First of all, let me inform 'A.B.' that the Arab firemen that serve on British vessels are as truly British as 'A.B.' himself. 'A.B.' has surely forgotten that a big majority of Arabs lost their lives for the sake of Britain, and these are more than ready to do so again if needs be, and they have every right today to sail the seas on the level of Englishmen. But I suppose they are not a matter of importance to 'A.B.' simply because they are coloured . . . 'A.B.' goes on to say that he pays his union to look after his interests, and in his opinion the Arabs will not pay the union. But in my opinion they are the only party that keeps the union going. I have come to the conclusion that 'A.B.' is prejudiced against the Arabs and the only way he can get at them is through the local paper. But in case he would prefer to meet an Arab face to face I will not write under a *nom-de-plume*.

Signed ALI SAID, 79a East Holborn, South Shields[37]

Let me inform 'JUSTICE' there were Arabs in Shields and other parts of England long before the Union was formed, and many of them the first to join before an Englishman. If he doubts my statement, I have proof to show him; or if he writes to the president, Mr Wilson, he will find my statement quite true. I have no wish to argue further. It is a waste of time and energy, but, as long as the Union Jack flies in certain parts of Arabia, so will the British Arab continue to sail on British vessels and also to domicile in this country. My advice to 'Justice' and his previous supporters is to content themselves as all their letters put together will not move the British Arabs from this country. In case this proves unsatisfactory, their only alternative is to appeal to higher authority, such as the India Office or other responsible parties, where perhaps they will get satisfaction. I have men in my house who have been in England since 1906.

Signed ALI SAID, 79a East Holborn, South Shields[38]

Answering 'W.H.' may I ask why it is a setback because Arabs are allowed in the union? It is necessary simply because the Arab, being a Britisher, would not be allowed to sign on a British vessel unless he is a member of the Sailors' and Firemen's Union. But how his being in the union can affect other contributors I fail to understand. The reason why Arabs are accepted in preference to Englishmen is simply for their ability in work and for discipline given while carrying out their duty. Speaking of poverty, 'W.H.' seems to have great experience with my country. I wonder if he has seen poverty amongst the Arabs either there or in England? I think not. If the majority of Englishmen would take an example from the Arabs they would not know what poverty meant, because instead of making the public house a going concern, they would be like the Arabs—put value on to what takes good honest working for money. As to my 'sentimental rubbish' as 'W.H.' terms it, I have no wish to appeal to the emotions of anyone; it isn't necessary. I am only trying to makes the likes of 'W.H.' see how dense they are simply because they will not meet plain facts in the face. What 'W.H.' bears against the Arabs is neither 'prejudice' nor malice, but something worse. The green-eyed monster has him fast in his clutches, and 'W.H.' is not strong enough in will to try to get out of them.

Signed ALI SAID, 79a East Holborn, South Shields[39]

Re the coloured seamen of home ports is there not one Englishman who knows a good word to say of the Arabs? One cannot but think of the altered opinion of these so-called coloured seamen since 1914–18. Is their war service so soon forgotten? It must be admitted that there are hundreds in this country who have no right to be called British, but whose is the fault that they have many of them obtained registration certificates? On the other hand there are hundreds settled in this country since they finished their war service and are living peaceably and are good citizens. What is more they were born in Aden and as such pay homage to the English flag. Yet they are stated to be aliens, and have as their nationality 'Seamen'. If one knows what nationality this is, well, they are ultra-clever. Apart from all this, what is the N.S. and F.'s Union going to say about and do with the hundreds of pounds paid by these men in contributions? Many are forced to pay the whole of their debts which they have incurred during unemployment before they can sign on. Is there no Englishman who will brave the prejudice of his fellow countrymen by saying a good word for those who are of a different religion, and look to a Christian country to treat them in a Christian manner.

Signed G.Y. of P.C.[40]

We live in a country that professes to be Christian, but which pays little heed to that teaching, that 'one is your father, even God, and all ye are brethren'. Colour should not make the above void, not parrot phrases such as 'once an Arab always an Arab', a saying which is generally meant to suggest a lot more than is said. Instead we should remember that character is not something confined to white skins, nor depravity to brown skins, for they are both to be found under both black and white skins, and our colleges and universities are proving that many a noble soul inhabits a dusky skin. As regards our own seamen being unemployed because of them, let us put the responsibility on the proper shoulders, namely those who employ them because of their cheapness for that is where the trouble lies. That is why they will still be coming here in increasing numbers even though they should have difficulty in finding lodging room, and it is to our shipowners at the other end that we must look for the remedy.

Signed C. BERGMAN, 2 Challoner Terrace East, South Shields[41]

In answer to C. Brown, I repeat that we Arabs are not here by choice. If our country was not monopolised by the white man we would have no need to seek our bread elsewhere. My experience of the white man is that he is not satisfied with having his own country, but he must needs covet and possess the coloured man's too. Give us, I say, our own country and you are welcome to yours, and my advice to you and others is not to kindle already smouldering fires or they may some day flare up and affect greatly the white race in the coloured man's country.

Signed T. SALEH, 35 Laygate Street, South Shields[42]

How many white men get ships and after cashing advance notes lose their ship through drink? Many a poor widow who cashes the note is robbed of the money. I can safely speak of one respectable widow that she has been robbed of practically £100 or more by white men cashing advance notes and forged notes and leaving ships. You won't find an Arab do such a mean, dirty trick. Some white men do want work, and some are too lazy to work, even when work has been found for them. They are quite content to sponge their drinks as long as they have the dole or the Guardians to keep them and their families.

Signed JUSTICE[43]

Give any Arab a chance to go down the mines or any other work he is put to and I will guarantee however hard it is he will not shirk his job. Half the Englishmen on the dole are there through their own fault, being too lazy to look for work. When they receive the dole what do they do with it? Nothing but gamble and waste money on horses and drink. As to all the talk about Britishers not wanting to be employed in the same vessels as Arabs, well I am disgusted with our so-called Britishers. If Arabs are not needed in England send them, their wives and children to Aden. I for one would gladly go and I know then what would happen; the bread you are taking from them will be taken from England in various ways.

I wonder if Fairplay One and Two know where all their foodstuffs come from? What is there in England to boast about; only coal and vegetables. They are forgetting it is the coloured man's country they depend on. What would England do if Arabs were to do the same to them as England is doing to the Arabs.

Signed ARAB'S WIFE[44]

... much has been said for and against these unwanted, but honest coloured British citizens, and very human children of God. Man was made in God's own image by God himself. This Jewish God had no special idea of colours. In fact nowhere in the Bible is it mentioned what colour the first man was. This religious and racial prejudice is (to anyone who has studied history and theology) the outcome of an old Christian dogma of self-aggrandisement and barbaric egoism. If the Arabs are

97

useful, keep them, but if no longer useful exterminate them, repatriate them. They have colour; they are heathens and unclean. In short an 'eyesore' in the town to our sanctimonious Christians. And if they do get £9 per month instead of a handful of dates? What did our Christian, capitalistic shipowners get by means of their service? Mohammed, an Arab camel driver, delivered his people from the cruel tyranny of the Christians in 570 AD. We are different now, we have changed all that, we are more charitable, more civilised, intellectually superior. Yes, Sir, we have learnt the art of hypocrisy to a fine art. I have translated this from my husband's written views—an Arab.

Signed MRS SAID RODMAN, Frederick Street, South Shields.[45]

V Regulation and repatriation: the Orders of 1920 and 1925

At the end of the First World War strong pressure was brought to bear on the Home Office by the Board of Trade and the National Sailors' and Firemen's Union to restrict the entry of Arab seamen who could not prove that they were British subjects.[46] By 1920 the short-lived post-war boom in shipping was over. Arab seamen, it was argued, competed for jobs in an overstocked labour market and caused grave discontent among British sailors. On the Tyne, the Superintendent of the South Shields Mercantile Marine Office reported in January 1920 that as quickly as he arranged for the repatriation of Arab seamen they were replaced by other Arabs who landed without interrogation even though they offered no proof that they were British subjects. Under existing conditions British seamen and firemen were averse to sailing with coloured seamen who were becoming restless and troublesome.[47] A report from the Mercantile Marine Office at Blyth in November 1920 states that

> The number of Arabs now employed in the Mercantile Marine
> has increased to such an extent as to cause uneasiness on the
> part of white men and unless some steps are taken in the near
> future with a view to arresting the increase and ultimately to
> diminishing the number of Arabs employed it is feared that
> some serious trouble will arise.[48]

The emphasis was now to be on regulation and repatriation. Arab seamen wishing to enter the United Kingdom would be required to prove their nationality. The India Office, who were asked for their comments, observed that from the political point of view there was a good deal to be said for maintaining the practice of treating all Arab seamen on the same footing as British subjects. But they accepted that this argument could not be pushed too far in the face of strong objections on other grounds.[49] At this time, imperial interests were to be overruled as the Board of Trade in particular pressed for stringent controls over the entry of Arab seamen into Britain. A letter from the Board of Trade to the Chief Inspector at the Aliens Branch of the Home Office dated 4 December set out their demands:

> We are glad to learn that the arrangement made by the Home Office, to refuse Arab seamen leave to land when they arrive as passengers without proper papers showing them to be British subjects, is working satisfactorily; and the Board of Trade would also like Arab seamen to be refused leave to land when they arrive as members of a ship's crew without proof of British nationality, and would (but for the refusal) be discharged and allowed to enter this country.
>
> ... the Board of Trade regard the position as so serious, by reason of the unemployment among British seamen, as to justify an instruction that not only Arabs but any coloured seamen signed on abroad should be refused leave to land unless they can produce evidence of British nationality. The only exceptions we think should be allowed are a) a seaman who can prove that he has a home of his own in this country and b) a seaman who has been engaged at a very distant foreign port, whose repatriation it would be almost impracticable for the shipowner or shipmaster to arrange for.
>
> The seaman in a) may have been originally engaged in this country and may have been signed on abroad after having become distressed; if he has a home in this country it would be harsh to keep him out. This suggestion goes somewhat beyond your proposal, because we do not want the coloured alien to be allowed leave to land even if he is a bona-fide seaman, in view of the unemployment among British seamen, and the probability that the alien coloured seaman would become a public charge, and provoke discontent and disturbance among British seafarers at the ports.
>
> We think there is no reason for treating alien coloured seamen other than Arabs differently from Arabs; they are equally undesirable immigrants at the present time.[50]

Under the Aliens Order, 1920, immigration officers were instructed to refuse coloured seamen permission to land unless they
could prove that they were British subjects, or that they were living
in Britain or that they had signed on in Britain for a round trip (for
the full text of the Aliens Order 1920 see Figure 9, p.101). These
measures, however, proved difficult to enforce. Under the terms of
the Order, ships engaged in the coastal trade, which included the
northern coast of France and the Low Countries, were not required
to report alien crew members to the immigration officer on every
arrival at a British port. Crew lists were only examined by the
immigration officials every six months. It proved relatively easy
for Arabs to join such vessels at a continental port and land
undetected. The police complained that when Arabs who had
reached this country through unauthorized channels were apprehended it was impossible to obtain a conviction. They argued that
this was because the courts required the police to prove that the
offender had been warned by the immigration officer, in a language
he understood, that he had been refused permission to land.
Repatriation was difficult to enforce because the Arabs would not
divulge the names of the vessels on which they had arrived.[51]

The frustrations experienced by immigration officials and police
in their attempts to prosecute Arabs who landed illegally is illustrated by a case which came before the South Shields magistrates
in March 1924. An Arab seaman was detained by the River Tyne
Police, South Shields and charged with being an alien and having
landed unlawfully in the United Kingdom without the permission
of an immigration officer. The man stated that he had arrived in
the country six weeks before, having travelled from Le Havre in
France to Hull as a stowaway. He either would not or could not
give the name of the ship on which he had travelled. After remaining
in Hull for a week he came to South Shields. He possessed four
discharge certificates in the name of Hassan Karika. When questioned he admitted that the discharge papers were given to him by
another man and that his real name was Hassan Yaya and that he
was born in Aden. His solicitor argued that as the man was born in
Aden he was a British subject and therefore did not come within
the jurisdiction of the Aliens Order. It was up to the prosecution to
prove their case that the man was not a British subject. The Clerk
of the Court pointed out to the magistrates that the onus of proof
of nationality rested with the individual concerned and that he had
failed to produce any evidence to prove his statement that he was
born in Aden and was therefore a British subject. One of the
immigration officers drew the magistrates' attention to the fact that

ALIENS ORDER, 1920.

NOTICE TO MASTERS OF ALL BRITISH AND FOREIGN VESSELS FROM FOREIGN, INCLUDING VESSELS ARRIVING COASTWISE FROM FOREIGN.

(This Notice should be retained for permanent reference).

PASSENGERS :

Report. The Master must report to the Immigration Office (by telephone or otherwise) as soon as the ship arrives, if he has any passengers on board—including British subjects, distressed British seamen, passage workers (i.e., all persons who are signed on the articles at a nominal rate of wages) and stowaways.

Inspection. The Immigration Officer will then visit the ship. Every passenger must produce his passport or other papers to the Immigration Officer before leaving the ship.

CREW LISTS :

The crew list on prescribed form must be filled in by the Master and be delivered to the nearest Immigration Office within 24 hours after the arrival of the ship.

Coloured Seamen. The crew list should include the names of all Coloured Seamen.

All-British Crews. If there are no aliens or coloured seamen among the crew, the list should be marked " NIL " and delivered to the Immigration Office.

Coastwise Ships. If the ship is coastwise from foreign only the particulars at the head of the crew list need be filled in, and the form should then be delivered to the Immigration Office after the Master has signed the second declaration at the foot of the form.

CREWS :

Discharge. Under the Aliens Order no alien member of a crew (including a passage worker) may land for discharge or transfer to new articles, or if discharged on board ship may land, without the permission of the Immigration Officer. To obtain this permission the Master must send the aliens who wish to be discharged, accompanied by a ship's officer, to the Immigration Office. Each alien must bring his passport and other papers with him. The Board of Trade and Foreign Consuls will not pay off or transfer an alien until his passport has been endorsed by the Immigration Officer " for discharge."

Temporary Shore Leave. Under Article 1 (4) of the Aliens Order, 1920, and on condition of departure in the same ship alien members of the crew who are not to be discharged at this port will be granted TEMPORARY SHORE LEAVE DURING THE SHIP'S STAY IN PORT, but this permission does not apply to any alien upon whom a refusal notice is served by the Immigration Officer.

Desertions. The Master must report immediately to the Immigration Office the DESERTION of any alien member of his crew.

W. Haldane Porter,
H.M. Chief Inspector,
Aliens Branch,
Home Department.

(*1240) Wt. 7427—97. 5,000. 7/27. T. S. 135

Figure 9. The Aliens Order of 1920. (PRO HO 45/14299 Part I. Reproduced by kind permission of the Controller of Her Majesty's Stationery Office)

numerous complaints had been made about the number of coloured seamen arriving in the country as stowaways. The solicitor for the accused man pointed out to the bench that if they were in any doubt as to whether the man was a British subject or not, the accused was entitled to the benefit of the doubt. The magistrates decided that a doubt existed and the man was discharged. The immigration officer concluded:

> This being to my mind a very clear case on which to get a decision and the fact that the accused had not a scrap of evidence to produce that he is a British subject, it is with some concern that I point out that should any future case of this description be brought to the notice of the Magistrates, the man has only to swear on oath that he was born in a British possession and the case will fall to the ground and any chance of stopping the practice of these men arriving as stowaways will be lost.[52]

The problems associated with the implementation of the Aliens Order of 1920 were discussed in detail in a report by Mr E.N. Cooper, Superintending Inspector, Immigration Office, Liverpool in March 1921, based on his enquiries at a number of British ports. In his opinion the Arabs were the main problem. As long as employment was good, these coloured seamen managed to live fairly comfortably but their presence in the United Kingdom had become socially very undesirable and had given rise to a good deal of trouble. He pointed out that the police were very anxious to get rid of all except a handful who had acquired permanent domicile. He felt that numbers could only be reduced gradually as the men chose to return voluntarily to their homes or to take their discharge at foreign ports. Efforts should therefore be concentrated on the best means of preventing the arrival and landing of more men. In order to accomplish this the Colonial Office should be approached to discuss the question of placing coloured seamen on native articles (seamen on native or Lascar articles had to be repatriated at the shipowner's expense). Cooper regarded this as essential if control was to be made more effective. This would need new legislation so that in the meantime he urged the Board of Trade to instruct British consuls to warn masters that if coloured seamen were engaged abroad the shipowners would in all probability be required to repatriate the men.[53]

In January 1923 the Seafarers' Joint Council sent a deputation to the Board of Trade to discuss the question of 'the employment of

Arabs to the detriment of British seafarers'. The deputation consisted of representatives of different sections of seafarers engaged
in the Mercantile Marine—the Imperial Merchant Service Guild,
the Marine Engineers Association, the Mercantile Marine Service
Association, the National Sailors' and Firemen's Union, and the
Shipconstructors and Shipwrights' Association—but the two union
delegates dominated the proceedings. Representatives from the
Home Office and the Ministry of Labour were also present.
Introducing the deputation, the Vice-Chairman of the Seafarers'
Joint Council, Mr T.W. Moore, began with an emotional appeal on
behalf of British sailors. These men had served their country during
the war and were now on the verge of distress and starvation because
Arabs were displacing them on board ship. He urged the Board of
Trade to intercede with the shipowners to request that employment
should be given to Britishers rather than Arabs and recommended
that a committee should be set up to get rid of this 'evil' by
repatriating Arabs to their own country. He then called upon the
two union delegates, Mr J. Henson and Mr Walsh.

Henson claimed that the employment of Arab seaman was not
merely a national but an international problem, affecting not only
the United Kingdom but also the continent of Europe and the
United States of America. In the union's opinion the Arabs competed with British seamen by unfair methods because they were
always prepared to bribe the employers in order to get employment.
At some ports Arabs were claiming the right of employment over
the Britisher and when they were passed over they threatened union
officials with knives and razors. Union officials were not going to
allow themselves to be insulted and threatened by 'a class of man
of the type of the Arab'. Arabs were not British subjects but aliens
and Henson complained bitterly of the assistance which Arabs
appeared to receive from many colonial officers and British consuls
which allowed these men to enter the United Kingdom. He called
upon the Board of Trade, together with the Home Office and
Colonial Office, to find ways not only of restricting the influx of
Arab seamen but, given that many of these men were of 'a dangerous
type', to deport those already in the country so that British seamen
would be able to get the jobs to which they were entitled.

Walsh, the union delegate for South Shields, stated that the Arabs
believed that no British seamen had the right to employment until
they, the Arabs, had got jobs. He claimed that seventy-five per cent
of the firemen employed on the Tyne were Arabs, and that as a
result British seamen were walking about starving. He appealed for
urgent government action. Instead of paying British seamen the

dole, the Arabs should be repatriated and 'our men' allowed to work. The Board of Trade had the powers to deal with this grave problem, and should exercise those powers. Arabs were coming into the country every day and being employed while British seamen were being displaced. What would happen if the unemployed men marching from Glasgow or Liverpool to London found that their jobs were being taken by Arabs? There would be revolution right away and no government would stand it.

Much of the discussion centred on the question of the nationality of Arab seamen. Henson argued that as far as the union was concerned Arabs should be considered as alien seamen. Nearly every Arab seaman coming into Britain claimed to be born in Aden and the general opinion among Arabs was that they were British subjects. They claimed that Aden was a British colony but the union maintained that it was simply a protectorate as far as Britain was concerned. Many Arab seamen had never seen Aden. Stricter regulations should be enforced and claims to British nationality thoroughly investigated. Henson claimed that from personal experience not one Arab in a thousand possessed a British passport. Haldane Porter for the Home Office disputed this and stated that the Immigration Authority had supplied many more than that.

Viscount Wolmer, for the Board of Trade, felt that it was important to recognize that there were three categories of Arab seamen: those who had passports proving that they were British subjects; those who had married English women and had settled down in Britain; and the class of purely alien Arabs who were trying to come into the country. The first two categories had certain rights and claims which must be recognized. As far as the third category was concerned, according to his information, the number of such alien Arabs coming into this country was not increasing as the union asserted.

Nevertheless he assured the union representatives that the terms of the Aliens Act were being strictly enforced by the Home Office. If the union knew of any cases where this was not being done, they should bring them to the attention of either the Home Office or the Board of Trade and the matter would be carefully investigated. The Government fully recognized the seriousness of the present situation where British seamen returning from the war found their jobs taken by these foreigners. However it was much easier to point out the evil than to find a remedy.

With reference to the union's suggestion that Arab seamen should be placed on native or Lascar articles, Viscount Wolmer stated that this could only be done by legislation. But he agreed that it was a matter for the Government to consider. He felt that the power of the Board of Trade to influence the shipowners on the problem of Arab seamen was limited but again he assured the delegation that the matter would be carefully considered. Repatriation would be a very drastic step in dealing with the problem and although it was not impossible, it raised very grave issues not only in this country but in the British Dominions abroad and in the East. Mr Moore, on behalf of the deputation, was encouraged that there was at least agreement on the principle for which they were struggling and hoped that the officers of the Board of Trade could help to resolve the conflict of opinion over the exact scale of the problem that faced them.[54]

The next development emerged from an initiative during 1924 by Mr Cooper, Superintending Inspector, Liverpool, in consultation with the Chief Constables of Cardiff and South Shields. Immigration officials and police clearly felt that greater control over coloured seamen already in the country and more effective action to restrict the entry of others into the United Kingdom could be achieved by introducing a system of registration. Stricter control and regulation was difficult because of the lack of proper means of identifying individual coloured seamen. The solution was to insist that every coloured seamen who could not prove by documentary evidence that he was a British subject, should be required to provide himself with a document by which he could be readily identified and on which his entry into the United Kingdom, if duly authorized by the grant of leave to land, could be recorded. A memorandum on the registration of coloured seamen by Haldane Porter of the Aliens Branch of the Home Office dated 3 November 1924 makes it quite clear that the proposed system of registration was aimed at the Arabs.[55] Replying to a letter on this subject from Haldane Porter, William Scott, the Chief Constable of South Shields observed:

> I beg to inform you that I quite agree with your suggestion, and think it only right that all these so-called Arab seamen who cannot prove by documentary evidence that they are British subjects, should be treated as Aliens, and should be registered. The issue of registration certificates to these men, would I think, give the Police an extra hold over them, and it would prevent them using each other's discharge books when ashore. I am entirely in favour of these men being registered as Aliens when they cannot prove otherwise.[56]

In March 1925 the Home Secretary made a Special Restriction Order under Article 11 of the Aliens Order 1920 imposing an obligation to register with the police upon all coloured seamen found in the United Kingdom on or after the 6 April. Chinese and Japanese were exempt and the Home Office made it clear that this measure was introduced to deal with the problem of the Arabs.[57] Although the Order applied generally throughout the United Kingdom, the new scheme of registration was only applied initially in certain districts, the South Wales ports, the Tyne ports, Liverpool and Hull—ports where the majority of Arab seamen congregated. The authorities acknowledged that when the scheme was first brought into operation there would be a number of seamen who would be unable to show that they had been given leave to land. The issue of a certificate would regularize their position but they would be identifiable. However if registration was refused there was no way of getting rid of them and they would remain outside police control.[58] In such cases the police were therefore instructed to issue a certificate of registration unless there was clear evidence that the man had landed irregularly and that it was considered possible to deal with him for the offence.[59] After a period of six weeks from the date when the new order came into operation, no coloured alien seamen would be entitled to obtain a certificate of registration unless he could show that he was already in the United Kingdom on 6 April 1925 or had been given leave to land since that date. The new Order was welcomed by the Shipping Federation and the National Sailors' and Firemen's Union.

Experience of implementing the Order quickly disclosed a number of difficulties for the authorities. Coloured seamen who were living outside the designated ports and who were unregistered were unable to sign articles before a Marine Superintendent at one of the designated ports, because instructions had been issued that no coloured seamen could be engaged unless he provided proof that he was a British subject or that he possessed a certificate of registration. There was particular concern that difficulties would arise when dealing with coloured alien seamen who were found without proof that they had been given leave to land, since they would be able to claim that they had arrived at a port where registration was not required. To ensure stricter control, the Special Restriction Order was extended to all police registration areas as from 1 January 1926. Another problem was that of coloured seamen who claimed British nationality but were unable to provide satisfactory proof. While the authorities acknowledged that in a number of these cases the claim to British nationality was well-founded, they emphasized that in the absence of documentary proof such claims could not be accepted.[60]

By the end of 1927 the total number of coloured seamen registered under the 1925 Order in the United Kingdom was 8,301; almost half of the seamen were registered at Cardiff and South Shields. The vast majority of the 1,255 coloured seamen registered at South Shields were Arabs. In October 1927 the Home Office had decreed that every coloured seaman who was entitled to register had had time to do so,[61] but doubts were expressed that the Order was dealing effectively with the problems it was intended to meet. A conference was therefore called at the Home Office on 26 January 1928 at which officials of the Immigration Office and the Board of Trade together with the Chief Constables of Cardiff, South Shields and Hull were present.

Sir Haldane Porter, Chief Inspector, Aliens Branch, stated that the main difficulty arose in dealing with those coloured seamen who managed to enter the country irregularly. Until recently the immigration officers, assisted by the Shipping Federation, had been able to dispose of most of these men by sending them to certain continental ports or by obtaining berths for them for discharge abroad. Unfortunately they were now being refused leave to land at continental ports such as Antwerp, Rotterdam and Le Havre, and it was difficult to discharge them abroad so that their disposal was becoming almost impossible.

William Scott, the Chief Constable of South Shields, reported that although men were continuing to land irregularly he thought that the numbers were decreasing. His experience was that the men who arrived irregularly found their way into the coasting trade. He paid tribute to the usefulness of the Order and to the good work done by the immigration staff in helping to enforce it. He agreed with the Chief Constable of Cardiff that it was difficult to get the magistrates to convict seamen who landed without leave. Wilson, the Chief Constable of Cardiff, had complained that magistrates were too ready to accept the defendant's statement that he was British and required proof of irregular landing which was almost impossible for the police to obtain. He suggested that the Order should be amended to place the onus on the defendant of proving that he had been given leave to land. Dowson of the Home Office explained that this had been considered but the difficulty in altering the law of evidence in this way had been thought too great. Dendy of the Board of Trade stated that arrangements for signing on only coloured men who could produce evidence of British nationality or a registration certificate had worked well and that boarding-house keepers were beginning to realize that the smuggling in of stowaways was ceasing to pay.

Cook, Immigration Inspector, London, reported that there had been a large influx of Arabs at the time of the coal strike in 1926 and that many of them were not included in the crew lists of the vessels in which they arrived. He suggested that something might be done to check the employment of coloured men in the coasting trade, if the co-operation of the London owners of coasting vessels could be enlisted. Summing up the meeting, Haldane Porter was reassured that the general opinion appeared to be that the Order was useful. There was general agreement also that the present arrangements should continue to be strictly enforced. Any relaxation in the direction of making registration easier would merely encourage irregular landings and would not help in the ultimate disposal of the difficult cases.[62]

A Home Office memorandum dated November 1927 highlighted the problem of dealing with coloured seamen who landed irregularly and were found later thereby presenting the authorities with a dilemma. If these men were refused registration they would be unable to get employment on a ship and this would limit their chances of making their own way out of the country. If they were allowed to register, their position would be regularized but they would then seek employment and compete in an overstocked labour market. The practice adopted in such cases was to decline to register the man and to mark any papers he might possess with the words 'Registration deferred'. This prevented the man from obtaining registration in another district and as his registration was deferred rather than definitely refused it avoided a case being made against the authorities that the Order required him to be registered. Yet it was alleged that coloured seamen continued to be smuggled into the United Kingdom at the instigation of coloured boarding-house masters, and although this movement had been checked by the 1925 Order, it had not been stopped by deferring registration. There was always the possibility that a certificate might eventually be issued and the problem was to convince the boarding-house keepers that the game was not worth while. Various alternatives were explored but it was concluded that there seemed to be no alternative to continuing the system of deferred registration. This was unsatisfactory because there was always the risk of its validity being challenged in view of the terms of the Order.[63]

In March 1928 Mr Adams of the Office of the High Commissioner for India approached the Home Office to discuss whether there was any practical means of relieving the distress of those seamen who, after being refused registration under the 1925 Order, applied to the High Commissioner for verification of their claim to birth in British India. The memorandum reporting these discussions does not state the nationality of the seamen referred to but they were almost certainly Arabs who claimed to be born in Aden. Mr Adams pointed out that enquiries into these claims normally took on average three months and during that time the applicant was unable to obtain work and frequently had to exist on the charity of his fellow countrymen. He suggested that in such cases the seamen might be granted temporary certificates of registration until the enquiries into their claim to British nationality had been completed; the certificates might then be withdrawn when the applicant had been proved to be either a British subject or an alien. To support his recommendation he argued that the number of applicants who were found to be aliens was very small. A Home Office official examined the relevant statistics and found that up to 20 March 1928 the claims of sixty-seven applicants had been investigated. Of these only thirty-four had proved to be British subjects; twenty had been found to be British protected persons, and thirteen were either known to be aliens or unidentified. It was his impression that since the end of March the proportion of rejected applications had increased. He concluded:

> I do not think that the distress of the 50% who are British could justify us in condoning, even temporarily, the irregular landing of the 50% who are aliens . . . As soon as it became known that temporary certificates of registration were being issued to seamen who had applied for these certificates of nationality, the boarding-house keepers would persuade men who knew they were aliens to apply for verification of bogus claims to British nationality. The men would then be able to get employment, and cash in their advance notes for the benefit of the boarding-house keeper. It is known that boarding-house keepers are now beginning to feel the pinch of having to keep in idleness seamen whose irregular landing they have encouraged or connived at; and that this indirect financial pressure on the boarding-house keeper is one of the means of checking irregular landing. The proposed issue of temporary certificates of registration would lead to the relaxation of this pressure at a time when it is producing its best results. If this prediction proved correct Mr Adams' proposal would recoil on his own head by giving him a large amount of additional and unnecessary work in dealing with bogus claims to British nationality.[64]

A memorandum from the Immigration Office dated January 1929 admitted that Arab seamen were continuing to arrive at United Kingdom ports, particularly Southampton, in considerable numbers. The authorities were powerless to stop the flow because if they were rejected both the French and Belgians were now refusing to re-admit them. As there appeared to be no satisfactory means of blocking the flow of Arab seamen at British ports, it concluded that the only hope was to persuade the French Government to try and stop the movement at Marseilles. A report had been received from the Acting British Vice-Consul at Marseilles which confirmed that there were no restrictions placed on the entry of Arab seamen at that port. The memorandum recommended that the British Foreign Office should be asked to approach the French authorities in this matter in order to persuade them to establish some effective form of control at that port and to impress on them the importance of the problem to the British authorities.[65]

In February 1930 Chief Constable Wilkie, reporting to the Watch Committee, South Shields, admitted that the number of Arab seamen in the town was increasing and that these men experienced little difficulty in getting into the country through irregular channels. Although permission to land was refused in many cases, shortly afterwards the alien seaman was found presenting himself at the Aliens' Department for registration. He had made it his practice to bring all such cases before the Justices. But the results obtained so far had not had any effect, and so long as fines of only 5s. to 40s. were imposed he believed that the aliens would continue to come here. He felt that he was entitled to greater assistance from the Justices than he had received in the past and that he was entitled to ask them to impose punishment which would act as a deterrent. There were those who argued that these offenders had served on British ships during the 1914–18 war but in his opinion by permitting them to reside here and by providing them with un-employment insurance benefit when they were unable to work, any service rendered by them in the past had been handsomely repaid.[66]

Several official reports on the application of the 1925 Order stated that with few exceptions the coloured seamen in Britain had welcomed the opportunity of obtaining a certificate of registration because this gave them a definite status in this country and was aimed at preventing the arrival of more coloured seamen who would compete with them for employment. Yet protests were voiced and there were many coloured seamen who objected to this dramatic change in their status. Instead of being treated as British subjects, they now became aliens and were required to report regularly to the police. Few could meet the rigorous requirements set by the police as proof of British nationality. In Cardiff there is evidence that the police used a range of dubious practices to compel registration.[67]

In April 1925 Dr Abdul Majid of the Islamic Society wrote to the Under Secretary of State of the India Office that the police in South Shields were compelling coloured seamen in the town to register as aliens whether the men were British or aliens. A number of these men came from Aden and its hinterland and having examined their papers he was satisfied that they were British Indian subjects. They had been very loyal during the war and remained loyal subjects of His Imperial Majesty. The effect of the 1925 Order would be to deprive these loyal subjects of His Majesty of their status. If registration was necessary, these men were therefore anxious to register as British subjects. The letter was forwarded to the Under Secretary of State at the Home Office for comments on the actions of the South Shields' Constabulary. The Home Office replied that there was nothing in Dr Abdul Majid's letter that should concern the India Office and observed that if the Arab seamen in question were in a position to establish that they were British subjects there was no need for them to register under the Order. They drew attention to the fact that in such cases it was the responsibility of each individual to prove that he was not an alien. They concluded that the Home Office was well aware that Dr Abdul Majid was ready to take up the cause of coloured seamen 'whether in general or in particular and whether on good cause shown or otherwise'.[68]

There is evidence that the police in South Shields required certain Arab residents who were not seamen and who claimed to be British subjects to register under the 1925 Order. It was also alleged that the police had set a time limit for these men to produce evidence of nationality. The Home Office took this matter up with the Political Resident, Aden and requested that any police action in these cases should be suspended until particulars had been received from Aden. A letter from the Home Office to the Chief Constable, South Shields dated 30 July 1926 stated that information received from Aden indicated that the men in question were not British subjects but British protected persons and therefore aliens liable to registration under the Aliens Order. Nevertheless the Secretary of State for Home Affairs recommended that these men be exempt from registration and that the police should take similar action in the case of other coloured men, *other than seamen*, who could show that they were from the Aden Protectorate and therefore entitled to the status of British protected persons.[69]

An interesting insight into the application of the 1925 Order is provided by a case which came before the South Shields' police court in December 1929. Farah Ali, an Arab seaman, was charged with being found in South Shields without permission of an immigration officer and also with having in his possession a certificate of registration on which the endorsement had been altered without lawful permission. Mr Muir Smith, the solicitor defending Ali, contended that Ali was a British subject. During the war Ali had been torpedoed three times on British ships and his war service had been recognized in 1919 by the Mercantile Marine as a British subject when he was presented with a war medal. In 1925 he had been required to register under the Special Restriction (Coloured Alien Seamen) Order at Cardiff and his certificates showed that he had served on British ships from 1923 to 1927. In 1927 he went back to Yemen and that appeared to have cancelled his previous registration. A police officer reported that when Ali presented himself at the Immigration Department at South Shields, he found that his registration certificate had been stamped and crossed by an immigration officer which meant that the person holding the certificate had been refused permission to land. The stamp had been altered and mutilated so as to make it indistinguishable. Ali argued that he thought his registration had been wrongly endorsed and he had therefore tried to erase it. The Chief Constable stated that the defendant could not be a British subject because he had registered as an alien. The chairman of the court concluded that the court was not satisfied that the defendant was a British subject and fined him 40s. for each offence.[70]

Five

South Shields the Storm Centre: The Rota System and the 'Arab Riot' of August 1930

I The National Union of Seamen steps up its campaign against the Arabs

While there was some popular feeling in South Shields that was highly critical of the National Union of Seamen because it accepted Arabs as union members (see Chapter Four, p.87), throughout the inter-war period union officials had in fact called for strict regulation and control over the Arabs to protect the jobs of white seamen. In 1929 the NUS stepped up its campaign against Arab seamen at British ports and on 9 December sent a deputation to the Board of Trade on this subject. Several members of parliament representing a number of port cities were present and the deputation was introduced by Commander Kenworthy, MP for Central Hull. The deputation stated that many white British seamen were unemployed because of the high proportion of Arabs and coloured seamen being shipped at ports in South Wales, the north-east and the Humber. They claimed that fifty-seven per cent of all the firemen shipped from these ports were Arabs or coloured seamen. It was argued that the introduction of oil burning and motor vessels had reduced the demand for firemen by as much as seventy-five per cent and that the influx of Arabs simply made it more difficult for white seamen to find work.

The Arab boarding-house masters were attacked for helping to smuggle Arabs into the country and for the corrupt methods they used in the lucrative business of supplying Arab and coloured crews.

The spectacle of coloured men fighting for a job while white men stood by was often seen on the north-east coast and on these occasions, it was claimed, NUS officials were often in danger of suffering grievous bodily harm. The deputation emphasized that Arabs were a social menace. There were growing numbers of half-caste children at these ports and many were illegitimate. When these children grew up they would be unable to find employment and would become a burden on the state.

The deputation called for action to ensure stricter control over the Arabs. They suggested that all Arabs and coloured seamen should be re-registered immediately and those found to have entered the country since 1925 in contravention of the Order in Council should be deported. The language test should be more frequently and more rigidly applied. The system whereby Arab and coloured seamen were supplied through the boarding-house keepers should be stopped, Arab boarding-houses and cafes should be placed under stricter police supervision and their licences should be reviewed periodically. Each discharge book should contain a photograph and fingerprints to prevent it being used by another seaman. If necessary a committee composed of the National Union of Seamen, the Board of Trade and the Home Office should be appointed to investigate thoroughly the whole question of the employment of Arab seamen. The Ministers who received the deputation promised to give these points their fullest consideration. A report on the deputation published in the NUS newspaper, *The Seaman*, concluded:

> It must be understood that we have no kick with the Arab as such, but charity begins at home, and with the elimination of these men who would be better off in the countries of their birth, employment would not only be found for our own at present redundant firemen but room could be found for ex-miners and ex-naval ratings, of which so many will be available especially of the latter, for if the disarmament programmes are carried out these men will add their quota to the already difficult problem of unemployment.[1]

At the same time *The Seaman* published a number of articles, often reprinted from other newspapers, in an effort to discredit Arabs and to praise the superiority of white crews.

Ali Said, one of the leading Arab boarding-house masters in South Shields, appealed to the Secretary of State for India against the attitude taken by the National Union of Seamen towards Arab and coloured seamen. In a letter dated 27 December 1929, he condemned the article reporting on the deputation to the Board of Trade in *The Seaman* as shameful from beginning to end and unworthy of the NUS. He pointed out that Arab, Indian, Somali and other coloured seamen were members of the NUS and yet the union was prejudiced against them. Why, he asked, did the NUS accept coloured seamen as members? It was little wonder there was such discontent amongst these men when they were subject to such 'vile treatment'. Because Arabs and Somalis were linked to India through Islam, they looked to the India Office as their guardian and asked for assistance in ensuring that they received fair treatment. He argued that Arabs were not recognized as British subjects simply because they were unable to offer proof of their status. Nevertheless, as much of Arabia, like India, was under British Protectorate, they claimed British protection and justice. On behalf of his fellow countrymen, he appealed to the India Office to take steps to maintain their rights.[2]

As the campaign against the Arabs continued, Dr Khalid Sheldrake, Life President of the Western Islamic Association, visited South Shields in March 1930 to express his support for the Arab seamen. Accompanied by the association's secretary, Mr Abdulla Day and Mr Muir Smith, a local solicitor who acted as the Arabs' legal adviser and spokesman,[3] Dr Sheldrake addressed a meeting of 170 Arabs at Chapter Row on 18 March. He appealed to all those present to work together to fight their case. The situation was critical and it was difficult for isolated groups to fight on their own. Unity was vital if action was to be taken speedily.[4] Sheldrake's appeal for unity indicates that there were serious divisions within the Arab community and although he gave no details it seems probable that it was the perennial problem of rivalry between the Arab boarding-house masters.

Sheldrake told the meeting that he had accompanied Mr Muir Smith to the Home Office and the House of Commons where Mr Muir Smith had fought hard in the interests of the Arab seamen. Mr Muir Smith also addressed the meeting and for the benefit of the audience his speech was translated into Arabic. In an interview with the local newspaper Mr Muir Smith referred to the serious plight of those Arab seamen who had been refused registration under the 1925 Order. There were about one hundred of these unregistered seamen in the town; some had been unemployed for nearly two years and were having to be kept by the boarding-house masters. The police authorities, he stated, argued that there were already enough Arab seamen in the town and that it was undesirable to increase the number. He had asked the Home Office either to register these men so as to enable them to obtain ships or, if they were determined not to register any more men, to pay their debts which were due to the boarding-house masters and then to repatriate them. Speaking of the Arab community as a whole in the town, Mr Muir Smith claimed that many were British citizens and genuinely came from Aden and the surrounding district which was British territory. But because there was no proper system of registration of births there they could not provide documentary proof of their nationality. Some had been in South Shields for twenty years and had a creditable war service. He considered that it was the duty of the Colonial Office to look after these men. During his visit to London he had taken the opportunity to see Mr Chuter Ede, the MP for South Shields, who was interesting himself in this matter.[5]

A few days later, Mr Muir Smith announced that as a result of the preferential treatment being given to white men by the National Union of Seamen, the Arabs were contemplating withdrawing from the union and setting up a union of their own for coloured seamen only. He stated that currently there were 2,000 coloured seamen in the NUS each paying one shilling a week. With £100 a week the Arabs would be able to finance and maintain a union of their own. He maintained that this would mean less contact with other seamen and there would be fewer clashes with the white seamen when men were signing on if the Arabs had their own offices. No action appears to have been taken to implement this suggestion and there is no evidence of any attempt to organize support for the initiative among Arab seamen at other ports. Concluding his announcement, Mr Muir Smith stated that the Arabs in South Shields were very alive at this time to the question of organizing themselves 'industrially, socially and religiously'.[6] It is perhaps significant that during Sheldrake's visit he had called for a strengthening of the South Shields branch of the Western Islamic Association which declared itself to be non-sectarian and non-political. Several new members had been enrolled at the meeting and the urgent need for a mosque, school and Muslim cemetery was expressed. One of the Arab boarding-house masters, Hassan Mohamed, had already arranged for a local firm of architects to prepare a plan for a mosque[7] (see Chapter Eight, p.216).

In April 1930 the National Union of Seamen sent another deputation to the Board of Trade including representatives from the north-east coast, the Humber, Bristol Channel and Antwerp. Once again it complained about the increasing employment of Arab firemen at a time when 21,000 British seamen were out of work, including nearly 3,000 at the Tyne ports. It claimed that the problem was particularly acute on the weekly boats which did not sign on their crews before a Board of Trade official. Allegations of bribery and corruption to secure employment and of social abuses due to the alliances of Arabs with white women were repeated. The NUS representatives reported that they had opened discussions with the shipowners to rectify these abuses and to see whether some restriction could be placed on the employment of Arabs on British ships at a time when so many British seamen were unemployed. The Board of Trade was sympathetic and promised to have the whole matter investigated thoroughly. The NUS indicated that they would continue their discussions with the shipowners and report back to the Board of Trade.[8]

In a long letter to the *Shields Daily Gazette* entitled 'Playing the Game', Dr Sheldrake strongly criticized the National Union of Seamen for mounting a general attack against Arab seamen through its deputations to the Board of Trade and through articles in its journal. He deplored the action of the union in turning against its own members and seeking to deny them employment. He was sure that fair-minded people would agree that any organization which deliberately tried to arouse racial hatred must be condemned. The main thrust of his argument was that this question should be seen from the point of view of the British Empire because the constant attacks made on Arabs in this country were bound to have repercussions in lands under the control of the empire. He pointed out that the British Empire was the largest Islamic power in the world and that King George V had more Muslim subjects than Christians. The Arabs had nobly played their part on behalf of the empire and its allies on both land and sea. Not averse to rewriting history, he declared that the Arabs had willingly and proudly proclaimed themselves British during the First World War and rejected overtures made to them by Britain's enemies. He was convinced that if the Arabs had not sided with Britain and fought side by side with British soldiers then Britain would have lost the campaign against the Turks in the Middle East. Arab seamen, he stressed, by proclaiming themselves British had suffered in enemy countries. Some were interned and all employment of Arabs on enemy ships was terminated. Since the end of the war, this policy had continued. As a result Arabs could no longer find employment on ships of other nationalities, even those of Britain's former allies, because the Arabs had voluntarily placed themselves under the protection of Great Britain. Consequently Arabs naturally sought to continue working on British ships. They willingly became members of the National Union of Seamen and had paid their contributions regularly.

Because Arab seamen were law-abiding, sober and industrious they were well-liked by the shipmasters.

Dr Sheldrake acknowledged that there was serious unemployment in the country but argued that the present government was doing its best to grapple with this problem. Unemployment could not be settled in a day or even a year and government ministers deserved support and encouragement and should not be worried by 'particular groups with an individual axe to grind' presumably a reference to the National Union of Seamen. He also referred to the weighty problems the Government faced abroad, particularly in India and Egypt, and noted that it was in these lands that attacks on Arabs in Britain were sure to have serious repercussions. He concluded:

> We desire peace in the Empire and friendly relations with all states, including those peopled by that great race, the Arabs, and it is up to every Britisher who holds to our traditions to see to it that fairplay is given to the Arabs in our midst and that they should not be penalised by Britishers for themselves claiming the protection of the Empire and fighting under the Union Jack side by side with out own sailors and soldiers.[9]

Dr Sheldrake's impassioned plea to think of the empire appears to have fallen on deaf ears in South Shields, though it clearly attracted some attention nationally. Support came from B. Williams of London who strongly condemned the actions of the National Union of Seamen against the Arab seamen in Britain and claimed that there were many in the trade union movement who felt the same as he did. In a letter to the *Shields Daily Gazette* he wrote:

> These Arabs are part and parcel of our Empire and it is the duty of every Britisher worth his salt to see to it that they get a sporting chance. The non-registration of these men for employment is absurd and reflects ill upon our hospitality. We allow foreigners from every land to work here in Britain, and it seems that some people would prefer a Russian or other nondescript to an Arab, whose forefathers brought civilisation to Darkest Europe. The NUS should support these Arabs and not commence a silly campaign against them. I am rather ashamed to think that our Arab friends should find themselves attacked by a British Union to which they belong and I know

118

that many here in London in the trade union world hold the same views.[10]

Arthur Field of the East-West Circle, London also came to the defence of the Arabs. In his letter to the *Shields Daily Gazette* he strongly condemned the actions of the National Union of Seamen and made a number of specific points about the union's position. He criticized the NUS for telling English seamen that by keeping the Arabs out their jobs would be protected, while at the same time telling the Labour Party and others that it would find employment on ships for British miners and the non-seafaring unemployed. He was appalled that any union should launch a campaign against a section of its own membership and seek to deprive them of jobs. Indeed the campaign against the Arabs was being financed out of the contributions paid by the Arab seamen. He pointed out that not all Arab seamen were aliens; many came from British protectorates or had received British protection. They were good seamen and appreciated by the masters of British ships. Only around one hundred Arabs were unregistered and yet the NUS claimed that there was 'an invasion of Britain by Arab seamen'.

The real picture was of a peaceful and industrious British-Arab population in various ports numbering around 10,000, many of whom had been here for up to twenty years. They educated their families and carried out their duties as British citizens. He argued that the NUS had neither destroyed the English boarding-house system nor had any real effort been made to weaken it so that until the English 'parasite' was eliminated, why should not his Arab counterpart stay in business. Field endorsed Dr Sheldrake's request that those Arabs who were British subjects or British protected persons should be registered and allowed to obtain ships and to earn their living. Those Arabs who were aliens should be repatriated after the debts they had incurred as a result of NUS action had been paid.[11]

Sydney le Touzel, the manager of *The Seaman*, was quick to reply to Field's stinging rebukes. In a letter to the *Shields Daily Gazette* he stated that the NUS had no quarrel with British Arabs but only with the 'alien Arabs' who were smuggled into Britain by the Arab boarding-house keepers to become their 'money-making machines'. This argument was to become one of the standard responses when the NUS was challenged about its campaign against Arab seamen. However, the fact that the union constantly drew attention to the social menace represented by the appearance of 'half-caste, illegitimate children' points to a much wider, racist assault on the

Arabs. Indeed Le Touzel's own journal had demanded the elimination and expulsion of Arab seamen not only so that employment could be found for unemployed white British seamen but also to provide jobs for ex-miners and ex-naval ratings. On the last point Le Touzel tried to argue that the recruitment of miners was not envisaged at the present time when 20,000 British seamen were idle but was merely seen as a possible source of supply for the mercantile marine in the future when it would be much better to give the British miner the chance of a job than 'the doubtful British Arab'. Given the statements made in previous issues of *The Seaman*, this argument is far from convincing.

Le Touzel went on to criticize Field for overestimating the size of the Arab population in Britain. Earlier in his letter Le Touzel had stated that there were 5,000 Arab seamen in the country—which represents a fairly accurate estimate. But he then went on to accept Field's figure of 10,000 as an additional reason for refusing to allow any more Arabs into the country. He drew attention to the fact that millions of white British workers were without jobs and that emigration was being encouraged as a remedy for unemployment and asked why Britons should emigrate to let Arabs take their place. Le Touzel then accused Field of 'lamentable ignorance' on the subject of the Arabs. His picture of the peaceful, industrious Arab was far from accurate. Knives were produced at the slightest provocation and violent disturbances were a common occurrence in South Shields and in other ports where Arabs congregated. Once again he drew attention to the large number of half-caste children who would inevitably become 'dole aspirants' and whose education was a charge on the British taxpayer.

Le Touzel denounced the Arab boarding-house keepers as 'parasites' and declared that the NUS intended to eliminate them as they were nothing less than crimps. He took issue with Field on the NUS's attitude towards the boarding-house system arguing that the late Havelock Wilson as president of the union had spent most of his life fighting against the crimping system. He argued that it was due to Wilson's efforts that today the English boarding-houses were purely lodging-houses and had nothing to do with the supply of seamen. On this subject he maintained that Field was mistaken as the NUS had fought a long and hard battle against the boarding-house masters for control over the entry of seamen into the labour market. In conclusion, Le Touzel suggested that Field should visit South Shields, Cardiff and Hull to see the Arab problem at first hand and the perniciousness of the Arab boarding-house keepers' system. He was sure that Field would then admit that he was misinformed and would withdraw his unworthy allegations against a great union which had fought for over fifty years to improve the pay and working conditions of British seamen.[12]

II The Seamen's Minority Movement takes up the Arab cause

In May 1930 the local branch of the Seamen's Minority Movement took up the cause of the Arab seamen in South Shields and to understand their role in the events which followed it is necessary to look briefly at developments in the National Union of Seamen after the First World War.[13] After many years of conflict, the war introduced a more harmonious relationship between the Sailors' and Firemen's Union[14] and the Shipping Federation, the organization representing the shipowners. Following the 1911 seamen's strike, the Federation had conceded a measure of recognition of the union, but the struggle between them to secure a monopoly of the labour supply continued. However the shipping boom of 1911–13 strengthened the workers' bargaining position and the outbreak of war brought a growing labour shortage. In 1917 unrest among the rank and file at a time when shipping was desperately needed and threatened by submarine warfare forced the Goverment to intervene and the Federation to concede a national joint board for the industry, known as the National Maritime Board. Under this agreement, the supply of seamen was to be jointly controlled by Federation and union. In theory a seaman could belong to any union, but the Sailors' and Firemen's Union, by far the biggest of any of the seafarers' unions, used joint control to enforce the closed shop. The Sailors' and Firemen's Union ensured that no rival organization was admitted to the Board simply by threatening to withdraw. The size of its membership ensured that this threat carried great weight. When the post-war depression in shipping drastically weakened the union's position, its leader, Havelock Wilson, clung tenaciously to the gains that he had already achieved. At a time of heavy unemployment and severe depression in the industry, strike action was avoided and his approach was to achieve the best possible bargain through negotiation.

In 1921 a new rival to the Sailors' and Firemen's Union appeared as a result of the amalgamation of the British Seafarers' Union and the Cooks' and Stewards' Union to form the Amalgamated Marine Workers' Union.[15] Wilson was determined to destroy the new union by ensuring that as far as ratings were concerned only members of the Sailors' and Firemen's Union were taken on. In this campaign he had the co-operation of the owners who were anxious to see a militant union killed off as quickly as possible. The machinery used to tighten control over the labour supply was the 'PC5' system introduced in April 1922. Under this system any sailor or fireman seeking employment was required to obtain a card, known as a PC5, from the Sailors' and Firemen's Union and get it stamped by both the union and the Shipping Federation. The Sailors' and Firemen's Union of course only accepted its own members and insisted on them being fully paid up. This meant real hardship for many seamen who, during a period of high unemployment, had been out of work for long periods. In practice the PC5 system meant that the owners agreed to employ only members of the Sailors' and Firemen's Union and in return the union agreed to keep the men in order. Not surprisingly there were many protests, especially from the TUC, but with little effect. The AMWU did not collapse immediately as the PC5 was not introduced universally for some time, but, as it had difficulty recruiting and retaining members, it was considerably weakened. When it attempted strike action, the Sailors' and Firemen's Union made every effort to break the strike.

In August 1925 sporadic strike action erupted at British ports and in London a communist-backed Central Strike Committee was formed with the active support of the seaman's section of the Minority Movement. From 1923 the Minority Movement was the name of the British section of the Red International of Labour Unions. The AMWU joined the strike but quickly clashed with the Central Strike Committee over how the strike should be run. By transferring seamen from one district to another to fill the place of strikers, the Sailors' and Firemen's Union, which was in daily consultation with the Shipping Federation, was able to ensure that ships sailed with only minor delays thus breaking the strike. In the following year, 1926, the year of the General Strike, the Sailors' and Firemen's Union was the only union that chose to disregard the strike call issued by the General Council of the TUC. Most seamen did not strike but the AMWU called out its members and some members of the Sailors' and Firemen's Union came out unofficially. Once again officials of the Sailors and Firemen's Union helped the Shipping Federation to break these strikes. Havelock Wilson achieved another victory in 1926 when the High Court ruled that the amalgamation of the British Seafarers' Union and the Cooks' and Stewards' Union was invalid because of a fraudulent ballot. The financial consequences of this decision destroyed the AMWU which quietly folded early in 1927.

Throughout the 1920s Wilson's union had shown increasing

readiness to accept the shipowners' wishes on wages and hours of work. Wage cuts were accepted in 1921, 1922, 1923 and 1925 with little consultation with union officials let alone the rank and file. The severe depression in shipping no doubt made some wage cuts inevitable but a less conciliatory attitude by Wilson might have resulted in less drastic cuts and somewhat shorter hours of work for the ordinary seamen.

The rank and file membership was bound to be scandalized by the extent of Wilson's co-operation with the shipowners, symbolized by a good deal of mutual wining and dining at a time when thousands of seamen were unemployed. Indeed for Wilson, harmonious relations with the employers had become not so much a necessary means to safeguard the union and its members as an end in itself. Once the PC5 system had been introduced, the union leadership had no need to take into account the views of the rank and file as the men were dependent on the union for their jobs. Any unrest which did emerge was seen as subversive and usually communist-inspired. The priority given to employer-union harmony, Wilson's strike-breaking activities and his lavish support for the breakaway company union in the Nottinghamshire coal mines increasingly isolated the NUS from the rest of the labour movement. In 1921 the union left the National Transport Workers' Federation and in 1922 it was disaffiliated from the Labour Party. The union's expulsion from the TUC in 1928 paved the way for the powerful Transport and General Workers' Union led by Ernest Bevin to launch its own seamen's section. But this was done only reluctantly because it was feared that such a section would be dominated by the Seamen's Minority Movement whose leading elements were members of the Communist Party. Byrne[16] has argued that in order to keep communists out of the TGWU Ernest Bevin devoted his energies to getting the NUS back into the TUC rather than to promoting a rival union. His opportunity came with Wilson's death in April 1929. Negotiations between the TGWU and the NUS began and resulted in an agreement by which the TGWU closed its seamen's section and the NUS withdrew its support for non-political unions and applied for re-affiliation with the TUC.

It is against this background of growing dissatisfaction among ordinary seamen with the activities of the NUS leadership that the Seamen's Minority Movement began holding meetings at the Mill Dam in South Shields, beginning in April 1930. At these meetings Minority Movement speakers denounced the methods employed by the NUS and the shipowners in bringing about a reduction in wages and longer working hours. They called upon all seamen who were dissatisfied with present conditions and who dared to voice their grievances to join the Minority Movement and form a new union run by seamen for seamen. This would fight against the NUS and the shipowners, smash the PC5 system and campaign for an increase in wages, shorter hours and better working conditions on board ship. The policy of the new union would be unity and solidarity to all seafarers no matter what their colour, creed or nationality. As a result of these meetings the Seamen's Minority Movement appears to have recruited about 300 members.

The South Shields' branch of the Seamen's Minority Movement first took up the cause of Arab and other coloured seamen in May 1930 after an incident at North Shields.[17] On 29 April there had been violent clashes at the New Quay, North Shields when a group of thirteen Somalis from South Shields were brought over to sign on the crew of the steamer *Cape Verde*, which traditionally carried a coloured stokehold crew. A large crowd of white men on the quay, not all of them seamen, tried to prevent the Somalis from signing on by blocking their way to the Shipping Office. Heavily out-numbered, the Somalis drew knives and razors and in the fighting which ensued a number of white men were wounded and one Somali was badly beaten by the crowd before the police intervened. No white men were arrested but three Somalis were found guilty of unlawful wounding and sentenced to between twelve and fifteen months in prison. The *Cape Verde* eventually sailed with a white crew. The local secretary of the NUS stated that North Shields had always been noted for its hostility to the engagement of coloured crews and very few were signed on. In most of the press coverage and in the subsequent correspondence about the incident the Somalis were referred to as Arabs.[18]

In a letter to the *Shields Daily Gazette* 'Swiftsure', speaking for the Seamen's Minority Movement, blamed the NUS for the incident at North Shields and argued that union officials had broken the National Maritime Board agreement which stated that no men should be brought from one port to another so long as there were sufficient men available at that port to man the ship. Administratively South Shields and North Shields were separate ports. The Arabs could not be blamed for taking a job when it was offered to them. He went on to criticize the NUS for stirring up racial feeling against the Arabs, a policy which was bound to have repercussions throughout the British Empire:

> It is hard lines that they [the Arabs] should have to suffer through official action and the policy which has been adopted

by the NUS to bring about racial feeling with the object of gradually ousting the Arabs and coloured men from British ships and ultimately from the NUS. I wonder what Havelock Wilson would think now could he return and see how his officials are working against the coloured seamen; he who often taunted the white seamen from public platforms that the funds of the NUS were kept up by the coloured seamen. These racial disturbances in England are bound to reflect elsewhere throughout the British Empire, who's proud boast is, justice and fairplay for all. Then by all means let us have it.[19]

In other letters to the local newspaper, 'Swiftsure' reiterated these arguments but went further and accused the NUS of stirring up racial feelings so that seamen would be fighting for jobs and divided and in no position to resist a further reduction in wages:

As I pointed out in my letter the other night, the root cause of the trouble could not be laid against the Arabs; I don't profess to know how the Arabs came to be in the country, or how long they have been here. The thing is they are here, and as British subjects must be treated as such. I say there is more behind these disturbances than the general public think. I am quite sure that if the public only knew how bad are the conditions of seamen, public opinion would be brought to bear on the subject and compel legislation to rectify the grievances.

I contended in my previous letter, the officials of the NUS could have prevented the riot which took place at North Shields, but have adopted a policy of stirring up racial feelings for the purpose of creating conditions where seamen will be fighting for jobs, so as to pave the way for the shipowners to force a further reduction of wages on the seamen and to keep them divided and so prevent the seamen from putting a united front against attack, which is going to be made on the already low wages and bad conditions existing. As it is the proud boast of the British Empire; justice and fairplay for all, then I say, by all means let us have it.[20]

In another letter 'Swiftsure' criticized the NUS for trying to create the impression that it was the alien Arabs and other coloured seamen who were responsible for unemployment among white seamen. The real cause, he claimed, was the large number of new men, the so-called 'first trippers', who were being signed up by the union for the sake of the £2 entrance fee. He argued that no new members should be allowed to join the union when so many men were unemployed.[21] This point was also made by 'Seaman' in a letter to the *Shields Daily Gazette* dated 24 May 1930.[22]

The Minority Movement's defence of the rights of the Arabs and other coloured seamen clearly outraged some South Shields' residents and touched the raw nerve of racial prejudice. 'British Able Seaman', for example, wrote to the *Shields Daily Gazette* indignantly:

> Now we are to have another new organisation that mark you is prepared to accept members from any nationality or creed. That is to say that British seamen who become members of the new minority movement union will have to live in the forecastle with Chinese, Arabs, Turks, Greeks, Russians, Bolshies etc. Well I think it will fizzle out, too or become an Asiatic union, then fade away the same as its predecessors, for no right-thinking Britishers would stand for such an organisation.[23]

III A rota system of registration for Arab seamen

While the Seamen's Minority Movement was campaigning in South Shields, the National Union of Seamen was continuing its discussions with the shipowners on ways of dealing with the abuses associated with the employment of Arabs. At a meeting held in London on 1 July 1930 they agreed to introduce a rota system of registration for Arab seamen at Cardiff, South Shields and Hull with effect from 1 August for a one-year trial period. It was based on a system of registering seamen signing on British ships which had been introduced at the port of Antwerp. A report on this system by the British Consul-General in Antwerp had been made to the Board of Trade in April 1930 and on 10 May of that year Commander Kenworthy MP and George Gunning, Assistant General Secretary of the National Union of Seamen, visited Antwerp to study how the system operated. Gunning's report describes the system in detail but its central feature was that seamen signing on British ships at the port were engaged in rotation so that those longest ashore had the first chance of employment. Although Gunning stated that the system applied to all seamen and that no distinction was made between the registration of any one nationality, coloured or otherwise, Kenworthy listed as one of the advantages the fact that preference could be and was given to British seamen in obtaining jobs on British ships. Both agreed that the system had proved effective in checking crimping, for which Antwerp formerly had a very bad reputation, and recommended its introduction in Britain.

Kenworthy argued that it should be applied to coloured seamen signing on European articles, i.e. Arabs, Chinese and Somalis, whereas Gunning singled out the Arabs because bribery and corruption were only associated with the employment of the Arab section.[24] Although the Government was keen to emphasize that the rota system was a private initiative by the union and the shipowners and that no government department could have managed it with existing powers, there seems little doubt that the system had the full backing of the Home Office and the Board of Trade.[25]

The rules of the rota system introduced at Cardiff, South Shields and Hull are presented in full as an Appendix, p.251. The Joint Supply Office at each of these ports was to keep a register in two parts, one for Arabs and the other for Somalis. Officers were to have complete liberty to determine the nationality of the crew. Those wishing to engage a coloured crew would be informed that it was not advisable to mix Arabs and Somalis and asked to specify which they preferred. In order to register, an Arab or Somali had to satisfy the Port Consultants that he was a bona fide seaman and was in this country lawfully. He was required to produce either a police registration certificate or a British passport together with discharges from one or more British vessels. If he satisfied these conditions, he was then issued with a pink numbered registration card to which his photograph was attached and was instructed to report at the office every fourteen days. The date of each report would be entered in the register and marked on the back of his registration card. When an Arab or Somali crew was required the relevant number would be called up for selection giving priority to seamen with the lowest number on the register who were recorded as unemployed. The existing crew could be re-engaged for another voyage but they were to be registered in the usual manner. On being engaged the seaman surrendered his registration card and when he returned to port he received a new card bearing a new number and the process would be repeated as before.

Soon after the London meeting of the union and shipowners, a notice was displayed in the window of the Shipping Federation Office at South Shields explaining the new scheme and requesting Arab and Somali seamen to apply at once to the local Joint Supply Office for instructions about registration. Announcing the new system to its readers, *The Seaman* reported:

> The agreement reached on the matter will give satisfaction to bona fide Arabs and will solve a very vexed question in addition to preventing any further racial disturbance. We have gained

127

our point, which was to regularise the method of employment of Arab and coloured labour, and by so doing eliminate the corrupt practices which have hitherto accompanied their employment.[26]

In contrast to earlier issues, the article contained no reference to the problem of half-caste children but argued that the rota system would be especially valuable to married Arab seamen. Furthermore, the NUS later announced that it would allow Arabs who were in arrears with their subscriptions to register under the new scheme so that they could obtain employment.[27]

News of the proposed new system immediately aroused opposition. On 8 July in a letter to the *Shields Daily Gazette*, William Harrison, the Secretary of the Seamen's Minority Movement in South Shields, denounced the rota system as a new form of control over the employment of Arab and coloured seamen. Speaking on behalf of the Arab seamen in South Shields, he stated that the Arabs had held a mass meeting the previous Sunday to discuss the proposed scheme and had completely rejected it as it was likely to lead to conflict with the white seamen. They had made it clear that they would not be used as strike breakers against the white seamen and did not want to be given preference for jobs over white seamen. They wanted to make it clear that they were not guilty of the charges of corrupt practices as alleged by the NUS and argued that the corruption, if it existed, lay with others. They had passed a resolution at the meeting to reject the rota system because it entailed constant re-registration at the end of each voyage and was likely to cause ill-feeling between white and coloured men.[28]

On 21 July 1930, at the suggestion of the Port Consultants' Office, Mr James Gray of the South Shields' Shipping Federation Office, Mr R.W. Clouston, District Secretary of the NUS, and Mr W. Coomber, Branch Secretary of the NUS, held a meeting with Arab and Somali boarding-house and coffee house keepers and other representatives in order to explain the new system to them and to seek their support. The *Shields Daily Gazette* did not publish details of the meeting and in an article headlined 'Colony divided' only reported that the Arabs were divided in their response to the rota scheme.[29]

The views of the Arabs who were opposed to the system can be found in letters to the local press from Ahmed Alwin, Ali Said and Abdul Ali who entered into a vigorous debate with Clouston about what actually transpired at the meeting. It is perhaps significant that Ali Said did not attend the meeting but stated that he had received a full account from those who were present. The main points made in all three letters are almost identical as is the language used. They demanded to know why the rota scheme, if it was such a good one, did not include the white seamen. They stressed that they did not wish to receive preferential treatment over white seamen and would not take part in any scheme whereby Arabs could be used against the white seamen to the disadvantage of both. Ali Said also drew attention to the fact that after the Arab boarding-house masters had been abused in every issue of the NUS's journal, Clouston now asked them to forget about it and to 'talk nice' to the men and try and persuade them to register. Some extracts from these letters are presented below:

> Well if this scheme is so good for getting employment for Arabs as stated by our Union official, Mr Clouston, why not the same for white men? But the Arabs are not so dense as not to see through this scheme. As they are British subjects they are entitled to all the rights of British seamen. They do not desire preferential treatment over white seamen and do not intend to take part in any scheme that may come in conflict with them. They are prepared to stand by the white seamen in any demand, and will not allow themselves to be placed on any scheme that may mean the scabbing of white seamen. Let me ask Mr Clouston if he will let white seamen ship when they are in arrears in their union, as he has offered the Arabs.
> Signed Ahmed Alwin, 42 and 43 Commercial Road, South Shields[30]

> I attended a meeting of boarding house masters on Monday afternoon which was called by the Federation and Union officials. Mr Clouston said he had a good way of finding work for us—to get us registered in the Federation Office and get our photos taken and placed on the registration ticket. I asked him if everybody was going to be registered and he said only Arabs and Somalis. I asked 'Why don't you make it for everybody?' He said 'Because I want to keep you men on one side as it will save a lot of trouble. I want you men to stay in the boarding houses and I will send for you as I want you. Only come down and report to the Federation Office every morning and then go back to the boarding houses and stay there until I send for you.' I asked him if he wanted to use us as blacklegs and he would not answer. I asked him who was responsible for all the trouble between white and coloured seamen but he refused to answer

but said he wanted to keep all the coloured seamen away from the Mill Dam. It is only a few months ago that Mr Clouston complained about us getting jobs from the boardingmasters, and now he wants us to go back to the system which he was one of the foremost to condemn.
Signed Abdul Ali, 1 Tiny Street, South Shields[31]

I want to make it clear that we do not want any preference over white seamen. When Mr Gray was asked who had given him instructions to get the coloured seamen registered, he said that he was acting under instructions from the ship-owners to endeavour to get all coloured seamen registered in the Federation Office by August 1 as the shipowners were going to start running all their ships from that date. As they have had all their ships running without the rota system, why can't they do the same again?

I would like to give Mr Clouston to understand that we are not going to allow our seamen to be used in any scheme which is likely to lead to a conflict. If the white seamen are registered first then our men will follow.

For months past in every issue of their paper, we have been abused, and now Mr Clouston is telling us it wasn't meant and wants to make use of us to serve his ends. But I want to make it clear that the coloured seamen are not going to accept the rota system. They are going to support the white seamen and not be used against them. I can give the white seamen a guarantee on that point.
Signed Ali Said, 77 East Holborn, South Shields[32]

Representatives of the Shipping Federation and the NUS attempted to answer these criticisms through letters in the local press. Mr Gray of the Shipping Federation stated that white seamen were not included in the rota system because their position was quite different from that of coloured men. The white men belonged to local families and especially in the colliers seafaring was often a family tradition so that when a man left a crew his place was taken by a son or nephew. It had never been their intention to apply the scheme to white men, although this was the practice on the Continent.[33] This was hardly a convincing argument.

Clouston for the NUS went to great lengths to explain what had happened at the meeting and to challenge the points put forward by Ali Said and Ahmed Alwin. He stated emphatically that he had simply explained the new scheme that had been agreed by the shipowners and union and denied that he had made any appeal to the Arab boarding-house masters or tried to interfere in their internal arrangements. He admitted that the union's 'so-called abuse' of the boarding-house masters had been brought up at the meeting but in his opinion the subject was irrelevant to the matter under discussion. On the one hand he tried to defend the rota system as 'in the interests of the Arab himself' and on the other to deny that it meant preferential treatment for the Arab. He believed that white firemen would recognize that the union was trying to remedy a grievance that they had complained about for many years. He claimed that a mass meeting of seamen, which included Arabs and Somalis, held in the Bristol Channel ports had unanimously approved the new registration scheme.

Clouston later produced the minutes of a meeting of the Barry branch of the NUS which confirmed support for the scheme.[34] However, Said Mabrouk, an Arab boarding-house keeper at South Shields, telephoned Miope Nagi, who kept a boarding-house at 1 Sophia Street in Cardiff, and was told that no Arabs in Cardiff had agreed to register and that they intended to boycott the registration completely.[35] Peter O'Donnell accused the NUS of packing the meeting at Barry with old age pensioners in order to pass the resolution and asked Clouston to provide the names of any Arabs or Somalis at the Bristol Channel ports who had actually signed the rota.[36] Ali Said rejected Clouston's explanations and replied:

> Arabs have not forgotten the things said about them but the Arabs have proved themselves along with other coloured seamen 100% whiter than those who have taken ships away this last week. I have come to the conclusion that we boarding house masters have stood quite enough of this abuse on corruption and intend in the future to put a stop to it.[37]

Ali Said appears to have been the leader of the Arab faction opposed to the rota system.[38] He established a close relationship with the local leadership of the Seamen's Minority Movement which had opened an office at 6 Brewery Lane, and begun peaceful picketing at the Mill Dam outside the NUS offices and the Board of Trade Office. The *Shields Daily Gazette* reported that there were many Arab seamen manning the picket line. The Minority Movement also held a series of meetings at the Mill Dam to win support for their cause. At a big meeting of seamen at the Mill Dam on 24 July addressed by Peter O'Donnell, Chairman of the South Shields

Committee of Action, supported by Fred Thompson, the national organizer of the Seamen's Minority Movement, and speakers from the Communist Party, Ali Said represented the Arabs opposed to the rota. Ali Said regularly attended meetings of the Seamen's Minority Movement and took an active part in advising the Arab seamen not to sign the new register.

O'Donnell strongly condemned the NUS and urged the men to refuse to sign the PC5 which the Minority Movement referred to as the 'slave ticket'. His members were not calling for strike action and were quite willing to sign on but they were determined not to pay for their right to work. He claimed that the Arabs had been '100 per cent' in refusing to sign the rota which would force them to become blacklegs if anything happened between the white men and the shipowners. A pamphlet signed by O'Donnell and W. Harrison on behalf of the South Shields Seamen's Committee of Action and distributed at their meetings declared that all the coloured seamen in the town were behind the Committee of Action. At the meeting it was stated that 1,100 white seamen in South Shields and 900 Arabs and Somalis were supporting the boycott of the PC5.[39] Given the size of the Arab and Somali community in South Shields, this figure is certainly exaggerated. A few days before, Thompson, the national organizer of the Seamen's Minority Movement, had told the *Shields Daily Gazette* that there were 800 seamen in the Minority Movement in South Shields out of a total of 2,500 men in the whole country.[40]

Despite the declarations of the Seamen's Minority Movement, there were Arabs and Somalis who were not opposed to the rota system and who were willing to accept the PC5 in order to sign on a ship. Little information has come to light on this faction or the number of its supporters[41] but one of its leaders was Hassan Mohamed,[42] an influential Arab boarding-house keeper of 132 Commercial Road, South Shields and a leading official of the South Shields Branch of the Western Islamic Association.

The earliest evidence to come to light on the Western Islamic Association's attitude towards the rota system is a long statement by the Life President, Dr Khalid Sheldrake, published in the *Shields Daily Gazette* on 9 September 1930. In this statement Dr Sheldrake recognized that opinion among the Arabs was divided and attempted to answer some of the objections that had been made to the scheme. He appealed to the Arabs of South Shields to accept the rota system or they would suffer further distress.[43] Later that month in a letter to the Secretary of State for India Dr Sheldrake expressed his support for the scheme and his opposition to the activities of Ali

Said.[44] The letter makes it clear that local officials of the Association in South Shields were in touch with Sheldrake on this subject and it seems probable that it was these officials who led and organized the faction in South Shields which advocated acceptance of the rota system and which encouraged Arabs and Somalis to continue signing on. Unfortunately, there is no evidence about the scale of support they received from the rank and file.

Although the Western Islamic Association had campaigned energetically against the NUS attack on the Arab section, it had always urged support for the Government at a time of economic depression and unemployment, and its hostility to the activities of the Seamen's Minority Movement would have been strengthened by the latter's links with the Communist Party. Rivalries between boarding-house masters and tribal differences may also have contributed to the division within the community. It is difficult, however, to explain why this rival faction did not campaign openly on the issue of the rota system at this time.

Some Arab seamen continued to sign on during this period. For example on 30 July 1930 when the steamer *Tacoma City* was engaging an Arab stokehold crew more Arabs went forward than were required for the jobs available and all were prepared to sign the PC5. Chief Constable Wilkie admitted, however, that trouble broke out at the Shipping Federation Offices when a crowd of Arabs tried to prevent other Arabs from signing on. Police officers were called in to assist in clearing the office and one Arab fireman was arrested and charged with having caused a breach of the peace. It turned out however that the man charged, Faid Hassan who lived at Muckble's boarding-house at 6 East Holborn, was one of the men actually trying to sign on. After being ejected by the police he tried to rush back into the office because he was afraid that he would lose his ship.

At the magistrates court, the Chief Constable asked permission to withdraw the charge and offered a police escort to the Mill Dam so that the man could sign on. The case was dismissed. It is interesting to note that Mr Muir Smith, the legal adviser to the South Shields branch of the Western Islamic Association, appeared for Hassan. Muir Smith is reported to have thanked the Chief Constable 'for having placed the case so fluently before the court' and stated that he did not wish to make any allegation against the police as they had a most difficult duty to perform. Discretion and tact was what had to be exercised and he thought that it was a fitting conclusion to the case if Hassan was now escorted by the police to ensure that there was no hindrance to his employment being completed and that he could get to sea at once. The job was being kept open for him.[45]

Various explanations for the introduction of the rota system are possible. One view is that on this occasion, as in 1925, the Shipping Federation backed the NUS's view and supported its virulent campaign against the Arabs and its efforts to ensure that white seamen obtained preference in employment on British ships.[46] A problem with this argument is that at a time when the Seamen's Minority Movement was attracting considerable support from among the coloured community, the introduction of further restrictions on the employment of Arab seamen was likely to drive more of them into the arms of a militant movement determined to destroy the NUS and form a new union. The strengthening of the Minority Movement was hardly in the best interests of either the NUS or the shipowners. Another problem is that the rota system fell far short of NUS demands which called for the elimination and repatriation of the Arabs.

It is interesting to speculate whether the rota system was in reality a compromise agreement introduced by the Shipping Federation and the NUS as a direct response to the challenge presented to them by the emergence of the militant Seamen's Minority Movement. Throughout the 1920s the NUS had carried out a blatantly racist campaign against Arab seamen and against the activities of the Arab boarding-house masters. As the total number of Arabs employed in British shipping was relatively small,[47] it could be argued that the union was using this issue, which it knew aroused deep-rooted racial prejudice among many white seamen, to divert atttention away from the consequences of the conciliatory attitude of the NUS leadership towards the shipowners. This, as we have seen, had resulted in a series of wage cuts, long hours of work and poor working conditions for seamen. Yet despite the fact that the NUS at this time was in practice a company union for the Shipping Federation, the shipowners had a very different attitude towards the Arabs. Some shipowners were obviously keen to employ Arabs and there were certainly companies operating from north-east ports that instructed their captains to engage Arab firemen and made supply contracts with Arab boarding-house masters. We know that Arab seamen had a good reputation for being sober and hardworking, but it seems more probable that they were engaged to increase competition for jobs and thus keep wages low, and because a loyal Arab section might be useful in strike breaking in the event of a conflict arising with the union.

The militant activities of the Seamen's Minority Movement and their demands for an end to the PC5, for wage increases and improved working conditions, presented a threat to both union and shipowners. In response to this threat it is possible that the shipowners put pressure on the NUS to accept a compromise agreement on the question of the Arabs. On the one hand, the rota system gave assurances to the majority of the Arabs that they would continue to be employed on British ships. On the other, the fact that Arabs were to be re-registered under the new rota and the activities of the boarding-house masters curbed enabled the NUS to present the scheme to its white membership as a successful conclusion to its campaign against the Arabs. Both shipowners and union may have hoped that the assurances of employment for Arabs provided by the rota system would weaken the appeal of the Seamen's Minority Movement and that a loyal Arab section might be useful in strike breaking in any future conflict with the Minority Movement. For example, one of the arguments put forward by O'Donnell of the Seamen's Minority Movement against the rota system was that it made the Arab seamen a section apart, stripped them of one of the fundamentals of trade unionism, i.e. collective bargaining with other seamen in the union, and allowed the shipowners to impose any conditions they wanted on them.[48] After almost a decade of racial abuse from the NUS, it is not surprising that many Arabs greeted the announcement of the rota system with deep suspicion and questioned the motives of both union and shipowners.

IV Violence erupts at the Mill Dam 2 August 1930

At first, picketing outside the NUS and Board of Trade Offices on the Mill Dam by the Seamen's Minority Movement was peaceful. Seamen, many of them Arabs, stood opposite these offices and urged seamen not to sign the PC5 and there was some derisive cheering and booing of NUS officials as they went about their duties. When the crowd got too close to the entrances to these offices it appears that they were dispersed by the police patrolling the area but without incident. The leaders of the Minority Movement held regular meetings at which they campaigned vigorously against the PC5 and, after the rota system was announced, against that scheme. But peaceful picketing seems to have proved unsuccessful so that at the end of July O'Donnell proposed that passive picketing should be replaced by forcible efforts to prevent scabs shipping out. A manifesto distributed by the Tyneside District Party Committee of the Communist Party at this time congratulated the seamen of South

Shields on their militant stand against the Shipping Federation and the National Union of Seamen and urged them to abandon passive resistance which had failed to prevent men signing on and to adopt a fighting policy of strike action for the demands of the Minority Movement and the Committee of Action. The escorting of scabs by the police, the manifesto proclaimed, exposed the Labour Government, which controlled the police, as protectors of strikebreakers and enemies of the working class:

> The seamen are fighting this triple alliance of shipowners, Labour Government and the Fascist Union of Seamen, the NUS. To smash this alliance and win through to victory the seamen must adopt strong measures and break with the policy of passive resistance ... Effective action must be taken to prevent scabs signing on and thus defeating your fight—this cannot be done by passive resistance—No seamen should be allowed into the Shipping Federation or NUS offices until your demands are agreed to by the Shipping Federation and Shipowners. Passive resistance has failed to hold up a single ship and thus reveals itself as a useless and dangerous policy. Active prevention of blacklegs signing on will hold up the ships and enable you to declare these ships 'black' and call upon seamen and dockers in all ports to see these ships get no crews and no dockworkers.[49]

The manifesto also pointed to the magnificent solidarity shown by the Arab and Somali seamen with their white comrades which demonstrated the essential unity of the workers of all lands against their common enemy, the capitalists. While Arabs and British workers were fighting shoulder to shoulder against British capitalists, the Labour Government, which was serving the interests of the British capitalists, was sending gunboats against the Arabs in Egypt as it sent aircraft to bomb Arabs in Palestine. The seamen's fight demonstrated the identity of interest between the colonial and British workers against the same enemy—the British capitalists and their Labour Government. The manifesto called upon seamen of all nationalities to assemble at the Mill Dam, South Shields on 1 August, 'Red Day', at 7p.m. for a united demonstration with the Central Committee of Action and to join a march to the Market Place where there would be communist and non-communist speakers, seamen speakers, white, Arab and Somali speakers. Readers were urged to join the Communist Party and an application form for membership was attached to the manifesto.[50]

The temperature at the Mill Dam was clearly rising fast. O'Donnell was charged with intimidating a seaman, Robert William Coverdale, on 29 July and threatening him with violence if he signed on the SS *Gothic*. It appears that Coverdale was a former militant who had actually introduced O'Donnell to the Minority Movement and O'Donnell had been deeply shocked to see him cross the picket line and sign the PC5. O'Donnell was later convicted of making a threat and intending to use violence.[51] On the 30 July the *Shields Daily Gazette* reported that John McAlhone, a delegate of the NUS, had been attacked by two Arabs near Whitehill Point Ferry landing but his assailants had then run away making identification difficult.[52] On the 1 August the *Shields Daily Gazette* carried a long article by a special correspondent which argued that the activities of the Minority Movement were part of a communist plot to plant the seeds of revolution. It claimed that the workers were being hood-winked. The Minority Movement was making demands that it knew could not be accepted under the prevailing economic conditions. But its aim was to induce the workers to fight for these impossible demands so that suspicion, hatred and discontent would be intensi-fied, thus strengthening the 'spirit of revolutionary struggle'.[53] The *Daily Worker* announced that sympathy strikes had broken out in Liverpool, Barry and Stepney where men were refusing the PC5.[54]

The explosion came on Saturday, 2 August, when a 'riot' broke out at the Mill Dam. There are two very different versions of the events of that day. What might be regarded as the official version is that presented by the prosecution at the trial which subsequently took place at Durham County Assizes in November 1930.[55] Accord-ing to this version, a meeting of the Seamen's Minority Movement took place at the Mill Dam at 11 a.m. which was addressed by O'Donnell. About 150 Arabs and 100 white men were present and fifteen policemen were on duty stationed in small groups on and around the Mill Dam. By this time the Arabs, who are described in the brief for the prosecution as normally quiet but easily led and readily worked up to a state of excitement, were very discontented as a result of what they had been told at previous meetings held by the movement. O'Donnell addressed the meeting and is alleged to have said:

> We have been carrying the fight on for a fortnight now pacifist methods have had no result, they are no use, we'll have to use force. Have you no guts at all? We have been on for a fortnight and you have not stopped a ship signing yet. The coloured men are 100%, they have never allowed a coloured man to sign.

Have you whites no guts? I've got a summons, I have to go there on Tuesday, I don't expect to get Justice.[56] I expect I'll have to go the whole hog—If you had as much guts as me the fight would not last long—You have got to stop that rotten Union over there and their agents the police making you sign the PC5.[57]

Another speaker, Dowell, then addressed the meeting and is alleged to have said:

I am a miner but I have come down here to help you seamen to smash that rotten Union, the NUS and the police who are backing them and the Federation up and making seamen sign the PC5. We have tried passive resistance and failed, we will now have to use force.[58]

While the meeting was in progess a number of Arabs, who had just signed off the SS *Linkmoor*, came out of the Shipping Federation Office and were going up Coronation Street in order to be photographed as required by the rota system. They were intercepted by Ali Said and returned with him to the meeting which at that time was being addressed by Harrison. He is alleged to have said:

We have been on for a fortnight now fighting in your interests, and what is the result; the whites are still signing on—the Arabs are a hundred per cent, no coloured men have signed on—You call yourselves Britishers—you call yourselves whites—you have no guts in you—you allow scabs and blacklegs to sign on—Why don't you stop them? These Arabs (pointing to the Arabs who had returned with Ali Said) are just paid off, they cannot sign on without the PC5—now is your chance—the whites are signing every day—the Arabs are a hundred per cent—you won't stand up yourselves—They are standing by you—you will have to use force to put the shutters up in that scab Union. The police are on their side—the police are always on the side of the capitalists —South Shields must be the storm centre—All the other ports are looking at us as an example.[59]

At 12.32 p.m. Superintendent Pilling telephoned for an additional six policemen who duly arrived. Shortly before 1 p.m. officials of the Shipping Federation and the NUS shouted for firemen. A number of white men entered the office and there was a rush of Arabs into the office. Harrison, O'Donnell, Dowell and Smit (a

Dutch seaman serving on British ships and a member of the Committee of Action of the South Shields Seamen's Minority Movement) stood in front of the crowd who were lined up from the footpath in Coronation Street past the lamp to Brewery Lane, shouting 'Don't go in men—don't let the scabs sign—all stand fast'. Ali Said went among the Arabs talking to them and they became excited. He was warned by Inspector Wilson. White men were selected for the firemen's posts and a number of Arabs had to be ejected from the Shipping Office and one was arrested for obstructing the police in clearing the office.

Shortly after 1 p.m. two men, Hamilton and Bradford, left the Federation Office and Harrison told Inspector Wilson that one of them had something up his sleeve and that the other had a razor. Hamilton was found to have an ebony ruler up his sleeve which he had taken from the Shipping Office and the police told him to return it. The ruler was never brandished in a threatening way nor was any razor seen. O'Donnell then approached Superintendent Pilling and Inspector Wilson and said that there was likely to be trouble if the white men took the Arabs' jobs and he would not be responsible for it. The police replied that they held no brief for either party but were there to see that there was no disturbance. If there was trouble they would deal with it and they would deal with O'Donnell for inciting the men.

About 1.20 p.m. there was another call from the Shipping Federation Offices for firemen. As two of the men selected were walking through the crowd from the Federation Offices to the offices of the Board of Trade, Harrison, O'Donnell, Dowell and Smit stood in front of the crowd shouting, 'Don't go in men, don't let the scabs sign on—now's your chance to get stuck into them.' Ali Said shouted to the Arabs in Arabic, 'Stop them'. The Arabs proceeded to rush towards the two men, brandishing 'loaded sticks', razors, knives, clubs and chair legs and to throw stones. The police on duty drew their batons and used them in an attempt to quell the disturbance and stop the fighting which had erupted all around the Mill Dam. They were assisted by ten River Tyne police and fifteen borough police reinforcements.

During the clashes many Arabs and a number of policemen suffered minor injuries. Four policemen were stabbed by Arabs and one of them was seriously wounded. During and after the disturbances nineteen Arabs and two white men (William Carnaby, a British seamen, and George Verschelde, a Belgian seaman who had been employed on British ships for many years; both active members of the South Shields Minority Movement) were arrested on charges of rioting; three of the Arabs were also charged with wounding police officers and six of the Arabs and one of the white men were also charged with assaulting police officers. Later in the day Ali Said, Harrison, O'Donnell, Dowell and Smit were arrested on charges of inciting to riot.

A very different version of the events was given by the South Shields Seamen's Committee of Action in their manifesto issued two days after the events:

> Despite the lies and misrepresentation of the capitalist press, seamen who witnessed the events on Saturday realise that it was definitely provoked by the scabs and thugs of the NUS aided by the Police.
>
> The position was, that despite repeated appeals and calls for men to 'sign on' the mass of seamen stood solid—the closing of the Federation and NUS offices was delayed because of their inability to get crews. The white seamen stood solid along with the coloured seamen in refusing to blackleg. Realising the effect that this must have upon seamen in other ports, provocation and terrorism was resorted to.
>
> A scab, who had throughout the struggle in South Shields, attempted to sow dissension amongst seamen, did his best to incense the seamen by getting one of his kind to follow his lead. He deliberately stood or paraded in front of the picket line, inciting the seamen by showing that he was prepared to scab. He openly displayed weapons which he threatened to use against the picket. He used every method possible to give the police the opportunity they sought.
>
> Eventually he attempted to break through the crowd of seamen towards the office of the Board of Trade. He taunted the seamen and eventually drew a stick or whip with which he smashed at any within reach.
>
> The seamen, incensed at the methods employed against them, fought back and attempted to prevent him reaching his destination. This was the signal for the attack by the police. Batons were drawn and the charge made. The seamen stood their ground against this brutal onslaught. They gave blow for blow until with the arrival of reinforcements of police they were divided into groups, and unmercifully beaten up by the police and then placed under arrest.
>
> Not content with this, the quarters of the coloured seamen were raided, and those showing any resistance were arrested immediately. Late on Saturday night further arrests took place,

this time with the deliberate intention of beheading the militant movement of South Shields, with the intention of leaving the seamen without leadership. The active elements of the Committee of Action were arrested.

The Capitalist press has attempted to represent the events of Saturday as a fight between white and coloured seamen for jobs. They represent it as an attack upon the white seamen by the coloured seamen. THIS IS UNTRUE. It was because of the solidarity existing between both sections of seamen that the fight took place. They are again attempting to incense the white against the coloured seamen. They aim, in common with the shipowners, the NUS and the Police to break the solidarity of the seamen in South Shields.

They hope to smash the Committee of Action and to enforce the acceptance of the PC5 and the rota system. They must be prevented by the action of seamen themselves.

Today 26 seamen are awaiting trial on various charges, because they have dared to fight against the blackmailing instrument of the PC5 and the rota scheme for the coloured seamen. They stand together in the capitalist courts because they have dared to fight for better conditions for their wives and families. This is the fight of all seamen, no matter what their creed or colour. Those in jail are making sacrifices in the interests of us all. We who are outside must do our utmost to carry on the struggle to a successful issue. We, like those inside, must stand solid together. We cannot let them down.[60]

The documents that have survived from the trial are those prepared by the prosecution.[61] Statements taken by the police from witnesses to the events and the statements made by witnesses called during the subsequent trial at Durham County Assizes are mainly from police officers and officials of the National Union of Seamen and the Shipping Federation. There are very few statements from other people who were present and therefore a lack of independent evidence about the events that took place at the Mill Dam that Saturday afternoon. Nevertheless the statements by police officers do provide some additional information.[62] As well as uniformed officers, a number of policemen in plain clothes were present at the Mill Dam that day but they were unarmed. Inspector Wilson stated that the police were expecting trouble and that they were ready for it. All the police witnesses denied that the two men, Hamilton and Bradford, had incited the crowd or had used abusive language towards the Arabs or that they were armed, though it was admitted that they had not been checked for weapons. They stated that most of the crowd at the Minority Movement's meeting were Arabs and that white men in the crowd expressed contempt at the speeches by the movement's leadership. Hassan Mohamed, an Arab boarding-house master who was opposed to the activities of the Minority Movement, tried to calm the Arabs and prevent them going into the Shipping Office.[63] The police maintained that the Arabs must have hidden their weapons under their coats and that if they had seen the Arabs carrying weapons they would have taken them from them. Nevertheless the police admitted that they had not searched the Arabs after the first rush towards the Federation Offices when the police intervened to clear the premises. No police batons were drawn before the riot but in one or two instances the police struck Arabs before being struck themselves. Inspector Scott admitted that before the riot he moved about the Mill Dam for a short time swinging a truncheon, but it was a weapon that he had taken from an Arab. Detective Inspector Wilson stated that when he arrested and charged the Arabs, six of them replied that they had gone to the Mill Dam that day to try and get a job.

The brief for the prosecution at Durham Assizes draws the attention of Council to some of the points that emerged from the cross-examination of prosecution witnesses by the defence at the hearings before the justices at South Shields in August. In cross-examination Inspector Scott evidently stated that he took a weapon from the man Hamilton but then admitted that he had made a mistake which he attempted to correct when the depositions were being read over. Scott maintained that he did not in fact take any weapon from Hamilton. The defence accused the police of acting 'in consort' with the Shipping Federation and the NUS and used as evidence the fact that they frequently used the office telephones and had meals there. The police admitted that they made frequent use of the office telephones because the public telephone on the Mill Dam was surrounded by a crowd of men and they could not use it to receive calls from their headquarters. But they denied that any meals were taken in the offices by members of the police.

As regards the allegations made by the Seamen's Committee of Action that the disturbances were caused by Hamilton and Bradford branishing a ruler and a steel-lined whip and taunting the crowd 'to come on', the document states that these allegations had been denied by all witnesses who saw them. However, neither Hamilton nor Bradford were called to give evidence. The document states that one had gone to sea and the other was unable to attend the court because he was ill. The defence had argued that as the crowd that morning did not show any weapons and had no opportunity of getting them then they could not have used the weapons produced at the trial. Council was asked to note that many of the weapons could be folded while others could readily have been hidden in their clothing. The stones used were probably found on a piece of vacant land known as the Mill Dam Cut. The police denied that they charged the Arabs before the Arabs drew their weapons and rushed towards the two men going to the Board of Trade Offices. They stated that no order was given to draw batons but each man did so in order to assist in protecting the two men and in self-defence. The document states that these facts were corroborated by one or two of the civilian witnesses. In answer to the allegation that the police struck Arabs before being struck themselves, the police admitted that this was true in one or two instances because the officers were attempting to stop the rush of Arabs. It was also alleged that police action on 2 August had been the culmination of their previous treatment of Arabs about which complaints had been made. It was stated that no complaints had in fact been received by the police. Dowell, who conducted his own defence, stated that he and other leaders of the Minority Movement who were on the picket line that afternoon did their best to control the crowd and to prevent them getting out of hand. The document states that this was admitted by some witnesses but denied by others.[64]

Turning to the statements of the civilian witnesses, two said that they had assisted the police. A seaman, John Shirley, stated that about 1.20 p.m. he saw three men leave the Shipping Federation Office and go towards the Shipping Office. As they were going across the road the Arabs, armed with sticks and stones, made a rush towards them. One of the Arabs pulled a knife and tried to strike him but though he was unarmed he struck him with his fist and the man fell to the ground. He took hold of another Arab and put him up against the wall of the Shipping Office and then joined in the fighting elsewhere. He later had difficulty identifying the Arab with the knife and is described by the prosecution as an unreliable witness. Septimus Richardson, a ship's steward, stated that he was in the crowd that day looking for a job. When the Arabs started using batons, knives and bricks, he took hold of one Arab but Carnaby hit him on the head and he had to let go. He said that he never struck anyone and had simply defended himself. His feelings were like everyone else's: he had the wind up and was frightened.

James Bainbridge, a labourer, stated that he was at the Mill Dam that afternoon and saw some white men leave the Federation Office and go towards the Shipping Office. He heard Verschelde shout out to the Arabs, 'Now's your time, now get at it'. A police constable tried to calm the men and was stabbed in the back by an Arab. Under cross-examination he stated that he knew Verschelde and some of the Arabs fairly well. As he was unemployed, he had been spending quite a lot of time around the Arab boarding-houses and some of the Arabs had helped him in his misfortune. He identified a number of the Arabs arrested but because he suffered from poor eyesight the prosecution considered him an unreliable witness.

Norman Livingstone, a mess-room steward, stated that he was at the Mill Dam on Saturday, 2 August, looking for a ship. He saw two men going from the Federation Office to the Shipping Office. When they were nearly there he heard a shout in Arabic which he did not understand and then there was a rush of Arabs. He turned round and saw an Arab making a stab-like blow at the back of one of the police constables. He had felt afraid during the disturbance. Joseph Nicholson, institute keeper of the Seamen's Mission at South Shields, who was not called as a witness, in his deposition stated that at about 1.20 p.m. on Saturday, 2 August, he had been on the roof of the Seamen's Mission when he saw a crowd of Arabs attack two white men with sticks. The police intervened and a free fight took place. He saw Carnaby, whom he had known for five years, attempt to hit one of the detectives by striking him with his fist.

Harry Crichton, a medical doctor, stated that he was called to police headquarters in South Shields on Saturday, 2 August, and treated one of the police constables who had been wounded. Under cross-examination he also stated that he examined those who were concerned in the disturbance. He found that about eighteen of the prisoners who were brought in were suffering from general bruising to the scalp but owing to the number of men examined he could not say definitively whether the injuries were from behind or from the front.[65]

The other documents that are of interest are the set of background notes on each of the prisoners prepared by William Wilkie, the Chief Constable of South Shields, for the Durham Assize Court.[66] Of the twenty-five men charged in connection with the events on 2 August, all but four had no previous convictions recorded against them. The convictions against Peter O'Donnell and Salem Kaleb were associated with the Minority Movement's campaign during the previous month; O'Donnell had been convicted of intimidating a seamen and Kaleb with assaulting an official of the National Union of Seamen. Abdul Mayal had only one conviction in 1922 when he had been charged with shooting at another Arab with intent to murder. The charge had been reduced to one of assault and he had been committed to prison for one month.

Ali Said in contrast had a string of convictions dating back to 1911 which included keeping a disorderly house, brawling, allowing prostitutes to assemble in his refreshment house, obtaining money under false pretences and wounding three Arabs by stabbing them with knives. In 1919 during a violent dispute with a rival boarding-house master, he had been charged along with four Arabs with the wilful murder of two Arabs and with inciting the four Arabs to murder. Although there was clear evidence against him of incitement to murder, he was found not guilty and discharged (see Chapter Three p.62). In November 1929 he had been charged with receiving stolen property and even though part of the stolen property had been discovered in a cupboard in his private rooms at the boarding-house he was found not guilty and discharged. The Chief Constable pointed out that he had taken an active part in obstructing the successful working of the rota scheme and identified himself with the South Shields Seamen's Minority Movement. He had been observed daily on the Mill Dam mixing amongst the coloured seamen. The Chief Constable was in no doubt that Ali Said exerted a great influence over the Arab seamen generally and he concluded: 'He is cute and crafty, in all cases where there has been trouble with the Arab population in South Shields, it has always been found that he took part in fomenting trouble'.[67]

Dowell, Smit, O'Donnell and Carnaby were described as un-employed, although from their discharge books both Smit and O'Donnell had been in regular employment until April and June 1930 respectively. Two of the Arabs, Abdul Ali and Ahmed Mohamed, had no proof of legal landing and were unregistered, and therefore had not worked since their arrival in Britain. But from the entries in their discharge books, most of the Arab seamen arrested had been in regular employment until April and June 1930. Saleh Ahmed for example had actually signed on after the announcement of the rota scheme and had been discharged at Rouen on 18 July 1930. All the men had discharges marked 'very good' for character and ability and general conduct. Nine of the Arab seamen had been employed on British ships since the First World War. The Arab seamen arrested ranged in age from twenty-three to fifty years. One of them, Abdul Mayal, was married to an English woman and had one child. Mohamed Ahmed had a British passport and had not therefore been registered as an alien. From the addresses given at the trial, over half of the Arabs came from two boarding-houses, that of Said Mabrouk at 2 Laygate Street and Salem Abuzed at 25

East Holborn. None of the men were from Ali Said's boarding-house.

When the prisoners arrested in connection with the disturbances came before the South Shields Police Court on 12 August 1930, Mr J. Muir Smith protested and stated that although he was the solicitor for the Western Islamic Association which had a branch in the town, the Minority Movement had instructed a solicitor and council to represent all the white and Arab men with the exception of Abdul Asig of 3 Ferry Street[68] and had inaugurated a fund for their defence. On behalf of the Western Islamic Association he wanted to make it clear that the Association had not authorized the fund and that as the Association's solicitor 'not a penny piece had come into his hands'. If anyone had contributed to the fund on the understanding that the money was to go to the Western Islamic Association then they were mistaken. It was all well and good if the prisoners wished to be represented by the barrister appointed by the Minority Movement but he felt that the Arab prisoners themselves should have been consulted on the matter.[69] Other sources reveal that a fund to pay the legal expenses of the men charged was set up under the auspices of the International Class War Prisoners' Aid Committee.[70]

Later in the proceedings at the South Shields Court, Muir Smith asked for his client, Abdul Asig of 3 Ferry Street, to be discharged. He could prove that on the day in question Abdul Asig did not go to the Mill Dam until 1.15 p.m. He went into a coffee ship for a meal and later, when a police officer entered in pursuit of another Arab, Abdul Asig was knocked to the floor at the same time and arrested. There was no evidence against him and no witness had identified him as one of the men taking part in the disturbances. It would be a great hardship if Abdul Asig was detained at the court and prevented from joining his ship on which he had been employed regularly for a number of years. He could produce witnesses to testify to the man's good character. The prosecution made no objection and Abdul Asig was then discharged.[71]

Some of the points made by the defence appear in press reports from the trial at the Durham County Assizes which opened on 17 November 1930. Dowell, who again conducted his own defence, stated that Harrison had complained to Inspector Wilson and Superintendent Pilling that the man Bradford had threatened him with a razor but that both officers refused to intervene. In spite of the provocative attitude of Bradford and Hamilton, there was no trouble until about 1.30 p.m. when Hamilton produced a steel-lined whip and flourished it before the crowd shouting 'Come on, you

black ——; try and stop me signing on.' Provoked beyond endur-
ance, white and coloured men made a rush towards the Board of
Trade Offices. This was the signal for the police baton charge. Only
Arabs were struck although there were large numbers of white men
there. Hamilton had struck at prostrate Arabs with his whip and
Arabs standing or walking about in Holborn were struck by the
police. About a hundred men were injured. He argued that the
police wanted just the provocation that Hamilton and Bradford had
provided to give them an excuse for instituting a reign of terror,
arresting the Minority Movement leaders and dividing the seamen.[72]

William Carnaby denied that he had assaulted anyone. George
Verschelde stated that Bradford and Hamilton were drunk and he
had seen them defending themselves. Bradford had an open razor
and Hamilton a stick down his trousers. Both O'Donnell and
Harrison denied that they had advocated the use of force. O'Donnell
stated that the actual words that he had used in his speech were,
'When men are faced with force they have got to use force.'
Harrison, who stated that he was no longer on the Minority
Movement Committee and had left the movement altogether, said
that he had never advocated the use of force except in a trade union
sense. Mr Norman Harper, who appeared on behalf of Ali Said,
stated that there was no evidence that his client knew that the Arabs
were carrying weapons or of what he actually said to the Arabs as
he walked among them. When he shouted just before the Arabs
rushed towards Bradford and Hamilton, he was not saying 'Stop
these men' but 'Stop, don't attack'. As a prosperous boarding-house
keeper and cafe proprietor it was unlikely that he would do anything
to jeopardize his position. Mr Hylton-Foster, who appeared on
behalf of Harrison, O'Donnell, Smit, Verschelde and Carnaby,
pointed out that no weapons were found on either Verschelde or
Carnaby, and submitted that if the riot had not taken place nothing
would have been heard of the Minority Movement's meeting that
morning. The language used by the Movement's leaders at the
meeting was, 'the ordinary sort of drivel these folks used'.[73]

The trial ended on 20 November 1930. In passing sentence the
judge, Mr Justice Roche, described Ali Said as the main organizer
of the Arab attack and sentenced him to sixteen months imprisonment and recommended him for deportation. Harrison, O'Donnell
and Dowell were each sentenced to eight months' imprisonment.
The judge stated that he did not regard them as professional
agitators but rather as minor actors in the campaign. He hoped that
the National Union of Seamen and the Shipping Federation would
help them to find work. Carnaby was sentenced to three months'

imprisonment without hard labour and Smit to four months' hard labour with a recommendation for deportation. Two of the Arab seamen, Raggi Omar and Abdul Assig, were acquitted. The charge against Ibrahim Ahmed of wounding a police constable with a knife was dropped because of insufficient identification, but he was convicted of rioting and sentenced to twelve months' hard labour and recommended for deportation. All the other Arab seamen were given sentences varying from three to sixteen months. The judge recommended deportation for all but two of them; Mohamed Ahmed, who could not be deported because he was a British subject, and Abdul Mayal, presumably because he was married to an English woman. With reference to the Arabs the judge commented:

> I think it is very undesirable that men so liable to be influenced should be in this country at a time when there is obviously slackness of trade and it is very difficult to get ships. These men in idleness are dangerous I think here.[74]

The next day the *Shields Daily Gazette* reported great public interest in the judge's recommendations with regard to the deportation of the Arabs. The article pointed out that although for many years local magistrates had recommended deportation for certain Arabs brought before them, few cases had actually succeeded because the final decision lay with the Home Secretary. It questioned whether the judge's recommendations would carry more weight than those of the magistrates.[75]

V Were the disturbances on 2 August a 'race riot'?

In the popular press of the day the events of Saturday, 2 August 1930, were referred to as a race riot. Byrne[76] however has pointed out that it was different from the race riots of 1919 because of the involvement of the Seamen's Minority Movement and has argued that press efforts to treat the fight as a race riot were an outstanding distortion of the facts designed to conceal a desperate effort to break the strike. Reviewing the limited and often contradictory evidence available to us on this episode unfortunately raises more questions than answers when we attempt to reconstruct and explain what actually took place.

One question relates to the degree of support for the aims of the Seamen's Minority Movement. It would appear that no Arabs had accepted the rota by 2 August, although opinion among them about the system was divided, and therefore no Arabs were eligible to sign on. In contrast, some white seamen continued to accept the PC5 and to ship out. Indeed Fred Thompson, the national organizer of the Seamen's Minority Movement, admitted a couple of weeks later that their campaign against the PC5 did not have popular appeal among the mass of seamen signing on British ships and that strike action was not the answer against a powerful capitalist enemy. He confessed that the fight against the PC5 could never be anything more than a fight of the unemployed.[77] The Arab seamen from the SS *Linkmoor* had been prepared to register in order to re-engage as members of the crew but had been persuaded by Ali Said not to sign the rota. The *Linkmoor,* which normally carried an Arab stokehold crew, sailed with white firemen. The evidence, therefore, does not support the version of events in the Committee of Action's manifesto that white seamen stood solid with coloured seamen, that ships were unable to get crews and that the police intervened to break a successful strike that had brought shipping to a standstill and might have spread to other ports. Furthermore, the evidence indicates that with the exception of Verschelde and Carnaby, all the men who took part in the attack on Bradford and Hamilton were Arabs. There is no evidence that any other white seamen came to their assistance after the police baton-charged them. In fact we know that at least two white seamen, Shirley and Richardson, fought against the Arabs during the disturbances and assisted the police. Despite important differences between the events in 1919 and 1930, racial prejudice clearly played a part in this episode.

Another question concerns who actually provoked the crowd to attack the two men, Bradford and Hamilton. According to the prosecution, it was the speeches by the leaders of the Minority Movement which worked the crowd up into a state of excitement and triggered off the attack. In the words of Detective Inspector Wilson, 'They worked the Arabs up to boiling pitch and then left them.' The witness James Bainbridge stated that he heard Verschelde shout at the Arabs just before the attack, 'Now's your chance, get at them'.[78] The Seamen's Minority Movement, however, claimed that Bradford and Hamilton, acting as agents of the NUS, deliberately provoked the pickets by threatening them with weapons in order to provide the police with an opportunity to intervene and smash the movement in South Shields. The evidence indicates that the speeches by the Minority Movement leaders had become more militant, but Harrison for example denied that he advocated the use of force except in a trade union sense. Dowell stated that he and other pickets in front of the men tried to control the crowd and calm them. His statement was supported by some witnesses but denied by others. None of the civilian witnesses stated that they saw either Bradford or Hamilton carrying any weapons. Verschelde stated that the two men were drunk and that Bradford had an open razor and Hamilton had a stick down his trousers. Dowell on the other hand said that Hamilton had produced a steel-lined whip which he had used to threaten the Arabs.

The police witnesses maintained that Bradford and Hamilton were unarmed and did not incite the Arabs but merely shouted to the pickets 'I don't care about you, I want my bread and butter.' Constable Addison, nevertheless, admitted that the police did not check either man for weapons and there is the statement by Inspector Wilson under cross-examination that he took a weapon from Hamilton, a statement which he later withdrew.[79] Such contradictory evidence makes it difficult to assess the role of Bradford and Hamilton in these events. But the fact that neither man, even though they were key witnesses, was called to give evidence and Inspector Wilson's admission that he made a mistake under cross-examination about taking the weapon from Hamilton, must raise doubts about their innocence.

Then there is the question of Ali Said's role in the events. The police accused him of moving among the Arabs at the Minority Movement's meeting and inciting them. Three police witnesses stated that later, just before the attack, they saw him pointing to the two men Bradford and Hamilton and shouting in Arabic 'Stop them'. Norman Livingstone stated that as Bradford and Hamilton approached the Shipping Office he heard shouting in Arabic and then the Arabs attacked.[80] At the subsequent trial at the Durham Assizes the judge described Ali Said as the main organizer of the Arab attack. He believed that the Arabs must have come prepared for a fight and Ali Said was the only person to tell them to bring weapons.[81]

Although the evidence against Ali Said was not particularly strong, he received the harshest sentence of any of the men arrested; sixteen months' imprisonment and deportation. The evidence available indicates that Ali Said was the only boarding-house master to have been closely associated with the leaders of the Seamen's Minority Movement in South Shields but we do not know whether he shared their ideological commitment or whether the association was simply a marriage of convenience.[82] As a boarding-house keeper, the rota system threatened his role as a supplier of labour and therefore his livelihood. He was certainly in a position to exploit the fears and suspicions that the rota system clearly aroused among many of the Arabs. Because of the hostility displayed towards them by the NUS, it is not surprising that many Arabs in South Shields suspected that there were more sinister motives behind the new scheme and that it was a means to drive them out of the country. One of the rumours circulating was that any Arabs who signed on under the new system would be taken on a short voyage and then dumped in another country with no possibility of returning to South Shields. Another claimed that Arabs returning from a voyage would not be allowed to land even though they were registered. Another claimed that seamen returning from a voyage would not be able to rejoin their ship but would be replaced by men whose names were at the head of the rota.[83] However inaccurate and misleading, it is not difficult to understand how such rumours circulated and were believed. Many of the Arab seamen had only a limited knowledge of English, even those who had lived in Britain for many years, and new regulations could easily be misunderstood and misinterpreted. In such matters the men looked to the boarding-house masters for guidance and advice and one suspects that a certain amount of disinformation about the rota system was deliberately spread by opponents of the scheme. There is a strong possibility that Ali Said engaged in such activities to strengthen opposition to the rota system.

These fears and suspicions may have been more powerful in arousing the anger of some of the Arab seamen than the rhetoric of the Minority Movement's leaders and may help to explain why Arab seamen who had been in regular employment on British ships for many years and had good discharges for character, ability and general conduct, took part in the attack. For contrary to the judge's statement at the end of the trial, only two of the Arab seamen arrested had been unemployed for any length of time and the majority had been employed on a regular basis until the announcement of the rota system at the beginning of July 1930. If Arab seamen were 'dangerous in idleness' then one might have expected the men who took part in the attack to have been drawn from the one hundred or more Arabs in South Shields who were unregistered under the 1925 Order and therefore unable to work and excluded from the new rota system.

Of course there remains the question of what triggered off the actual attack. Against a background of fear and suspicion about the real motives of the rota system, the sight of white seamen taking jobs held by Arabs on that day may have provided sufficient provocation without threats or racial abuse from the two men, Bradford and Hamilton. O'Donnell, for example, stated that he warned the police that there would be trouble if the white seamen took the Arabs' jobs and that he would not be responsible. Arabs had continued to ship out until the rota system became effective on 1 August. But on 2 August no one had signed the new register and as no Arabs were eligible to sign on, white firemen were engaged. However it is difficult to explain why violence did not break out when the Shipping Federation called for firemen shortly before 1 p.m. On that occasion a number of Arabs rushed into the offices where several white seamen were signing on. Federation officials evidently asked them to leave as a white crew was being taken and there was no work for Arabs. Several Arabs had to be removed from the office by the police and one man, Ali Hamed from Muckble's boarding-house, was arrested for obstruction.[84] Violence did not flare up until around 1.20 p.m. when there was a second call for firemen. Inevitably, this brings us back to Bradford and Hamilton despite the contradictory evidence about their role in the events.

Finally there is the question of the role of the police in these events. Inspector Wilson stated that the police were expecting trouble and were prepared for it. When O'Donnell warned the police that there was likely to be trouble between the white seamen who were signing on and the Arabs, Superintendent Pilling replied, 'We hold no brief for either party and are here to see there is no disturbance', whereas Inspector Wilson stated, 'We will meet trouble if it comes and also deal with you for inciting these men.' Under cross-examination by the defence, Wilson stated, 'These meetings have been getting hotter and hotter every time. It was in my mind there was sure to be a burst. We were prepared for the burst.' Detective Constable Davison under cross-examination stated, 'These speeches were leading up to a disturbance. It was not for me to say whether they should have been allowed to go on from day to day.' Detective Constable Atkinson admitted under cross-examination that no attempt was made to search the Arabs for weapons when they tried to occupy the Federation Offices before the fighting broke out.[85] But if the police were expecting trouble why did the Chief Constable allow the meetings to continue when he had the power to refuse permission? It is possible that the police were waiting for an outbreak of violence so that they could intervene and arrest the leaders of the Minority Movement and Ali Said and put a stop to their militant campaign against the NUS. One suspects that Ali Said may have been a more important target for the police than the leaders of the Minority Movement because of his role in resisting the rota system and the influence that he exerted over many of the Arab seamen.

Six

After the Storm

I Resistance to the rota system collapses

At the end of September 1930 the Chief Constable of South Shields reported to the Watch Committee that for some days after the fighting at the Mill Dam on 2 August Holborn had been in an unsettled state and it had been necessary to keep large bodies of police in readiness for any further outbreaks of violence. He was pleased to say that tranquillity had practically been restored to the neighbourhood and although one or two Arab boarding-house masters were still inclined to be unreasonable, he did not anticipate any recurrence of the events at the beginning of August. Nevertheless, he was still refusing to give permits for meetings at the Mill Dam.[1] Resistance to the rota system had continued, and, according to the Shipping Federation, Arabs did not begin to register until 27 August 1930.[2]

During the early part of August the Seamen's Minority Movement continued to picket the Shipping Federation Offices on the Mill Dam but Thompson, the movement's national organizer, and Thirlbeck, the leader of the Sunderland Seamen's Minority Movement, were arrested when they attempted to hold meetings there. Few Arabs were present and Thirlbeck stated that they were keeping away from the Mill Dam because they would be blamed if there was any further trouble.[3] A bulletin issued by the South Shields Seamen's Committee of Action on 6 August declared that the fight against the PC5 and the rota scheme would continue but admitted that their pickets had been unable to prevent seamen from signing on.[4] A second bulletin issued on 11 August pointed to the weaknesses of the movement's campaign and accused the NUS of dividing the movement's forces by inducing white firemen to take the jobs of coloured seamen who refused to sign under the rota system. It declared that the white men were being used to force the rota system on the Arabs and that later the rota would be used to reduce Arab wages as a preliminary to reducing wages for all seamen.[5] Although the seamen were urged to fight on, by September 1930 there is little doubt that the movement's campaign for the abolition of the PC5 and the rota system had been defeated.

After the events of 2 August, several Arabs appealed to the India Office for assistance against the injustice of the rota system. Abdulla Ali blamed the NUS for all their suffering and claimed that the union had only turned against Muslims. His letter continued:

> We very deeply request our brothers in the Muslims' Depart-ment in England as to see into the matter and give us the necessary help as all the coloured seamen are being on shore for certain months unemployed nearly fainting with starvation as they have no one to feed them except the boarding house keepers which have now failed into great loss by supporting us for the past months.
>
> We at present request your Muslim brothers to see into the matter and to kindly assist the living of our people. We also request your honour to send a man to Shields and other seaports and to see how Muslims are treated by the unions.
>
> . . . some of our men have not had a chance to sign for 10 months so this is the reason I am begging of you to help all our people not just myself for we see nothing but starvation ahead for us for we are like a lot of convicts with nothing to eat and all this is through the union. We also have men who have been ashore from 2 years and they do nothing whatever to help them and we have no one here who could assist us in our trouble and this is the reason we call on you and hope and pray to God that you will answer this appeal and do your best for us.[6]

With no Arab seamen signing on because of the rota system, the Arab boarding-house masters now faced financial ruin. Five of them (Ali Hamed Dheli, 95 and 103 West Holborn, Abdo Mohsen, 33 East Holborn, Ahmed Cassem, 105 East Holborn, Muro Mocassar, 59 East Holborn and Cassim Ali, 55 East Holborn) wrote to the India Office on 10 September enclosing lists of the number of unemployed seamen they were maintaining and the amounts these men owed them (see Figure 10, p.155). Some of the men had been unemployed for over a year. They blamed the rota system for the unemployment and stated that their men refused to accept the new

Mr. ALI HAMED DELHI,

SEAMEN'S BOARDING HOUSE AND
REFRESHMENT HOUSE KEEPER,

95 and 103, West Holborn, South Shields.

Mohamed Silam, Debt, he owes me	£45 0 0	Mathana Rajeb, Debt, he owes me	£71 10 0
Saleh Hassan, Debt, he owes me	£33 0 0	Guide Hassine, Debt, he owes me	£34 10 0
Naser Assam, Debt, he owes me	£30 0 0	Mohamed Said, No. 3, Debt, he owes me	£47 0 0
Abdul Milek, Debt, he owes me	£20 0 0	Hassen Ahmed, Debt, he owes me	£53 0 0
Abdulla Salim, Debt, he owes me	£35 0 0	Guide Said, Debt, he owes me	£21 0 0
Ahmed Mahomed, Debt, he owes me	£31 0 0	Ali Ahmed, Debt, he owes me	£46 10 0
Mohamed Ahmood, Debt, he owes me	£51 0 0	Redman Guide, Debt, he owes me	£60 0 0
Hassan Mohamed, Debt, he owes me	£49 0 0	Maldi Said, Debt, he owes me	£41 0 0
Said Fada, Debt, he owes me	£29 0 0	Mohamed Murshud, Debt, he owes me	£35 10 0
Mohamed Ali, Debt, he owes me	£39 0 0	Daifulla Mehsen, Debt, he owes me	£69 0 0
Saleh Mohamed, Debt, he owes me	£42 10 0	Nag Saleh, Debt, he owes me	£30 0 0
Saleh Hamed, No. 1, Debt, he owes me	£61 0 0	Ali Mohamed, Debt, he owes me	£41 0 0
Nassar Ali, Debt, he owes me	£41 0 0	Mohamed Hussen, Debt, he owes me	£43 0 0
Said Saleh, Debt, he owes me	£34 0 0	Ahmed Mahomed, Debt, he owes me	£40 0 0
Mohamed Said, No. 1, Debt, he owes me	£36 10 0	Ali Hamed, Debt, he owes me	£45 0 0
Saleh Messen, Debt, he owes me	£41 10 0	Mohamed Abdulla, Debt, he owes me	£39 0 0
Mohamed Hassan, Debt, he owes me	£51 0 0	Mohamed Shemson, Debt, he owes me	£75 0 0
Ali Ahmed, Debt, he owes me	£61 10 0	Ali Mohamed, Debt, he owes me	£30 0 0
Ahmed Hassen, Debt, he owes me	47 10 0	Ali Mosleh, Debt, he owes me	£29 0 0
Garnum Chuman, Debt, he owes me	£81 10 0	Mohamed Newmann, Debt, he owes me	£48 0 0
Sala Hamed, No. 2, Debt, he owes me	£39 10 0	Zaid Abdulla, Debt, he owes me	£29 0 0
Krist Mohamed, Debt, he owes me	£48 10 0	Saleh Nasser, Debt, he owes me	£51 0 0
Mohamed Said, No. 2, Debt, he owes me	£49 10 0	Salah Abdulla, Debt, he owes me	£29 0 0
Ahmed Saleh, Debt, he owes me	£35 10 0	Mohamed Abdulla, Debt, he owes me	£33 0 0
Ali Batash, Debt, he owes me	£24 10 0	Wais Abdul Kader, Debt, he owes me	£61 0 0
Mohamed Mosley, Debt, he owes me	£69 10 0	Hamood Alwa, Debt, he owes me	£71 0 0
Ahmed Alwen, Debt, he owes me	£51 0 0	Ali Ahmed, Debt, he owes me	£81 0 0

SIR, WEDNESDAY, 10/9/1930.

Enclosed list of Arab Seamen unemployed, and the debt they owe me only, up to the present date, all are in the National Seamen's Union, paying 1/- per week ; unemployment being due to this Rota Scheme brought forward by the National Union for Seamen and the Federation Officials.

The Arab and Somali refuse to take the Rota Scheme, because it is not justice to number the said two races of Coloured Seamen, and not every other coloured race, namely, Malaya, Chinese, Indian, African, and not to mention the Foreigner, such as Maltese, Greeks, Norwegian, Danish, Swedish, and many others.

This list of Arab Seamen's names are proved British Subjects, or Protected persons, their proofs having been forwarded from Aden through the Colonial Office, London, and therefore are entitled to all help and aid a Britisher can give them in or out of England.

This only refers to the said mentioned Arabs, and does not include any other Arab or Somali who has taken the Rota-Scheme or intends to do so in the future.

This tribe of Arabs mentioned are natives of Dheli, Towahi, Aden, Arabia, and wish to seek employment on British Ships in the old way and not under the Rota System, as early as can possibly be done, as some of them have been idle over one year, or more, and any funds of any description will be gladly received, or the last resource for the N.U.S. to pay all the said mentioned Debts and send the men to their own home.

Signed yours,
ALI HAMED,
born Mehakum, Dheli,
Towahi, Aden,
Arabia.

Present address :—103, West Holborn, South Shields.

Figure 10. Copy of letter from Ali Hamed Dheli to the India Office. (PRO CO 725/21/9)

scheme because it only applied to Arabs and Somalis and not to other coloured seamen, let alone foreigners, and was therefore unjust. The men wanted to seek employment on British ships in the old way and not under the rota system. They appealed for any kind of financial assistance and in the last resort suggested that the NUS should pay the men's debts and send them back to their own country.[7] The letters were passed on to the Colonial Office which replied that it could take no responsibility for the debts of the Arab seamen as that was a matter between the men and the boarding-house masters. If any seamen were destitute, the boarding-house masters should take the matter up with the South Shields Public Assistance Committee. The Colonial Office pointed out that the prevailing unemployment affected British seamen as well as Arabs and was due to the general trade depression and not to the rota system.[8]

Ali Said, who had been released on bail pending the trial at the Durham Assizes in November 1930, was also active during this period. The police were convinced that Said, together with another boarding-house master, Ali Hamed Dheli, was doing his utmost to foster opposition to the rota system. Early in September the two men issued a statement that the India Office was going to give relief to all Arabs who refused to register under the rota system. The Chief Constable immediately contacted the India Office where officials assured him that there was no truth in the statement. Neither Ali Hamed Dheli nor Ali Said had visited the India Office, although they believed that Ali Said had received money from some of the Arabs in South Shields for that purpose. Chief Constable Wilkie was of the opinion that if these efforts could be frustrated then the Arabs on the Tyne would accept the new system.[9]

The Arabs in South Shields remained divided over the rota system. On the 26 August fighting broke out at the Mill Dam between seamen who were opposed to the rota system and those who wanted to accept it. Three Arabs were charged with assault and others with causing a breach of the peace. When the case came before the magistrates, two of the Arabs who had been assaulted stated that they wanted to withdraw the charges because they had settled their differences with the man accused of attacking them who belonged to their own tribe.[10] A few days later, Dr Sheldrake of the Western Islamic Association, who had made no public statement on the rota system since it was announced in July, made a long appeal to the Arabs of South Shields to accept the new scheme or they would only suffer further distress. But first on 8 September 1930, together with Mr Muir Smith and Hassan Mohamed, the secretary of the local branch of the Association, he announced that the Aga Khan, a patron of the Association, had handed over a cheque to purchase land for a mosque in Commercial Road and had promised a substantial sum for the actual building.[11]

The next day, in an article published in the *Shields Daily Gazette*, Dr Sheldrake stated that he had spent many months in negotiation with several government departments on the question of the rota system and had come to the conclusion that the Arabs should accept it. By not signing the new register, they had already lost many ships which had previously carried an Arab stokehold crew. All the seafaring community in Britain, not only the Arabs but the white seamen too, was suffering from the depression in shipping and whether the rota system was in force or not, employment prospects would not improve until there was an economic revival. He believed that the rota system had one positive aspect. Men who registered could be called up as ships demanded Arab crews and there could be no interference by anyone outside if the engineer or captain was instructed to pick an Arab or Somali crew. In the past, he stated, there had been obstruction 'from a certain quarter' and under the rota system this would cease.[12]

In talking to the Arabs in Shields he found opinion divided on the rota system. Some, he stated, suspected a trick and feared that they would be driven out of the country. He assured them that these fears were 'absolutely absurd'. If opinion remained divided he could foresee trouble and he thought that the Arabs would be well advised to try the rota system. Mr Chuter Ede, MP for South Shields, had pointed out to him that the rota system was here to stay at least during the present depressed state of shipping. Sheldrake also warned that there were implications for the British Empire. After months of idleness, and finding their hopes of employment dashed, the Arabs in Britain had written to their fellow countrymen in Arabia and this had created difficulties in relations between the Arab States and Britain. As no evidence exists on this point, it would appear to be a figment of Sheldrake's imagination.

He pointed out that, unlike the white seamen, Arab seamen did not receive unemployment benefit and would have starved if the boarding-house keepers had not provided them with food and shelter. Sheldrake claimed that about 240 Arabs had already registered under the rota system in Cardiff[13] while in South Shields a considerable number had registered the day before and several more had promised to do so that day. At the end of the article he gave some insight into the rivalries within the Arab community by protesting against the activites of those individuals who made collections among the Arabs to send men to London 'for religious and other purposes'. Such activities contravened the rules of the local branch of the Western Islamic Association. He stated that when the South Shields branch was formed the Arab boarding-house keepers in the town had agreed to regularize collections from the men and that money could only be withdrawn on four signatures.[14] These protests were clearly directed at the activities of Ali Said and Ali Hamed Dheli.

The activities of these two men were also the subject of a letter from Dr Sheldrake to the Secretary of State for India dated 18 September 1930. In the letter Sheldrake writes that it had been brought to his attention that after visiting the India Office Ali Said and Ali Hamed Dheli told the Arabs of South Shields that the Indian Government would assist unemployed Arabs in the town if they did not register for employment under the rota system. He reported that Ali Said, even though he was on bail, was causing mischief and that the statements of the two men had aroused suspicion in the minds of 'Arabs of repute' in the town who were officials of the local branch of the Association and that they had written to him on the subject. He continued:

> Both men are well known to me as trouble makers and if their statements are left unchallenged will result in a further deadlock in shipping, more distress for the men (which the rota system would obviate) and possibly cause further trouble to the police.
>
> In writing to you I feel that I am only doing my duty to the vast number of coloured seamen, who are in a pitiable condition, and trouble might be obviated.
>
> I know that from Cardiff also you will have received a request for assistance in maintaining a large number of coloured seamen. The situation is difficult, and I have no desire to place any difficulties in your way in dealing with the situation.
>
> The statements of these two men, however, are responsible for much worry to the Muslims who are desirous of registering for employment, but fear to do so, owing to their statement that the relief to be accorded by the Indian Government is for men who refuse to accept the condition of employment laid down by the shipowners, i.e. the rota system.[15]

A reply on behalf of the High Commissioner for India dated 6 October 1930 states that neither Ali Said nor Ali Hamed Dheli had been interviewed at the India Office or at the Office of the High Commissioner and no promise had been made that seamen who did not register under the system would be assisted. The Chief Constable of South Shields had been informed of this.[16]

A number of Arabs in South Shields immediately challenged Dr Sheldrake's statements. In a letter to the editor of the *Shields Daily Gazette*, Mohamed Ahmed and Saleh Ali of 41 West Holborn, stated that Sheldrake's opinions did not represent those of the Arabs of South Shields and that he had never been consulted or asked for assistance in the recent trouble. They denied that Arabs were signing the new register in considerable numbers at South Shields and claimed that only a few Somalis, who had 'nothing to do with the Arabs', had signed. They accused Sheldrake of being in collaboration with the officials of the Shipping Federation and the NUS and of championing the rota system on behalf of the shipowners. Claiming to speak on behalf of the Arab seamen of South Shields, they challenged the legality of the rota system and expressed their determination not to accept it. Finally, they pointed out that if anyone wanted to collect funds from the Arab seamen to send representatives to London then they were free to do so without applying to the Western Islamic Association for permission.[17]

Ahmed Mohamed of 41 Commercial Road—which turned out to be a false address—also claimed to write on behalf of the Arabs in South Shields. In his letter he stated that only about thirty out of 600 Arabs in the town had signed the new register and these men had not signed of their own free will but had been forced to do so by a boarding-house master. He also challenged the legality of the new scheme and claimed that it actually applied to all seamen, but that this fact was being kept secret from the white seamen. Mohamed's claim is another example of the inaccurate and misleading information about the rota system circulating in the community. He also demanded that those Arabs who were without police registration should be allowed to sign the new rota and get employment.[18]

Peter O'Donnell, Chairman of the South Shields Seamen's Committee of Action, who had been released on bail pending his trial at the Durham Assizes, claimed to write on behalf of the 400 Arabs in South Shields who were members of the Seamen's Minority Movement. He argued that Dr Sheldrake was ignoring the main aspect of the Arabs' struggle, namely that by registering they were being forced into the hands and control of the shipowners and were forfeiting one of the fundamentals of trade unionism—collective bargaining with other seamen. He appealed to Dr Sheldrake to give advice to the Arabs on religious matters but where their bread and butter was concerned to allow them to make up their own minds.

159

He insisted that the Arabs would continue to fight the rota system and he asked Sheldrake to support them and not to stand apart but to take a tip from their religion to 'Care for your brother whether he be of any colour.'[19]

According to figures released by the Shipping Federation, on 22 September 1930 363 Arabs had registered under the rota system at South Shields and sixty-six Somalis; fifty-eight Arabs and twenty-seven Somalis had obtained ships.[20] Some protests continued until the end of the year but by the end of September active resistance to the new scheme had been replaced by passive acceptance. The reasons for this change are unclear. One factor may have been the failure of Ali Said and Ali Hamed Dheli's efforts to persuade the Arabs that the India Office would provide assistance to those men who refused to sign. The India Office had made no such promises and in the middle of September the Chief Constable stated that if the activities of these men could be frustrated then he was confident that the majority of the Arabs in South Shields would accept the rota system. Another factor may have been the intervention of Dr Sheldrake and the Western Islamic Association who may have succeeded in winning over the majority of the boarding-house masters to accept the new scheme. Whether his activities were significant or not, it is still difficult to explain why Dr Sheldrake did not intervene at an earlier date but waited until the beginning of September to lend his public support to the Arab faction which favoured acceptance of the rota system. Of course it is possible that by the beginning of September the majority of the boarding-house masters in the town had realized that the new scheme was here to stay, that attempts to oppose it had failed and that they had no alternative but to bow to the inevitable.

Since 1 August when the rota system became effective, no Arab crews had been signed on, so that the boarding-house masters were receiving no income at all from their men and each day saw ships which had traditionally carried an Arab stokehold crew engage white firemen. On the 14 October the Chief Constable of South Shields wrote to the Home Office that a total of 455 Arabs and Somalis had registered leaving only about fifty men unregistered and that each day saw one or two names being added to the rota. He reported that the scheme was working satisfactorily and that he would be sorry to be' without it. Crowds of coloured seamen no longer gathered around the Shipping Offices and this was a great help to the police.[21]

II Unemployed Arab seamen apply for indoor relief

On 29 September 1930, in a dramatic new development, a hundred unemployed Arab seamen applied for and were granted indoor relief. By the evening forty-five men had actually taken up residence at the Poor Law Institution at Harton, commonly known as the South Shields workhouse. It was reported that the boarding-house masters had declared that they could no longer keep these men. Some of the men had not had a ship for eighteen months. As the South Shields Public Assistance Committee had refused to grant them outdoor relief they had no alternative but to advise their boarders to enter the workhouse.[22]

In Cardiff, in contrast, the Public Assistance Committee, after dragging its feet for some months, did provide outdoor relief to destitute Arabs. Five shillings a week was paid for each man to the boarding-house master after strict investigation into the eligibility of all the men boarding there. The local press greatly exaggerated the number of Arabs receiving relief and the size of the bill to the ratepayers.[23] According to the *Shields Daily Gazette*, an unnamed Arab leader told their reporter that as many as 500 unemployed Arabs would soon apply to be admitted. It was reported that the men would be accommodated in a special ward, provided with a special diet and allowed to leave the institution during the day to look for work. Extra staff would have to be engaged to deal with the influx.[24]

The event hit the national headlines. The *Daily Herald* reported the matter on the 1 October with the headline, 'Arabs besiege workhouse—ratepapers say "send them home" '.[25] An editorial in the *Shields Daily Gazette* warned against sensational and exaggerated versions of the case[26] but gave prominence to a statement by 'a local businessman in public office' who protested that many of these Arabs would be institutional guests 'for the rest of their lives'. He continued:

> This is the Arab boarding house masters' doing. They have got the best out of these men and they are now shifting their responsibilities upon the town. Let these men go back to their motherland. It would pay us to send them back or to help to do so, because I can see we shall be having the Arabs permanently settled upon us if we are not careful. It is a problem surely but it ought to be tackled boldly and firmly now in the economic interests of the borough if we don't want to have a millstone around our necks.[27]

Another angry ratepayer, who wrote to the local newspaper under the name of 'Sida', protested:

> I see that these men are to be fed on mutton, poultry, pancakes etc. Very nice indeed. Compare that with their native diet, mealies; three or four or more eating out of the same vessel, the husk of a big melon.
>
> Arabs come here by choice and if they cannot supply their own food why should the ratepayers. I do hope the public men of Shields won't be dictated to by Arab boarding house masters.[28]

Other letters to the editor urged repatriation and one writer even suggested that the Arabs should be accommodated in a discarded passenger ship or government vessel that might also be used for other Arabs to allow slum clearance in Holborn.[29]

Said Mabrouk, in reply to these protests, stated indignantly that he had been a boarding-house master in South Shields for ten years and had always kept his men together. Not one of his forty-four boarders had applied for indoor relief. He had kept them through many difficulties and intended to continue doing so.[30] The *Shields Daily Gazette* also published letters from a number of Arabs and their wives who made a spirited defence of their unemployed countrymen who had sought indoor relief. Elsie Cassim of 90 Adelaide Street, South Shields maintained that if these men had been justly treated they would have been working for their living and not begging for it. She continued:

> As to settling down to comforts and becoming institutional guests, I should like our worthy citizens to understand that the Arab is no sponger, nor does he indulge in comforts for which he cannot pay and that the step they are taking is a great blow to their pride and to that of those connected with them. I would add in conclusion that the boarding house masters are in no respect to blame. The present crisis has been brought about by the blundering of the NUS and the sooner they put the matter right the better for all concerned.[31]

Ahmed Alwin, 43 Commercial Road, South Shields blamed the actions of the NUS and the Shipping Federation for reducing the Arabs to penury and forcing them to become a charge on the ratepayers. They were responsible for this debacle and it was they who should be criticized by the citizens of South Shields and not the unfortunate Arabs.[32] Peter O'Donnell also blamed the NUS and the shipowners and stated that if the rota system were abandoned the problem of Arabs at Harton would disappear.[33]

In a long and rather pompous letter, Dr Sheldrake of the Western Islamic Association expressed a very different view of the problem. He appealed to the ratepayers of South Shields to consider the wonderful sacrifice made by the boarding-house masters who had maintained their men for so long. As a result, they had been forced to mortgage their property and even their furniture and yet they still maintained hope that their boarders would find employment. He was happy to observe that since registering under the rota system a number of Arabs had obtained ships but he acknowledged that the present state of shipping was terrible and that many thousands of coloured and white seamen were idle. On 2 October he had discussed the matter with Sir Umar Hayat, Member of the Council of the Secretary of State for India, and had supplied him with all the facts. The problem was being discussed by the India Office in consultation with other government departments but nothing could be arranged definitively until these discussions were completed. Because the Arabs of South Shields came under the local branch of the Western Islamic Association, he was devoting every minute of his time to this pressing matter. He assured the citizens of South Shields that he was doing his best on behalf of the Arab seamen and that he wished to ensure that they could pursue their calling without hindrance so that by paying their rates and taxes they might benefit the town. He was also putting forward the case of the boarding-house masters who had practically ruined themselves keeping the men through their long period of unemployment. The whole trouble was caused by the economic depression and its effect on shipping. When trade recovered both white and coloured seamen would quickly find employment and more seamen would be required.[34]

Speculation that as many as 500 Arab seamen might invade the South Shields workhouse proved to be a wild exaggeration. By 1 October it was reported that only ninety-seven Arabs had accepted indoor relief and that eleven men had gone leaving a total of eighty-six. Some of the eleven men had secured ships.[35] Colonel Chapman, Chairman of the South Shields Public Assistance Committee, stated that his committee was not unduly perturbed and intended to deal with all cases of destitution as required by law.[36] By 3 October it was announced that all the unemployed Arab seamen who had sought refuge in the Harton Institution had discharged themselves that morning following a decision by the

South Shields Public Assistance Committee the day before to apply to magistrates for deportation orders in cases of aliens. The next day the *Shields Daily Gazette* gave a different explanation for the departure of the Arabs from Harton. They reported that it followed a decision by the Public Assistance Committee to restrict the Arabs leaving the institution to the same hours as other inmates. According to this report, officials explained to the Arabs that the rota system would guarantee them their turn for ships and that they would be called for when required, but that the men were not satisfied with this arrangement.[37] In a letter to the editor of the *Shields Daily Gazette*, Elsie Cassim stated that the real reason why the Arabs had left Harton was because of public comment and open insults levelled at them which made them feel too proud to accept the ratepayers' charity.[38]

Despite the departure of all the Arabs from Harton, popular demands for their repatriation continued to be voiced. One irate South Shields resident stated that this issue was of such vital importance that in the forthcoming municipal elections any candidate who did not favour repatriating the Arabs was not worthy of support.[39] The Public Assistance Committee proceeded with their efforts to obtain deportation orders for the men who had accepted indoor relief.

The Chief Constable was convinced that Ali Said and Ali Hamed Dheli were the prime movers in this episode and expressed a suspicion that 'the communist element' in the town was fostering trouble in the matter. He wrote to the Home Office asking for their urgent assistance to secure deportation orders.[40] Certainly there is some evidence that Ali Said was involved. For example, Mr Moran, the relieving officer, stated that Ali Said was with some of the men when they presented themselves for admission orders for the Harton Institution.[41] One of the men who applied to be admitted to Harton declared that he was destitute but was then seen in a shop in East Holborn with a £5 note. When challenged he stated that he did not have the money but later admitted he had received it from Ali Said.[42] However, press reports suggest that it was the boarding-house masters, or at least some of them, who advised their men to apply for indoor relief and accompanied them when they presented themselves for admission. Small groups of men from at least twelve different boarding-houses and refreshment houses entered Harton and it would appear that they were not advised that as aliens they risked deportation if they went into the workhouse. For example, in December 1930 when a number of Arab seamen who had entered Harton were summoned with a view to their deportation, Mr Muir

Smith, their solicitor, asked Mr Moran, the relieving officer, if it was pointed out to them that they were aliens and that if they went into the workhouse they might be sent out of the country. He replied that it was not part of his job. Mr Muir Smith then asked him, 'Batches of men very much like sheep were anxious to get into the Institution and you did not think fit to tell them what the consequence would be?' Mr Moran replied, 'No sir.'[43]

The whole episode was almost certainly a protest but it is unclear why such action was organized and what it was supposed to achieve. It seems unlikely that it was part of the movement to oppose the rota system because by this time the majority of Arabs had registered. It may have been simply a protest against the refusal to grant the Arabs outdoor relief but if this was the case one might have expected action to have been taken earlier when the boarding-masters faced financial ruin because no Arabs were being shipped. Alternatively it may have been a protest against the authorities' refusal to register about a hundred Arabs in the town who were unregistered under the 1925 Order and were therefore not eligible under the rota system. In the past, boarding-house masters had been able to secure work for some of these men on the weekly boats but the introduction of the rota system put an end to this source of employment. The boarding-house masters therefore found themselves faced with the burden of keeping men who were ineligible for work. Whatever the motives, the consequence of this action was that in December 1930 forty-four Arab seamen were summoned at the South Shields police court for being aliens who had entered the country within the last twelve months and who within the last three months had been in receipt of poor relief. The object of these proceedings was for the magistrates to certify these facts so that a recommendation could be made to the Home Secretary for the men's deportation.[44] Deportation orders were later made against all but four of the men. There seems little doubt that these men were used by others and were the innocent victims of this particular fiasco. On 29 January 1931 thirty-eight of the Arab seamen who had had deportation orders made against them left South Shields under police escort for London where they boarded the P & O liner *Nankin* bound for Aden.[45]

Once the majority of Arab seamen had accepted the rota system, the main problem facing the police authorities in South Shields was the hundred or so Arabs who were unregistered under the 1925 Order and therefore ineligible to sign the new register. This problem appears to have been more serious on the Tyne that at the South Wales ports or Hull, suggesting that Arabs seeking to enter the country irregularly favoured the north-east ports. On 15 September 1930 the Chief Constable of South Shields wrote to the Chief Immigration Officer on this subject expressing his concern that these men might become a charge on the rates of the town. He believed that the influx of coloured seamen into the borough had ceased and that the number of unregistered men was unlikely to increase. As a result he suggested that this matter could be resolved if these men were gradually granted registration.[46]

This question was discussed at a Conference of Immigration Inspectors held in the Home Office on 14 October 1930. Mr Stovell, the Immigration Inspector from Newcastle, did not support the suggestion and argued that if registration were granted to these men the news would quickly spread and unregistered men from other parts of the country would rapidly drift to the Tyne in increasing numbers. Although the rota system was proving a success, he pointed out that the rate at which Arab seamen on the register were being shipped from the Tyne was slow because of the continued slump in shipping. There were about 534 coloured men at present at South Shields and a colony of 400 was ample in normal times to meet requirements. Since it was introduced 429 Arabs had been signed under the rota system and of these only 160 had found work, leaving 338 unemployed. Inspectors from other areas agreed and it was felt that if the Chief Constable's suggestion was adopted it would merely encourage a new influx of Arabs. Indeed it was claimed that judging from the numerous reports relating to the refusal of leave to land to Arabs, there appeared to be no decline in the attempts by this category of seamen from abroad to gain admission to Britain. This influx was being successfully checked not by the introduction of the rota system but by the energetic and ceaseless activites of the police and immigration officers. The meeting concluded that these men should not be granted police registration and that their compulsory removal from the United Kingdom might be considered.[47]

In the end no large-scale deportations of unregistered Arab seamen took place. Apart from the thirty-eight Arab seamen who were deported following the large scale applications for indoor relief on 29 September 1930, the only group of Arabs to be deported from South Shields were the fifteen men, including Ali Said, sentenced at Durham Assizes for their part in the disturbances at the Mill Dam on 2 August 1930.[48] Nevertheless, the threat of deportation procedures appears to have been sufficiently real[49] for the boarding-house masters to have resumed responsibility for these men, at least for a time. According to the Chief Constable's report, by April 1935 there were only twenty-four coloured alien seamen in South Shields who were unregistered under the Special Restriction (Coloured Alien Seamen) Order of 1925.[50] Presumably, once the authorities had made it clear that these men were not to be registered and indeed had threatened deportation, they either left of their own accord or were encouraged to do so by the boarding-house masters. The local authorities continued to deny unemployed Arab seamen outdoor relief and the vast majority of Arabs refused to apply for indoor relief at Harton because it would prevent them from looking for work at the riverside. There is some evidence to suggest that Arab seamen who succeeded in obtaining employment helped to support men living in the same boarding-house who were unable to get ships. For example, in April 1936 the *Shields Gazette* reported that every time an Arab seaman was paid off a vessel with £50 or £60, he handed the money over to the master of the boarding-house where he lived when ashore to be used for the maintenance of his fellow lodgers. The *Gazette* commented that without this 'free-masonry' among the Arabs, they would have been reduced to accepting indoor relief at Harton long ago.[51] Some Arabs simply paid the boarding-house master whatever they could.

III New restrictions imposed on Arab seamen

The limited number of jobs available for Arab seamen was further reduced in 1935 with the passing of the British Shipping (Assistance) Act. Pressure from the NUS and the Transport and General Workers' Union had ensured that in order to enjoy the government subsidy on merchant shipping, shipowners had to agree to employ only British crews.[52] This was a serious blow to the Arabs as the vast majority were registered as aliens under the 1925 Special Restriction Order and as a result could not be employed on ships receiving the new subsidy. In September 1935 the *Shields Gazette* reported that since February of that year more than a dozen Tyne-owned vessels, which had traditionally carried an Arab stoke-hold crew, had replaced them with white firemen.[53] In August 1935 the fifty or so Somali seamen in South Shields protested to the Foreign Office about the discrimination by shipowners against coloured seamen but received no reply. A deputation appealed to the Mayor of South Shields asking him to approach the Government to stop the discrimination against their employment on British ships or failing that to arrange their repatriation to Somaliland. One of the Somalis in the deputation had been out of work for four years and another for one year.[54]

At the same time, action was taken to impose new restrictions at Aden on Arab seamen wishing to travel to Britain in search of employment. Early in 1935 the Home Office issued instructions that in view of the persistence of acute depression in the shipping industry resulting in high rates of unemployment among white and coloured seamen in Britain, 'Adenese' seamen should not be issued with certificates of nationality and identity at Aden which would enable them to proceed to Britain to look for work unless they had a record of residence in the United Kingdom and of service in British ships 'closely antecedent to the date of their applications for such certificates'. These restrictions were to apply to British subjects and British protected persons.[55]

The British Resident at Aden pointed out in a letter to the Colonial Office that the new restrictions, imposed since February 1935, had the effect of throwing permanently out of employment British protected persons who had been seamen and who had been visiting their native country and of preventing young men from adopting a profession followed by people from some parts of the protectorate for generations. There had been protests from the Amir of Dhala, one of the principal chiefs of the protectorate. The Resident appreciated the necessity of preventing Arabs from Aden and the protectorate becoming stranded in the United Kingdom but thought the restrictions 'unduly harsh' and suggested that they be modified in order to leave an opening to former seamen and to young men who wished to adopt this profession. He recommended that a limited number of certificates should be issued to seamen provided that the cost of their repatriation, where necessary, was guaranteed by the Amir of Dhala or another chief of similar good political and financial standing or by a well-to-do merchant from Aden.[56]

The Home Office however was adamant that the restrictions should remain unchanged. The Colonial Office was informed that on average half the coloured seaman population in Britain was unemployed and that the supply of coloured seamen was far in excess of present and future requirements. Great prominence had been given to the lack of employment amongst seamen in the discussions on the British Shipping (Assistance) Act and as a result the Tramp Shipping Subsidy Committee was actively encouraging the employment of British seamen who were currently unemployed. In these circumstances the Home Office could not agree to any action which might assist in adding to the coloured seaman population.[57]

The restrictions appear to have been strictly enforced. For

example, when the Amir of Dhala recommended that one of his subjects, Abdul Malik Abdulla, should be given a certificate of nationality and identity to proceed to the United Kingdom in search of employment as a seaman, the Chief Constable's Office in South Shields reported in April 1935 that although Abdulla had served on British ships since 1913, he had left England in March 1933 for Mecca. The report continued:

> Abdulla has no dependants in this country, and, should he be permitted to return, it is very unlikely that he would obtain employment for some considerable time, as owing to the displacement of Aliens in favour of British crews, unemployment among coloured seamen shows a tendency to rise, and, as Abdulla would automatically be at the bottom of the Coloured Seamen's Rota, it would be from one to two years before he could hope to obtain a ship. Owing to his long absence from the United Kingdom, he would be unable to obtain unemployment benefit, and would in consequence become a charge to Public Assistance Committee.[58]

Thus, even though Abdulla had lived and worked in Britain for some twenty years and had left the country for only two years, presumably to make the pilgrimage to Mecca and to visit his family, this was regarded as 'a long absence' and sufficient to recommend that he be prevented from returning to the United Kingdom.

In response to the restrictions imposed by the British Shipping (Assistance) Act, many Arab seamen in the United Kingdom applied to become British naturalized subjects. By 1938 the Aliens Department of the Home Office indicated that about 2,000 coloured alien seamen had acquired British citizenship and that such naturalizations largely accounted for the drop in the number of coloured alien seamen registered under the Special Restriction (Coloured Alien Seamen) Order of 1925 in the United Kingdom from 5,198 in 1931 to 2,407 in 1938. The figures for South Shields, where the majority of coloured alien seamen were Arabs, show a decline in numbers from 827 in 1935 to 283 in 1938.[59] The *Shields Gazette* reported that during the first three weeks of January 1936 thirty Arab seamen had applied to the Home Office for naturalization and that altogether more than fifty had sought to change their nationality during the last three months. The report commented that these applications were something of a gamble. The Arabs had to pay the sum of £1, which they could ill afford, to make the initial application and they forfeited the money if the application was unsuccessful. The total cost of naturalization could be as high as £15 if the services of a solicitor were employed.[60]

Early in 1936, certain Arabs in South Shields approached the mayor, Councillor Edmund Hill, and asked him to write to the Aga Khan and the Nizam of Hyderabad drawing their attention to the fact that many Arabs in the town were almost destitute as a result of prolonged unemployment and requesting financial assistance. The mayor agreed and in his letter he pointed to the serious effects of the British Shipping (Assistance) Act on Arab seafarers in the town and explained that they could not be given outdoor relief and had refused accommodation in the Harton Institution. There was no reply from the Nizam of Hyderabad but in August the Aga Khan sent a cheque for £100 to be used for the relief of distressed Arab seamen in the town. After some discussion about how best to distribute the money, a police enquiry identified sixty-five Arabs who were most in need of assistance; sixty-four of the men received £1 10s. 9d. each and one man, Saili Abdullah of Maxwell Street, who was a married man with children, received £1 12s. The *Shields Gazette* commented that most of the money would be handed over to the Arab boarding-house keepers but the men would not complain as the boarding-house keepers continued to give their men food and shelter even when they were destitute.[61] In a predictably racist comment, 'A Shieldsman's Diary' in the *Shields Gazette* commented that

> . . . the situation contains enough explosive material for a real spot of bother in the traditional Mill Dam manner. Let the denizens of any particular lodging house suspect that they have been discriminated against, however fairly from the viewpoint of English people, and the tribal passions are likely to boil over with disastrous results. Then again, who is going to put the Arabs through a 'means test' in order to determine whether they are genuinely in need of assistance? The Mayor frankly admits that he cannot spare the time for it. Moreover, if I know anything of the Arabs, it won't have to be a means test so much as a brisk exposition of 'third degree' methods if the truth is to be brought to light. I don't know whether it has occurred to the Mayor but a possible way out would be to hand the money over to one or other of the social organisations in the borough . . . Of course, a truly humorous solution of the difficulty and one that would appeal to a large section of the townspeople, would be to stack the money in the centre of the Market Place

and let them fight it out. Meanwhile, I have confidence in the Mayor's ability to cope with his coloured burgesses. Not only can he imitate their speech and gestures to perfection, but he understands their queer, unhumorous attitude to life.[62]

In March 1938 Sir Bernard Reilly, the Governor of Aden, wrote to the Secretary of State for the Colonies requesting that the restrictions imposed on Adeni seamen in 1935 be reconsidered. He stated that these restrictions had been strictly obeyed but that certificates had been issued to Adeni seamen to enable them to travel to France in search of employment. Since January 1936, however, the French authorities had begun to enforce their own regulations more strictly with the result that Adeni seamen who were unable to qualify for admission to the United Kingdom were being refused entry into France. As the qualification required for entry into the United Kingdom was a record of residence there and of service in British ships closely antecedent to the date of their applications, these regulations affected all younger Adenis, whether they were natives of Aden or of the Aden Protectorate. If other countries were to adopt similar restrictions the Governor feared that the majority of these young men would be excluded from the occupation which they and previous generations of Arabs had followed and which offered some relief from the economic hardships of their own country. As these men were British subjects or under British protection, it would be unfortunate from the local political point of view if Britain was seen to be taking the lead in closing the door to them. The Governor appreciated that existing restrictions were due to economic conditions and not to racial distinctions but drew attention to the fact that since 1935 there had been an improvement in the shipping trade. For this reason and in view of the recent action by the French authorities, he requested some relaxation of the present rules and suggested that an annual quota should be allowed for Adeni seamen irrespective of previous employment or residence in the United Kingdom.[63]

The Colonial Office took the matter up with the Home Office and the Board of Trade emphasizing the Governor's reference to the unfortunate impression likely to be created if, as a result of present restrictions against entry to the United Kingdom, British subjects or British protected persons were prevented from obtaining employment as seamen. A meeting was arranged at the Colonial Office on 13 October 1938 between the Governor of Aden and representatives of the Colonial Office, the Home Office and the Board of Trade to consider whether it would be possible to improve the prospects of employment in Britain for Adeni seamen. At the meeting Sir Bernard Reilly explained the position from the Aden point of view emphasizing in particular the political aspect. He pointed out that while he fully recognized the difficulties of admitting Adeni seamen without restriction into Britain, if some relaxations were not made the supply of Adeni seamen would gradually dry up altogether. He thought it was undesirable for Britain, the country responsible for the protection of these seamen, to be the one which took the lead in excluding them. Such a situation had a bad effect, especially at the present time when it was important to do nothing to alienate still further Arab sympathies from Great Britain. The Italians in particular might exploit the situation by offering the men employment in their East African colonies and reminding them that they could get more from the Italian Government than from the British which was their protecting power.

Mr Cooper from the Home Office explained the difficulties of admitting more coloured seamen into the country at a time when there were many more coloured alien seamen than could be found jobs. He produced statistics showing that as of 1 July 1938 almost half of all the coloured alien seamen registered under the Special Restriction (Coloured Alien Seamen) Order were unemployed. These statistics were presented by nationality and it is significant to note that they reveal that Arab seamen experienced somewhat lower levels of unemployment than all coloured seamen taken together. For the country as a whole 453 Arabs were recorded at sea and 203 on shore; for South Shields there were eighty-one Arabs at sea and sixty-six on shore. Cooper went on to explain that the effect of admitting more Arabs would be to create an extra charge on the unemployment fund and on other social services and there would be fewer jobs for the coloured seamen already here. However, he recognized that these objections might be overridden by political considerations and thought that a small quota of perhaps fifty Adeni seamen a year might be sanctioned in order to avoid closing completely the outlet for Arab seamen from Aden.

Mr Norman from the Board of Trade mentioned the objections of the National Union of Seamen to any increase in the numbers of coloured seamen but pointed to the advantages of having an adequate supply of seamen available in the country 'in case of emergency'. From that point of view he thought it might be undesirable to maintain a complete bar to the entry of Arab seamen to this country and thus lose this recruiting ground, especially as the Arab seamen had a good reputation as workers on ships. Both the Home Office and the Board of Trade representatives were impressed by the important political implications which came into the case and agreed to give sympathetic consideration to admitting an annual quota of fifty Adeni seamen into the country.[64] This was eventually approved in February 1939. A Colonial Office note commented: 'I gather that although there is no justification for bringing more Adenese seamen into the UK, the Home Office will agree, on general grounds of policy, to a quota for the admission of fifty Adenese seamen annually.'[65] Whereas imperial interests had been overruled after the First World War when stringent controls were imposed on the entry of Arab seamen into Britain, by 1939 as the war clouds gathered once more over Europe, political considerations came to the fore again and secured a small concession for Arab seamen wishing to enter Britain.

Seven

Mixed Marriages and Moral Outrage

I Arabs and white girls

The arrival of Arab seamen in the town provoked not only resentment because they competed with white seamen for jobs but also a moral panic as a result of the association of Arabs with white women. The voices of moral outrage were loud and clear and those of officialdom exploited widespread popular fears of moral danger from 'the Arab menace'. In the years following the First World War allegations of immorality, feelings of sexual competition and jealousy, fears of miscegenation and the need to defend the purity of the white race, the problem of a growing number of half caste children and the dangers of disease were all used by the authorities to justify tougher restrictions on the Arab population. These issues also provided a powerful weapon for the National Union of Seamen in its campaign to discredit the Arabs during the inter-war years. Moral dangers were also evoked in debates in the Town Council to support demands that the number of Arabs in the town should be limited and that they should be strictly segregated and confined to the Holborn area. Not content with forcing the Arabs to live in the most overcrowded parts of the town, they were then accused of being responsible for the slum conditions prevailing there.

From the outset the relationship of Arabs with white girls aroused hostile feelings among the townspeople. After one of the earliest racial disturbances in South Shields in April 1913, when a white crowd attacked Ali Hassan's refreshment shop in East Holborn, a police inspector commented that the Arabs living in the district were a great attraction to girls in the neighbourhood and this fact had

174

provoked the anger of the English residents.[1] During the First World War the number of Arab seamen in the town increased dramatically. They were mostly young men who were either single or, if they were married, had left their wives and children at home in the Yemen. There were no immigrant women. Those seeking female companionship were able to meet white girls in the Arab boarding-houses and refreshment houses, where young girls were often employed as domestic servants. But girls from other parts of South Shields and from neighbouring towns were also attracted to Holborn. Some came to visit girlfriends working there or a married sister, but there were also girls who were no doubt attracted by the fact that the Arabs were earning good wages at this time, liked to wear fine clothes and were generous with their money when they came ashore. After a voyage of six months an Arab seaman could easily have amassed the sum of £50 and 'such wealth may have been a solvent of any racial prejudices on the part of white girls'.[2]

In a case reported in the *Shields Daily Gazette* in July 1916 one young Arab seaman, named as Jasin Ali, claimed to have spent £40 on a girl with whom he had been cohabiting for the last five months. They had stayed in various temperance hotels in Newcastle and South Shields and he had bought her clothing and other things. However the relationship did not last and when the girl refused to have anything more to do with him, Ali traced her to an Arab cafe in the Market Place at South Shields and threatened to murder her. The police intervened and Ali complained that the girl had £51 belonging to him. He was charged with committing a breach of the peace and fined 5s.[3]

Many of these liaisons between young Arab seamen and white girls were no doubt temporary and those resulting in marriage and permanent settlement in the town appear to have been limited in number. Most of the boarding-house masters, refreshment house keepers and shopkeepers married white girls and settled down in the town and so did a number of seamen, but by 1930 the settled community numbered only forty to fifty families. Some of the unions between Arabs and white girls were stable and happy, others ended in separation and divorce. When couples separated, responsibility for any children was normally taken by the father. The majority of Arab seamen, however, remained temporary migrants who returned to their home villages and to their families in Yemen after a few years when they had accumulated sufficient savings.

Any form of intimate association between Arabs and white girls was regarded as offensive to the local townspeople and provoked loud cries of moral condemnation. The police were particularly vigilant in their efforts to protect the town's moral welfare. For example in December 1921 the police charged Mohamed Saleh, a boarding-house keeper, with having allowed his premises at 27 and 29 East Holborn to be used 'as a place where idle and disorderly persons assembled'. The police stated that they had visited the boarding-house to look for a seventeen-year-old girl named Miller reported missing by her mother. The girl had had a child by an Arab when she was only sixteen years old. They had found the girl and her baby in one of the upstairs rooms with an Arab seaman known as Siff Norman and had taken her back to her mother. On that occasion there were two other girls in the house and the police reported that they had frequently found white girls there, 'at all times of the day and up to eleven o'clock at night,' and that Saleh had been cautioned on an earlier occasion about having young girls on his premises. Eight of the girls that the police had seen there had been convicted at the police court at different times. The police had received complaints about girls as young as thirteen years there and regarded the conduct of the house as offensive. When Victor Grunhut for the defence, asked in what way the conduct of the house was offensive, Inspector Wingfield replied, 'They [the girls] were sitting drinking tea and cuddling up to the Arabs.' In the eyes of the police this was clear evidence of immorality! Further cross examination by the defence revealed that some of the girls seen by the police at the house were actually employed there or were married to Arabs, others were visiting their Arab 'sweethearts'. Questioned by the Chief Constable, Mary Mamont, who was married to an Arab and worked at Saleh's boarding-house, admitted that she had seen girls of sixteen and seventeen there, sitting among the Arabs having tea. 'Was there ever any love-making?' asked the Chief Constable. 'There was kissing and that', replied the witness.

Mr Grunhut, for the defence, argued that if Saleh had not been an Arab, the case would never have been brought before the bench. The Chief Constable no doubt felt it his duty to try and stop friendships or cohabitation between English girls and Arabs but Grunhut was satisfied in his own mind that whatever anybody did they would not stop any girl keeping company with an Arab if she chose to do so. He continued:

> You must not be prejudiced because this man is an Arab. Inspector Wingfield was very fair when he was asked whether it was the girls who ran after the Arabs or the Arabs after them. It was half and half. They will go; they will keep company with them; and they will marry them. That may not be right from

our point of view, but there is a tremendous difference between that and committing a criminal offence.

The girl Miller had been ostracised by her own family and her English friends. According to her own story she had been put out. Where was she to go? She could only go back to her Arab friends where she could get a good night's rest for herself and her baby. There were legitimately married women there, and so far as was known they were doing no harm.

The Bench must wipe out the colour question. Most of those girls had unfortunately made alliances with the Arabs. Which was the better: that those girls should go to this place for cups of coffee or tea or go and become drunkards elsewhere? Were mothers so keen on protecting their daughters as they should be? It seemed to him they were—but when it was too late. If a mother could not keep her daughters away, the Chief Constable could not.

You cannot turn these people out on to the streets . . . They have the right, just as we have, of the freedom of their lives. Just as a person may visit the Ritz, these people can go here with the same freedom, provided of course, that the place is not used for immoral purposes.[4]

Despite the eloquent defence presented by Victor Grunhut, the bench decided to convict Saleh who was fined 50s. Alderman Lawson, the presiding magistrate, remarked that the evidence had demonstrated that idle and disorderly persons had gone to the house, a fact which might have had serious results. The case was fully reported in the *Shields Daily Gazette* under the heading 'White girls and Arabs—What the police saw in Holborn.'[5] Clearly there was nothing to prevent moral condemnation from being spiced with a measure of titillation.

White girls were also a source of rivalry between Arabs, sometimes between brothers, between shipmates or between seamen from different Arab boarding-houses. These rivalries occasionally ended in violence and in one case the death of a girl. A few examples will illustrate this point. During the trial of the boarding-house keeper Nasser Abdulla in March 1919 for the murder of his brother and partner Faid, there was speculation that sexual jealousy may have been a motive. Nasser had known Faid's young English wife, Margaret, before they were married. She used to write letters for him. Faid had been afraid of telling his brother about the marriage and it was some seven months before Nasser found out. Nasser had refused to speak to his brother for three months, never spoke to

Faid's wife and sometimes used to hit her. Eventually Nasser was acquitted because he was able to prove that he was elsewhere at the time of the murder.[6]

In August 1917 a quarrel broke out between two shipmates, known as Said Abdul and Ahmed Sali, over a girl named Lizzie. They had met the girl in Holborn after coming ashore and the three of them had visited a number of Arab boarding-houses in the district. But when the girl rejected Abdul for Sali, a quarrel broke out between the two men during which Abdul wounded Sali with a knife.[7] In another case earlier the same year rivalry between seamen from different boarding-houses over a girl ended in violence when Mohamed Ali, who lived at Muckble's boarding-house, attacked and wounded Said Ali from Abdul Rahman Zaid's boarding-house. Said Ali had evidently been keeping company with a girl named Ellen Pears but on the night of the incident the girl had been out with Mohamed Ali. Said Ali saw them together and when he went to talk to the girl Mohamed Ali rushed at him with a knife wounding him in the back. Mohamed Ali was sentenced to prison for one month.[8]

A rather different case was reported in June 1931 when Ahmed Alwin, a refreshment house keeper of 43 Commercial Road was accused of wounding a man called Mohamed Abdul. It appears that Abdul had frequented Alwin's refreshment house for some six years and earlier that month had gone off with Alwin's wife. The wife's daughter by a previous marriage had stayed with Alwin and on the day of the incident she was standing in the doorway of the shop when Abdul passed by. Alwin claimed that Abdul had kissed his hand to the girl and shouted 'I have taken your wife and now I am going to have the girl like a sheikh.' A fight broke out between the two men during which Abdul was injured. The magistrates accepted that Alwin was the aggressor but given the circumstances they decided to reduce the charge to assault and fined him 20s. A recommendation by the prosecution for deportation was rejected.[9]

A far more serious incident occured in March 1923 which resulted in an Arab seaman, Hassan Mohamed, being sentenced to death for the murder of Jane Nagi and executed at Durham Gaol in August 1923. Jane Nagi, née Brown, was from Jarrow and had been married to an Arab seaman named Mahomed Nagi who had died about a year before the incident. After the death of her husband, Jane, who was twenty-five years old, had returned to live with her father in Jarrow but during the day had worked as a domestic servant in one of the Arab boarding-houses in Holborn. During the nine months before her murder, she had been keeping company with Hassan

Mohamed and had received considerable sums of money from him from time to time. A few days before the murder Jane had gone to Cardiff to meet Hassan when his ship docked there and had returned with him to South Shields. On the afternoon of 12 March Jane had visited Salem Ali's refreshment house at 107 East Holborn. She was drunk and stated that she was looking for trouble. When Hassan arrived they quarrelled. She attacked him scratching his face and used abusive language. Both then left but returned to the refreshment house in the early evening. Hassan asked her if she would go out with him but she refused and declared that she was finished with him. Hassan then left the cafe for a few minutes and on his return he went into the kitchen where Jane was sitting on the sofa, pulled out a revolver and shot her. She died a few minutes later. The proprietor, Salem Ali, a servant and two Arabs were in the kitchen at the time and witnessed the shooting. Hassan tried to run away but was stopped by Salem Ali and disarmed. At the trial Hassan maintained that the fatal shot was fired by another Arab during a scuffle but he was found guilty and sentenced to death.[10]

The incident provoked a strong condemnation of marriages between white girls and coloured men from the Deputy Coroner of South Shields. He commented:

> It is a sordid case, and I am sorry to say that in my experiences of inquests at South Shields I have come into contact with a number of cases in which white women have married coloured men. I feel very strongly on the point, not that it has any bearing upon this case, but it seems a great pity that white women should marry men of a different nationality altogether and that trouble more or less arises from such unions.
>
> I don't consider it is fair to the children who may be born in any such marriages and it seems to me that steps should be taken to prevent these unions if possible. I am sure we should not have been here today had such a wedding as was contemplated in this case not been about to be celebrated.[11]

Nevertheless, this was tame stuff compared with the views of the local authorities in Cardiff where the Chief Constable in particular assumed the role of moral policeman and demanded legislation to make sexual relations between coloured seamen and white women a criminal offence. In his view the half-caste children who resulted from these unions possessed 'the vicious hereditary taint of their parents' and were seen as unemployable; for the girls there was only domestic service in the lodging-houses and inevitably prostitution.[12] A report published in 1930 based on an investigation into the colour problem in Liverpool and other ports, including Cardiff and South Shields, commissioned by the Liverpool Association for the Welfare of Half-caste Children, endorsed this view concluding:

> The problem of the half-caste child is a serious one, and it appears to be growing in most of our seaport towns. The coloured families have a low standard of life, morally and economically. It is practically impossible for half-caste children to be absorbed into our industrial life and this leads to grave moral results, particularly in the case of girls. The white women themselves mostly regret their marriage with a coloured man and their general standard of life is usually permanently lowered.[13]

Commenting on her visit to South Shields, Miss Fletcher quoted the Chief Constable who stated that there were only sixty-five half-caste children in the schools there because 'the Arab child dies at a very young age on account of the prevalence of tuberculosis and venereal disease.' On the basis of visits to eight coloured families in the town she concluded:

> Most of the children were young, but the mothers were already feeling that there would be no future for them when they grew up and showed that they realised their responsibility in having brought these coloured children into the world.[14]

The report conveniently recommended that the only way to prevent the growing number of 'contacts of an undesirable nature', between coloured men and white women at the nation's seaports was to prohibit the employment of coloured men.[15]

II Popular feelings on mixed marriages

In South Shields popular feelings on the subject of mixed marriages, expressed in the many letters to the editor of the *Shields Daily Gazette*, were far less restrained than those of the town's deputy coroner. Some respondents blamed the white girls who married Arabs, describing them as 'shameless', 'poor and misguided', 'lacking in self-respect' and 'bringing disgrace on their parents.' Mixed marriages were 'wrong', 'detestable', 'against nature' and 'filled the mind with horror'. Some argued that God never meant there to be mixed marriages and urged the churches to step in and stop these marriages taking place at the registry office. It was assumed that the girls were only attracted to Arabs for their money, not for love. The Arabs were accused of picking only the prettiest girls, leaving the 'ugly ducklings' for the white men. Arabs were described as inferior, intellectually and morally, to white men and their unions with White girls were regarded as a threat to the purity of the town. Such intermingling undermined the white race and led to moral decline. Unions between Arabs and white girls resulted in 'a surfeit of half-caste children' and an increase in immorality. A view commonly expressed was that the children of such unions were 'outcastes' and that 'no mixed breed child was as good as a child of white parents'. The number of Arabs in the town, the number of mixed marriages and the number of half-caste children were greatly exaggerated, presumably to make the threat which they were alleged to present appear all the more serious. There was general agreement that the solution to the problem was to deport the Arabs to their own country together with their wives and children. A number of extracts from these letters are presented below by way of illustration.

'Burgoo' wrote:

> I was impressed by the remarks of Mr Boulton, the deputy coroner, upon the question of white women and black men marrying. I think it is about time this subject was brought to the notice of the 'powers that be'. As an Englishman and one who is proud of the fact, I shudder to think of what the population of this country must degenerate into if these marriages are allowed to continue. Take Shields as a case in point; the Arab colony numbers several thousands, I believe, say three. Assume that half of these are married to white girls or are contemplating marriage. Their children will grow up and be educated as white children are. When the male portion of these attain manhood they will naturally marry and when looking for wives will not confine themselves to Holborn. Then there will be trouble in roost. I can imagine my feelings were I the father of a marriageable daughter who presented a half-caste Arab as her future husband. Possibly some misguided persons will say that given the benefit of a decent education and holding a good job, the parentage of these half-castes should not be held against them. But the Arabs who go as firemen in British ships are not quite the elite of Egypt and birds of a feather flock together even in marriage. I am a firm believer in heredity. However, even if a ban were placed upon these marriages that

would not worry the dusky gentlemen of Holborn. So the only remedy I can suggest to counteract this evil is to deport them back to their native land to eat rice, sell oranges and the other things the Lord put them on earth for.[16]

'Englishman' wrote:

I am in entire agreement with 'Burgoo'. I not only think that these mixed marriages should be prohibited, but I feel that in the interest of our town's purity it would be a good thing if our swarthy friends were given the 'order of the boot'. It must be a very common kind of sense that can visualise with equanimity a future South Shields largely populated with the issue of these white and black marriages. As an Englishman who has seen something of coloured people, I submit sir, that it is against nature that they should intermarry with whites. They are in every way inferior, and they ought not to have equal rights with white men in a white man's country. Give them their natural rights by all means. Ship the lot of them back to their own country and give the South Shields of the next generation a chance to be wholesome. 'East is East and West is West'.[17]

'J.C. of Tyne Dock' wrote:

. . . Many reasoned thinkers agree with Plato that 'Society will only put itself on the pathway leading to the highest physical, mental and ethical excellence when it recognises the necessity of regulations in the interest of the whole organism, by which bad, weak, diseased and socially deficient members are weeded out, or at least prevented from reproducing their kind, and the race continued by the proper mixture of the essentially fit.' However revolting this may be to some minds, the very idea of mixed marriages is ten times more so.

In the white race, by the perpetuation of the race, we know ourselves to be vitiated stock. As one goes through life one sees many cases of uncleanness and impurity and wonders. But what excuse can one find for a white girl marrying a coloured man. The very contemplation of it fills some minds with horror. Think of the native traits which are handed down to the half-caste, possibly a blighted, cramped existence, life itself being an unescapable prison.

I do not blame the men, who evidently cannot, at present, be ejected; but the white girls who go and mix up with such men

182

Plate 12. Arab mourners at the funeral of Ahmed Saleh at Harton Cemetery, South Shields in February 1935. (Courtesy of the *Shields Gazette*)

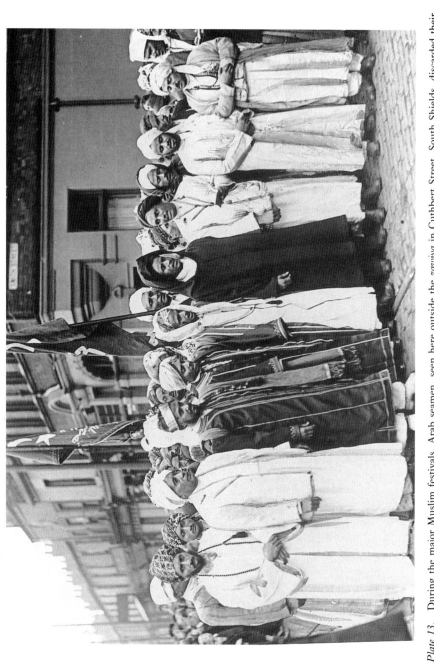

Plate 13. During the major Muslim festivals, Arab seamen, seen here outside the *zawiya* in Cuthbert Street, South Shields, discarded their European clothing for Yemeni dress or the Arab dress of North Africa. (Courtesy of the *Evening Chronicle*, Newcastle upon Tyne)

Plate 14. Children from the Arab community lead a procession through the streets of South Shields on Monday 16 August 1937 to mark the festival of al-Ihtifal commemorating the death of the founder of the 'Alawi *tariqa*. Sheikh Abdullah Ali al-Hakimi is third from the left. (Courtesy of the *Evening Chronicle*, Newcastle upon Tyne)

Plate 15. Prince Hussein (third from the left), one of the sons of Imam Yahya of the Yemen, and part of his entourage at the boarding-house of Said Hassan (first right) during the prince's visit to South Shields on 21–22 May 1937. Mrs Hassan is standing at the back of her husband. (Courtesy of the *Shields Gazette*)

Plate 16. Sheikh Abdullah Ali al-Hakimi (right) presenting gifts to fourteen-year-old Norman Abdo Ali who had learned the Qu'ran in one year. The presentation took place at the end of Ramadan, early December 1937. (Courtesy of the *Shields Gazette*)

Plate 18. Maud Deans, the wife of Said Saleh Hassan. Her first husband, the boarding-house master, Ali Hassan, died in January 1914. Her mother's family were wealthy shipowners in Whitby. (Courtesy of Mr Norman Hassan)

Plate 17. Said Saleh Hassan (right) began shipping out of North-East ports in 1908 and later married Maud Hassan, the widow of Ali Hassan. Said Saleh Hassan was killed in October 1917 when his ship, the *SS Zillah*, was torpedoed off Murmansk. He referred to himself as a 'Huraifi', probably a sub-tribe of the Shamiri. (Courtesy of Mr Norman Hassan)

Plate 20. Norman Hassan (left) pictured with one of his father's kinsmen, Amin Kaid, also known as Azig Abdul (back), and another Yemeni friend, Nasser, in 1927. Amin Kaid was a seaman who lodged at Abdul Sophie's boarding-house in Thrift Street, South Shields. (Courtesy of Mr Norman Hassan)

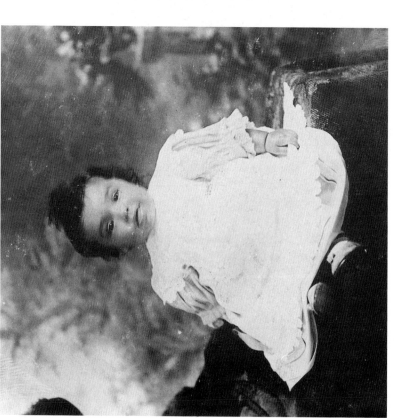

Plate 19. Said Saleh Hassan's son, Norman, was only a few months old when his father died at sea. He was one of the first children born into the Arab community in South Shields and later became a professional footballer before going to sea in 1936. (Courtesy of Mr Norman Hassan)

Plate 22. An Arab seaman who lodged at Ali Hassan's boarding-house taken before the First World War. Possibly he is Ali Bakcush, a North African, who later settled in South Shields and opened a barber's shop at 21–23 East Holborn. (Courtesy of Mr Norman Hassan)

Plate 21. Amin Hamed, pictured here as a young man, was born in South Shields in 1918 or 1919, the son of a Yemeni seaman and his English wife. Like many of the sons born into the Arab community, he followed his father into seafaring. (Courtesy of Mr Norman Hassan)

Plate 24. Two unidentified Arabs in South Shields probably taken before the First World War. Until the late 1930s Arabs in South Shields rarely wore Yemeni dress when they were ashore but preferred European suits. However, like the man on the left, they sometimes wore a fez. (Courtesy of Mr Norman Hassan)

Plate 23. One of the early Arab seamen to marry and settle down in South Shields, pictured here with his wife just before the First World War. (Courtesy of Mr Norman Hassan)

even living with them. It seems to me that the majority of these girls are not sufficiently enlightened as to their position.[18]

'A Holborn Resident' wrote:

> I would like 'Arab's wife' first to understand that no mixed breed child is or ever will be as good as the child born of white parents. As regards dirty white children, well, if an Arab child was never washed it would never be known, as black is a good standing colour. As to Arabs never being in prison for neglect, as many of these Arabs' wives have never been married they cannot prosecute any Arab they co-habit with. They have no claim on them. It is only luck, in many cases I know, that has saved the Arab from prison. A white man can be found and identified but it takes you all your time to identify the Arabs. How many Arabs have escaped prison for lashing their so-called wives with whips and sticks? Only on one occasion was the law lucky enough to get the Arab. There is no escape for a white man for such conduct ... 'Arab's Wife' says build an Arab school. I wonder if she thinks the education authorities are mad. I say send the Arab children over to Aden and then they will be united and educated among their own.[19]

'Adsum' wrote:

> With all due respect to the Arab community, I maintain that no self-respecting white girl is going to marry an Arab for love alone. Then what is it that draws them? Not the Arab's beauty, surely! No, it is the dress that these men can offer, the pleasures they can indulge in. When these are the bait, with a little kindness thrown in the type of man does not matter.
>
> Furthermore, the Arabs can always be relied upon to pick the prettiest girls: the ugly ducklings being left for the white man, with the exception of the girls who have their self- respect. Also an Arab can get a job where a white man has not a look in; they refuse to sell themselves cheaply. 'An Arab's Wife' says the Arab children are as good as the white children. True, but are the mothers that bear them as good as their white sisters?
>
> There are dirty people wherever you may go but these are a class unto themselves. There are poor white people who are scrupulously clean, both with themselves and their children, many of them having to go to bed in the suit they were born in, until their clothes are washed. But they are clean? Again,

'An Arab's Wife' says that all Arab children are both clean and well-clothed. Does she refer just to her own children or does she go about blindfolded?

In conclusion, let me say that so long as there are girls with no self respect, so long will there be these detestable mixed marriages. If a white woman is good enough for a white man, why is not an Arab woman good enough for an Arab.[20]

Only a few writers sought to challenge these racist views but they included a number of white women married to Arabs who protested vigorously at the attacks made on them, their husbands and children. They pointed out that a woman had the freedom and the right to marry whoever she wished. Arab husbands treated their wives and children well, better than many of their white counterparts. Their children were as good as white children and were clean and well-fed, unlike many white children. One Arab's wife suggested that if the townspeople did not want white children to mix with black they should build an Arab school. Supporters from the white community argued that black and white were equal and that Arabs should have the same rights as white people in Britain. A common political point raised was that if the white man got out of the coloured man's country then the Arabs would be willing to return to their native land and that their wives and children would be happy to accompany them. Extracts from some of these letters are given below.

'West Holborn' wrote:

> I take the liberty of answering 'Burgoo', 'Englishman' and 'Clinker's' letters and would like to remind them that their words have no effect upon either the Arabs in Holborn or their wives or children. We only put them down as those of ignorant people who have nothing else to do but mind other people's affairs instead of their own. And as for giving us the 'Order of the Boot', as he names it, why doesn't he try? Why doesn't he send a letter to Parliament?
>
> They must not think the Arabs or their wives or families are afraid of going back to Aden for the men themselves love their country the same as Englishmen love theirs. It is under the English flag.
>
> There isn't much said about the hundreds of Arabs who were sunk in the war years. Of course that is nothing, because they are coloured: but there would have been if they had been white. The Arabs did their share in the war and some of the people

who are so eager to get a ship and send them back to Aden, Arabia, their home, will perhaps find the reparation for their countrymen who were sunk in war time for Britain. There are as good men in the coloured races as there are in the white.[21]

'Common Sense' wrote:

Allow me to answer 'White Girl', 'Englishman' and 'Clinker'. Firstly, when God made the world, he made all men alike both black and white. And why does He allow the marriages to continue if, as 'White Girl' says, they were never intended to be. Let me tell 'White Girl' I have lived the better part of my life in Holborn and have found nothing in it to be ashamed of, although it be named the Arab colony. Does she expect to find poisonous vapours just because an Arab takes up his abode there? Let me add that if everyone was as clean in person and in deed as the coloured people there would not be near the disease there is.

Secondly, what about reversing 'the order of the boot' and have the white men kicked out of the black man's country. What more disgrace is there in a white girl marrying a black man than a white man marrying a coloured woman which I know to go on in tropical countries?

'Englishman' is not the only individual that has seen something of coloured men; I also have but I speak as I find, and do not follow one's example, 'Kick a dog when it is down'. I don't see in what way they are inferior and why they should not have equal rights even if it be a white man's country; be they black, green or yellow, they have every right to be protected.

I again contradict that an Arab is an Egyptian. I am speaking of Arab birth and not the different countries they are found in. 'Burgoo' said that an Arab was not the 'elite of Egypt'. Lastly, let me point out that even if they do come from the desert, that is no reason why they should not be looked upon as gentlemen.[22]

'A White Woman of Six' wrote:

I am a white woman, having a family of six (four sons and two daughters) and I say that there are just as good Arabs as bad.

I have often noticed when in a car if any white woman or girl were standing they would get up and offer them their seat: that shows respect to us white people. On the other hand there are dozens of white men who would sooner see one drop than give up a seat in a crowded car.

As for the coloured men being inferior, well, it may be only in stature, but they are kind and gentle to their wives and children and that is more than a great deal of the so-called white men can say.

Even if the coloured gentlemen of Holborn had to resort to sell oranges they would do it willingly to support the white wife they chose to share their lives and their kiddies; they look after their own and take care of what they have. Again I say that is more than a lot of our so-called white men do. If white girls find happiness and kindness and comfort in their Arab husbands, I think that is all that is required.[23]

'An Arab's Wife' wrote:

In reply to 'Holborn Resident's' remarks about coloured children mixing with the white children I think they are equally good. The Arab children get the same education as the English and some better. Can anyone prove that any Arab's child has ever been taken from the school dirty? No they can't, but I know hundreds of English children that have. The Arab children are both clean and well clothed. How many white men have been sent to prison for child neglect? A coloured man has never been.

They talk about the Arab leaving his wife after a few years of married life. Yes, if he comes and finds her with another man, but the Arab is not like the white man who lets his wife work to keep him. Because the Arab has blood not like the white man they next talk about the VD hospital. Well, out of the Arab population there have been twenty-six who attended there. I would like to know if the white man has never been there.

If they do not want the white children to mix with black, let them build an Arab school. Good luck to the black man if he can get every house in Holborn so long as he can pay the rates. If there is any charity looked for the black man is always the first to put his hand in his pocket. So let fair be fair.[24]

'White Woman' wrote:

No matter what colour for we are all flesh and blood, and I think that C. Brown is going a little too far by writing as if every Arab's wife is shameless. If talk like this still keeps going on we will do all in our power to take proceedings against such scandal and show narrow minded people that we can claim British protection. As for our kiddies being outcastes I think those who say that do not know the meaning of the word; one thing we can send our children to school clean and tidy, and they can come home to a good dinner. We have not to send them to the school for tickets, nor yet apply to the police station for boots for our kiddies.

No doubt there are some shameless girls down our quarters but not those who have a man and a good home to keep them, and if C. Brown only went around some of the public houses there would be more shameless women than in Holborn.

If the white men were out of our coloured man's country, we would be quite willing to go back with our men to their country.[25]

III   The Arabs and the threat of disease

The moral issue was also used in debates in the Town Council by those councillors who demanded that limits should be placed on the number of Arabs coming into the town. By 1929 a new threat was raised, the threat to the health of the townspeople from disease and in particular the prevalence of tuberculosis among the Arab community.[26] These debates provide a valuable insight into the attitudes of local officials towards the Arabs. At a meeting of the Town Council on 6 February 1929, Councillor Cheesman objected to a decision taken by the Watch Committee to approve an application by Ali Hamid of 2 East Holborn for a licence to use 67 Coronation Street as a seamen's lodging-house. He argued that it was not fit and proper for Arabs to live among white people no matter how thick the veneer of civilization might be. He said that he spoke from personal experience having lived in their country, studied their languages, customs and general conditions of their lives. He was in favour of a coloured man's country for coloured men, and a white man's country for white men. Coloured men were being brought into already overcrowded parts of the town at the rate of 250 a year and it was estimated that there were about 2,000 of them in the borough. The town was already overcrowded and yet these men were concentrating in slum areas that ought to be cleared away. How were they going to get rid of the slums if Arabs were allowed to settle down in them making them worse than they were before? Councillor Cheesman argued that the Arabs presented a real danger to the health of the townspeople and referred to the fact that in 1927 forty-five coloured men were treated at the VD clinic, the majority of them Arabs. In addition, these men were helping to maintain a high rate of unemployment among the seafaring community who had to be supported by state benefits or by the ratepayers of the town. If there were not so many lodging-houses licensed to Arabs there would not be so many of them coming into the town. He asked the Council to begin to deal with this matter at once by refusing to grant this licence. Councillor Linney seconded the motion stating that he did not regard the Arabs as desirable neighbours and that they should not be encouraged. If more licences were granted to Arabs, it would only encourage the importation of more Arabs into the borough. Their presence in the town in such large and increasing numbers was objectionable. The motion to refuse the licence was carried by thirty-three votes to five.[27] It is interesting to note that the number of Arabs in the town was greatly exaggerated by Councillor Cheesman in his statement to the Council, a well-known racist tactic to draw attention to the alleged threat posed by coloured immigrants. By arguing in favour of a coloured man's country for coloured men and a white man's country for white men, he demonstrated that anti-imperialist sentiments could be employed to support racist attacks on coloured people at home.

At this time there were numerous references to an 'Arab invasion' and a great deal of confusion about the number of Arabs who had settled in the town. In response, in January 1930 the *Shields Daily Gazette* published the results of an enquiry they had carried out into official sources on this question. It pointed out that there were between forty and fifty Arab residents in the town and in addition a floating population of between 250 and 300 men. The Arab residents were mainly lodging-house keepers, cafe proprietors and tradesmen in a small way of business. The majority of Arabs were seamen whose numbers fluctuated according to the demands of the shipping industry. These men had no homes nor home ties in South Shields and lived in the boarding-houses while they were ashore. The report continued:

> It is altogether a mistaken impression that is getting about that the Arabs are descending upon us in hordes like the Assyrians of old. The fact is they are fewer than many previous years and getting fewer, thanks to the strict surveillance of a vigilant police. He is an elusive little chap to deal with, this soft-eyed dusky compatriot of ours, and occasionally we have examples of how, in spite of everything we can do, he breaks the cordon

of police supervision and is smuggled away for a time. But that kind of story is usually told in the Police Court, the significance of which will be understood.

These are the facts the people of South Shields should know, having regard to the nonsense that is being written and talked about of our Arab invasion. At the same time, I hold no brief for the Arab as a desirable citizen of this town.[28]

The Council's decision to deny Ali Hamid a licence met with an angry response from a number of Arab boarding-house keepers, including Hassan Mohamed, the local secretary of the Western Islamic Association, and Ali Said. On this issue, at least, the two men appear to have been in agreement. In a letter to the editor of the local newspaper, Hassan Mohamed protested against the statements made by Councillors Cheesman and Linney and made the point that although the Arabs had restricted themselves to the 'slums' their houses were clean and properly conducted and subject to strict police supervision. He wrote:

According to Councillors Cheesman and Linney the Arabs in South Shields appear to be the most undesirable people in the world. Yet we owe allegiance to the British Government and claim its protection. In the Great War Arab seamen from the port of South Shields lost their lives in hundreds. I also understand that the Christian religion teaches one man to love another as his brother, and surely if he does not, he cannot love his God.

We have tried to live together in South Shields without annoying others and have restricted ourselves to the 'slums'. We invite any Councillor to inspect our houses (which are also subject to strict police supervision) and see for himself if they are not clean and properly conducted.

If Arabs come to the town, is it not better for them to stay with their own countrymen? Licensed boarding houses do not increase the number of Arabs any more than the building of an hotel would bring more visitors to the town.

Arab seamen have to be 'permitted' to land in this country and when they arrive have also to be registered as 'coloured seamen'. This means considerable restriction of numbers.

We pay our rents and rates and no Arab has a pauper's funeral. A Britisher is welcomed and honoured in our country, and we may be more loyal to the Crown than many who seem to despise us. Surely because the sun has baked us brown we

are not to be disowned. The British nation boasts of Freedom
and Justice to all. We only ask for this, and it is only the
narrow-minded or selfish people who refuse it.[29]

The day before Ali Said had written:

The Arab community in South Shields is not a menace and the
remarks made by Councillor J. Cheesman seem to me purely a
racial prejudice. We are loyal British subjects as seamen of the
Merchant Shipping. Licences to Arab boarding house keepers
are essential as it is only Arabs who can manage Arab seamen.
English people will not give them room because of their religion
and customs. Mr Cheesman does not seem to see this, neither
does he see the position of the Arab in England as a seaman.
He does not show any legal reasons why the Arab seaman is a
menace to the public. We pay rates and taxes and spend money
in England. His criticism is not a worthy public sentiment. It
is the duty of a councillor to promote peace and not antagonism.
No unprejudiced Englishman can agree with his remarks. The
Government does not accept it.

So we ask Englishmen to give British justice to British
subjects, immaterial of colour. I trust Englishmen will offer us
sympathy as brotherhood is claimed much in England.[30]

But the matter did not end there. Ali Hamid made a new application
requesting that the licence for his boarding-house at 2 East Holborn
be transferred to the new premises at 67 Coronation Street. The new
application was approved by the Watch Committee and came before
the Town Council at their meeting on 1 May 1929. The mayor,
Alderman Dunlop, supported the recommendation but Councillor
Smith objected, arguing that the time had come when they should
severely limit the number of Arabs entering the town. He refered
to a statement by the medical officer that thirty-three per cent of
the Arabs were tubercular and argued that it was bad for the
community as a whole. He pointed out that if it was good enough
for Englishmen, Irishmen and Scotsmen to be subjected to rigorous
medical tests before they were allowed to enter the Colonies, he
thought that it was only fair that the coloured man should have to
submit to a similar test. Councillor Cheesman returned to the attack,
stating:

It is not safe for a woman to walk down Holborn. It is hardly
safe for a white man to walk down Holborn there is that much

freedom (Nonsense). It appears on the surface that there is very little we can do to stop them, and the fault lies with this Council owing to its laxity. Are you willing there should be additional accommodation so that more and more of these people shall come into the town? You have got to consider that Blyth and Sunderland and Newcastle and all the ports in the United Kingdom—excepting the few that hold the registers—have never allowed these people to come into their towns? But they know by the action of this Council that South Shields welcomes them with open arms.[31]

But in this debate some support was expressed for the Arabs. Alderman Lawson supported the original recommendation and argued that if the application was rejected they would be doing a serious injustice. The Council now had an opportunity of doing a simple act of Christian charity to these people. Councillor Cheesman's comments were nothing more than the product of a mind prejudiced against Arabs. If all the crimes attributed to the Arabs by Councillor Cheesman were true then it was only fair to assume that the sequel would be found in the police courts. But this was not the case and from his experience as a magistrate he could say that in proportion to their number the Arabs were not in the court as often as Englishmen. He thought a good deal could be said on behalf of the Arab in the matter of international sentiment: 'If you take another man's country from him and adopt that man as your own, you can not very well refuse him access to your country.'[32]

When the matter was put to the vote, Councillor Smith's amendment was rejected by twenty-five votes to sixteen. Councillor Cheesman then moved that the licence be granted only on condition that no Arab or coloured seamen were taken as boarders. This was seconded by Councillor Donnelly who expressed concern about the trade union aspect of the Arab question. He had been informed by officials of the Shipping Federation that a surplus of fifty Arabs would be sufficient to man all the ships at the present time but they had far more than fifty Arabs and there were British firemen walking the streets who ought to be manning ships but were shut out. Councillor Noble opposed the amendment and argued that every individual who came into the town, whatever their nationality, was subject to the laws of the town and of the country and that was all they could ask of any man. With regard to the question of morality, he could quote a case against the white man for every case they could quote against a coloured man. In fact the morals of the European and the Englishman were just as bad as could be found among the coloured people. Indeed he believed that the worst forms of immorality were found in civilized countries. The amendment was rejected and the mayor's resolution agreed to.[33]

Defeat did not deter Councillor Cheesman and his allies who lost no opportunity in council meetings to point to the increasing number of Arabs entering the town, the danger that they presented and the urgent need to impose restrictions on them. At the Town Council's meeting on 5 June 1929 Councillor Cheesman took exception to the granting of a licence by the Watch Committee to Said Hassan for a bus service between South Shields and London. He used this issue as a excuse to suggest that all the committees of the corporation should combine to deal with the question of Arab and alien population as it seemed to him that there were a great many interests involved in this difficult problem. He could not imagine, for instance, that the value of property would be increased by people of this description living in a particular locality. Restrictions had been imposed on Arabs at other ports with the result that they were being registered in South Shields in increasing numbers. South Shields was rapidly becoming a dumping ground for other places as far as the Arabs were concerned.

In reply, Alderman Lawson stated that the previous speaker had given no specific reason why the licence should not be granted and that all he was doing was to air his prejudices. Councillor Scott disagreed and argued that there were too many Arabs in the borough. He refered to the appalling conditions existing in Holborn and to the fact that these coloured men were marrying white women. He resented the fact that an Arab boarding-house keeper could spend £2,000 on a bus, when some English lodging-house keepers could not even pay their rent. In the end the council agreed to grant the licence.[34]

At a meeting of the Town Council on 8 January 1930, Councillor Smith objected to a decision taken by the Watch Committee to allow the transfer of a lodging-house licence from one Arab to another. After what had happened in recent months as far as the Arabs were concerned, he thought that the least the Watch Committee could do was to take every opportunity to limit these people. He drew attention to the large number of white seamen who were on the unemployed register and condemned the system which existed between the Arab boarding-house keepers and certain ship's engineers for the supply of crews. The Arabs were prepared to pay big prices for lodging-houses in scheduled areas and he believed that about £200 was at stake. Councillor Smith then drew attention to the moral danger and reminded the Council of the medical officer's report three years before which stated that a third of the Arabs were tubercular. He was satisfied in his own mind that of the 450 Arabs in the borough there were 400 too many; '450 too many,' suggested Councillor Purvis. Councillor Watson seconded and supported Councillor Smith's views. He argued that the council should take action to reduce the number of Arab boarding-houses in the town.

Councillor Smith's amendment was also supported by Councillor Lawlan who described the Arabs as 'undesireable aliens'. He stated that there was a movement throughout the country with regard to the Arab question and that the Government was now looking upon it as a serious menace. He thought that South Shields had enough trouble without these people and this was an opportunity to do away with a licence that should never have been renewed. Councillor Scott agreed and argued that in the cause of morality they ought to make a start on reducing the number of Arabs in the town. These Arabs were marrying white women and there was a pretty mix-up down in Holborn if only they knew it. Councillor Scott suggested that the Arabs ought to have been confined to one area and not allowed to spread all over the town but he defied anyone to say that Holborn was worse than any other part of the town. On this occasion no one spoke in support of the proposed transfer and the amendment was carried with twenty-eight votes for and none against.[35] The debate was fully reported in the *Shields Daily Gazette* and provoked an angry letter to the editor from 'Disgusted' who wrote that more than enough had been said about the Arab problem. Holborn had always been an alien area and was not a so-called heaven before the Arabs came.[36]

On 3 April 1930 the *Shields Daily Gazette* carried the headline, 'Tuberculosis scourge in Shields. Heavy deathrate among Arab seamen. Fighting the disease—Town's black spots'. The article which followed reported on the meeting of the Town Council the night before at which Alderman Druery, the Chairman of the Health Committee, reported that tuberculosis was greater in the slum districts of the town than in other parts and that the death rate in Holborn Ward was unduly heavy due to the excessive mortality among Arab seamen. He proceeded to state that the incidence of tuberculosis in the borough was higher than average for the country and on four occasions the deathrate from the disease had been the highest in England and Wales. He continued:

> In our own borough the excess is principally confined to wards where housing conditions are unsatisfactory, chiefly in the older

parts of the town. Shields and Holborn Wards stand out pre-eminently as the wards with the largest amount of slum property, and the death rate in Holborn is unduly heavy, owing to the excessive rate of mortality among Arab seamen resident in that quarter. There have been 154 deaths in 14 years; but even if these deaths were deducted, the rate is still high in that ward.

Shields and Hilda Wards have also been affected by the Arab residents, but to a much less extent. Tyne Dock and Laygate have many dwellings of poor quality, but there are several wards in the town which compare most favourably with other districts. This information regarding the death rate among Arabs, I ought to say, has not been submitted in any partisan spirit, but simply as a contribution towards assessing the factors causing the excess in the local death rate from the disease.[37]

The association of Arabs, overcrowding, slums, disease and death was too good an opportunity for the ever vigilant Councillor Cheesman to miss and he immediately called attention to one aspect of Alderman Druery's remarks, 'the menacing factor of the Arabs'. He asked for permission to move the following addendum to the paragraph referring to unhealthy areas:

That we view with alarm the abnormal percentage of deaths among Arabs and other coloured subjects in the borough, from tubercular disease and urge upon the Minister of Health the necessity for immediate legislation to fix and restrict them to areas to reside in.[38]

The mayor stated that he could not accept the addendum or an amendment along these lines whereupon Councillor Cheesman withdrew his amendment but said that he would give notice of a motion on the subject for the next meeting.[39]

IV Slum clearance and proposals to segregate the Arabs

An opportunity to segregate the Arab community from the rest of the townspeople arose in early 1935 following the announcement of a major slum clearance scheme affecting large parts of Holborn. The Arab boarding-houses and most of the houses occupied by Arabs and their families were threatened with demolition under the proposed scheme. On 28 January 1935 the *Shields Gazette* reported that most members of the Housing Committee favoured rehousing the Arabs in a four or five storey block of tenement flats in the Commercial Road area. The report stated that unless the council provided the Arabs with specific accommodation when their houses were pulled down there was a danger of them penetrating into 'good class residential areas in South Shields'; this had already occured in a number of isolated cases. Members of the council were opposed to allowing them to migrate along with displaced white slum dwellers to the new housing estate at West Harton or to the projected housing estate in Prince Edward Road. Public opinion was inclined to the belief that they should be kept together. The week before, a deputation from the Housing Committee had visited Liverpool to inspect tenement blocks built by the City Council in centrally situated areas and on his return Alderman Dunlop, chairman of the Housing Committee, told the *Shields Gazette* that his deputation had been highly impressed by what they had seen. Although he would not recommend building flats for the 'rank and file' of displaced slum dwellers, Alderman Dunlop was of the opinion that they provided 'an excellent solution of our difficulties with regard to the Arabs'.[40]

Earlier that month in an interview with the *Shields Gazette* Alderman Dunlop had stated that: 'The position in South Shields is that we are not going to have any more flats here if we can avoid it, outside those which may possibly be put up to re-house the coloured population.'[41] The proposal was not without its problems and the committee was particularly concerned about the high cost of the flats (estimated to be £31,600) and the absence of legislation that would enable the council to compel the Arabs to live in the flats once they were built.[42]

The scheme for the tenement flats was greeted with alarm among the Arab community. The *Shields Gazette* reported:

> Alarm and resentment have been aroused among the Arab colony in Holborn by the announcement that the Housing Committee of South Shields Town Council are considering a scheme for the erection of a five-storied block of tenement flats to house them when their present dwellings are razed to the ground under the slum clearance drive. The Council's aim is to segregate, if possible, the coloured inhabitants, numbering about 400, and prevent them from penetrating into residential areas or migrating along with the displaced white slum dwellers to West Harton. Storm clouds are gathering in Holborn. Over cups of coffee in dingy, drably-furnished cafes Arab tongues

wagged furiously as news of the Council's proposal to rehouse them in one big block of tenement flats percolated through the coloured colony. It is feared that unless extreme tact and diplomacy are employed by the authorities in handling this delicate matter, the hugh concrete edifice, if and when, it is erected, will not only be a Tower of Babel but a place of hate[143]

In interviews with the local press, prominent Arab residents voiced their concerns about the council's re-housing plans. Fears were expressed that the boarding-house keepers, cafe proprietors and shopkeepers would lose their businesses and would find it difficult to get back the money owed to them by their former lodgers. Would they be compensated for the loss of their businesses and how would Arab seamen survive without the Arab boarding-houses? They anticipated trouble if Arabs from different tribes were housed together in the same block and pointed out that Arabs who were married would be unwilling to live in the same building as single men. They were adamant that the council could not compel them to live in the proposed flats but they were also opposed to moving out to West Harton because most of the Arabs were seafarers and they would be too far away from the River Tyne and the Shipping Office. Salem Abuzed, a boarding-house master of 25 East Holborn, told a reporter from the *Shields Gazette*:

> There are more than 50 different tribes among the Shields Arabs, with customs and ways of their own. If they put us all together there is bound to be trouble. No other Council complains about us as much as they do in South Shields . . . In Cardiff the Arabs are allowed to live where they like. Why should we be put in what is nothing more or less than a camp? We are not soldiers. During the war I was in Ruhleben prison camp in Germany. I know what a camp is like. England is a free country and they cannot do things like this to us. If the Council carry out this plan of putting us all together we shall leave the town. A much better scheme would be for them to build 3 or 4 different blocks of flats so that the Arabs and other coloured peoples could split up as it was thought best. In any case it will be a disaster for me personally. Altogether my countrymen owe me something like £2,000 which I have spent on food and clothes when they were without ships. When they get back to sea again they always pay me back, but if I am no longer a boarding house master it will be very different.[44]

Abdul Ali of East Holborn declared that:

> It is not humanity to put us on one side as if we were lions or tigers or horses. Perhaps the Council think they can charge people a shilling at the gate for coming to look at us. Then again we do not want to go out to West Harton with the white people. It is too far out for one thing and we must live somewhere near the shipping office. The Council cannot compel us to go and live in these flats they are talking about. So long as we pay our rents and rates we can live where we like.[45]

Said Mabrouk of 2 Laygate argued that:

> If Arabs and Somalis are put together there will be serious trouble. In my own case I have bought a boarding house some years ago. Are the Council going to compensate me for the loss of it and the loss of my business?[46]

Abdu Osman of 59 East Holborn stated:

> This plan is causing much fear and anger among my people. For one thing some of them are married and very naturally they do not want single men in the same building. Out in Aden we have respect for the white people, but here they have no respect for us. I do not know how many of the Arabs can live if their shops and businesses are taken away from them and there are no longer boarding house masters to look after them and keep them when ships are difficult to get. They certainly could not pay rent to the Council.[47]

When the Housing Committee's proposal came before the Town Council at their meeting on 6 February 1935, it met with a great deal of criticism. It transpired that the matter had come to the Housing Committee at the end of its meeting when few members were present and had been decided on the casting vote of the chairman. Alderman Curbison moved that the matter should be referred back to the Housing Committee and that plans for a different kind of dwelling should be prepared. He was shocked to find that Alderman Dunlop, who was on record for expressing his opposition to the building of flats in South Shields, should now be promoting such a scheme. He pointed out that each flat would cost

£480 and that the coloured people were going to be forced to live in them. He continued:

> I do not know what Alderman Dunlop will do when he goes to an international Socialist conference and some of these coloured brethren come and ask him why he seeks to force their countrymen into this class of house. I do not know how he will answer. I could not answer, if I voted for this resolution as an international Socialist.
>
> ... I quite agree we are entitled to house these people, but my point is this: be a man black, brown or red, he is a human being, and I cannot as a Socialist, believe in the fact of the human brotherhood and say that my fellow men, if they are coloured, have to have something different from what I have.
>
> If you build these flats there is no law by which you can compel these people to go into them, and then what happens will be that if you cannot force them in, then you will want to force the working classes of South Shields into them. Surely we are not going to spend £32,000 by building blocks of flats with all the amenities five storeys high, and then find we cannot get tenants for them?[48]

Alderman Curbison concluded that in his opinion the Holborn area was capable of accommodating the people presently living in the area after it had been cleared and that they should rebuild and re-house the people in the same area and not proceed with the construction of colossal flats. Councillor Laybourn seconded Alderman Curbison's recommendation and Alderman Richardson asked whether the Arabs could be compelled by law to go into the houses if they had the means to pay for the house they occupied. The mayor replied that the council could not compel anyone to live in a house, but had to give them the option of a house. Councillor Smith advised the council not to send the matter back to committee:

> Our problem is to deal with the white population first, but the Arab population has given the committee a great deal of trouble ... If the committee had wanted to be slack they could have taken no notice of the problem and when houses were ready transferred the Arabs to West Harton and other sites, and mingled them up with our own people. That could have been and would have been permitted under the Act.[49]

He assured members that this matter had been carefully considered and that every possibility had been explored. There were simply not enough sites in Holborn on which to build houses. They would build houses if they could get the land but every site was already taken for rehousing the white population and there was still a shortfall. When the matter was eventually put to the vote, the amendment referring the question back to committee was carried by twenty-five votes for and seventeen against.[50]

When the Housing Committee met on 19 February, Alderman Curbison led the opposition to the proposed flats. He advocated the building of separate dwellings on the cleared riverside sites in Holborn and contended that there was sufficent land for both housing and industrial development there. But his concern was not for the Arabs:

> The coloured population say they will not live in them [the flats]. I am not worried about that, but what I am worried about is that I believe this is the beginning not so much to house the coloured population in this monstrosity, in which human nature was never intended to live, but it is an attempt to force our white people ultimately into them.[51]

Despite these fears, the committee decided by one vote to recommend again to council that the Arab families should be re-housed in a block of flats.

Strong opposition to the proposal continued to be voiced at the meeting of the council on 12 March 1935 at which a large scale model of the proposed flats was placed on the Council Chamber table. Alderman Curbison again moved an amendment that the council reject the proposal and that the Housing Committee seek to acquire sites in the Holborn area on which to build the ordinary type of working-class houses. Councillor Gompertz, who supported the amendment, stated that the Arabs should be treated like human beings. In his opinion the proposed block of flats was the worst type of dwelling for Arabs, knowing how susceptible they were to quarrelling. He would not like to be an Arab on the top floor against whom an Arab on the bottom floor had a grievance. Councillor Lawlan asked whether white people would be expected to fill those parts of the block that were not filled by coloured people. Councillor Laybourn argued that to build the proposed block of flats would be a retrograde step. If the council wanted to keep the Arabs together, they should provide suitable housing for them in which they would agree to live and not a veritable 'Tower of Babel' and a 'storehouse of inflammable material likely to burst into flames at any moment.' Councillor Brown stated that he did not believe that the Housing Committee were particularly enamoured of the scheme but that they were up against a deadlock. The committee did not have the land on which to build the houses they wished, time was running out when the dispossessed people would have to be re-housed and they were anxious to keep the Arabs in one area. This scheme was the best they could do. Alderman Dunlop, Chairman of the Housing Committee emphasized the serious nature of the problem facing them. They were 'up against the wall' because they could not get the land on which to build houses, and he added:

> We have a coloured problem to meet and I have sworn that as long as I had anything to do with housing, the coloured people would have to be in a colony by themselves, and not mixed up among the white people, and I am going to try to keep my promise to the people of South Shields.[52]

He pointed out that the block of flats would be divided into three distinct portions which would be useful if experience proved that trouble arose through differences of caste. However he did not think that there would be trouble because the people would be only too pleased to get out of the hovels they were living in at present. If for some reason the coloured people would not go into the flats, they would be let to white people. Alderman Curbison's amendment was defeated seventeen votes against and eleven votes for.

Councillor Lawlan then moved that the matter be sent back to committee for further consideration and asked:

> Do you think for a moment that these coloured people, accustomed to living in boarding houses, would take these flats? Who would take the upper stories, and who is going to carry things up five flights of stairs? Do you understand the condition the stairs would be in? It is altogether wrong.[53]

Alderman Curbison supported the amendment. He maintained that the question of housing the coloured population in the Holborn area had not occupied the Housing Committee for two hours during the last three years and claimed that the proposal was an insidious attempt to house the white working class of South Shields in this type of dwelling. Councillor Bainbridge, speaking against the amendment, explained that the flats were not intended for the Arabs living in boarding-houses but for those occupying ordinary dwellings. He referred to the borough engineer's report which stated that adequate sites for building houses were not available in the Holborn area. Consequently the committee was 'between the devil and the deep blue sea'. The amendment was defeated, eleven votes for and nineteen against.

In a final attempt to stop the proposal, Councillor Gompertz moved a further amendment that the matter be sent back to committee and that no further plans for blocks of flats should be submitted. He pointed out that tuberculosis was a serious menace to South Shields and the coloured population was particularly susceptible to this disease. Yet it was proposed to house the people most susceptible to tuberculosis in a building of a type condemned by all the foremost authorities as providing conditions under which this disease was bred. He called on the council to oppose it and thought the Housing Committee would be well advised to consider the matter again. Councillor Lawlan seconded the motion, stating that the coloured people were up in arms against the proposition and that it would be a very difficult thing to force people against their will. In spite of these arguments, Councillor Gompertz's amendment was defeated with twelve votes for and fifteen votes against and the Housing Committee's proposal was accepted by the council.[54]

It is significant that throughout the debate about the proposal to re-house Arab families in a block of flats, little or no consideration was given to the views of the Arabs themselves. The Housing Committee was determined to segregate the coloured population and prevent them moving into white residential areas, while those opposed to the proposed block of flats were hostile to the scheme mainly because they feared that this type of dwelling would be inflicted on the white working class. There appears to have been no debate about the relocation of the Arab boarding-houses due to be demolished under the Holborn slum clearance programme, even though they housed about half the Arab community.

In an interview with the *Shields Gazette* on 18 March 1935 John Reid, the borough engineer of South Shields, stated that in the council debates a fact which was not sufficiently emphasized was that only Arab families would be housed in the new block of flats and no single Arabs would be expected to live in it. He stated that there were seventy-one coloured men living with their families and 196 Arabs living as lodgers in the boarding-houses. The 196 men living in lodgings posed 'a quite distinct and separate problem'.[55] If we accept that there were around 400 Arabs in the town at this time, then these figures ignore the fact that there must have been over a hundred Arab seamen, probably single men, living in unfurnished rooms as sub-tenants. No consideration was given to their plight.

But the matter did not end there. At a meeting of the Town Council on 10 April 1935 Councillor Harris moved that the resolution passed by the council at its meeting on 12 March approving the plans for the block of flats in Commercial Road be rescinded and that the Housing and Town Planning Committee be instructed to submit plans for the erection of self-contained houses on one of the sites subject to slum clearance. He criticized the proposed flats on the grounds that they would bring coloured aliens of various races and religious sects into close proximity and that there would be danger in case of fire. Councillor Ewart seconded the motion and stated that if the Arabs wanted to quarrel it was a job for the police and not for the council. Alderman Curbison also supported the motion and said that he had been told authoritatively that Arabs were procuring houses in another part of town. Councillor Lawlan compared the problem in South Shields with that in Hull and said South Shields should see that they did not get too many of these people. When the vote was taken the council was equally divided[56] and as a result three alternative schemes were submitted to the Housing Committee by the borough engineer on 21 May 1935. These were for two blocks of three-storey flats, sixteen blocks of two-storey flats and eight blocks of two-storey houses. The committee approved the scheme for eight blocks of two-storey houses which would provide fifty-five self-contained dwellings in the Commercial Road area. Although the other schemes provided more dwellings, the overall cost of the self-contained houses was lower. This scheme was approved without discussion at the council meeting held on 13 June 1935[57] and with that decision the debate about re-housing the Arabs in a block of flats finally came to an end.

But fears about Arabs moving out of Holborn into white residential areas continued. In an article entitled 'Coloured men moving uptown' published in Sepember 1935, the *Shields Gazette* reported that as the demolition of individual houses proceeded in Holborn, Arabs were moving into houses in Winchester Street and Saville Street off Ocean Road and quite recently they had reached Cuthbert Street and Maxwell Street off Laygate Lane. Clearly, demolition of houses occupied by Arabs in Holborn had started even before preliminary work had begun on the re-housing scheme in Commercial Road, leaving those Arabs displaced to find their own accommodation.

The article also pointed to the plight of those Arabs who

owned businesses in Holborn, such as boarding-houses, cafes and general stores, who all risked losing their livelihood as a result of the demolition scheme. For example only three shops had been included in the proposed block of flats and none were scheduled in the scheme for self-contained houses. The Arab boarding-houses, it was reported, were not going to be demolished until last, 'in an effort to minimize the tendency of the coloured population to spread.'[58] Concern over the re-housing of the Arabs was voiced again in May 1936 when the Town Council discussed delays in construction on the site of the Cornwallis Square Clearance Area. Councillor Laybourn pointed out that the object of the Cornwallis Square scheme—now reduced from fifty-five to forty houses—was originally to re-house the Arab population. The Arabs were speading all over the town and he was concerned that if the houses were not constructed soon the Arabs would find living accommodation 'in places where their presence was not desirable.'[59]

In March 1937 Dr Lyons, the Medical Officer of Health for South Shields, in a special report on clearance and re-housing schemes prepared for the Housing Committee, urged the Town Council that the housing of coloured men and their families should be given further consideration. He emphasized that the Arabs occupied the worst houses and as slum clearance in Holborn continued they were displaced into other unsatisfactory parts of the town. Unwelcomed by their new neighbours, there was further depreciation of poor premises. He put forward the suggestion that part of the new Commercial Road estates might be set aside for the use of the coloured community.[60] This suggestion was followed up by a deputation representing the women of the Arab community who met the mayor on 31 March 1937 to press their claim that part of the new housing estate in Commercial Road be set aside for the exclusive use of the Arabs. Commenting on the meeting, the mayor, Councillor Smith, stated that he had been impressed with the arguments put forward by the deputation and was in sympathy with most of them. He had agreed to put their views before the Council. He reported that the Arabs definitely wished to be housed in one locality, particularly in the interests of their children who, the women claimed, were avoided by other children because of their colour. They also wanted to live close to the site near Holy Trinity Church where they proposed to build their mosque. As British subjects, the Arabs claimed the right to the same type of housing as that provided for white people who were being transferred from the Holborn clearance area.[61] It is interesting to note that in a earlier interview, the mayor had put forward another argument for segregation, that it would allow better control over the Arabs. He told the *Shields Gazette* in March 1937:

> From one point of view it would be an advantage. We have to administer the Aliens Act and if the Arabs were domiciled in one particular part of the town it would be much more simple for the authorities to get in touch with them.[62]

After the meeting, the deputation expressed confidence that they would obtain modern houses in the Commercial Road estate.[63]

In October 1937, when the allocation of housing in the Cornwallis Square and Commercial Road development began, a group of sixteen white residents sent a petition to the Housing Committee insisting that they be allotted new houses along Commercial Road rather than in Cornwallis Square at the rear. Interviewed by a reporter from the local newspaper, one petitioner stated:

> I don't want to get mixed up in any fights with the Arabs, so leave me out of it. So far as I am concerned, you can say that I signed the petition because I think we have more right than anyone else to be given houses on the front. We have lived on the front, many of us nearly all our lives and we shouldn't be put in the square at the back because of someone else.[64]

Another petitioner argued:

> But the trouble is that if the Arabs are allowed to live in Commercial Road with us behind them, we will have to pass them to get to our houses. Why should we have to do that? We were here first and we should have first choice.[65]

In reply to these demands, an Arab spokesman stated that they did not want any trouble and that those people who had lived along Commercial Road for a long time should be allowed to stay there. Councillor Brown, the Chairman of the Housing Committee, stated that the arguments put forward would be considered when the matter was discussed by the committee.[66]

At the next meeting of the Housing Committee on 14 October, it recommended to the Town Council that the white residents should be allocated new houses on the front of Commercial Road and Windmill Hill and that Arab families be grouped together in Cornwallis Square at the rear. An Arab who had lived on Commercial Road for many years told the local newspaper that he did not mind moving into Cornwallis Square so long as other Arab families moved there too. He stated that all along the Arabs had wished to live together. Councillor Brown pointed out that while this recommendation solved the problem of the Commercial Road area, it did not settle the entire Arab housing question in South Shields. If the entire Arab community was settled in one place, as had been suggested, they would need a much bigger estate than Cornwallis Square because, 'there are so many of them and they are so very scattered.'[67]

After some three years of acrimonious debate in the Housing Committee and Town Council over the re-housing of the Arabs, thirty-seven families, about half of the total number of Arab families in the town, were resettled in modern and well-equipped houses in Cornwallis Square constructed in 1937. There was clearly a strong desire by local officials to segregate the Arabs in one area but, it would seem, an unwillingness to spend the money necessary to re-house them all in decent dwellings. Arabs could apply to the Housing Department for council accommodation, but were only permitted to rent within the Cornwallis Square development. In theory, Arabs were free to purchase or rent a house or flat privately in any part of the town but in practice they faced discrimination and prejudice from estate agents and white tenants. Collins refers to a case reported in the local press in June 1940:

> Colour prejudice against coloured tenants is confirmed by Estate Agents who are suggesting that the obvious way out is to segregate the coloured people and set aside a certain area in the town for them to live in. Mr V—— said it was particularly noticeable in tenemented properties where there were common yards, white tenants objected to coloured people living in the same building. If landlords agreed to a coloured tenant occupying the premises, the white tenants objected and would state their intention of leaving.[68]

As the demolition of slum properties in Holborn proceeded, most Arabs moved south of Commercial Road and the Newcastle and South Shields Railway line into the streets of nineteenth-century terraces made up mainly of two-storey 'Tyneside' flats to the east of Laygate Lane where the seamen were still only a short distance away from the Shipping Offices on the Mill Dam. Fears that the Arabs were spreading all over the town were not justified. When Collins visited the Laygate area in the late 1940s, he found the Arab families confined mainly to four streets where they occupied flats of from one to four rooms. White families were also living along these streets. In contrast to the modern houses in Cornwallis Square, these flats were not equipped with bathrooms and the lavatories were located in the backyard. Many of the buildings were in a poor state of repair and were poorly furnished. Most families occupied over-crowded rooms. Some single men also lived in rented rooms, which were locked when the men were at sea and the key left with the landlord.[69] The general stores and cafes and later the Arab boarding-houses were re-established in this area, the boarding-houses often occupying the larger dwellings on Laygate Lane.

The new settlement pattern of the Arab community that emerged after the slum clearance programme in Holborn was determined partly by the policy of the local authorities, partly by the racial prejudice of white residents and partly by the wishes of the Arabs themselves. The Arabs preferred to live together in order to retain the social cohesiveness of their own group rather than be absorbed into the life of the host society. Nevertheless, segregation was never complete. In Laygate, as in Holborn, Arabs and white families lived side-by-side in the same streets.

Eight

Religious Revival and Political Rivalries

I Religious beliefs and observances among Arab seamen

The vast majority of Arab seamen from Yemen belonged to the Shafi'i school of Sunni Islam (see Chapter Two, p.40). At the Arab boarding-houses in South Shields, Arab seamen arriving in the town for the first time were able to observe basic Islamic beliefs and rituals. In some, if not all, the boarding-houses a room was set aside for the five daily prayers (*salas*) observed by Muslims and until the *zawiya* or small mosque was established in the town in the late 1930s, the principal congregational prayer for the week, held at noon on Friday, also took place there. Before the arrival in South Shields of Sheikh Abdullah Ali al-Hakimi, a Sufi of the 'Alawi *tariqa* or religious brotherhood, who quickly established himself as spiritual head of the Muslim communities in South Shields and Cardiff, there was no full-time imam or religious leader. In each of the boarding-houses the duties of imam were carried out by one of the seamen. As most Arab seamen were unable to read or write in Arabic, few were able to read the Qur'an but all could repeat from memory in Arabic the prayers and verses used in their rituals and all had some knowledge of the narratives and stories contained in the Qur'an. In April 1936 a reporter from the *Shields Gazette* visited the prayer room in one of the Arab boarding-houses and the scene he described must have been similar to that found in other boarding-houses in the town:

Five times every day a hundred Arabs living in a model lodging house within a stones throw of South Shields ferry landing don red and white checked cotton drawers and with bared feet, turn their faces towards the East. Outside 'windy hammers' in the neighbouring shipyard hiss and roar and on the TIC pontoon the warning bell tinkles the quarter hours away. Inside the gaunt brick building there is perfumed silence broken only by the high, wailing chant of the imam exhorting his dusky countrymen to remember that God is great and that prayer is better than sleep. Next week, if he is lucky, the imam may be sweating in the stokehold of a Newcastle steamer, shovelling coal into hungry furnaces for £8.15s. a month. But the Star and Crescent will still reign in Spring Lane, only another imam will be leading the prayers.

Through the courtesy of Abdul Mussem, proprietor of the largest boarding house in South Shields, I was permitted a glimpse the other day of the mesjid or prayer room of his establishment. With their legs tucked beneath them they squatted barefoot, their faces about a yard from the wall. The air in the room was heavy with frankincense. As I stood there an Arab throatily shrilled a final chant of praise, crept to the door and slithering his feet into a pair of leather slippers at the threshold, padded off in the direction of the kitchen. 'Now you have seen' said Abdul Mussem, closing the door quietly behind us. 'But please remember, no photographs'.[1]

Special facilities were provided at the Arab boarding-houses for prayers during the month of Ramadan, held sacred by Muslims as a month of fasting and prayer,[2] and it was there that the major annual religious festivals were celebrated, the *'Id al-Fitr* (The Feast of Breaking of the Fast) marking the end of Ramadan, and the *'Id al-Adha*, (The Feast of Sacrifice) marking the end of the pilgrimage and known locally in South Shields as the 'Muslim Christmas'.

Until 1928 a few Arab boarding-house masters had been granted permission by the South Shields Corporation to slaughter a sheep in accordance with Muslim rites in the backyards of their houses each year for the celebration of the *'Id al-Adha*. But when it was discovered that other Arabs were doing the same thing without permission, the local authorities banned the practice for everyone. For example, in March 1935, when Abdu Osman, a general dealer of 59 East Holborn, who was licensed by the council to kill animals at the municipal abattoirs for consumption by the Arab population, applied for permission to kill a sheep on his own premises for the *'Id al-Adha*, the request was refused. Mr W.A.C. Hill, the

208

corporation food inspector, told the local newspaper that the manner in which the animals were being killed in the backyards of houses constituted a menace to public health. Abdu Osman expressed the view that while the Muslim com munity was content to abide by the law on this matter in the ordinary way, they thought that an exception could have been made in the case of this particular festival.[3] In 1936 it was reported that because of the continuing depression in the shipping industry, few Arabs in the community could afford to spend upwards of £3 on a single sheep to celebrate the '*Id al-Fitr*.[4]

Sydney Collins, the anthropologist who carried out research on the Muslim community in South Shields in the late 1940s, concluded that the giving of alms, fasting and the daily and seasonal rituals were the most assiduously observed features of religious life among the Arabs.[5] We know that some of the Arab seamen also undertook the pilgrimage to Mecca or *hajj*. For example it was reported that in 1930 several Arabs from South Shields went by means of Cooks Tours as far as Jeddah in Saudi Arabia and from there to Mecca with other pilgrims.[6] But until the arrival of Sheikh Abdullah Ali al-Hakimi, religious observances appear to have remained a private affair restricted to the boarding-houses and private homes. There is no evidence of the colourful processions through the streets of the town on the occasion of the major religious festivals until the late 1930s. For many years the burial ceremonies for Arab seamen who died in the town were one of the few public manifestations of the Islamic faith in South Shields.[7] Taking part in the procession to the cemetery and in the service held at the grave are duties which one Muslim owes to another. One of the earliest accounts of a Muslim funeral in the town is from January 1916. The *Shields Daily Gazette* carried the following description of the event:

A burial carried out with Mahommedan rites is a unique spectacle locally and accordingly the funeral of Farah Abdoo, an Arab fireman, which took place at Harton Cemetery yesterday, attracted a considerable amount of public attention and was largely attended. The deceased died at Harton Hospital on Tuesday. After being washed seven times in accordance with the observances of the Mahommedan religion, the body was dressed in the deceased's ordinary clothes, sprinkled with perfume, and then wrapped in new linen and enclosed in a handsome oak coffin with brass mountings. Later the remains were removed to the residence of Ali Nasser of 29 East Holborn, where the body was prayed over night and day by a number of the deceased man's friends up to the time of the interment. The funeral was a very large one. There was a beame and a score of carriages. A singular feature of the proceedings was that while passing through the streets of the town, the mourners did not ride but marched in procession in front of the hearse, with the High Priest at their head. On reaching the outskirts, however, they entered the coaches and rode the remainder of the journey to the cemetery. The High Priest from Aden who happened to be visiting the district, was present and conducted the service. On the arrival at the cemetery the body was taken straight to the grave, where the High Priest read prayers from the Koran. The mourners themselves filled the grave. The cost of the funeral was equally borne by members of the Arab colony in South Shields.[8]

The 'High Priest' refered to in the newspaper article was presumably either a religious scholar, a member of the *'ulama* (the body of religious scholars) of Aden, or a Sufi sheikh. There is no information about the purpose of his visit to South Shields during the First World War, but we know that he stayed with each of the three Arab boarding-house keepers, Ali Said, Muhammad Muckble and Abdul Rahman Zaid, probably to avoid causing any friction between them.[9]

Other reports suggest that a funeral ceremony was very much a community affair when tribal and ethnic differences were put aside and the occasion used to strengthen the bonds between all sections of the Muslim community in the town. This point is illustrated in one of the most detailed descriptions of a Muslim funeral ceremony reported in the *Shields Gazette*, which took place in February 1935:

Squatting round a yawning grave in Harton Cemetery yesterday afternoon, two hundred of the Faithful offered up prayers to Allah. They were the Arab mourners at the funeral of Ahmed Saleh, the South Shields donkeyman who died dramatically in Durham Gaol on Sunday while awaiting trial on a double murder charge, sequel to a stabbing affray on a ship at Blyth.

Turning their cloth caps round so that the peeks pointed to the rear, they crouched on all sides of the open grave, and with palms uplifted in front of them, chanted and prayed for more than a quarter of an hour.

Wearing a green and white velvet muffler, the Imam led the service, and in a high-pitched voice of peculiar sweetness and melancholy intoned the age-old prayer of the Moslem, 'La illaha

i'la Ihahu ... wa Muhhumadun rasullu Ihahu—God is great
. . . there is no other God but God, and Mohammed is His
prophet.'

Like the murmuring of bees, the great concourse of coloured
men droned the words after him, examining earnestly the palms
of their hands, occasionally tapping their foreheads. Towards
the end of the service the mourners scooped great handfuls of
clay and soil onto the coffin below and almost completed the
task of burial. 'Ahmed Saleh' the name of the dead man
constantly recurred during the chanting.

Five motor cars containing the principal mourners headed
the cortege to the cemetery and more than 150 other Arabs
walked behind. Shemeri, Malaiki and Shari—the three great
sects among which the Shields Arabs are principally divided
—sank their tribal jealousies and attended the funeral in force.

Darker skinned Somalis and one or two Indians were also
included among the crowd by the graveside. An unusual feature
of the ceremony was the large number of white women present.

Saleh's body was brought back to South Shields from Durham on Tuesday immediately the inquest was over. It was lifted
from the plain oak coffin in which it had been conveyed and
taken into a Thrift Street boarding house where the dead man's
brother lodged. There it was washed by fellow countrymen and
purified in accordance with the Mohammedan faith, scented
and wrapped round in plain white calico.

Practically every detail connected with the funeral was carried
out by the Arabs themselves with painstaking care and attention.
Eight of them carried the coffin on their shoulders from the
hearse to the graveside. The others surged gently round it, not
pushing or shoving, but purposefully darting in and out of the
little knot in an effort to allow as many as possible to touch the
unpolished oak in which their compatriot's remains were being
borne.

Many of them had gay-coloured scarves of orange and blue
round their necks contrasting strangely with the silk-hatted,
black frock-coated habit of the undertaker, Mr A.W. Wilson
of Derby Street, who takes charge of the majority of Arab
burials.[10]

The article also indicates that women did not usually attend such
ceremonies in large numbers. Collins also found that in the late
1940s few women were present at such ceremonies and that if they
did attend they travelled in a separate carriage to the cemetery, stood

away from the grave outside the group of men and took no active part in the rituals. Collins adds that after the ceremony the men made a circle clasping hands with male relatives of the deceased before returning to the *zawiya* where the mourners performed some further ritual prayers.[11]

Other religious rituals regulating the individual Muslim's life cycle were of course circumcision and marriage. According to Collins, a male child of an Arab father was circumcised in a hospital three weeks after birth. The men told Collins that they preferred the ceremony to be performed on the eighth day as in their home villages but the English mothers would not allow this to be carried out at such an early age. After the child had been circumcised a Dedication Ceremony was held either at the *zawiya* or at home.[12]

Marriages according to Muslim law do not appear to have been carried out until the arrival of Sheikh Abdullah Ali al-Hakimi in the late 1930s (see below, p.228). Until that time some Arabs presumably married in the local register office, and there is evidence that marriages between Arabs and local women were also performed at both the local Anglican and Roman Catholic churches. Many Arabs and their partners, however, appear to have preferred common-law marriages. Indeed concern that Arabs living in European countries were unable to marry according to Muslim law and were forsaking their religious obligations may have been one of the factors which led the 'Alawi *tariqa* to extend its missionary activites from North Africa to Europe. We know that both Sheikh Abdullah and his deputy in South Shields and Cardiff, Sheikh Hasan Ismail, possessed a diploma or licence from the leadership of the *tariqa* authorizing them to conduct marriages according to Shari'a (Islamic religious) law. An English translation of the original Arabic text of the diploma or licence granted to Sheikh Hasan Ismail by the Committee of the *Nahdat al-Sufiya al-'Alawiya* in Egypt in 1941 has survived and reads as follows:

> In the name of God the Merciful, the Beneficent, and the blessings of God upon our Master Muhammad and his Family and Companions and Peace.
>
> Peace be to God who brought together Adam and Eve in the beginning, and created her from him, and from the two brought forth many men and women. And blessings and peace upon the best of his creations (i.e. Muhammad) to whom revelation was made. 'And verily we have sent prophets before you and have made for them wives and descendants.' (And blessings be) upon his family and his comrades who came after him. 'Do not marry

or otherwise behave outside the limits laid down by Shar'i law and that which it permits.'

To continue, since there are many Muslims scattered throughout the countries of Europe, who desire to marry; and since there is not found among them anyone who assumes for them the duty of joining them in marriage according to the Holy Book, the Committee of the Nahdat as-Sufiya has seen fit, for the benefit of the children of the Tarikat al-'Alawiya, that a member of the blessed 'Alawiya community should be permitted to perform the marriage ceremony for them, and to admonish them and those who belong to them in the matters of their Moslem religion, one who is competent for this purpose. And their choice has fallen upon the Saiyid Shaikh Hasan Ismail ash-Shamiri, on whom the blessing is bestowed, since he is a man suitable for this, and knows the duties of marriage and what is incumbent upon the married couple in religious and worldly matters.

The 'Ulema, whose signatures are attached to this diploma recommend him with the corroboration of God in secret and in public.

And let him not proceed to anything until he knows the command of God and His Prophet regarding it; as God Almighty said 'That which the Prophet gives you, take it; and that which he forbids abstain from it.'

Written on the 11th of Jumadi al-Ula A.H. 1360-the 6th of June, 1941.

Signed:

Hussain ibn Ahmed al-Buzidi, one of the 'Ulema of al-Azhar, Imam and Khatib and Mudarris.

Jadhil al-Wartalani, one of the 'Ulema of al-Azhar

al-Hiiali Muhammad at-Tahir, one of the 'Ulema of al-Azhar

Khalil 'Abdu' l-Kadir, Mudarris of the Cairo Ma'had in al-Azhar

Seal of the Committee of the Nahdat as-Sufiya al-'Alawiyah in Egypt.[13]

During the 1920s there is evidence that some Christians saw opportunities for Christian missionary work among the Arab colony in South Shields. In August 1926 in a long article in the *Shields Daily Gazette*, one Christian, who had visited the Arab colony in Holborn during a recent stay in the town, emphasized the importance of studying comparative religion and the need to appreciate the historical significance and ethical value of other religions. Unlike

213

the last century when many regarded Islam as an invention of 'the evil one', it was important, he argued, that the value of the great work of the Prophet Muhammad be seen from the historical point of view. He pointed out that the Qur'an encouraged all its readers to study the New Testament and also bore witness to the miraculous birth and sinless character of Jesus Christ. He continued:

> What a glorious opportunity for the Christian missionary to say to his Mohammedan hearers: He of Whom your holy book speaks with such great honour as the 'Word of God' is the same as is mentioned in the opening chapter of St John's Gospel: 'In the beginning was the Word and the Word was with God, and the Word was God . . . And the Word became flesh, and dwelt among us.' And it is about Him, Jesus Christ, that I have come to speak to you today.[14]

He thought that one of the positive results of the First World War was a more favourable attitude in Muslim countries towards Christian missionaries.

> As we think of these encouraging features, we are forced to the conclusion that God is preparing man everywhere for a great advance for the triumph of the Cross over the Crescent. What a cause for thanksgiving. What an opportunity for the Christian Church to set apart special men to preach the Christian faith to Muslims. Such special men obviously require special training and equipment for their great and difficult mission.[15]

He recommended that a cleric with experience of Christian missionary work in the Muslim world and a knowledge of Arabic so that he could read the Qur'an in that language, should be appointed to work as a missionary or chaplain in charge of the Arab colony in South Shields. He should be given a free hand in all his religious and social work among the Arabs. He concluded: 'Here is real missionary work only waiting for the right man to undertake it. No need for him to traverse oceans in a P & O liner to reach his far-flung parish—here it is in South Shields.'[16] His suggestion does not appear to have been taken up by any of the local Christian churches and there is no evidence of any of the Arab seamen converting to Christianity. However, we know that some of the English wives of Arab seamen converted to Islam. For example in a letter to the editor of the *Shields Daily Gazette* in November 1930, Elsie Cassim of 93 Adelaide Street, who ran an Arab boarding-house, wrote proudly, 'I am not coloured, but I have embraced the Islamic religion, the customs of which I admire and respect.'[17] In 1938 there were twenty women converts in the community.

II The Islamic Society and the Western Islamic Association

A number of international Islamic organizations were active in the town during the first half of the twentieth century. The first organization to take an interest in the Arab community was the Islamic Society. The society appears to have emerged from one of the earliest Islamic organizations in Britain, the Pan-Islamic Movement headed by Abdullah Sohrivardi and by 1915 its activities had begun to appear in the journal *Islamic Review and Muslim India*. Several of its members belonged to the British Muslim Society and the Woking Islamic Mission. Its stated object was, 'to promote the religious, moral, social and intellectual advancement of the Muslim world', and its patrons numbered several members of the British Government including Balfour, Chamberlain, Lloyd George and Baron de Rothschild.[18]

After the violent clashes in South Shields between Arabs and White seamen in February 1919, the President of the Islamic Society, Dr Abdul Majid, an Indian barrister with chambers in London, and the society's secretary, Mr S.G. Sathe, visited South Shields. Dr Abdul Majid, as we saw in Chapter Four, p.84, held a watching brief for the Islamic Society at the trial of the twelve Arab seamen charged with rioting. During his visit, Dr Abdul Majid held meetings with the Mayor of South Shields and announced the establishment of a branch of the Islamic Society in the town. This committee included the Arab boarding-house keepers and representatives of seamen from different parts of the Muslim world, Arabs, Indians and Malays. Its primary aim, according to Dr Abdul Majid, was to look after the economic, moral and religious welfare of Muslims in the town, and he stated that he hoped that the branch would receive the patronage of prominent citizens in the town and in this way bring about better understanding between the Arabs and other sections of the community.[19] Dr Abdul Majid continued to take up the cause of Arab seamen in South Shields during the 1920s. For example in 1925 after the Special Restriction (Coloured Alien Seamen) Order was introduced, Dr Abdul Majid wrote to the India Office to complain that the South Shields police were compelling all Arab seamen there to register as aliens. He informed the Under Secretary of State at the India Office that he was satisfied that the

Arabs were British Indian subjects and emphasized that they had been very loyal during the war and were still loyal subjects of His Imperial Majesty. He claimed that as a result of this order loyal British subjects were being deprived of their status. He asked the India Office to intervene on behalf of these men and get the Home Office to modify its order so that the Arabs would not be required to register or that they should be registered as British subjects.[20] It is not clear from the correspondence whether he was acting on behalf of the Islamic Society.

Apart from Dr Abdul Majid's intervention in 1925, there are no traces of the Islamic Society's activities among the Arab seamen after 1919 but ten years later in 1929 another Islamic organization, the Western Islamic Association, began to take an interest in the Arabs of South Shields. In August 1929 it was reported that the Western Islamic Association, which had its headquarters in London, had enthusiastically endorsed a scheme proposed by the Arab residents to build a mosque in South Shields. Plans were being prepared for a mosque designed according to Islamic architectural traditions with centre dome, small domes and minarets and capable of accommodating 300 worshippers to be built on a site near Academy Hill and Payne's Bank in East Holborn. The mosque would not only cater for the spiritual welfare of the Arab community in the town but also serve as a recreational and educational centre. Hassan Mohamed, an influential boarding-house master in South Shields, was named as the leading figure in the movement to build the mosque. The report stated that for some time Hassan Mohamed had organized religious services for the Arabs in a part of his boarding-house in Commercial Road.[21]

The origins of the Western Islamic Association are obscure and its relationship, if any, to the Islamic Society is also unclear. All we know is that in 1930 it was headed by Dr Khalid Sheldrake, who took the title of 'Life President'. Sheldrake was one of a number of British converts to Islam who were associated with the Woking Muslim Mission. Like other British converts to Islam at this time, we can assume that Sheldrake was a member of the upper classes. In 1915 he held the post of Honorary Secretary of the British Muslim Society and contributed a number of articles to the journal *Islamic Review and Muslim India*. The Woking Muslim Mission had been established in late 1913 and from the outset had attracted a strong group of British converts to Islam, notably Lord Headley. Most of these converts were from the middle classes and the aristocracy and many had lived and worked in India or in other Muslim countries.

216

Sheldrake claimed that the Arabs in ports such as South Shields and Cardiff came under the local branches of the Western Islamic Association and early in 1930 he took up the cause of the Arab seamen by strongly criticizing the National Union of Seamen for mounting a general attack on the Arabs at British ports (see Chapter Five, p.117). By March 1930, when Sheldrake visited South Shields, a branch of his association had already been established in the town with Hassan Mohamed as the local secretary. During the visit, Sheldrake repeated his support for the construction of a mosque in the town and for the provision of a separate Muslim cemetery. He was particularly concerned that the children of the community should be brought up in the Muslim faith. Dr Sheldrake told the local press that the Western Islamic Association was a large body with branches and representatives throughout 'the whole of the civilized world' and evidently showed the *Shields Daily Gazette* reporter letters of support from eminent Muslims in all parts of the world including several 'royal personages'. He stressed that his organization was not antagonistic towards Christianity or Judaism but that it merely wished to ensure that there was adequate provision for Muslims in South Shields to practise their faith. It was reported that the local branch of the association had been strengthened as a result of Sheldrake's visit and that a large number of officials and a strong working committee had been appointed.[22]

Like the Islamic Society, the Western Islamic Association declared itself to be non-political and in its support for the Arabs was careful to avoid any criticism of the British Government. In defending the rights of Arab seamen, one of Sheldrake's main arguments was their loyalty to the British Empire and to the British Crown. Like the Islamic Society, it also became active among the Arab seafarers during a period of acute tension and unrest. As we have seen, the Western Islamic Association urged acceptance of the government-backed rota system and its officials sought to counter the activities of those Arabs who chose resistance and solidarity with the radical alternative provided by the communist-led Seamen's Minority Movement. The day before Sheldrake made his first public statement in support of the rota system, he handed over a cheque from the Aga Khan, a patron of the Association, to purchase a site in Commercial Road for a mosque and announced that the Aga Khan had promised a substantial sum for the actual building.[23] A few weeks later it was reported that the Aga Khan would visit South Shields the following year under the auspicies of the Western Islamic Association to lay the foundation stone of the mosque.[24] In fact the mosque was never built and no more was heard of the proposed visit by the Aga Khan. Indeed in 1935, Sheldrake, who was then living in India, is reported to have sold the land in Commercial Road back to the South Shields Corporation without informing the local Arab leadership who knew nothing about the sale. The report states that the project had not progressed because of differences of opinion between the Aga Khan and the Nizam of Hyderabad, the scheme's main backers.[25] It seems likely that the offer of financial assistance for the religious aims of the Arab community was used to help diffuse tension and win acceptance of the government-backed rota system and when this was achieved the project was quietly abandoned.

After 1930 there are no references to the activities of the Western Islamic Association or its local branch in South Shields. Hassan Mohamed, the Association's local secretary, sold his boarding-house in 1932 and left for France where he died in 1938.[26] The branch appears to have survived but to have declined in importance. In November 1936 Yussif Hersi Sulliman, a Somali boarding-house master who had taken over as secretary of the local branch of the Western Islamic Association after the departure of Hassan Mohamed, became secretary of the newly established branch of an organization known as the 'Zaouia Islamia Allawouia Religious Society of the United Kingdom' founded by the 'Alawi Sheikh Abdullah Ali al-Hakimi.[27] The Cardiff branch of the Western Islamic Association still owned three houses and had some money in a local bank in 1942 but the Muslim community had divided largely along ethnic lines.[28] These divisions were avoided in South Shields.

IV Sheikh Abdullah Ali al-Hakimi and the 'Alawi *tariqa*

In contrast to the Islamic Society and the Western Islamic Association, which were London-based organizations led by professionals whose education and social class gave them access to senior levels of government, a Sufi brotherhood, the 'Alawi *tariqa*, became active among the Arab seafarers of South Shields in the late 1930s.[29] It was more firmly rooted in the Arab community and its leaders were drawn from the same tribal background as the seamen and lived among them. The word *tariqa* means '(spiritual) path or way' and in Islam has come to denote an order or brotherhood of those Muslims who follow this path. The initiate, known as *faqir*, passes through various stages of spiritual attainment until he reaches a degree of understanding which entitles him to be called *sufi*. Few reach the higher grade of 'Guide' *murshid* or sheikh.

The 'Alawi *tariqa*, an offshoot of the great Shadhili order, was founded in 1918 by a North African sheikh, Ahmad ibn Mustafa al-'Alawi. Sheikh al-'Alawi lived at the Mediterranean port of Mostaganem in Algeria and it was there that he built his *zawiya*, a mosque used as a regular meeting place of the order. He had studied the outward form and the inner meaning of knowledge under a sheikh of the Shadhili order but on revealing his own saintly powers, his teacher had placed himself under al-'Alawi who then founded a new *tariqa* which became known by his name. By the 1930s Sheikh al-'Alawi had disciples throughout North Africa and his order had extended its missionary activities to Muslims living in France and Holland.[30] He had many disciples among Yemeni seamen and before the Second World War Yemenis belonging to this order were found in Marseilles and in the Channel ports of Rouen and Le Havre.[31] The 'Alawi order was first established in England in 1936 by one of Sheikh al-'Alawi's pupils, Abdullah Ali al-Hakimi, who founded what became known as the 'Zaouia Islamia Allawouia Religious Society of the United Kingdom' with *zawiyas* in Cardiff, South Shields, Hull and Liverpool.

The reasons why the 'Alawi *tariqa* was particularly active among Yemeni seamen in Europe is unclear. This particular order had few adherents in Yemen though many of the seamen would have been brought up under an Islam strongly influenced by Sufism in their home villages and as a result would have been susceptible to the teachings of the 'Alawi *tariqa*. As we have already stated, one of the factors which led the 'Alawi *tariqa* to extend its missionary activities to Muslims in Europe may have been its concern that these men, mainly Arab seafarers, were not marrying according to Muslim law. It is perhaps significant that the leadership of the *tariqa* in England devoted considerable efforts to ensure that the children of Arab seamen and local women were brought up as good Muslims. Abdullah Ali al-Hakimi was himself a Yemeni and Sheikh al-'Alawi may have instructed him to work among his fellow countrymen in Europe. Collins notes that the sheikh was said to have started his work on Tyneside on the authority of the head of the *tariqa* to whom God had revealed his choice.[32]

Sheikh Abdullah's origins are obscure but he was clearly a well-educated man and was the author of two books on religion and Sufism. In addition to his religious calling he was also a merchant[33] with business interests in Aden and was well-connected within the Yemeni merchant community there. He appears to have met his spiritual guide, Sheikh al-'Alawi, in Morocco in the late 1920s and to have been appointed a *muqaddam* or sectional leader within the tariqa. When he came to England he was in his mid-thirties and had previously lived and worked in Algeria, France and Holland. He arrived in South Shields towards the end of 1936 and remained there until May 1938 establishing his *zawiya* in a former public house, the Hilda Arms in Cuthbert Street. Within a period of less than eighteen months he brought about profound changes in the religious life of the Arab seafarers in the town and their families.

Setting about his work with great energy, Sheikh Abdullah appears to have encouraged something of a religious revival among the town's Arab community. Religious life was regularized and dramatized. New rituals and practices were introduced and special attention was given to the religious instruction of the children of the community, boys and girls. In May 1938 it was reported that 150 children were attending evening classes in Qur'anic studies at the Sheikh's *zawiya* in Cuthbert Street.[34] Weekly classes for religious instruction were also provided for those wives of Arab seamen who had converted to Islam and, perhaps for the first time, they were encouraged to take an active part in the religious life of the community. At least one of the English wives learned to read the Qur'an and study religious books in Arabic. Collins felt that one of Sheikh Abdullah's most outstanding achievements was the en-thusiasm and devotion for Islam that he inspired in the English wives.[35] These women clearly held the Sheikh in high esteem and responded enthusiastically to his teachings. Some forty-five years after the Sheikh's departure from South Shields, one of the English wives, by then a widow, kept a framed photograph of the sheikh in her living room and spoke of him with great affection. Collins argued that in the face of prejudice because they had married Arabs, the English wives found a new sense of dignity and confidence through Islam. One of the wives told him: 'Before the Sheikh came, we felt that we were only Arabs' wives, but after we felt differently. We felt better. We had our own religion and priest and we were proud of it'.[36] In March 1937, only a few months after the Sheikh's arrival in South Shields, the BBC's outside broadcast service recorded the Arab children and a group of women from the community chanting *nashids* or praises of God as part of the 'Northern Notions' pro-gramme relayed from Newcastle.[37]

Elaborate and colourful processions through the streets of the town were organized to mark the major Muslim festivals, occasions when members of the Arab community were able to make a strong public declaration of their faith. Muslims from other parts of the north-east sometimes took part in these processions and groups of Arabs from Cardiff also participated in the festivities. On these occasions many of the seamen discarded their European clothing for Yemeni dress or the Arab dress of North Africa. Indeed the order's spiritual leader, Sheikh al-'Alawi, had emphasized the dangers of adopting European habits of thought and life and in particular had condemned Muslims who wore modern European dress.[38] Green banners inscribed with the words *la ilaha illa 'llah* (There is no God but God), together with a white crescent and stars, were always carried aloft at the head of the procession and those taking part chanted 'Alawi *nashids* or praises to God. The local press often referred to the *nashids* as 'Koranic hymns'. These processions attracted hundreds of curious onlookers including holidaymakers visiting the town, and were reported in some detail, though with numerous inaccuracies, in the local press which was obviously intrigued by the 'picturesque pagentry' of these occasions. For example in February 1937 the *Shields Gazette* reported on the celebrations for *'Id al-Adha*:

Over 200 Mohammedans marched through the streets of South Shields to celebrate the festival of Id-el-Arifa. Brilliantly coloured tarbushes, caftans and kuffiehs made contrast with the vivid green banners of Islam and the pure white vestments of the women and girls. The different racial types and their strange headgear gave the festival a cosmopolitan flavour rarely found in an English town.

At the head of the procession which moved off from Cuthbert Street shortly after 8.30 am was the Sheik himself, tall, bronzed and black-bearded. Many of the followers had just a white or coloured cloth wrapped loosely about the head. Some were wearing long cotton garments, loose-fitting and often gaudy. Others had baggy trousers while one was dressed in a brown blanket. Women and girls brought up the rear of the procession all dressed in spotless white satin or artificial silk, their necks adorned with bright beads. Among them were the young girls who were to rise and address the gathering of the Faithful.

Chanting and praying, the procession moved slowly to Unity Hall, where devotions took place, and there, for nearly six hours, prayers were said, chants intoned and the gathering addressed on the merits of the Koran and the strength of Islam. Each worshipper carried his own prayer mat, and as the crowd filed in through the door shoes were taken off and piled in heaps at either side. Then the men arranged themselves, sitting, squatting or kneeling on the floor, their eyes turned eastwards and towards the Sheik who sat facing them. The women were not allowed to kneel nor use prayer mats but were provided with chairs in a corner of the room, where they sat throughout the ceremony, breaking out at times into the monotonous, wailing chants which were part of the devotions.

Green, white, yellow, red and spotted turbans bobbed up and down in rhythmic motion as the Moslems took part in the service, each man intent upon his devotions but keenly aware of the part he had to play. The Imam, Sheik Abdulla, addressed them and spoke from the Koran, after which girls read essays they had written on the subject of Islam and the Koran, at times reciting long passages from the Holy Book. 'Those who believe in one God believe in the Koran. Those who believe in the Koran believe in God. But those who do not believe in the Koran do not believe in God,' declared one small girl as she read out her essay.

The service was only a part of the devotions. The ceremonial meal, at which mutton was the chief dish, followed and the guests were invited to partake of their host's food in accordance with the custom of the East.[39]

In December 1937 the *Shields Gazette* described the procession organized by Sheikh Abdullah as part of the celebrations to mark *'Id al-Fitr*:

Unity Hall, headquarters of South Shields branch of the Seaman's Union, became a temporary mosque for four hours yesterday. Nearly 150 South Shields Moslems dressed in their multicoloured prayer robes assembled at the home of Sheikh Abdulla Ali in Cuthbert Street and formed a religious procession to Unity Hall. They carried their beautifully-worked prayer mats and chanted hymns of the Koran as they walked to the mosque. The occasion was the celebration of Ed-el-Fatia, which marks the end of the festival of Ramadan.

A four hour session of prayers and meditation conducted by the leader of the Moslem community, began at 9 am and was attended by more than 100 men and 40 children. Many intricate questions were addressed to 14 year old Norman Abdo Ali, who has mastered the Koran in a year and to Norman Abdul Adem aged 10, and Hegir Hamid aged 8, who have also proved apt pupils in learning the Koran. All three answered satisfactorily and without prompting. A copy of the Koran, together with other gifts, was presented to Norman Abdo Ali, by the sheikh in recognition of his feat.

The return procession to the sheikh's home was watched by many people who gathered in Station Road to see the parade pass. Sheikh Abdullah told the Gazette reporter at the conclusion of the celebration, that he was delighted with the way the three children had answered the questions put to them. Asked if Norman Abdo Ali sought to be a Moslem priest, he said 'The boy is anxious to become a priest and in all probability he will eventually journey abroad to Algeria for his final training.'[40]

In addition to celebrating these two festivals, Sheikh Abdullah introduced a third annual festival to commemorate the death of the founder of the order, Sheikh al-'Alawi, who died in 1934. Such festivals were a feature of the religious life of all communities where the 'Alawi *tariqa* was active. The first of these festivals to be held in South Shields was in August 1937. The *Shields Gazette* reported:

The stately figure of Sheikh Abdulla Ali, in his flowing Eastern robes, surrounded by tiny Arab children chanting Koranic hymns in their shrill voices, moved through the streets of South Shields yesterday morning at the head of one of the most impressive Moslem processions seen in the town. It was a colourful climax to a weekend of prayer, the three-day festival of El-Ehteffel [al-Ihtifal] during which the Moslem community of Shields in common with brethren of their faith throughout the world, remembered His Highness Sheikh Ahmed Bin Mustapha Ali Allaoue, highest priest in the Moslem world during the last century, who died three years ago.

Yesterday's procession was watched by hundreds of people and provided an unusual sight for holidaymakers in the town. Scores of visitors ran alongside the procession as it passed from the Sheikh's home in Cuthbert Street to the temporary mosque in Spring Lane, and scores of cameras 'snapped' the colourful parade. The procession was not as big as had been expected, but the 200 Moslems taking part included about 30 visitors from Cardiff and Moslems from many parts of Northumberland and Durham.

Among those who came from outside the town was Mr Ahmed Lennard, a British Moslem and a personal friend of the sheikh. He was converted to the Moslem faith some months ago and made a special journey from London to take part in the procession. It had been hoped that the Imam of Woking would be present in response to an invitation from Sheikh

Abdulla Ali but he was unfortunately unable to attend. Police
officers helped to keep the crowds back as the procession moved
off from the Sheikh's home, the sun shining on the multicoloured prayer gowns of the men and the white robes of the
women, and the breeze curling round the green flags of the
Moslem faith which were carried high in the air.

It was a scene which struck a strangely contrasting note with
the modern surroundings and the wisps of incense trailing from
the wrist of one Arab added to the picturesque nature of the
scene. At the temporary Mosque the Moslems gathered round
their Sheikh and sang hymns until he gave the signal for them
to enter the Mosque. Inside he conducted a service which lasted
for several hours. The prayers were followed by feasting.[41]

One of the new religious rituals introduced by the 'Alawi *tariqa*
that is not reported in the local accounts of these festivals is the
ceremony known as the *dhikr*, or the 'mentioning' of the name of
Allah. The late Professor R.B. Serjeant, one of the leading experts
on south-west Arabia, was privileged to attend one of these ceremonies in South Shields on a visit to the town during the Second
World War and has left us the following description of the ceremony
held in a large room in a boarding-house in Spring Lane which
served as a temporary mosque:

On arrival in the building, the various elements of the procession
dissolved and a circle was formed in the zawiya for the
performance of the dhikr. Those who took part discarded their
European clothing to put on the *futa* or coloured cotton skirt,
a white shirt, and the turban of their native land. In all there
may have been a hundred men in the circle of the dhikr, with
Sheikh Hasan [Sheikh al-Hakimi's deputy] and a singer in the
centre. All joined hands and at a motion from the sheikh began
to sing or chant 'la ilaha illa 'llah', at the same time jerking up
and down from the knees while the singer intoned, chanting
praises of Allah.

At what seemed to be a signal given by the sheikh, those in
the circle began to breathe deeply, uttering a respiratory 'ah' in
rhythm with the movement of the knees (said to be the 'ah' of
the name of God, Allah). Simultaneously the entire circle began
to jerk up and down, continuing the action automatically, as if
not of their own will. The sheikh and singer inside the circle
remained unaffected by the trance-like state of the dhikr, which
lasted perhaps for half an hour until it was stopped by the sheikh

and the singer ceased to chant. The action is so vigorous that I consider it nearly impossible for anyone to perform of his own accord. When the sheikh perceives that the participants have had enough, he makes the dhikr stop: were he not to do so, they would continue until they dropped to the ground with exhaustion. One man, indeed, did carry on the spasmodic movements after the others had finished, and had to be patted on the back until he recovered from his ecstatic state. Later in the day there were more dhikrs; and sometimes as many as five or six are performed on these occasions, for as it is said in the mystic language, 'Mention the name of God until they say you are mad'. Another form of the dhikr as practised by the Mevlevis in Turkey has been described by European travellers who know the sect as the 'Dancing Dervishes'.[42]

Professor Serjeant also observed that one of the English wives had learned to perform the *dhikr*.

The 'Alawi *tariqa*, in the form of the 'Zaouia Islamia Allawouia Religious Society', seems to have attempted to formalize the long established system of voluntary offerings within the Arab community and each member of the society's local branches was required to pay a weekly contribution. These funds, administered by a local committee, were used to pay for the annual festival commemorating the death of Sheikh al-'Alawi, for the repatriation of seamen who became ill or were too old to work, for the funeral costs of any seamen who died destitute and possibly to assist seamen who were unemployed. The extent to which the *tariqa's* organization supplemented or replaced that of the individual boarding-house keepers is unclear. Both the Islamic Society and the Western Islamic Association had made efforts to regulate the system of making voluntary collections among the Arabs. For example, when the South Shields branch of the Western Islamic Association was formed, the Arab boarding-house masters agreed to collect money from their men on behalf of the association and money was only to be withdrawn on the signatures of four of the local officials. Voluntary contributions to the *tariqa* also paid for the personal expenses of the Sheikh and the upkeep of the *zawiya*. Wherever a branch of the *tariqa* was established, it was required to pay the expenses of a teacher to instruct the children in their religious obligations and scholarships were awarded to those with special ability so that they could continue their religious studies in the Middle East. In South Shields, Sheikh Abdullah was responsible for teaching the children during the period he remained in the town.

When Collins visited South Shields in the late 1940s a booklet setting out the main rules of the 'Zaouia Islamia Allawouia Religious Society' was circulating among the Arab seamen. He gives the following extracts:

> No other person than a true believer and a sincere friend of Islamic faith may become a member. Each member on joining automatically becomes a brother, and only good feelings towards each other will be tolerated. The sole purpose and aim of the Society is for the propagating of the religion of Islam and no other interests will be allowed to intrude.
>
> Once a member has been expelled, on no account can he be re-admitted to membership. Each member must pay a contribution towards the society—minimum of 1s. and the maximum of 2s. 6d. a week. From this amount the rent of the Zoaia [zawiya] and all other incidental expenses will be paid, the balance to be banked.
>
> Each branch shall also be entirely self-supporting. No member can be transferred temporarily from one branch to another. Any member who whilst ashore fails to pay his subscriptions for six weeks, automatically falls out of benefit, if he fails to pay for three months, he must leave the society, unless satisfactory reasons can be given. The objects of the society shall be to hold processions for Islamic Allawaia annually, to last three days—the Society to pay all expenses. More money for this purpose may be obtained by a loan (to be repaid) from another branch, or from extra subscription. The holding of the three days' celebration is compulsory, because it not only strengthens the Society but the religion as well.
>
> Any member being ill, aged or regarded as incurable, the management committee shall have the power to send him home provided that he is destitute and has paid his subscription up to date. Should a member die destitute in this country, then the committee shall have power to bury the deceased member and defray all expenses. If after burial it is found that the deceased left any assets, then the Society shall be entitled to reimburse itself of such expense.
>
> In the event of any member getting into trouble of his own making, the Society shall take no part in any of his affairs. If there is evidence of a miscarrage of justice, then the Society shall help, in so far as the committee thinks fit.
>
> If more than fifteen members find themselves residing in a port that has no Zoaia branch there, then the committee will

pay the rent of a room for them. Each branch of the Society must send a representative to visit other branches so that he can try and strengthen the Society and give instructions to the Islamis.

Wherever there is a branch of the Zoaia, the Society will pay the expenses of a teacher, who will instruct the children and others in the Islamic Religion. Scholarships will be awarded to children of special promise to enable them to attend at an approved High School (Religious School in Arabia, Iraq, Aden etc.)

If members have quarrels or anything between them, the committee will act as arbitrator.[43]

The influence of one of the *tariqa's* English solicitors is apparent from the text of this unique document which represents one of the few pieces of literature from the 'Alawi brotherhood in Britain that has come to the attention of researchers.

Sheikh Abdullah diligently cultivated contacts with local officals in South Shields such as certain councillors, the mayor and the Chief Constable. For their part the local authorities appear to have welcomed the establishment of the *tariqa* in the town. By strengthening the religious organization of the community, the *tariqa* provided a useful mechanism to control the behaviour of its members and exert social discipline. At a time of continuing high unemployment when many Arabs were destitute and unrest was always a possibility, the *tariqa's* activities did not challenge the status quo and self control was a supplement to social control.[44] As far as the British authorities were concerned, the energies of the seafarers were better spent pursuing their religious ambitions than associating with radical movements such as the communists. The founder of the *tariqa*, Sheikh al-'Alawi, had spoken out against all anti-religious movements and in particular against Communism.[45] Indeed, another reason for the *tariqa's* missionary drive in Europe may have been to counter communist propaganda among Arab seafarers at European ports.

Soon after his arrival in South Shields, Sheikh Abdullah wrote to the mayor and Chief Constable to request that a small part of Harton cemetery be set aside for use by the Muslim community, adding that he hoped that the local authorities would help them in all matters concerning their religion.[46] The request was approved by the Parks and Cemeteries Committee but when the Sheikh asked if the amount of land allocated to them could be doubled, the committee refused and withdrew the original offer. At a meeting of the Town Council on 8 March 1937 Councillor Hill spoke in support of the Sheikh's application and made a strong plea for equity in the treatment of the town's Muslim population. Extracts from his speech were published in the local newspaper:

> I have taken a great interest in these people and I have found that they possess ideals of a very high religious order, while we must agree that they are certainly self-respecting and law-abiding citizens. They have always desired to live together as one community and the Council had at times encouraged the segregation of the Moslems to which they had raised no objection whatever. Now a great drive was being made by the Islamic Association to strengthen the old faith and a mosque was to be built ... These people are entitled to their rights. While this Council has always pursued a policy of isolation for the Moslems in life, the Parks and Cemeteries Committee now ask them to come amongst us in the same burial ground when they are dead.[47]

Councillor Hill moved that the community be granted the exclusive right to bury Muslims in a quarter section of the Harton Cemetery to be selected by the Parks and Cemeteries Committee. Councillor Laybourn seconded the amendment commenting:

> We live in an age of tyranny when the rights and privileges of certain sections—the small minorities and particularly the coloured minorities—count for nothing. Although they are small in number in the town they represent a world-wide religion whose influence has been equally as potent as that of Christianity in the formation of mankind. I want the Council to grant these people the same rights as we would grant to our own.[48]

Councillor Hill's amendment was approved by twenty-seven votes to seven.

But there was one issue where Sheikh Abdullah's religious zeal led to conflict with the local authorities and that was over marriages according to Islamic law. One case in particular hit the headlines and involved the Sheikh himself. Early in 1937 the Sheikh had befriended three young children who had been taken into care in the Cottage Homes at Cleadon after the death of their father, an Arab seaman. He sought custody of the children, two girls aged eight and sixteen and a twelve-year-old boy, so that he could educate them and bring them up as Muslims. The Sheikh was particularly concerned about the young boy and felt that without a proper education the only career available to him would be seafaring. Having been informed that custody would only be granted if he married, the Sheikh chose the nineteen-year-old sister of the three children to be his wife and they were married according to Islamic law. The entire family then went to live at the Sheikh's home in Cuthbert Street. But the town's Public Assistance Committee declared that the marriage was not legal and insisted that unless he went through a Register Office ceremony to legalize his marriage under English law his adopted children would have to return to the Cottage Homes. Sheikh Abdullah refused to submit to a Register Office ceremony and declared that he was already married according to his own religion and that if he went to the Register Office he might lose his licence as a 'priest'. He told a reporter from the *Shields Gazette*:

> Although I am a British subject and have every respect for British laws, I cannot possibly as a good Moslem consent to be married at a Register Office when, in the sight of my religious brethren, I am already married. I am being penalised for doing good. The boy has no father and I wanted to open his eyes with teaching. Nobody is better fitted than I am to undertake this task of looking after and educating these children. You must believe when I say that if I go to the Register Office to be married, they will take away my licence as a priest. My wife, also does not desire that we should go through a second marriage. She is content with the legality and binding character of the first.[49]

During the interview he produced a document in Arabic that was the licence or diploma from the leadership of the *tariqa* authorizing him to conduct marriages according to Islamic law.

The affair took a dramatic turn in August when the children's English mother, who had remarried and was living with her husband, a white seaman, in Tyne Dock, arrived at the Sheikh's home in Cuthbert Street and demanded that the children be returned to her. When he refused the mother threatened to apply to the magistrates for a summons against the Sheikh. A week later one of the children, the sixteen-year-old girl, decided to go and live with her mother, but the younger children expressed their wish to stay with the Sheikh. The Public Assistance Committee appear to have delayed taking action in this matter but in September, before the Sheikh left South Shields for a visit to Algeria, he left the two children temporarily in the care of the Cottage Homes stating that he was anxious to ensure that they were properly cared for during his absence and that he would make formal application for their custody on his return.[50] Just how the case was finally resolved is not reported. The Sheikh's young wife Miriam, the children's sister, died in childbirth in December 1937, and it seems probable that the two younger children remained in the care of the Cottage Homes. There is little doubt that Sheikh Abdullah carried out marriages in South Shields according to Islamic law, and a strong suspicion that he may have advised the couples against going through a second ceremony at the Register Office. Later, when he was living in Cardiff, the police there reported that they suspected that he was carrying out marriages illegally. They thought that he performed marriages according to Islamic law without sending the couple to the Civil Registrar for the marriage to be carried out under English law and concluded that if this was the case then the Sheikh was liable to criminal prosecution.[51]

Sheikh Abdullah's concern that the children of the Arab community should receive religious instruction and be brought up as good Muslims resulted in some friction with the Roman Catholic Church over the religious upbringing of children of Arabs married to Roman Catholic women. One case came to light in February 1938. It was reported in the local press that a Roman Catholic woman married to an Arab for ten years wished to see her children brought up as Roman Catholics. Two of her children had attended Peter and Paul Church in Tyne Dock for mass and the father had not objected until recently when he insisted that they attend classes at the *zawiya* to learn the Qur'an. The children were continuing to attend mass at the church secretly and were carrying tiny Catholic prayer books in their pockets which they were compelled to hide when they went to the mosque. The report followed a letter to the *Shields Gazette* from the children's grandmother who wrote:

> Is this Arabia or Shields? Do the people of Shields realise the hold that the religious leaders of the Moslem community are getting in our town? Some poor children have been taken away from the church schools to attend the teachings of the Koran in Cuthbert Street. Can the Education Committee, the priests or the ministers do anything to stop this?[52]

The letter prompted the *Shields Gazette* to ask, 'What is the future of the children of marriages between white girls and dark-skinned followers of Mohammed? If the mother still adheres to her own religion, shall the children be Moslem or Christian? Who is to decide?' Interviewed by a reporter from the *Shields Gazette*, Sheikh Abdullah emphasized that no-one was ever approached to become a Muslim and that the white wives of Arabs were not compelled to convert to Islam or to take part in Muslim ceremonies. Nevertheless it is clear from the interview that he expected the children of Arabs married to Catholic women to be brought up as Muslims. Canon J.B. Byrne of St Bede's Church was equally insistent that the children of such marriages must be brought up as Roman Catholics. He told the reporter that there were only a few cases of Roman Catholics married to Arabs in South Shields but such cases presented difficulties because there was always a danger to the Catholic party in the marriage and to the children. He felt that such cases could only be dealt with individually.[53] It is unclear whether or not this was an isolated case but there are no other reports in the press on the subject during this period.

IV The new campaign for a mosque

The arrival of Sheikh Abdullah in South Shields gave new impetus to the long-established plan to build a mosque there. On arriving in the town, Sheikh Abdullah had established his *zawiya* in a former public house, the Hilda Arms, in Cuthbert Street. Part of the building was converted into a prayer room capable of accommodating sixty people with an adjacent room where wor- shippers could change their clothes and a bathroom in which ritual ablutions were performed before prayer. Rooms on the first and second floors were used as living quarters by the Sheikh. For many years before that, a large room in a boarding-house in Spring Lane had served as prayer room for the community and was large enough to hold fifty worshippers. Collins states that Sheikh Abdullah suggested that this prayer room should be closed after he opened his *zawiya* but the boarding-house master refused. As the boarding-house master, probably Abdul Mussem, was also a Sufi and was highly regarded in the community because of his generosity and piety, his prayer room continued to attract supporters. For a time the community spit into two religious groups giving their support to one or other of the two *zawiyas* but eventually they were reconciled and the two *zawiyas* became complementary rather than rivals.[54] We know that by August 1937 both the *zawiya* in Cuthbert Street and the prayer room in Spring Lane were being used to celebrate the festival of *al-Ihtifal*.

Nevertheless it is clear that during the celebrations of the major Muslim festivals the two *zawiyas* could not accommodate all the worshippers and rooms were also needed for teaching the children and wives the Qur'an. A new campaign for a mosque began in December 1936 after a big religious rally at the Mill Dam. A mosque committee was formed with Sheikh Abdullah as chairman and, as secetary, Gulam Hasson Shah, an Indian Muslim who had set up in business as a boarding-house master in the town early in 1936 after previously living in New York. Interviewed by the *Shields Gazette*, Gulam Hasson Shah told the reporter that the main reason the Muslim community wanted to build a mosque was to ensure that their children received instruction in the Muslim faith. The committee would first look for a site in Holborn and then appeal to leading Muslims in the empire, such as the Aga Khan and the Nizam of Hyderabad, for financial support.[55]

In May 1937 Sheikh Abdullah, Councillor Edmund Hill, the Deputy Mayor of South Shields and 'business adviser' to the mosque committee, and Abdul Ali Hadi, who had replaced Gulam Hasson Shah as secretary of the committee, met several prominent Muslims who were in London for the Coronation of King George VI at a reception at Grosvenor House. The deputation, it was reported, was received by Seif al-Islam Hussein, one of the sons of Imam Yahya of the Yemen, Crown Prince Saud of Saudi Arabia, and Sultan Abdul Karim of Lahej and the Prince of Mukalla from the Aden Protectorate and expressed high hopes of securing the necessary financial support for the mosque.

Some months before, the committee was reported to have opened negotiations to purchase Zion Hall in Laygate for conversion into a mosque but this proposal appears to have been dropped in favour of a new purpose-built mosque. In June 1937, 150 pamphlets containing an illustration of the proposed mosque and an appeal for financial contributions were sent to Muslim leaders throughout the world. The mosque was estimated to cost £3,000 and some £500 had been raised from local subscriptions. The pamphlet emphasized that the seafaring community at South Shields was poor but possessed ideals and spiritual ambitions of a high order. Councillor Hill, whose meetings with 'Moslem potentates' had attracted much interest in the local press, announced that they were on the brink of success and he was confident that substantial contributions would begin coming in within the next few days.[56] His confidence turned out to be mistaken and after almost a year no further progress had been made in securing funds for the mosque.[57]

At the end of 1938 hopes revived that the mosque scheme would go ahead, this time with financial assistance from the British Government. In late October 1938 the BBC's Arabic programmes' organizer, Stewart Perowne, who had previously served as information officer in the Aden Secretariat, visited South Shields to make preparations for recording the 'Id al-Fitr celebrations to be held the following month. The BBC planned to broadcast the recordings as part of Britain's propaganda campaign in the Middle East. Mr Conner, the BBC's Newcastle director, told the local press that this was something the Italians had overlooked in their propaganda campaign among the Arabs. The BBC officials were accompanied by Sir Bernard Reilly, the Governor of Aden, who emphasized that he was in no way connected with the broadcast but was interested in visiting the Arab community in South Shields as most of them were from Aden. The party visited several Arab boarding-houses and met leading members of the Arab community.[58] It appears that there was some discussion about the community's plans for building a mosque because the next month Sir Bernard wrote the following letter to Abdul Mussem:

Peace be upon you and the mercy of God and His blessings.

On this blessed day we wish to you all a happy Feast and prosperity. To our sorrow we cannot be with you today, but we send you this letter now so that you may know that we do not forget you and that the Government and the people of Aden also remember you always though you are far from them in a strange land.

We have heard that you hope to build a mosque. We are happy to know this and we wish to hear more of it, so that we may see whether we can find any help for you. First, therefore, please write a letter to our assistant, Perowne, and tell him all details. When we receive that letter from him we will give the matter consideration. May you continue preserved.[59]

As Abdul Mussem was illiterate, Yussif Hersi Sulliman, the secretary of the South Shields branch of the 'Zaouia Islamia Allawouia Religious Society', sent the following letter to Mr Perowne through the Chief Constable of South Shields:

On behalf of the Moslem Community of South Shields, which number about 645 including 20 women and 55 children, most of whom are Arabs and the remainder Somalis and Indians. I would like to inform you that we are desirous of building a mosque in South Shields to replace our temporary one in

Cuthbert Streeet. We have on several occasions tried to get a site for the building but find through lack of funds that we are unable to do so. We have however arranged with our members who are working to subscribe 6d per week. Through this we have at present £125 in the Bank, we had more than that but the remainder has been spent on visits to London trying to get assistance for the object in view for the building of a mosque but could easily find one if we had sufficient money to cover the cost of same. I am sure whatever you or your friends can do to assist us in this matter would be greatly appreciated by all Moslems not only in South Shields but the whole of the world. Our present weekly income is at the rate of about £7.10s per week but varies according to the number of persons employed. So I will again repeat that your services in assisting us will be appreciated. Attached is a plan of a Mosque that we were intending to build some time ago.[60]

In his accompanying letter, Chief Constable Alex Wilson commented, 'The Arabic community in South Shields are generally well-behaved, law-abiding and worthy of support in their endeavours to obtain suitable accommodation for observing their religious rites.'[61]

As the war clouds were gathering once more over Europe both the Governor of Aden and the Colonial Office pointed to the possible propaganda value in considering some measure of financial support for the South Shields mosque project. The Governor of Aden wrote to the Secretary of State for the Colonies:

> Both at Cardiff and South Shields, Mr Perowne and I found that the main desire of these small Moslem communities was to possess mosques, for which object they had collected among themselves a certain amount of money, but not sufficient to carry out their purposes. These Arabs work as seamen, but are liable to periods of unemployment, and their means are, therefore, very limited. I should be glad if I could assist these Arabs in England ... most of whom come from the south-western part of Arabia of which Aden is the natural outlet. If some financial assistance could be given to them to attain their desire for mosques, I consider that this help would be deeply appreciated not only by the immediate recipients, but also in the outside Muslim world, and especially in that part of it in which these people have their homes, namely Aden, the Aden Protectorate and the Yemen. Help in the cause of their religion,

which is so dominant a factor in the minds of Arabs, would be useful in countering those influences which have been endeavouring to sow distrust between Arabs and the British.[62]

A Colonial Office memorandum on the Governor's proposal commented:

> In normal times we can be sure that the Treasury would not consider any such proposal, though it is the sort of thing which the Italian or German Government would actively support for propaganda purposes, and with less justification. But in view of the present desire to placate Arab opinion . . . there is some little hope that a properly considered plan might be given some support.[63]

In the end these proved empty promises and no money was forthcoming for the South Shields mosque. In Cardiff the 'Alawi *tariqa* by its own efforts succeeded in converting some terraced houses in Peel Street into a mosque and in 1941, after the building was destroyed by enemy bombing, the Colonial Office did agree to finance its rebuilding.

During the war years the BBC made recordings at a number of the religious festivals held in South Shields for their broadcasts to the Middle East. For example in June 1942 the BBC recorded the celebrations to mark the festival commemorating the death of Sheikh al-'Alawi and extracts were broadcast to the Middle East a few days later. At the service, which was led by Sheikh Hasan Ismail, prayers were offered for the Allies' victory and before the procession messages were recorded by Arabs in South Shields to their friends and relatives in the Middle East. One seaman, who had been away from his home in Aden for a number of years, sent a message to his mother and hoped that England and the democratic countries would win the war.[64] It is therefore ironic that at a time when the British authorities were keen to use the Arab communities in Britain to counter Italian propaganda in the Arab world, the Arabs of South Shields were eagerly tuning into the Arabic news broadcasts from Rome. The local press reported in February 1938 that the Arabs in South Shields were unable to receive the BBC Arabic Service because their radio sets were old and they could not afford to buy the new short wave sets that were capable of picking up the BBC Arabic broadcasts. Nevertheless they declared that they were under no illusions about the Italians and would prefer to listen to the BBC. One Arab resident told the reporter:

We know that Italy is against England and Russia and we know
that we cannot always accept as the truth the news broadcasts
from the Rome station, but they explain the news in such a way,
make it seem almost like a story, that it is easy for us to
understand ... We know that it is not because they like the
Arab that they do this for us. We know Italy is not doing this
to help the Arabs but to upset the world for their own benefit.[65]

Sheikh Abdullah had left South Shields for Cardiff in May 1938
in order to take charge of the scheme to build a mosque there. He
was due to return to South Shields for the annual festival commemorating the death of the founder of the *tariqa* but had to cancel
because he was leaving for a visit to Paris, Marseilles and Algiers.[66]
He returned to South Shields in November 1939 for the celebrations
to mark the end of Ramadan and then left for Aden where he had
a *zawiya* at Sheikh Othman and where his family were living. Two
Arab boys from South Shields, Norman Abdul Ali and Norman
Cassim, accompanied him as far as Cairo where they were to
continue their religious education at the headquarters of the *tariqa*
in that city. On the way to Aden Sheikh Abdullah completed the
pilgrimage to Mecca. Before leaving South Shields the Sheikh sent
his good wishes to the mayor and Chief Constable thanking them
for their kindness and support for the local Muslim community.[67]
During his absence from Britain, his deputy, Sheikh Hasan Ismail,
assumed the leadership of the *tariqa* in Cardiff and South Shields.

The religious life of the Arab community in South Shields seems
to have lost some of its vigour after the departure of the charismatic
Sheikh Abdullah and the rigours and deprivations of war-time may
also have contributed. The women converts to Islam, in particular,
must have regretted his departure. They were no longer permitted
to take part in the processions that continued to mark the major
Muslim festivals and became merely onlookers.[68] They were
deprived of the use of a room in the *zawiya* for their meetings and
presumably the classes organized to teach them the Qur'an also
came to an end. Collins states that some of the men had objected
to the Sheikh's attitude towards the women converts and had
opposed his efforts to encourage their participation in the religious
life of the community and suggests that they may have been deprived
of their meeting room in the *zawiya* even before the Sheikh left
South Shields.[69] Classes in religious instruction for the children were
also discontinued perhaps because there was no one qualified to
instruct them after Sheikh Abdullah's departure.[70] A similar fate
befell the classes for Arab children in Cardiff.

V Political rivalries among the Yemeni seafarers

Even before his departure from Britain for the Middle East at the end of 1939, Sheikh Abdullah appears to have developed political ambitions and during the 1940s and early 1950s he became an outspoken critic of the Imam's regime in the Yemen and one of the leaders of the Free Yemeni Movement. From the late 1930s the Free Yemeni Movement had brought together many of the opponents of Imam Yahya's regime in the Yemen. The movement called for material reforms, the building of roads, schools and hospitals, and an end to the Imam's policy of isolation. One of its main sources of support was among Yemeni communities overseas.[71] A printed manifesto of the Free Yemenis was circulating among Yemeni seafarers in Cardiff and South Shields as early as 1941.[72] It is unclear exactly how Sheikh Abdullah became associated with the Free Yemenis. However, we know that in the summer of 1943 while he was living in Aden he visited Ta'izz in Yemen where he met two of the movement's leaders, Nu'man and Zubairi. The fact that he was quickly arrested and expelled from the Yemen on the orders of Seif al-Islam Ahmad, the Crown Prince, suggests that he was already identified as a member of the Free Yemeni leadership.[73]

On his return to Britain after the Second World War Sheikh Abdullah remained in Cardiff but was active in spreading his political message among the Yemeni seamen in South Shields, Hull and Liverpool. When leading Free Yemenis announced the formation of the Grand Yemeni Association (GYA) in Aden in January 1946, the first Yemeni community overseas to voice its support was that in Britain. Unlike previous attempts to organize the Free Yemenis, the GYA had a constitution and a newspaper of its own. In November 1946, in response to the founding of the GYA in Aden, Sheikh Abdullah formed 'The Committee for the Defence of Yemen' and declared that henceforth his committee would celebrate the birthdate of the GYA newspaper, *Saut al-Yaman*, as a holiday. They pledged themselves to publicise the GYA cause, to send representatives to Yemeni communities in the USA, Africa and Europe and 'to set up a permanent delegation to visit Arab and Islamic capitals so that the leaders of the Arabs and the Muslims will understand the need to help solve the Yemeni problem'.[74]

The committee was still operating in 1948 and its members in Cardiff, South Shields, Hull and Liverpool continued to meet regularly.[75] In December 1948 Sheikh Abdullah began publishing his own newspaper, *Al-Salam*, from the Nur al-Islam Mosque in

Peel Street, Cardiff. It contained regular articles attacking the Imam's regime. The paper was funded by his friends and supporters in Aden and although most copies were destined for North Africa and the Middle East, *Al-Salam* was also distributed among the Yemeni seamen in Britain. In South Shields, copies were sold from the *zawiya* in Cuthbert Street.

One of the editions of *Al-Salam* circulating in South Shields carried an open letter from Sheikh Abdullah to the Imam of the Yemen complaining bitterly about the great suffering of the Yemeni people under the Imam's rule. It illustrates Sheikh Abdullah's hostility to the Imam's regime:

> Your Majesty, I hope you will allow me to speak to you openly in a newspaper than to write to you in a private letter and allow me to express my feeling of pain and bitterness. I am expressing this about the Yemeni peoples' affair who are lost as in a very deep sea and I am now trying to do what is right and in the interest of our people and country. I am only trying to do a duty. A Moslem should advise another Moslem, to tell him to do what is right and to avoid what is wrong . . .
>
> Your Majesty, you must have known that during the time the Turkish government was occupying our country with an army of eight to nine million, we were a colony of the Turks. It's the people whom you are having as subjects now who fought against the Turks and cleared entirely the Turkish invaders from Yemen. Since then, your Majesty, your ancestors were Kings of Yemen until today. Since then you have been an independent government and up to this time you haven't done anything which is good or to be remembered for the people, such as establishing schools and mending roads . . . It is not fair, your Majesty, that the Royal family should be living a very happy life while thousands of your subjects are perishing of hunger. You do not know that the authorities under you are not acting as responsible authorities but as business men, selling and buying the subjects of the country?
>
> Yemen is an agricultural country and very rich and could support about ten million if there was a responsible administration who could run the subjects and country in a modern way. But the poor Yemeni had become so hungry in his country that he must leave Yemen and go to another foreign country to earn his living.
>
> Your Majesty, do you think it fair that you should ask for a tax from the land or money of your subjects who have not

enough crops from their fields and then mortgage their land until such a time that the possession of the land becomes the government and the destitute Yemeni flee from their country. Your Majesty I suppose you didn't believe the engineers whom you employed and who told you that the land is very rich and there is petroleum, gold, silver, mica and coal and some of these minerals could be seen on the surface. But you did not try to operate these schemes and open jobs for your subjects since with your family you were happy and prosperous.[76]

Until Sheikh Abdullah and the Free Yemenis began campaigning among Yemenis living at British ports such as Cardiff and South Shields, the Imam of the Yemen appears to have ignored these communities. There is no record that he intervened to protest against the British Government's policies to control and regulate Arab seamen during the inter-war period or against the racist campaign to which these men and their families were subjected at this time (see Chapter Four, p.79). Yet there seems little doubt that the Imam knew of the campaign against his subjects in Britain as he had informants among these port communities and recognized that his country benefited from the remittances that the seamen sent back to their families in Yemen. Many of the seamen would have suffered from the oppressive taxation system of the Imam's officials in their home villages and few could fail to have compared conditions in Britain with the backward state of their own country and the lack of almost all modern amenities. In these circumstances the Free Yemeni Movement was bound to attract support. Nevertheless, it would be a mistake to assume that all the Yemeni seamen or even the majority were opposed to the Imam whose position as spiritual as well as temporal ruler no doubt commanded respect. Furthermore, expressions of loyalty to the Imam, however superficial, might earn his thanks and even a reward. After all most of these seamen had families in Yemen and intended to return there one day.

In May 1937, while Prince Hussein, one of the sons of Imam Yahya, was visiting Britain for the Coronation of King George VI, he was invited to South Shields by Said Hassan, one of the leading boarding-house masters in the town, and received a warm reception from the Yemeni community there. The *Shields Gazette* described his visit in some detail:

In the early hours of today, Prince Seifal Islam Hussein, 30-year-old son of the King of the Yemen, left South Shields after a lightening visit to the Moslem community of the town—a

239

visit which had been eagerly awaited by excited Arabs and their children. Inside a South Shields Arab boardinghouse last night, the Prince, surrounded by his retinue, dined and talked while outside groups of Arab children showed their pleasure and excitement by chanting hymns from the Koran.

About 9 oclock last night the Prince, accompanied by his private secretary and a bodyguard of three, arrived at Wolsingham airport, Newcastle, having flown from London in a specially chartered plane. He was met by Mr Said Hassen, who was accompanied by his wife and Mr Y. H. Sulliman, a member of the local mosque committee. The Prince and his retinue came on to South Shields by car ... There was an enthusiastic scene when the Royal visitor arrived at Said Hassen's boarding-house in Chapter Row. Outside, a crowd of Moslems waited to greet him, while scores of children stared in fascination at the dignified figure of the Prince. It made a colourful picture against the drab settings of the street as Prince Hussein, in his brightly-coloured robes, stepped from the car and passed through the guard of Moslems drawn up outside. He smiled and bowed as he entered the door. Elaborate arrangements had been made inside the boarding-house for the Prince's reception, and when the welcomes were over, thanksgiving was offered in the prayer room for the Prince's safe arrival. In an interview, the Prince, with Said Hassen acting as interpreter, described how he was enjoying this first visit to England and said he was particularly pleased to be able to visit South Shields.[77]

A few days' later when Prince Hussein visited the Arab community in Cardiff, he was presented with a massive silver casket containing an address of loyalty and welcome. It stated that the Arabs of Cardiff sent a message of homage to the prince's father the Imam and wished the prince, his father and members of his noble dynasty long years in the service of Islam. Sheikh Abdullah travelled from South Shields to take part in the presentation.[78] Prince Hussein was considered a favourite of the 'ulama or religious scholars and more pious than any of his brothers. He was killed in the turmoil which followed the assassination of his father in February 1948 in which the Free Yemenis were directly involved.

In 1942 Imam Yahya requested permission from the British Government for the Saudi Arabian Minister in London to look after the interests of his Yemeni subjects in Britain for the duration of the war. Although the Imam's request made reference to the need to protect Yemenis in Britain (chiefly seamen who were often stranded there)[79] it is likely that the real reason for his concern may have been the fact that he had discovered that Free Yemeni propaganda was circulating among these communities. When Crown Prince Ahmad became Imam in 1948 after his father's assassination, he appears to have embarked upon a more energetic campaign to counter the influence of Sheikh Abdullah and the Free Yemenis among the Yemeni seafaring communities living in Britain. The new Imam heartily disliked Sheikh Abdullah, feared his propaganda and was convinced that Sheikh Abdullah's activities were supported and even financed by the British Government.[80] There is no doubt that Sheikh Abdullah was sympathetic to the British and admired British methods of government. During the 1940s he maintained a regular correspondence with Tom Hickinbotham, a long serving senior British official in Aden who eventually became Governor in 1951, and proved a useful informant on the activities of the Imam's agents in Britain. Whether his co-operation extended beyond this is unclear. The Imam certainly believed that Sheikh Abdullah was a British agent.

At the beginning of August 1948 two representatives of Imam Ahmad, Sayyid Hasan bin 'Ali Ibrahim, a trusted aide and private secretary to his brother Prince Abdullah, and Sayyid Abd al-Rahman Abd al-Samad Abu Talib, held meetings with Yemeni communities at Cardiff, London and Liverpool. A number of Yemenis from South Shields attended the meeting held at the Cairo Hotel in Bute Street, Cardiff on 4 August. According to a report of the meeting from one of Sheikh Abdullah's informants, the two representatives of the Imam carried with them a letter from Imam Ahmad. In it the Imam accused the British Government of complicity in the assassination of his father because he claimed Britain had always wanted to control the Yemen and declared that agents of the British in Aden had planned and financed the assassination. This was clearly a reference to the Free Yemenis. He thanked all those loyal Yemenis who had written letters to him pledging their allegiance which he had received through Sheikh Hasan Ismail (Sheikh Abdullah's deputy) and ordered them to contact the Yemen Youth Association in Aden (probably the *Jam'iyat al-Shabab al-Yamaniya*—the Yemeni Young Men's Association set up to mobilise support for the Imam). But he warned that letters were not enough against an imperialist enemy and against those who declared that they were true Muslims but who were the supporters of the imperialist enemy. The Imam was no doubt referring to Sheikh Abdullah and the Free Yemenis. Imam Ahmad called upon loyal Yemenis to unite and to appoint true and faithful leaders to whom they should report in secret and who in turn would report to him through Sayyid Hasan bin 'Ali Ibrahim. In this way their movement would become stronger. The informant then listed the names of those persons who had been appointed as leaders of the movement in the different port cities and commented that these were the men who had been working for a secret organization for the last eighteen months. Abdul Rakib Abdul Rahman Shamiri, Abdul Wahab Mosa Shamiri and Mohamed Dowah Shamiri were named as the officials of the South Shields branch of the pro-Imam movement.

After the meeting, the men who had attended were ordered to leave and a special session was held in secret between the branch leaders and the Imam's two representatives. The informant reported that a lot of Yemenis at the meeting were upset and stated that they could not spy or cause trouble as they held British passports and would face difficulties if the British authorities found out that they were Yemenis. Some felt that it would have been better if the organization had been kept secret. Nevertheless, although there were disagreements among the Yemenis, he felt that the pro-Imam organization was growing stronger because it received financial support from the Yemen Government.[81]

Whether or not this report represents an accurate account of events at the meeting, there is little doubt that Imam Ahmad attempted to weaken Sheikh Abdullah's position among the Yemenis in Britain and kept himself well-informed of his opponent's activities. The feuding between the two rival groups, the supporters of the Free Yemenis led by Sheikh Abdullah and the pro-Imam faction led by Hasan Ismail, took place mainly in Cardiff, the major centre of Yemeni settlement in Britain, in the late 1940s and early 1950s and was carefully monitored by the Cardiff City Police. Few open disturbances occurred. The nearest approach to anything like a breach of public order took place at a meeting called by Hasan Ismail on 25 February 1951 to try and resolve the differences between the two rival factions during which the Cardiff City Police were forced to intervene. The meeting was quickly dispersed and no real harm was done.[82]

Both factions had their followers in South Shields and it seems probable that, as in Cardiff, support for the rival groups was along tribal lines. Sheikh Hasan Ismail and most of the men chosen to lead the pro-Imam organization were Shamiris whereas Sheikh Abdullah was a Dhubhani. Supporters of Sheikh Hasan Ismail were reported to have been in the majority, not surprising as the Shamiris were probably the most numerous tribe among the Yemeni seafarers in Britain. The rivalries between the two factions rarely came to the surface in South Shields although there is some evidence that each faction tried to discredit the other by making false reports against them to the police.[83] Collins, who was carrying out his field research in South Shields at this time, found that these rivalries had weakened the 'Alawi *tariqa* and that some Muslims criticized the order for being more of a political than a religious group.[84] By the early 1950s he observed that the *tariqa* was virtually inactive and that most of its activities had been taken over by the local branch of the Moslem League[85] which had been founded after the Second World War by Gulam Hasson Shah.

In May 1952 Sheikh Abdullah announced that he was ceasing publication of *Al-Salam* in Cardiff and returning to Aden where he intended to relaunch the newspaper. One of his two sons was working with the Free Yemenis there. His reasons are unclear but opponents of the Free Yemenis in Aden are reported to have declared that Sheikh Hasan Ismail, described as 'the emissary of the Imam', had achieved his objective in ousting Sheikh Abdullah from Britain.[86] Officials at both the Foreign Office and Colonial Office expressed deep concern about Sheikh Abdullah's impending return to Aden. By this time he had become something of an embarrassment to the British authorities who were anxious not to offend the Imam.

After the assassination of Imam Yahya in 1948 the Foreign Office had instructed the Governor of Aden to ban all political activities of the Free Yemenis there. Britain was anxious to ensure that there were no grounds for allegations that the British authorities had supported any move to overthrow Imam Ahmad. The Foreign Office maintained that if Sheikh Abdullah was allowed to publish any kind of newspaper in Aden, whether political or not, Imam Ahmad would assume that he had gone there with the support of the British Government and would interpret this as a move directed against him and Yemen.[87] Sheikh Abdullah's request for a licence to publish his newpaper in Aden was therefore denied.

When Sheikh Abdullah arrived in Aden on 15 January 1953 he was welcomed by more than a thousand supporters of the Free Yemeni Movement who held him in high regard as both a religious and political leader. A few days later, however, when his luggage arrived, customs officials at Aden found arms and ammunition in one of the trunks containing religious books. They had evidently received a tip-off from the Cardiff police.[88] As it was illegal to import arms into Aden, Sheikh Abdullah was arrested and later sentenced to one year's imprisonment. Supporters of the Free Yemenis believed that the weapons had been planted by someone in the pay of Imam Ahmad while some Yemenis pointed accusingly at the British.[89] The sentence was later quashed by the East African Court of Appeal and Sheikh Abdullah, who throughout the case had protested his innocence, was released from prison on 17 July 1953.[90]

Three months later he was unanimously elected president of the Yemeni Union, an organization set up in 1952 by the Free Yemenis ostensibly to promote the social and religious welfare of Yemenis in Aden and elsewhere but widely recognized as a vehicle for propaganda against the Imam.[91] He held the post for less than a year and the circumstances of his death are as mysterious as those surrounding his arrest for importing arms. According to one account Sheikh Abdullah was admitted to Aden's civilian hospital early in August 1954 with a kidney infection and was given an injection with a poisoned syringe by someone in the pay of the Imam.[92] Others doubt this story and official British sources are strangely silent about his death. Of course by then he may no longer have been of interest to the British authorities. In June 1954 he told a British official that he was much hurt by the way he had been neglected by the British in Aden and their lack of sympathy for his aims which he considered were based on British democratic traditions.[93] His death went unrecorded in South Shields and in Cardiff the local press merely reported that he had died 'while travelling in the Middle East'.

Nine

The Post-War Years: Integration and Assimilation

In the inter-war period competition for jobs in seafaring, sexual jealousy and moral outrage at the intermarriage of Arabs with white women resulted in popular demands to control and regulate the Arab community. The Arabs of South Shields faced racism, discrimination and prejudice at both official and popular levels. In the post-war years prejudice against the Arab community has certainly declined although it has not disappeared altogether. By the late 1940s Arabs had been settling in the town for some fifty years. As one member of the community commented later, 'We've been here such a long time, everyone's got used to us.'[1] But probably the most important factor in explaining the decline in prejudice is the assimilation of much of the community into the larger society of South Tyneside and the loss of their Arab and Islamic identity. The Arabs themselves have virtually become invisible.

Since the Second World War, several factors have contributed to what some observers have described as the 'disappearance' of the Arab community in South Shields. In fact it is probably more accurate to interpret this process of change as one in which the Arab population and their descendants have gradually 'dissolved' into the general population of South Tyneside in much the same way as the Irish immigrants before them.[2] Many Arab seamen and their sons lost their lives during the Second World War either serving in the Merchant Navy in the Battle of the North Atlantic and on the Russian convoys, or in the British armed forces. Wartime losses in the Merchant Navy were very high. Some Arab families lost more than one of their members. For example in June 1942 Mrs Ali of 5 Cornwallis Square received the news that her son, William Norman

245

Ali, had been killed at sea through enemy action. He was only eighteen years old and had enlisted at the outbreak of war. Mrs Ali's husband had been lost at sea eighteen months before.[3] Carr highlights the case of Hasan Joseph Hamid, the eldest son of Ali Hamid, the man refused a licence for a seamen's boarding-house in 1929 by certain racist councillors because they claimed such establishments represented a threat to the townspeople. Hasan was shot down over Germany and taken prisoner in 1943 while serving his country as a Warrant Officer in the Royal Air Force.[4] Byrne has argued that the war record of the Arab seamen and their sons in a particularly dangerous service, the Merchant Navy, and in a 'just war' played a crucial role in the subsequent integration of the Arabs and their families into the South Shields community on equal terms.[5]

There were few new arrivals in the town from Yemen. Collins claims that in the late 1940s and early 1950s all the Arab seamen in South Shields were able to find employment.[6] Some continued to work on the steam-driven colliers which plied the coal trade up and down the east coast. For although diesel-powered ships were introduced after the Second World War, a few of the old colliers survived until the early 1980s. Certainly, despite a few isolated incidents immediately after the war, there appears to have been little or no discrimination against Arab seamen shipping from north-east ports and the National Union of Seamen made no distinction between its white, Arab and Anglo-Arab members.[7] But the decline of the British shipping industry in the post-war years threatened the jobs of both white and Arab seamen.

In the 1950s and 1960s a new influx of Yemenis into Britain found employment not in shipping but in heavy industry, especially in the steel and metal-working plants in Sheffield and Birmingham, though a few came to the expanding iron and steel works of Middlesbrough and Stockton in the north-east. As the demand for seamen declined, some Arab seafarers moved to the midlands where new employment opportunities were opening up in industry and in this way forged a link between the two phases of Yemeni migration to Britain.[8]

Whereas in 1960 there were still some 300 Arab seamen registered with the NUS office in South Shields, by 1986 the number had fallen to between fifty and sixty and all these men were over fifty years of age. By this time many were taking voluntary redundancy and returning to Yemen; there were few opportunities for sons to follow their fathers into seafaring, bringing to an end the former close association of members of the Arab community in a common occupational group. One old man, a former seamen about to return to Yemen after spending most of his working life in South Shields, proudly showed me a collection of photographs which he kept in his wallet. One set of pictures were of his children and grandchildren in South Shields, the other of his home village in Yemen and his relatives there. Although he had left the village as a young man and had never revisited it, he had kept in touch with his relations there and no doubt received a warm welcome on his return to a community that still regarded him as one of its sons. By the late 1980s only two Arab seamen's boarding-houses remained in the town, one in Brunswick Street and the other in St Jude's Terrace. Only a few seamen lodged there but these establishments had acquired a new and equally important role as social centres where elderly Arabs and Somalis living in and around South Shields could meet, talk, play dominoes, have a meal and sometimes chew *qat* (the stimulant leaf consumed daily throughout Yemen and of great social importance in Yemeni society); they also served as advice centres offering help and support. The famous Mill Dam, once the heart of this seafaring community and crowded with seamen 'walking the stones' as they waited to be hired, is now deserted and the Board of Trade Offices alongside, a derelict shell: a stark reminder of the dramatic decline in the town's major industry.

After the slum clearance programmes in Holborn beginning in the late 1930s, and the redevelopment of much of the riverside at South Shields, the Arab community had regrouped in the streets on either side of Laygate Lane with some families occupying part of the new housing estate built at the bottom of Laygate Lane along Commercial Road. The Arab boarding-houses, cafes and general stores were re-established in the Laygate area and it was here that Sheikh Abdullah Ali al-Hakimi opened his *zawiya*. But a new urban redevelopment programme beginning in the 1950s and continuing into the 1960s and early 1970s demolished most the streets of terraced houses east of Laygate Lane and the residents, including the Arab families whose homes had been demolished, were dispersed and rehoused in council properties scattered across the town. In contrast to the earlier slum clearance programme in Holborn, there was no question of segregating the Arabs and their families under this new redevelopment scheme. Today people of Arab descent are to be found living throughout South Shields.

But other factors have been at work, weakening the bonds uniting the Arab community. Even before the redevelopment of the Laygate area, Collins observed that members of the second generation, as soon as they reached adolescence, tended gradually to abandon the customs and values of the community, tried to free themselves from the network of social controls, and increasingly adopted the ways and values of British society. He found that very few young men attended daily prayers at the *zawiya* or took part in the annual religious festivals, although young children continued to participate in these festivities with great enthusiasm. Some young people sought to disassociate themselves from the Arab community. One Arab complained to him, 'Some of them pass us and pretend they do not see us. Playing white, I suppose.'[9] From other sources we know that some Arabs took English surnames, often their mother's maiden name, to disguise their Arab origins. Collins, writing in the early 1950s, concluded that the informal social controls within the community were weakening as far as the second and third generations were concerned. The young people were becoming more Anglicized and were tending to disregard the informal checks of the Arab community.[10]

Demographic factors may also have contributed to this trend. With few new arrivals into seafaring and the continued absence of immigrant women, young people in the community were inevitably forced to look for partners in the host society. Collins observed that when an Anglo-Arab man married an English girl the couple tended to move away from the Laygate area to settle in other parts of the town and in this way escaped the social controls of the Arab community. One woman married to an Arab told him that her son had married an English girl and was now living outside the Arab community. She complained that her son had been doing all the things of the 'present generation' and no longer listened to his father's advice.[11] Each successive generation tended to participate more fully in British society at the expense of identification with the Arab community and acceptance of its regulative systems.

It is a cruel irony that just as the dispersal of the community following the redevelopment of the Laygate area was substantially complete, the Arabs of South Shields at last succeeded in their ambition to acquire a purpose-built mosque. The Al-Azhar mosque in Laygate was opened in July 1972, some ten years after Sheikh Abdullah Ali al-Hakimi's *zawiya* in Cuthbert Street had been demolished as part of the redevelopment programme. At that time a new appeal had been launched for a mosque where the children of the community could be taught the Islamic faith and where other people could come to learn about Islam. The mosque with its large white dome and twin minarets quickly became a familiar landmark in the town. Abdul Ali, a disciple of Sheikh Abdullah and the 'Alawi *tariqa*, who had performed the duties of sheikh for some twenty years, retired at this time at the age of eighty-six years. He was a Yemeni and had originally worked as a seaman before he was appointed Imam. His retirement marked a break with the past, for the imams that followed him were not appointed from within the community nor were they Yemenis.

At the opening of the new mosque some of the older Arabs acknowledged that successful integration of their community into the general population of South Shields had resulted in assimilation and, for many, the loss of their Arab and Muslim identity. One member commented, 'The older generation was wrong, they have not kept the minds of the children.' Another was more hopeful, 'We are all over the place now . . . Years ago the community was in one area, but when we moved from Holborn, people were splintered all over the town, in new houses and on different estates—now we can get back together.'[12] In the years since the opening of the new mosque a number of people have moved back into the Laygate area after requesting a transfer from the Housing Department to one of the new council flats built there under the redevelopment programme. Most of them are older members of the community who stated that they wanted to return to the Laygate area in order to be close to the mosque. In December 1988 a Yemeni School for Arabic and Islamic Studies was opened next to the mosque providing evening and weekend classes in English, Arabic and Islamic Studies. After two years about thirty boys and girls were enrolled at the school.[13]

The leadership of the community remains with the older generation who were born in the Yemen. Among the first generation the development of a Yemeni identity has grown stronger as a result of the emergence of a Yemeni national movement and consciousness especially since the 1960s and in response to renewed efforts by the Yemen Government since the 1970s to re-establish links with the Yemeni communities in Britain. But it has not replaced earlier tribal and regional identities. In the past a seamen was a Shamiri, a Jubani or a Dalali, for instance, before he was a Yemeni, and there was little sense of unity apart from their identification with the wider Muslim community or *umma*. Attitudes have begun to alter but only to a limited extent. Although rarely observed by non-Yemenis, it is significant that different tribal loyalties have been one of the major factors in rivalries within the leadership of the community. Today the leadership presides over a community composed mainly of the older people and a small group of younger families who have resisted assimilation and retained their Arab and Muslim identity. The majority of people of Arab descent have dissolved into the larger society, sometimes without trace and often with their Arab surnames as the only tenuous remaining link with their Arab forbears. Claims that the practising Yemeni/Muslim community in South Shields numbers between 2,500 and 3,000[14] are misleading and greatly exaggerate the real situation. It is true that the leadership can point to some solid achievements in their efforts to strengthen community institutions, but the provision of religious education for the children of those families eager to pass on their Islamic traditions and values to their sons and daughters may not be enough to stem the continued decline of the community through intermarriage and assimilation.

The Rota System: Rules of Joint Supply Registration and Engagement of Somali and Arab Seamen

1. A Register shall be kept in the Joint Supply Office in two parts for (1) Somalis, (2) Arabs from other countries.

2. A white card shall be issued at the Joint Supply Office to any Somali or Arab who satisfies the Port Consultants that he is a bona fide seamen and is lawfully in this country. The white card shall only be issued after being stamped by the National Union of Seamen and the Shipping Federation.

3. Proof required shall be production of police registration certificate or a British Passport, and discharges from one or more British vessels.

4. On receiving a white card the holder will be instructed to procure three copies of his photograph, and to present himself for registration at an appointed time.

5. Certain hours will be fixed for registration at the Joint Supply Office on three days each week.

6. Any man who presents his white card and photograph at a Joint Supply Office at an appointed time shall be registered, either as a Somali or an Arab, and he shall surrender his white card in exchange

for his registration card (pink) to which his photograph will be attached. A photograph will also be attached to his discharge. He will be informed that he can offer himself for selection at the Joint Supply Office at any time when a crew is required, subject to his obtaining the National Maritime Board employment form before actual engagement.

7. When registered the man is to be instructed to report at the office every fourteen days. The date of each such report will be entered in the register and will also be marked on the back of the man's Registration Card (pink).

8. Officers engaging Somalis or Arab crews shall be informed that it is very undesirable to mix Somalis and Arabs of other races, and asked to specify which they prefer.

9. (1) When a requisition for a Somali or Arab crew is received the number required shall be called up for selection (except provided below) in the order of priority of their registration beginning with the lowest number standing on the register as unemployed. If required, further members will be called up in succession until the officer has selected a crew to his satisfaction.

(2) Provided that where men who have sailed in the vessel on the preceding voyage are to be re-engaged, they shall have priority over any others on the register but they are nevertheless to be registered in the usual manner.

10. When a man has been duly engaged, his ship shall be entered in the register and on his Registration Card (pink). He shall surrender the latter, and it will be filed in the Joint Supply Office. In the event of subsequent re-registration he will receive a new pink card and a new number, and the same procedure will be followed.

11. It is understood that every officer deputed to engage a crew shall have complete liberty to determine the nationality of the crew to be engaged, and shall be supplied accordingly, as long as there are men on the register, if Somalis or Arabs are required.

12. If no Somalis or Arabs are on the register at the port where the vessel is, or if there are insufficient the Port Consultants shall, if the ship's officer so desires, immediately communicate with the Port Consultants at another port keeping a register and arrange for the transfer of a sufficient number of men.

13. Where a man wishes to be transferred from one district to another his Registration Card (pink) will be marked accordingly by the District from which he is transferred, and he will be given a new number in the Register of the District to which he is transferred, but he will retain the same card re-numbered. If the District to which he is tranferred has no Register, the Joint Supply Office of the District at which he obtains employment shall take from the man his Registration Card (pink) and after marking on it the name of his vessel and date of engagement, send it to the port of registration.

14. The Register will come into operation on August 1st, 1930, and notice of the obligation to register will be given by advertisement and placards in the Joint Supply Office on July 20th, 1930.

Source: PRO HO 45/14299 Part 1.

Notes and References

Transcripts of Crown-copyright records in the Oriental and India Office Collections of the British Library and in the Public Record Office appear by permission of the Controller of Her Majesty's Stationery Office. Extracts from the *Shields Daily Gazette/Shields Gazette* are reproduced by kind permission of the *Shields Gazette*. References to documents in the Tyne and Wear Archives Service are made with the permission of the Chief Archivist, Tyne and Wear Archives Service, Newcastle upon Tyne. The quotation from the *Geographical Magazine* appears by kind permission of the *Geographical Magazine*, London. Extracts from *Coloured minorities in Britain: studies in British race relations based on African, West Indian and Asiatic immigrants* by Sydney Collins appear by kind permission of The Lutterworth Press. Extracts from 'An early Somali autobiography' are by kind permission of Professor Richard Pankhurst.

Abbreviations: IOR (India Office Records); PRO (Public Record Office); TWAS. (Tyne and Wear Archives Service); SG (*Shields Daily Gazette and Shipping Telegraph* to 2.4.1932; from 4.4.1932 *Shields Gazette and Shipping Telegraph*).

Introduction

1. For an overview of Arab migration to Britain and a study of the different phases of Yemeni migration see Fred Halliday, *Arabs in exile: Yemeni migrants in urban Britain* (I.B.Tauris, London and New York, 1992). Chapter 2 is devoted to the early seafaring communities. Sydney Collins studied the Muslim community in South Shields as part of his doctoral research on coloured communities in Tyneside. See Sydney Collins, *Moslem and Negro groupings in Tyneside*, Ph.D. thesis

(University of Edinburgh, 1952) and his book based on this research, *Coloured minorities in Britain: studies in British race relations based on African, West Indian and Asiatic immigrants* (Lutterworth Press, London, 1957).

1 The Earliest Arab Immigrants: The Pioneers

1. The figures are given in SG 25.8.1910 p. 3. There is no comprehensive history of South Shields in the twentieth century. A brief history of the town is included in *1835–1935 A hundred years of local government—a century of progress in South Shields* (County Borough of South Shields, 1935). For a detailed account of the nineteenth century see G.B. Hodgson, *The Borough of South Shields from the earliest period to the close of the nineteenth century* (Andrew Reid and Co., Newcastle, 1903).
2. SG 20.3.1917 p. 4.
3. SG 14.2.1925 p. 4.
4. I am most grateful to Mr Norman Hassan of South Shields for allowing me to consult papers belonging to Mr Ali Hassan.
5. Tyne and Wear Archives Service T95/152 Letter from the Chief Constable, South Shields to The Judge, Assize Court, Durham (undated). The letter gives background details on Ali Said and was prepared in connection with his trial at Durham Assizes in November 1930 on the charge of incitement to riot.
6. SG 2.9.1911 p. 4.
7. SG 17.8.1912 p. 3.
8. SG 15.4.1913 p. 4.
9. David Byrne, 'Class, race and nation: the politics of the "Arab issue" in South Shields 1919–1939', paper presented at a Conference on Ethnic Seafarers in the UK held at the University of Liverpool, 14–15 December 1992.
10. SG 16.4.1913 p. 2.
11. Neil Evans, 'The South Wales race riots of 1919', *Llafur*, vol. 3, no. 1 (Spring 1980) p. 9.
12. The Arab community in Cardiff also experienced rapid growth at this time. H.M. Superintending Aliens Officer, Cardiff reported to H.M. Inspector, London in March 1917: 'Since these days the Arab colony in Cardiff (which I believe is the largest centre in UK for these men) has increased almost a hundredfold, owing chiefly I think to the high rate of wages now obtainable by seamen and firemen . . . I have recently made a night tour of the Arab boardinghouses here, of which there are at least 25 with a floating population of some 500. The majority of these houses have sprung up since the commencement of the war.'

PRO HO 45/11897 332087/8: H.M. Superintending Aliens Officer, Cardiff to H.M. Inspector, London, 31 March 1917.
13. SG 19.5.1916 p. 5.
14. SG 30.8.1916 p. 4.
15. SG 16.5.1968 p. 12.
16. SG 12.4.1916 p. 2.
17. SG 11.3.1919 p. 2.
18. SG 16.4.1917 p. 4.
19. Byrne, op. cit.
20. PRO HO 45/11897 332087/17: Asst. Suptg. Immigration Officer to H.M. Chief Inspector, Home Office, London, 23, January 1920.
21. Harris Joshua and Tina Wallace, *To ride the storm—the 1980 Bristol 'riot' and the state* (Heinemann Educational Books, London, 1983, p. 14).
22. Ibid. p. 14–15.
23. F.T. Bullen, *The men of the merchant service* (Smith, Elder and Co., London, 1900), pp. 320–4.
24. Messageries Maritimes began as a French road transport company, Messageries Nationales. In 1851 it came to an agreement with the French Government to take on the state-owned packet service to Levant ports. In 1853 it was renamed Compagnie des Services Maritimes des Messageries Impériales. After the revolution in France in 1871 the company changed its name to Messageries Maritimes. On the history of the company and its rivalry with P & O, see Sarah Searight, *Steaming East: the forging of steamship and rail links between Europe and Asia* (The Bodley Head, London, 1991).
25. IOR R/20/A/444 Marine compilation 1875: A memorandum from the Shipping Master, Aden to the Political Resident dated 11 December 1874 complains that Arabs and Somalis are being engaged for Messageries Maritimes steamers by unauthorized agents. Other correspondence in the file states that this custom was in force when Captain Playfair was in Aden (Captain Playfair was First Assistant Resident, Aden between 1855 and 1859); the memorandum makes reference to the fact that the system of hiring firemen had existed for many years.
26. The correspondence on both these cases is to be found in IOR R/20/A/497 Marine and general compilation 1869. Letter from the Agent, Services Maritimes des Messageries Impériales, Aden to First Assistant Resident dated 26 March 1869; Letter from the Agent, Services Maritimes des Messageries Impériales, Aden to First Assistant Resident dated 20 October 1869.
27. IOR R/20/A/444 Marine compilation 1875 states, 'The privilege of shipping native seamen without the intervention of the Shipping Master having been provisionally granted to the French consular agent, it cannot be refused to the Dutch consul.' p. 651; Letter from the Marine

Department, Aden to the consuls of France, Italy, Austro-Hungary, Royal Dutch, and Imperial German dated 9 August 1875: 'I am directed by the Resident to inform you it has been ruled by the Government of India that Africans and Arabs who are foreigners and not British subjects may be engaged to serve at this port as stokers, firemen and seamen in foreign ships without the intervention of the Shipping Master and may be discharged in a similar manner.' p. 683.

28. IOR R/20/A/444 Marine compilation 1875 p. 651 refers to the fact that the engagement of Arab and Somali seamen for British P & O vessels had not yet arisen. P & O had been running mail steamers from Suez to India since the 1840s. IOR R/20/A/810 Marine 1895, p. 337, Letter from the representatives of key shipping companies, including P & O, Luke Thomas, and Aden Coal Company, to Major Ferris, First Assistant Political Resident, asking for permission to continue to employ Mr Hormusjee Bhicajee to procure Arabs to work as firemen in their companies' steamers.

29 IOR R/20/A/2134 Employment of seamen at Aden, 1910–1918, p. 579, Letter dated 1 March 1918 from DADIWT, Aden to Pudumjee Jeewanji, licence holder for supplying seamen to H.M. ships.

30. IOR R/20/A/2133 Employment of seamen at Aden 1906–8 p. 91 Shipping Master, Aden to First Assistant Resident 6 August 1906.

31. I am grateful to Mr Norman Hassan of South Shields for allowing me to consult papers belonging to Mr Ali Hassan.

32. Ibrahim Ismaa'il, a Somali of the Warsangeli tribe, wrote his autobiography describing his experiences as a seaman. This unique document remained unknown until published by Richard Pankhurst in 1977. See Richard Pankhurst, 'An early Somali autobiography 11', *Africa* (Rome) vol. 2, (1977), pp. 355–4.

33. Ibid. pp. 368–73.

34. IOR R/20/A/444 Marine compilation 1875 pp. 635–6 Shipping Master, Aden to Political Resident 11 December 1874.

35. IOR R/20/A/444 Marine compilation 1875 pp. 634–5.

36. IOR/R/20/A/2133 Employment of seamen at Aden 1906–08. Memorandum by Commander Dobson pp. 171–2.

37. See as an illustration, complaints against the two licensed brokers, Adan Ali and Mohamed Nassir, dated 1910 in IOR R/20/A/2134 Employment of seamen at Aden, 1910–18 p. 41.

38. Ibid. p. 87 Deputy Superintendent of Police, Aden to Shipping Master, Aden.

39. Ibid. p.41.

40. Ibid. p.87.

41. IOR R/20/A/444 Marine compilation 1875, p. 667.

42. IOR R/20/A/810 Marine 1895, p. 325.

43. See correspondence dated August 1908 in IOR R/20/A/2133 Employment of seamen at Aden 1906–08, pp. 497–9.
44. IOR/R/20/A/2852 Coolies and labourers. Memo to the Resident from the First Assistant Resident dated 1920.
45. The procedure is described in a Home Office memorandum dated 14 March 1917: 'It is quite a common occurence for seamen from Aden to work their way to this country, and after obtaining their discharge here, return to Aden as passengers; they apply for tickets to Messrs Thomas Cook and Sons, and as they never have proper passports that firm arranges to obtain from this Department permits to enable them to leave this country. They are seldom if ever able to support their claim to British nationality by documentary evidence, but unless there is reason to doubt it, the permits are issued on the submission of their particulars and photographs by Messrs Thomas Cook and Sons.' PRO HO 45/11897 332087/2 Memorandum from Home Office to Chief Constable, South Shields dated 14 March 1917.
46. PRO HO 45/11897 332087 and SG 12.3.1917 p. 3 and 20. 3.1917 p. 4. A note from H.M. Inspector, Home Office dated 14 May 1917 to the Superintending Aliens Officer, Cardiff implies that the case was dismissed at the suggestion of the Home Office because the result of the charges against the three boarding-house keepers had been 'an immediate threat of a strike of all Arab seamen on the Tyne.' PRO HO 45/11897 332087/9.
47. PRO HO 45/11897 Under Secretary of State, Home Office to Chief Constable, South Shields, 3 April 1917.
48. SG 20.3.1917 p. 4.
49. SG 17.2.1925 p. 4.
50. IOR R/20/A/444 Marine compilation, 1875, p. 651.
51. IOR R/20/A/2133 Employment of seamen at Aden 1906–08 pp. 497–498, Petition submitted to Captain A.J. Meek, Superintendent, Sheikh Othman 14 August 1908.
52. Ibid. p. 499.
53. PRO HO 45/11897 332087/12 Letter from Major-General J.M. Stewart, Political Resident, Aden to British Consul-General, Marseilles, 28 March 1917.
54. PRO HO 45/11897 332087/9 Letter from the Assistant Secretary, Marine Department, Board of Trade to Under Secretary of State, Home Office, 19 April 1917.

2 Aden and the Yemen: Emigration and Society

1. The following sections on the port of Aden and the Aden Pro- tectorate are largely based on the comprehensive study by R.J. Gavin, *Aden under British rule 1839–1967* (C. Hurst and Company, London, 1975).

2. Until 1869 steamers were not in a position to compete with sailing ships for the carriage of goods in bulk. However between 1869, when the compound steam-engine came into use, and 1885 with the introduction of the high pressure steel boiler and the triple-expansion steam engine, the steamer rapidly replaced the sailing ship for the carriage of freight. Ibid. p. 178.

3. IOR R/20/A/2852 Coolies and labourers.

4. Zaidis are often referred to as the 'fifth school of Islamic law'.

5. Shafi'is belong to one of the four schools or *madhahib* of Sunni or orthodox Islam. It is estimated that they were slightly more numerous than the Zaidis in the Imamate of Yemen.

6. M.W. Wenner, *Modern Yemen 1918–1966* (The Johns Hopkins Press, Baltimore, 1967), p. 36, note 13.

7. J. Leigh Douglas, *The Free Yemeni Movement 1935–1962* (The American University of Beirut, Beirut, 1987), p. 8.

8. On the Turkish occupation of Yemen see Gavin, op.cit., especially chapters five, eight and nine.

9. The following section on the Imamate draws heavily on Wenner op.cit.; P. Dresch, *Tribes, government and history in Yemen* (Clarendon Press, Oxford, 1989); Leigh Douglas, op.cit.; and Gavin, op.cit.

10. For a detailed discussion of Yemen's external relations under Imams Yahya and Ahmad see Wenner, op.cit.

11. Dresch, op.cit., p. 229.

12. R.B. Serjeant, 'The Yemeni poet Al-Zubayri and his polemic against the Zaydi Imams', *Arabian Studies* V, 1979, p. 92, note 71.

13. Dresch, op.cit., p. 229.

14. Quoted in Leigh Douglas, op.cit., p. 11.

15. PRO CO 539/3968 78009/1B Report on the visit to King of Yemen in Ta'izz, by the Governor of Aden, November 1948.

16. On the history of emigration from Yemen see J.C. Swanson, *Emigration and economic development: the case of the Yemen Arab Republic* (Westview Press, Boulder, Colorado, 1979), chapter four.

17. The recruitment of Arab labourers at Aden for employment overseas is discussed in IOR L/P&S/10/190 Aden recruitment of Arabs 1916.

18. Leigh Douglas, op.cit., p. 40.

19. Information on the tribal origins of seamen was collected from reports in a wide range of India Office and Public Record Office files. Petitions from seamen to the British authorities at Aden often give the tribal names of the petitioners. Reports on the deportation or repatriation of seamen from Britain also give information on this subject. The following Aden Government files were particularly helpful : IOR R/20/A/2133 Employment of seamen at Aden 1906–08; IOR R/20/A/ 2134 Employment of seamen at Aden 1910–18; and IOR R/20/A/2135 Employment of seamen at Aden 1925–33.

20. The Amiri and Haushabi were among the 'nine tribes' which came under British protection during the second half of the nineteenth century. Each 'tribe' contained several sub-tribes. The others denote groups of villages making up a *mikhlaf* or administrative unit headed by a tribal sheikh.

21. The Sha'ibi were one of the sub-tribes of the Upper Yafa'i and under British protection.

22. K.L. Little, *Negroes in Britain-a study of racial relations in English society* (Kegan Paul, Trench, Trubner and Co, London, 1947), p. 134, note 1.

23. PRO CO 725/21/9 Letter from Mr Dheli to the Under Secretary of State for India dated 4 December 1930 in connection with the introduction of the rota system at South Shields.

24. 'Sir Stewart Symes [Resident, Aden] explained some of the difficulties experienced at Aden in regulating the movements of native seamen, etc. The port of Aden was the natural place to which Arabs drifted from the protectorate and from all parts of south-west Arabia, and egress from it, especially by dhow, was hard to control. Further it was comparatively easy, by means of bribery, for Arabs not of protectorate origin to get chiefs in the protectorate to declare them to be their subjects.' PRO HO 45/14299   C79323/30 no. 34, minutes of a conference held at the Colonial Office on the 4th of September 1930 to consider the question of the maintenance and repatriation, etc., of Adenese seamen.

25. Pankhurst, op.cit., pp. 364–6.

26. Leigh Douglas, for example, argues that taxation was the major factor in the emigration of Shafi'is and that the large Yemeni communities in France, Britain and USA became established in the 1920s when the Imam's taxation system was becoming an in- creasingly heavy burden. Leigh Douglas, op.cit., pp. 13–14.

27. Walter B. Harris, *Journey through the Yemen and some general remarks upon that country* (William Blackwood and Sons, London and Edinburgh, 1893), pp. 228–30.

28. As late as 1948 the Political Officer, Northern Area reported on conditions in Sha'ib territory on the Yemen border: 'Shaib is down and out; women walk about in patched rags and I have seen children picking up odd seeds of grain from the dust and eating them on the spot. The country was set for a good harvest, but the rains have failed at a vital moment, and although the country is everywhere green, unless two more heavy downpours develop, over 80% of the harvest will fail.' PRO FO 371/68340   78009/3/48 The Governor, Aden to The Secretary of State for the Colonies, 8 September 1948 concerning operations against the Saqladi Sheikh p. 2.

29. IOR R/20/A/2134 Employment of seamen at Aden 1910–18, p. 775

Petition dated 8 May 1919 to First Assistant Resident via Shipping Master.

30. IOR R/20/A/4854 Correspondence with the Sheikhs of Juban. Letter from Major Merewether, Political Officer, Dthala to Lieutenant Colonel J. Davies, First Assistant Resident, Aden dated 19 October 1904.

31. PRO FO 371/68340 Report on operations in the Northern Area, August 1948, p. 5.

32. PRO CO 725/31/3 Letter from the Resident, Aden to the Secretary of State for the Colonies, 16 April 1935.

33. The correspondence on this subject is in PRO CO 725/31/3.

34. The correspondence is in IOR/R/20/A/1528 Nationality of Arabs in Aden vicinity.

35. It is interesting to note that in legal matters concerning seamen, particularly claims to the estate of a deceased Arab seamen, the Shipping Master, Aden normally insisted that claims by the man's relatives and heirs had to be verified by the claimant's sheikh. See for example the case of Ali Hassan, 11 Nelson's Bank, South Shields, a Shamiri, who claimed to be the lawful cousin and heir of Kassim Hassan, a seaman who died in 1934. He was required to produce a document from the Sheikh of Shamir testifying that he was the sole heir to Kassim Hassan's wages and possessions. PRO CO 725/43/1 Letter from the Shipping Master, Aden to the Assistant Secretary for Finance, Board of Trade, London, 10 December 1935.

36. For example a memorandum on Arab seamen by the Acting British Vice-Consul, Marseilles emphasizes the temporary nature of their emigration. 'It appears to be a recognised fact that such seamen leave with the fixed intention of accumulating a sum of, say three or four hundred pounds and returning therewith to their homes.' PRO HO 45/13392   493912/97 Memorandum on Coloured Seamen by the Acting British Vice-Consul, Marseilles, 11 December 1928.

3 The 'Big Men' of the Community: The Arab Boarding-house Masters

1. PRO CO 725/21/8 Letter from Chief Superintendent, Mercantile Marine Office, North Shields to The Assistant Secretary, Mercantile Department, Board of Trade dated 29 July 1930.

2. These regulations did not apply to seamen who were living with their families. Some single Arab seamen evaded the regulations by renting an unfurnished room in a house thereby becoming a subtenant and not a lodger. A few items of furniture would then be purchased often for a nominal or fictitious sum to satisfy the police or Sanitary Authorities (Little, op.cit., p. 40). A number of seamen who had married and

settled down in South Shields sublet rooms in their homes to single Arab seamen to help pay the rent. Certain Arab refreshment house keepers also took in seamen as boarders. Unlicensed boarding-houses were not unknown. For example in December 1921 Musid Mohamed was charged with receiving seamen into 23 and 24 Long Row, South Shields, premises which had not been licensed by the Sanitary Authority as a seamen's lodging-house (SG 24.12.1921 p. 3).

3. PRO CO 725/54/7 Letter from Chief Constable, South Shields to Under Secretary of State, Home Office, Aliens Department, London dated 15 November 1938.

4. SG 12.4.1935 p. 3.

5. A licence was granted for the bus service by the South Shields' Watch Committee in 1929. One councillor objected strongly to the granting of the licence but another defended the decision arguing that: 'This man paid £2,000 for this bus, and his licence is a privilege to which he is legally and morally entitled.' (SG 6.6.1929 p. 2). A detailed description of Said Hassan's business activities is given in SG 31.1.1930 p. 7.

6. SG 12.2.1925 p. 3.

7. SG 26.7.1939 p. 5.

8. SG 20.5.1916 p. 3.

9. SG 21.6.1921 p. 3. and 5.7.1921 p. 5.

10. Details of the case are given in SG 20.8.1921 p. 3.

11. SG 15.5.1914 p. 6.

12. SG 24.1.1919 p. 3.

13. SG 5.11.1931 p. 7.

14. SG 19.2.1919 p. 2; 25.2.1919 p. 3; 12.3.1919 p. 3; 13.3.1919 p. 3; 14.3.1919 p. 3; 19.3.1919 p. 2; 25.3.1919 p. 3; 26.3.1919 p. 3; 27.6.1919 p. 3; 28.6.1919 p. 3; 30.6.1919 p. 3.

15. SG 30.12.1924 p. 5.

16. SG 13.12.1921 p. 5.

17. SG 8.2.1929 p. 6. 'Freedom' in a letter to the *Shields Daily Gazette* replied: 'Arab boarding houses are not essential to British industrial welfare as they only exist to supply what displaces our own seamen and thus adds to the burden of our town and country' (SG 11.2.1929 p. 4).

18. SG 16.7.1921 p. 3.

19. SG 20.10.1921 p. 3.

20. I am most grateful to Mr Norman Hassan for allowing me to see papers belonging to Mr Ali Hassan.

21. I am most grateful to the late Mr Michael Muckble for allowing me to see letters belonging to his father.

22. *The Seaman* vol. 8, no. 442, (18 December 1929) p. 4.

23. PRO HO 45/11897 Deputation to the Board of Trade (Viscount

Wolmer) from the Seafarers Joint Council regarding the employment of Arabs to the detriment of British seafarers, Board of Trade, London, 15 January 1923, p. 5.

24. Ibid. p. 8.
25. PRO HO 45/14299 Part 1 Report on visit to Antwerp by G. Gunning, Assistant General Secretary, National Union of Seamen, 10.6.1930.
26. SG 23.7.1928 p. 4.
27. SG 13.2.1925 p. 6.
28. SG 9.5.1916 p. 2.
29. SG 12.2.1925 p. 3.
30. SG 1.6.1926 p. 4.
31. PRO HO 45/11897 Report on Coloured Seamen by E.N. Cooper, Immigration Officer, Liverpool dated 17.2.1921, pp. 4–5.
32. Anecdotal evidence from South Shields suggests that such practices were not exclusively associated with Arabs. There are claims that Shetlanders and Irish seamen also used bribery to secure jobs. It is interesting to note that in South Shields seamen from the Shetlands were commonly referred to as 'white Arabs'. There are also references to the nefarious role of moneylenders among the white seamen. One writer, for example, refers to them as 'hawks' who hovered around men who were signing on with wads of notes ready to lend money so that those in arrears with their subscriptions to the union could square up and obtain their PC5 (Letter to the Editor from 'A.B.' SG 28. 7.1930 p. 4).
33. SG 26.7.1929 p. 4.
34. Quoted in M.J. Daunton, 'Jack Ashore: seamen in Cardiff before 1914', *Welsh History Review*, vol. 9, no. 2 (December 1978) pp. 176–7.
35. North-east ports evidently had a better reputation with regard to crimping and other such practices than some other ports, e.g. London and Cardiff. Many seamen shipping from north-east ports were local men who went home to their families when they came onshore.
36. SG 2.6.1913 p. 4.
37. SG 19.5.1916 p. 5.
38. SG 5.6.1919 p. 5.
39. SG 28.6.1919 p. 3.
40. Violent clashes took place between Arab seamen around Muckble's boarding-house at 5 East Holborn in May 1916. At the subsequent trial, Mr Spence, defending four men from Muckble's boarding-house, stated: 'Witness thought there were two different tribes of Arabs engaged in the struggle.' The Magistrate's Clerk asked, 'Or two different boarding houses, which?' Constable Ryles said there were two different factions, whatever they were (SG 19.5.1916 p. 5).
41. The statement by the union official, Mr Walsh, does not make it clear in detail just how this rota operated. He stated: 'These Arab Boarding

Masters could not, as I say, agree among themselves, and therefore the Board of Trade and the Chief Constable and ourselves met and formed a plan whereby certain men should come in rota, and all the Arab boarding-house keepers and coffee-shop keepers who put up Arabs as boarders, were put on a list and each list as it came in, they went to this, that or the other house. That saved any trouble for a time, but now there is a big demand, and the principal boarding-house keeper in South Shields has been to me and, speaking in the name of all the establishments, he says he wants that scrapped, and he wants Arabs to be able to go out in the open and be picked the same as anyone else, to revert to the old system they had before.' PRO HO 45/11897 Deputation to the Board of Trade (Viscount Wolmer) from the Seafarers' Joint Council regarding the employment of Arabs to the detriment of British seafarers, Board of Trade, London, 15 January 1923, p. 8.

42. This matter was clearly discussed after the Mill Dam 'riot' in February 1919. Dr Abdul Majid, an Indian barrister practising in London and President of the Islamic Society, visited South Shields in March 1919 to mediate between the Arab community and the authorities. In a statement to the *Shields Daily Gazette* he pointed out that on the subject of the employment of Arabs he was making arrangements with the Government of India for these men to be selected from a 'waiting list' so that in future the precise number of men available would be known and that they would be engaged according to the length of time they had been ashore. He believed that this was the best way to solve the problem. He also stated that he had established a committee of Arab boarding-house keepers and representatives of seamen from different parts of the world such as Arabs, Indians and Malays, known as the South Shields branch of the Islamic Society, to protect the interests of the Muslims and look after their economic, moral and religious welfare (SG 11.2.1919 p. 2). The rota system that was eventually introduced appears to have included Somali seamen staying at the Arab boarding-houses as well as Arab seamen. For example, in February 1920 Mohamed Farah, a Somali fireman lodging at an Arab boarding-house at 10 Chapter Row, was charged with assaulting a Board of Trade official at the Mill Dam. Farah had been ashore for five months and twelve days without finding a ship. The solicitor defending Farah asked a Board of Trade official if regulations for shipping coloured men were being strictly adhered to and that if men were being taken in strict rotation why had this man been ashore for over five months. (SG 10.2.1920 p. 5).

43. SG 9.3.1923 p. 5.

44. Ibid.

45. SG 25.3.1927 p. 7.

46. SG 5.12.1924 p. 5.
47. Ibid.
48. SG 17.4.1928 p. 2.
49. SG 9.10.1928 p. 5.
50. See SG 18.2.1929 p. 5; 10.6.1929 p. 5; 17.6.1929 p. 5; 2.7.1929 p. 3; 4.7.1929 p. 3; 16.8.1929 p. 8; 16.11.1929 p. 6; 18.11.1929 p. 2.
51. PRO HO 45/11897 Copy of Extract of Report from the Mercantile Marine Office, Blyth, dated 5 November 1920.
52. PRO HO 45/11897 Asst. Suptg. Immigration Officer, Immigration Office, Newcastle-on-Tyne to H.M. Chief Inspector, Home Office, London, 23 January 1920.
53. PRO HO 45/13392 493912/42 Note of a conference held at the Home Office on 26 January 1928 p. 2.
54. PRO HO 45/11897 Memo signed C. Baines, India Office, dated 23.2.1920.
55. An interesting example is provided by a case which came before the South Shields magistrates on 20 March 1924 (PRO HO 45/11897 332087/86 Immigration Officers' Report, South Shields on the subject of Abdullah Ahmed alias Hassan Karika alias Hassan Yaya Coloured Seaman dated 20 March 1924).
56. IOR R/20/A/2852 Coolies and labourers. Letter from the Aden Residency to the Secretary of Administration dated 7 August 1920.
57. IOR R/20/A/2852 Coolies and labourers. Note by K.S. Dadina, Superintendent of Police, Aden dated 8.6.1920.
58. A useful insight into the activities of seamen's agents and their rivalries can be found in IOR R/20/A/3265 Re: certain Arab passengers who left Aden for Marseilles without passports, 1928. See also Dick Lawless, 'The role of seamen's agents in the migration for employment of Arab seafarers in the early twentieth century', *Immigrants and Minorities* April, 1995).
59. PRO CO 725/43/1 Letter from the Governor, Aden to the Secretary of State for the Colonies, 14 April 1937; See also IOR R/20/A/2473 Passports: impounding of registration certificates of seamen, dated 1936. All the correspondence in this file relates to allegations that certain Arabs from Yemen living in South Shields and Cardiff had fraudulently obtained British Indian passports through seamen's agents in Aden. Further allegations regarding trafficking in passports and certificates of nationality and identity were made in 1938 (See PRO CO 725/54/9 Letter from M.R. Cowell, Colonial Office, London to Sir Bernard Reilly, Governor, Aden dated 13 June 1938 and letter from Sir Bernard Reilly to Cowell dated 3 August 1938. In both of these cases, one of the men making the allegations was a former seaman, Hassan Abdul Kader Mackawee, who appears to have been in business in both South Shields and Cardiff. According to an enquiry made at

the request of the Governor of Aden into the allegations, Mackawee had attempted to establish himself as a seamen's agent at Aden but had rapidly lost clients and business because he had been misappropriating his clients' money. It is claimed that he threatened certain seamen who refused to deal with him that he would cause trouble for them when he went to Britain and would have them returned to Aden.

60. PRO CO 725/54/7 Copy of a report, no. 3337 dated 18 August 1938 from the Police Inspector, Crater and Report from Chief Constable's Office, South Shields on Salyman Hassan, dated 8 October 1938.

61. IOR R/20/A/3265 Re: certain Arab passengers who left Aden for Marseilles without passports dated 1928.

62. PRO HO 45/13392 493912/42 Note of conference held at the Home Office on 26 January 1928, p. 2.

63. SG 18.9.1929 p. 9.

64. PRO HO 45/12314 Home Office memorandum on the Coloured Alien Seamen's Order 1925 dated 24.9.1925 p. 5.

65. At a conference held at the Colonial Office on 3 May 1929, Mr Adams of the High Commissioner's Office, India, 'referred in particular to the insistent requests of certain boarding-house keepers in South Shields for the issue of these certificates to Adenese boarding with them.' PRO CO 725/19/6 Notes of a conference held at the Colonial Office on 3 May 1929, p. 2.

66. PRO HO 45/13392 Letter from H.M. Immigration Officer, Mill Dam, South Shields to H.M. Inspector, Newcastle dated 11 January 1928.

67. See the debate in PRO HO 45/11897 Deputation to the Board of Trade (Viscount Wolmer) from the Seafarer's Joint Council regarding the employment of Arabs to the detriment of British seafarers, Board of Trade, London 15 January 1923.

68. Numerous cases of Arabs charged with landing without permission of the immigration officer were reported in the Shields Daily Gazette; see for example SG 9.7.1925 p. 7; 7.12.1927 p. 5; 1.3.1928 p. 5; 17.12.1928 p. 5; 14.9.1929 p. 5; 6.12.1929 p. 11; 12.12.1929 p. 5. During one such case in March 1928 the Chief Constable of South Shields stated that Arabs landing without permission were giving the police a great deal of trouble. He stated, 'Fining these men is no punishment at all . . . Other people bring them into the country and the Aliens Department is determined to stamp it out if possible.' He also pointed out that when these men were fined, others paid their fines for them so that it was no punishment for them. They should therefore be sent to prison (SG 1.3.1928 p. 5). In December 1928 the police stated that they were having considerable trouble with Arab stowaways and during the past six or seven weeks about sixty or seventy of them had come into the town (SG 17.12.1928 p. 5).

69. PRO CO 725/21/8 Destitute Coloured Seamen. Report from Chief

Superintendent, Mercantile Marine Office, North Shields to Assistant Secretary, Mercantile Marine Department, Board of Trade dated 29 July 1930. These figures would be more meaningful if we had statistics for those Arabs employed at sea in 1922 and 1930 but these data are not available.

70. Extract from Report by the Chief Constable, South Shields to the Watch Committee reproduced in SG 20.2.1930 p. 5.

71. Men signing on British ships in the foreign trade were required to prove to the Mercantile Marine Superintendents by documentary evidence that they were either British subjects or had been given permission to land by an immigration officer.

72. PRO HO 45/11897 Copy of extract of report from the Mercantile Marine Office, Blyth, dated 5 November 1920.

73. PRO HO 45/11897 Report on Registration of coloured seamen, Aliens Branch, Home Office, initialled W.H.P., and dated 3.11.1924.

74. For details of the Special Restriction (Coloured Alien Seamen) Order of 1925 which came into operation at South Shields in April 1925 see Chapter Four, p. 106. One of the aims of the Special Restriction Order was to make the Arab boarding-house masters realize that it was no longer profitable for them to keep men who had no hope of obtaining certificates of registration and therefore stop them from importing others. It was even hoped that the masters might ask for the repatriation of some of the men in their charge. PRO HO 45/12314 476761/99 Report on registration of Arabs irregularly landed by Sergeant Gerald Broben, Detectives Department, Cardiff City Police, 20 May 1926.

75. The Assistant General Secretary of the National Union of Seamen reported in May 1930 that, 'While every endeavour has been made to put the Joint Supply system into operation in the Weekly boats, owing to the action of certain engineers and boarding masters, it is impossible to keep an effective check on the employment of coloured ratings in British ships.' PRO HO 45/14299 Part 1 Report on visit to Antwerp by G. Gunning, Assistant General Secretary, National Union of Seamen, May 1920.

76. PRO HO 45/14299 Part 2 Letter from H.M. Inspector, H.M. Immigration Office, Newcastle to H.M. Chief Inspector dated 9 January 1931.

77. PRO HO 45/13392 Memorandum on the working of the Special Restriction (Coloured Alien Seamen) Order, 1925, dated 17.5.28.

78. PRO CO 725/21/9 Letter from Abdul Sophie et al. to the Under Secretary of State for India, dated 1 October 1930.

79. PRO CO 725/21/9 Letter from Mohamet Muckble to the Under Secretary of State for India (undated).

80. PRO HO 45/14299 Part 1 Newspaper cutting from Daily Herald

attached to letter from the Chief Constable, South Shields to Home Office dated 1 October 1930.

81. PRO HO 45/14299 Part 1 562898/36 Home Office Minute initialled J.P. and dated 3.10.30. See also an interesting letter from Ali Saleh Alewa, 2 Mill Dam, South Shields to the High Commissioner, India House, undated but obviously written in 1932, in which he states, 'That we people of Aden amongst the whole of the British Coloured seamen throughout the Empire, have not been treated accordingly by the Federation Officials and been forced to take the rota system. In the first place, it was declared in their papers of 1930 that the rota system was meant so as to send the Arab Boarding House Masters into the limbo of forgotten things and not for the British coloured seamen.' IOR R/20/A/2473 Letter from Ali Saleh Alewa to the High Commissioner, India House, undated.

4 Unwelcome Guests: Competition for Jobs

1. In analysing the material from South Shields for this chapter I owe a great debt to the pioneering work of Neil Evans on the Black community in Cardiff. See notably Neil Evans, 'Regulating the reserve army: Arabs, Blacks and the local state in Cardiff, 1919–45', *Immigrants and Minorities*, vol. 4, no. 2 (July 1985) pp. 68–115.

2. SG 15.4.1913 p. 4.

3. SG 16.4.1913 p. 4.

4. SG 3.9.1914 p. 4.

5. SG 6.5.1916 p. 2. In 1915 the Admiralty came under pressure from the National Seamen's and Firemen's Union to exclude Chinese sailors and firemen from British transports and as a result issued a notice to owners of all transports and to mercantile marine officers that in Admiralty transports as far as possible crews should be British or British coloured persons. No other nationalities should be employed unless it proved impossible to engage British or British coloured crews (SG 9.11.1915 p. 9). Of course, at this time Arab seamen were classified as 'British coloured persons'.

6. SG 9.5.1916 p. 2.

7. SG 9.5.1916 p. 2.

8. SG 16.5.1918 p. 3.

9. There seems little doubt that the Imam knew of the campaign against the Arabs in Britain as he undoubtedly had informants among the port communities there and recognized that his country benefited from the remittances which the seamen sent back to their families in Yemen. It is therefore somewhat ironic that in 1923 Imam Yahya asked the Political Resident, Aden for British protection for his subjects in Abyssinia, a request which Britain readily agreed to. The Yemeni

community in Abyssinia at this time numbered around 2,000. The Resident commented, 'I think it desirable to help the Imam's subjects where possible in order to get the Imam into the habit of seeking our assistance.' In a letter to the British Minister in Addis Ababa dated 12 July 1923 the Resident wrote, 'The Imam is an independent ruler in the Yemen, with whom I am at present negotiating a treaty. I consider it very desirable that he should turn to His Majesty's representatives for assistance in his difficulties rather than seek aid from the French or the Italians' (IOR R/20/A/3085 Request of the Imam for the protection of his subjects in Abyssinia by H.M.'s representative there). Of course at this time Arabs in Britain maintained that they were British subjects—the status that had been granted them during the First World War—and any intervention on their behalf by the Imam would have undermined their case by confirming that they were in fact aliens. This may explain why the Imam did not protest against the treatment of his subjects in Britain. A more cynical reason may be that he was more concerned about the community in Abyssinia because it included many wealthy merchants.

10. The disturbances in Cardiff in June 1919 left three men dead, dozens injured and caused damage to property of over £3,000. For information on the race riots at other ports in 1919 see Evans, 1980, op.cit., pp. 5–29; Neil Evans, 'The South Wales race riots of 1919: a documentary postscript', *Llafur*, vol. 3, no. 4, (1983) pp. 76–87; Roy May and Robin Cohen, 'The interaction between race and colonialism: a case study of the Liverpool race riots of 1919', *Race and Class*, vol. 16, no. 2 (1974) pp. 113–26; Jacqueline Jenkinson, 'The Black community of Salford and Hull 1919–21', *Immigrants and Minorities*, vol. 7, no. 2 (1988) pp. 166–83; Peter Fryer, *Staying power: the history of Black people in Britain* (Pluto Press, London and Sydney, 1984), pp. 298–316; Joshua and Wallace, op.cit., pp. 20–7.

11. SG 13.1.1919 p. 3.

12. SG 15.1.1919 p. 3.

13. In 1919 South Shields had a much less favourable ratio of police to population than Cardiff or Liverpool. In South Shields the population per constable was 885; for Cardiff 624 and for Liverpool 332. Evans (1980), op.cit., p. 19.

14. SG 5.2.1919 p. 3.

15. SG 12.2.1919 p. 3.

16. No details are given about the man named as Abdul Zaid in the press reports but it seems probable that he was Abdul Rahman Zaid who kept a boarding-house in East Holborn and that this was where the chief engineer made arrangements to sign on the nine Arab firemen. Zaid would then have accompanied the men as usual when they went to the Shipping Office.

17. The main sources for these events are SG 5.2.1919 p. 3; 11.2.1919 p. 3; 12.2.1919 p. 3; 18.2.1919 p. 3; 5.3.1919 p. 3; 6.3.1919 p. 3.
18. SG 10.3.1919 p. 3.
19. See PRO HO 45/12314 Letter from Dr [Abdul] Majid to the Under Secretary of State for India dated 16 April 1925 and responses from the India Office and Home Office dated 18 April 1925 and 9 May 1925.
20. The report accompanying the interview with Dr Abdul Majid suggests that no fewer than 700 Arab seamen sailing from the Tyne lost their lives through enemy action during the First World War (SG 11.3.1919 p. 2).
21. SG 11.3.1919 p. 2.
22. Ibid.
23. Ibid.
24. Ibid.
25. SG 2.6.1921 p. 2.
26. SG 4.5.1922 p. 4.
27. SG 10.5.1922 p. 2.
28. SG 4.2.1925 p. 4.
29. SG 12.2.1925 p. 3.
30. SG 29.5.1926 p. 4.
31. SG 6.8.1927 p. 4.
32. SG 16.2.1929 p. 4.
33. SG 11.1.1930 p. 4.
34. SG 11.2.1935 p. 9.
35. SG 3.6.1921 p. 4.
36. SG 10.5.1922 p. 2.
37. SG 6.2.1925 p. 6.
38. SG 14.2.1925 p. 4.
39. SG 12.2.1925 p. 3.
40. SG 12.12.1929 p. 4.
41. SG 14.2.1929 p. 4.
42. SG 15.2.1929 p. 6.
43. SG 24.1.1930 p. 6.
44. SG 6.5.1930 p. 4.
45. SG 4.2.1935 p. 4.
46. PRO HO 45/11897 Document entitled 'Registration of Coloured Seamen' by Aliens Branch, Home Office, dated 3.11.1924.
47. PRO HO 45/11897 332087/17 Letter from Asst. Suptg. Immigration Officer, Newcastle to H.M. Inspector, Home Office dated 23 January 1920.
48. PRO HO 45/11897 332087/22 Copy of Extract of Report from Mercantile Marine Office, Blyth dated 5 November 1920.
49. PRO HO 45/11897 Observations by J.E. Shuckburgh, India Office

dated 4.3.1920 on papers dealing with the control of Arab seamen at South Shields submitted by the Home Office.

50. PRO HO 45/11897 Letter from G.E. Baker, Board of Trade to W. Haldane Porter, H.M. Chief Inspector, Aliens Branch, Home Office dated 4 December 1920.

51. See for example PRO HO 45/11897 Letter from Chief Constable, Cardiff to Under Secretary of State, Home Office, 24 September 1923.

52. PRO HO 45/11897 332087/86 Immigration Officer's Report on the subject of Abdullah Ahmed alias Hassan Karika alias Hassan Yaya dated 20 March 1924.

53. PRO HO 45/11897 332087/23 Report on Coloured Seamen by E.N. Cooper, Immigration Office, Liverpool dated 17.2.1921.

54. PRO HO 45/11897 Deputation to the Board of Trade (Viscount Wolmer) from the Seafarers' Joint Council regarding the employment of Arabs to the detriment of British seafarers, Board of Trade, London 15 January 1923.

55. PRO HO 45/11897 Memorandum on Registration of Coloured Seamen by W. Haldane Porter, Aliens Branch, Home Office dated 3.11.1924.

56. PRO HO 45/11897 Letter from Chief Constable, South Shields to W. Haldane Porter, Aliens Branch, Home Office dated 10 July 1924.

57. See PRO HO 45/11897 Letter from the Under Secretary of State, Home Office on the 'Registration of Coloured Alien Seamen (other than Chinese and Japanese)' addressed to Chief Constables and dated 23 March 1925. The first paragraph states, '. . . he [the Secretary of State] has come to the conclusion that in order to deal with the problem presented by aliens—particularly those of them who are Arabs—it is necessary that they should be required in all cases . . .'.

58. See PRO HO 45/11897 Memorandum on Registration of Coloured Seamen by W. Haldane Porter, Aliens Branch, Home Office dated 3.11.24.

59. See PRO HO 45/11897 Memorandum: Instructions as to the Registration of Coloured Alien Seamen (other than Chinese and Japanese) under the Special Restriction (Coloured Alien Seamen) Order, 1925 clause eleven.

60. See PRO HO 45/12314 Report on Coloured Alien Seamen's Order, 1925 by E.N. Cooper, Immigration Office, Liverpool, dated 24.9.25.

61. PRO HO 45/13392 493912/36 Extract from Minutes of Meeting of Aliens Branch Inspectorate held at the Home Office on 5 October 1927.

62. PRO HO 45/13392 493912/42 Coloured Alien Seamen: Note of conference held at the Home Office on 26 January 1928.

63. PRO HO 45/13392   493912/36   Special Restriction (Coloured Alien Seamen) Order 1925. Memorandum from the Aliens Branch Inspectorate dated 22.11.1927.
64. PRO HO 45/13392 Home Office Memorandum initialled N.C.B. and dated 17.5.1928.
65. PRO HO 45/13392 Memorandum initialled C.R. and dated 1.9.1929.
66. SG 20.2.1930 p. 5.
67. See Evans, 1985 op.cit., pp. 79–81.
68. PRO HO 45/12314 476761/10 Letter from Dr Abdul Majid to the Under Secretary of State, India Office dated 16 April 1925; PRO HO 45/12314 Letter from the Under Secretary of State, Home Office to the Under Secretary of State, India Office dated 9 May 1925.
69. PRO HO 45/12314 476761/71 Letter from the Secretary, Economic and Overseas Department, India Office to the Under Secretary of State, Home Office dated 22 January 1926; PRO HO 45/12314 Letter from the Home Office to the Chief Constable, South Shields dated 30 July 1926.
70. SG 6.12.1929 p. 11.

5 South Shields the Storm Centre: The Rota System and the 'Arab Riot' of August 1930

1. 'Deputation from the National Union of Seamen on the subject of Arab seamen received by the Board of Trade and Home Office', *The Seaman*, vol. 8, no. 422 (18 December1929) p. 4.
2. PRO CO 725/21/8 Letter from Ali Said to the Secretary of State for India dated 27 December 1929.
3. The Arabs of Cardiff also appeared to have acted through a solicitor in their efforts to resist the campaign against them (see Evans (1985), op.cit., p.81).
4. SG 18.3.1930 p. 5.
5. SG 19.3.1930 p. 2.
6. SG 22. 3.1930 p. 5.
7. SG 19.3.1930 p. 2.
8. SG 17.4.1930 p. 5.
9. SG 25.4.1930 p. 5.
10. SG 30.4.1930 p. 4.
11. SG 29.4.1930 p. 4.
12. SG 2.5.1930 p. 2.
13. This section is based on Basil Mogridge, 'Militancy and inter-union rivalries in British shipping, 1911–1929', *International Review of Social History*, VI (1961) pp. 375–415.
14. A national seamen's union was formed in 1887 at Sunderland as the National Amalgamated Sailors' and Firemen's Union. Between 1894

and 1926 it was known as the National Sailors' and Firemen's Union and from 1926 onwards as the National Union of Seamen.

15. It is interesting to note that according to the Minutes of the South Shields Labour Party and Trades Council, the AMWU did not accept coloured men as members. See South Shields Labour Party and Trades Council, Minutes of Meeting held on 24 September 1922. I am grateful to Miss Doris Johnson, Local Studies Librarian, Borough of South Tyneside Libraries for bringing this reference to my attention.

16. David Byrne, 'The 1930 "Arab riot" in South Shields: a race riot that never was', *Race and Class*, vol. XVIII, no. 3 (1977) p. 266.

17. The South Shields branch of the Seamen's Protection Society, a critic of NUS policies but a bitter rival of the Seamen's Minority Movement, also denounced the NUS for arousing racial antagonism and called on the Government to take action against the union because its actions were detrimental to the interests of the British Empire (see Letter from Allen Aitken, President, Seamen's Protection Society, South Shields to the Editor, *Shields Daily Gazette* (SG 6.5.1930 p. 4). However the society does not appear to have played a significant role in the resistance to the racist attacks against the Arabs in the town.

18. SG 30.4.1930 p. 2 and p. 5; SG 1.7.1930 p. 7.

19. SG 1.5.1930 p. 4.

20. SG 3.5.1930 p. 4.

21. SG 27.5.1930 p. 4.

22. SG 24.5.1930 p. 4.

23. SG 23.5.1930 p. 4.

24. PRO HO 45/14299 562898/2 Memorandum on registration system for seamen at certain European ports by Lt. Commander the Hon. J.M. Kenworthy, R.N., MP, and Report on a visit to Antwerp by G. Gunning, Assistant Secretary General, National Union of Seamen.

25. In a letter to the Colonial Office from A.S. Hoskin of the Board of Trade in October 1930, he states, 'We were not consulted in connection with the institution of the system and there seems to be no reason why we should interfere with it. We take the view that the selection of seamen for employment is a matter for the discretion of the shipowner and, so long as there is no breach of the law, there are no grounds on which we could officially intervene. The rota system is not illegal and, so far as we can judge, not inequitable; and there for the present the matter rests' (PRO CO 725/21/9 Letter from A.S. Hoskin, Merchantile Marine Department, Board of Trade to F.J. Howard, Colonial Office dated 5 October 1930). Yet in May 1930 in answer to a question in the House of Commons from West Russell, MP for Tynemouth, about the preference given to coloured seamen by some shipowners, Graham, President of the Board of Trade, stated that he had received a report from the British Consul-General at

Antwerp on the system of registering Arab seamen operating at that port and would be quite ready to consider the adoption of a similar system at British ports (SG 5.5.1930 p. 5). Later that month, when Commander Kenworthy presented his memorandum on the rota system at Antwerp, he stated clearly that it was drawn up at the request of both the Home Office and the President of the Board of Trade and for their information (PRO HO 45/14299 Part 1 562898/2 Memorandum on registration system for seamen at certain European ports by Lt. Commander the Hon. J.M. Kenworthy, R.N., MP).

26. PRO HO 45/14299 Part 1 'Rota system for British Arabs and coloured seamen agreed', *The Seaman*, (2.7.1930).

27. At a meeting between officials of the NUS and the Shipping Federation and Arab boarding-house masters at South Shields on 21 July 1930, Clouston, the District Secretary of the NUS stated: 'In commencing the registration we would register men who had been ashore 12–18 months, so as to give them all a chance to obtain employment seeing that inequality of opportunity was one of the chief reasons for the rota system, it would have been illogical to have insisted at the beginning of the registration that only financial members could register. Of course after obtaining employment and upon their application for re-registration, their position would naturally have to be reconsidered and dealt with, each case individually on its merits.' This statement was set out in a letter from Clouston to the *Shields Daily Gazette* to answer criticisms from Ahmed Alwin as to why white seamen were not to receive similar concessions. As far as the white seamen who were in arrears were concerned, Clouston merely stated that union officials tried to do their duty impartially and in the best interests of their members (SG 25.7.1930 p. 5).

28. SG 8.7.1930 p. 4.

29. SG 22.7.1930 p. 5.

30. Ibid.

31. SG 24.7.1930 p. 5.

32. Ibid.

33. SG 22.7.1930 p. 5.

34. SG 25.7.1930 p. 5; 26.7.1930 p. 4; 29.7.1930 p. 5.

35. SG 26.7.1930 p. 4; PRO HO 45/14299 Part 1 562898/19 Letter on unrest amongst Arab seamen by Sergeant T. Holdsworth, Detectives Department, Cardiff City Police, dated 26 July 1930.

36. SG 30.7.1930 p. 4.

37. SG 25.7.1930 p. 7.

38. We have no information about the internal politics of this faction. On the evidence available, Ali Said was the only Arab boarding-house master who became closely associated with the Seamen's Minority Movement. It seems probable that not all the Arab boarding-house

masters who were opposed to the rota were willing to become involved with the Seamen's Minority Movement and it would be interesting to know the extent to which Ali Said was able to influence the rank and file of Arab seamen in the town. It is perhaps significant that in one of his statements, Clouston of the NUS implied that he had discussed the rota system with Ahmed Alwin before the meeting with the boarding-house masters on 21 July so that Alwin would have an opportunity to explain it to the men (SG 29.7.1930 p. 5).

39. SG 24.7.1930 p. 5.
40. SG 23.7.1930 p. 5.
41. In sharp contrast to the faction opposed to the rota system, who wrote regularly to the local press to state their views, somewhat surprisingly there are no letters or statements from the rival faction. Had the editor of the *Shields Daily Gazette* received any letters from this group, it seems certain that he would have published them. Clouston, the NUS District Secretary, told the *Shields Daily Gazette* that at the meeting with Arab and Somali boarding-house masters on 21 July 1930 some of the Somali seamen had agreed to register under the rota (SG 24.7.1930 p. 5).
42. The Brief for the prosecution in the case of Rex vs. Ali Said and others states that during the disturbances at the Mill Dam on 2 August 1930 Hassan Mohamed had tried to calm the Arabs, that he took no part in the disturbances and held views contrary to those of the Arabs involved in the fighting (TWAS T95/152 Rex vs. Ali Said and others).
43. SG 9.9.1930 p. 5.
44. PRO CO 725/21/9 Letter from Dr Khalid Sheldrake, Life President, Western Islamic Association to the Secretary of State for India, India Office dated 18 September 1930. It is worth recalling that as early as 1919, after the disturbances in February of that year in South Shields, Dr Abdul Majid of the Islamic Society recommended the introduction of a 'waiting list' whereby Arabs would be engaged according to the length of time they had been ashore.
45. SG 31.7.1930 p. 5.
46. Evans (1985), op.cit., p. 107.
47. In reply to a question in the House of Lords from Lord Lamington, who feared that the treatment of Arabs in Britain might have repercussions in the east where these events might be exaggerated, Lord Ponsonby for the Government stated that the total number of Arabs in the United Kingdom was not large and that the 120,517 engagements of seamen for service in foreign-going ships during the first quarter of 1930 included 1,116 Arabs or 0.9 per cent (SG 3.6.1930 p. 5). The NUS, of course, claimed that the engagement of Arabs was a more serious problem on the weekly boats but that has yet to be proven.
48. SG 11.9.1930 p. 4.

49. TWAS T95/152 Manifesto of the Tyneside District Party Committee of the Communist Party, Great Britain (undated).
50. Ibid.
51. SG 5.8.1930 p. 5.
52. SG 31.7.1930 p. 5.
53. Byrne, 1977 op.cit., p. 271.
55. TWAS. T95/152 Brief for the prosecution, Rex vs. Ali Said and others, Durham County Assizes. A brief report on the events was sent by the Chief Constable of South Shields to the Home Office (PRO HO 45/14200 Part 1 562898 /22 Letter from Chief Constable, South Shields to the Under Secretary of State, Home Office dated 18 August 1930.
56. Presumably he was referring to the charge of intimidation against Coverdale.
57. TWAS T95/152 Brief for the prosecution pp. 5–6.
58. Ibid. p. 6.
59. Ibid.
60. TWAS T95/152 Manifesto to the Seamen of South Shields issued by the South Shields Seamen's Committee of Action and dated 4 August 1930.
61. These documents are contained in TWAS T95/152 Rex vs. Ali Said and others.
62. TWAS T95/152 Depositions of witnesses.
63. During the trial one of the police officers, Inspector Wilson, was reported to have stated that some of the Arab boarding-house keepers assisted the police in quieting the Arabs (SG 20.11.1930 p. 4).
64. TWAS T95/152 Brief for the prosecution, Rex vs. Ali Said, Durham County Assizes pp. 12–16.
65. TWAS T95/152 Depositions of witnesses.
66. TWAS T95/152 Background notes on each of the men charged prepared by the Chief Constable of South Shields and addressed to His Lordship, the Judge, Assize Court, Durham.
67. TWAS T95/152 Statement by William Wilkie, Chief Constable, South Shields addressed to The Judge, Assize Court, Durham.
68. Two of the Arabs arrested had the same name. The other man named Abdul Asig boarded at 21 East Holborn.
69. SG 12.8.1930 p. 5.
70. Communist International Records 539/3/305 R. Lovell to M. Stassova, MOPR (International Red Aid) Executive, Moscow 23.9.1930. I am grateful to Marika Sherwood, Institute of Commonwealth Studies, University of London, for this reference.
71. SG 19.8.1930 p. 5.
72. SG 19.11.1930 p. 5.
73. Ibid.

74. SG 20.11.1930 p. 5.
75. SG 21.11.1930 p. 5.
76. Byrne, 1977 op.cit., p. 272.
77. SG 18.8.1930 p. 4.
78. TWAS T95/152 Depositions of witnesses.
79. Ibid.
80. Ibid.
81. SG 19.8.1930 p. 5.
82. A Home Office official, reporting on a visit to South Shields at the end of July 1930, was of the opinion that the Minority Movement was exploiting the coloured seamen and that as a result there was co-operation between the Minority Movement agitators and the coloured boarding-house masters (PRO HO 45/14299 Part 1 Report on visit to North and South Shields on 29 July 1930 initialled J.H.M.).
83. Some of the fears and suspicions aroused among the Arabs by the announcement of the rota system are described in an article by Dr Sheldrake of the Western Islamic Association in the *Shields Daily Gazette* of 9 September 1930 p.5. As late as 21 September 1930, Mohamed Hamed, 2 East Holborn, South Shields, in a letter to the High Commissioner for India, stated that many Arabs were still ignorant of the rules of the new rota system. He maintained that as he was born in Aden and had a British Indian passport he was a British coloured seaman and therefore exempt from the new scheme (PRO CO 725/21/9 Letter from Mohamed Hamed to the Secretary of the High Commissioner, General Department, London dated 21 September 1930). In December 1930 an Arab boarding-house master from South Shields, Ali Hamed Dheli, wrote to the Under Secretary of State for India stating that he had proof that the men boarding with him were born in the Aden Protectorate and asking whether this was sufficient for them to be exempt from the rota (PRO CO 725/21/9 Letter from Mr Ali Hamed Dheli 95 and 103 West Holborn, South Shields to the Under Secretary of State for India and dated 4 December 1930).
84. SG 4.8.1930 p. 5.
85. TWAS T95/152 Depositions of witnesses.

6 After the Storm

1. SG 27.9.1930 p. 5.
2. SG 23.9.1930 p. 7.
3. SG 7.8.1930 p. 7 and 9.8.1930 p. 5.
4. TWAS T95/152 South Shields Seamen's Committee of Action Bulletin dated 6 August 1930.

5. TWAS T95/152 South Shields Seamen's Committee of Action Bulletin dated 11 August 1930.

6. PRO CO 725/21/9 Letter from Abdulla Ali, 1 Tiny Street, South Shields to High Commissioner for India, India House, London dated 3 September 1930.

7. PRO CO 725/21/9 Letters from Ali Hamed Dheli, Abdo Mohsen, Ahmed Cassem, Muro Mocassar and Cassim Ali to the Office of the High Commissioner of India, London dated 10.9.1930.

8. PRO CO 725/21/9 C 79323/30 Draft of letter from Colonial Office to M. Mocassar, A. Cassem and A. Mohsen dated 31 October 1930.

9. PRO HO 14299 Part 1 562899/36 Letter from the Chief Constable, South Shields to W. Porter, Aliens Department, Home Office dated 19 September 1930.

10. SG 26.8.1930 p. 5 and 29.8.1930 p. 7. It is interesting to note that the men who were charged with assault and breach of the peace came from three boarding-houses, Hassan Mohamed's at 132 Commercial Road, Abdul Massin's at 33 East Holborn and Abdu Osman's at 50 Commercial Road. As we know of Hassan Mohamed's involvement in the Arab faction which was in favour of accepting the rota system, Abdul Massin and Osman may also have been part of this group. The episode also suggests that opinion about the rota system may have divided certain tribes in South Shields, with some members opposing the scheme and others favouring its acceptance. The rota system also divided the Arab and Somali community in Cardiff and violence broke out between the different factions in August 1930 (see *Western Mail* 20.8.1930 p. 5 and 16.9.1930 p. 12).

11. SG 8.9.1930 p. 5.

12. Sheldrake declined to elaborate on this point and it is uncertain who or what he was referring to. It is possible that he meant the NUS or perhaps the rivalries between certain Arab boarding-house masters over the shipping of men.

13. By 16 September 1930 only sixteen Arabs and two Somalis had registered under the rota system at Cardiff according to the *Western Mail* 16.9.1930 p. 12.

14. For the full text of Sheldrake's article see SG 9.9.1930 p. 5.

15. PRO CO 725/21/9 Letter from Khalid Sheldrake, Life President, The Western Islamic Association, to the Secretary of State for India, India Office, London dated 18 September 1930.

16. The letter from the Office of the High Commissioner added that they only had responsibility for seamen who were British subjects from Aden colony. As it was understood that almost all of the Adeni seamen in South Shields came from the protectorate, Sheldrake's letter had been sent to the Colonial Office. PRO CO 725/21/9 Letter from the Office

of the High Commissioner for India to Khalid Sheldrake, The Western Islamic Association, dated 6 October 1930.

17. SG 10.9.1930 p. 4.
18. SG 11.9.1930 p. 4.
19. Ibid.
20. SG 23.9.1930 p. 7.
21. PRO HO 45/14299 Part 1 562898/42 Letter from the Chief Constable, South Shields to E.N. Cooper, Home Office, dated 14 October 1930.
22. SG 30.9.1930 p. 5.
23. Evans (1985), op.cit., p. 84.
24. SG 30.9.1930 p. 5.
25. PRO HO 45/14299 Part 1 Cutting from Daily Herald attached to Letter from Chief Constable, South Shields to W. Jagelman, Home Office dated 1 October 1930.
26. SG 30.9.1930 p. 4.
27. Ibid. p. 5.
28. SG 1.10.1930 p. 5.
29. SG 2.10.1930 p. 5.
30. Ibid.
31. SG 1.10.1930 p. 5.
32. SG 2.10.1930 p. 5.
33. Ibid.
34. SG 3.10.1930 p. 6. Dr Sheldrake seems to have misunderstood certain important details of the problem. For example, in the opening paragraph of his letter he refers to the Arabs seeking outdoor relief whereas the whole issue revolved around the fact that they had been denied outdoor relief and were therefore forced to seek indoor relief by entering the Harton Institution.
35. SG 2.10.1930 p. 5.
36. SG 1.10.1930 p. 5.
37. SG 4.10.1930 p. 5.
38. Ibid. p. 4.
39. SG 20.10.1930 p. 4.
40. PRO HO 45/14299 Part 1 562898/37 Letter from the Chief Constable, South Shields to The Under Secretary of State, Home Office, dated 3 October 1930.
41. SG 12.12.1930 p. 7.
42. SG 8.10.1930 p. 7.
43. SG 12.12.1930 p. 7.
44. SG 10.12.1930 p. 5.
45. SG 30.1.1931 p. 2.
46. PRO HO 45/14299 Part 1 Letter from Chief Constable, South Shields to The Under Secretary of State, Aliens Department, Home Office, London dated 15 September 1930.

47. PRO HO 45/14299 Part 2 562898/51 Extract from the proceedings of a conference of immigration inspectors held at the Home Office on 14 October 1930.

48. SG 24.12.1931 p. 1.

49. At a conference held at the Colonial Office in September 1930 to consider the question of the maintenance and repatriation of Adeni seamen, Mr Cooper from the Home Office stated that it was possible that if the circumstances warranted it the Home Secretary would be prepared to consider the question of the deportation of all coloured persons other than those who were British subjects, but that such a policy would be a departure from the normal procedure and would need careful consideration. PRO HO 45/14299 Part 2 562898/53 Minutes of a conference held at the Colonial Office on 4 September 1930 to consider the question of the maintenance and repatriation of Adenese seamen.

50. SG 10.4.1935 p. 1.

51. SG 16.4.1936 p. 5.

52. Evans, 1985 op.cit., pp. 85–6.

53. SG 3.9.1935 p. 5.

54. SG 3.9.1935 p. 5 and 4.9.1935 p. 5.

55. These restrictions were imposed by the Aden Passport Office in February 1935 on the basis of instructions from the Home Office in November 1934 (PRO CO 725/31/3 Letter from the Resident, Aden to the Secretary of State for the Colonies, dated 16 April 1935). The Resident's request for some modification to the instructions was rejected by the Home Office in July 1935 and the restrictions confirmed in a letter from the Secretary of State for the Colonies to the Acting Resident, Aden dated 23 July 1935 (PRO CO 725/54/9 Colonial Office Memorandum entitled 'The restrictions of facilities for Adenese seamen who wish to proceed to the United Kingdom in search of employment (1938)').

56. PRO CO 725/31/3 Letter from the Resident, Aden to the Secretary of State for the Colonies, dated 16 April 1935.

57. PRO CO 725/31/3 Letter from the Under Secretary of State, Aliens Department, Home Office to the Under Secretary of State, Colonial Office, dated 2 July 1935.

58. PRO CO 725/31/3 Letter from Constable R.J. Hetherington, Chief Constable's Office, South Shields to the Chief Constable, South Shields dated 24 April 1935 to be forwarded to the Under Secretary of State, Home Office.

59. PRO CO 725/54/9 Draft note of a meeting at the Colonial Office on 13 October 1938 on the question of the admission of Adenese seamen into the United Kingdom. The statistics on the number of coloured seamen registered under the Special Restriction (Coloured Alien

Seamen) Order 1925 were presented at the meeting by Mr Cooper of the Aliens Department, Home Office.

60. SG 20.1.1936 p. 2.
61. SG 16.4.1936 p. 5; 30.5.1936 p. 8; 7.8.1936 p. 6; 5.10.1936 p. 5.
62. SG 5.6.1936 p. 6.
63. PRO 725/54/9 Letter from Sir Bernard Reilly, Governor, Aden to W.G.A. Ormsby-Gore, Secretary of State for the Colonies, dated 16 March 1938.
64. For an account of the meeting see PRO CO 735/54/9 Draft note of meeting at the Colonial Office on 13 October 1938 on the question of the admission of Adenese seamen into the United Kingdom.
65. PRO CO 725/54/9 Adenese seamen: miscellaneous correspondence; note signed K.W. Blaxter and dated 1.2.39.

7 Mixed Marriages and Moral Outrage

1. SG 15.4.1913 p. 4.
2. Evans (1980), op.cit., p. 9.
3. SG 20.7.1916 p. 4.
4. SG 9.12.1921 p. 5.
5. Ibid.
6. SG 12.3.1919 p. 3.
7. SG 4.8.1917 p. 3.
8. SG 12.5.1917 p. 3.
9. SG 20.6.1931 p. 7.
10. SG 16.3.1923 p. 5; 5.7.1923 p. 3 and 8.8.1923 p. 3.
11. SG 16.3.1923 p. 5.
12. Evans (1985), op.cit., pp. 86–98.
13. M.E. Fletcher, *Report on an investigation into the colour problem in Liverpool and other ports* (Liverpool Association for the Welfare of Half-caste Children, Liverpool, 1930), p. 38.
14. Ibid. p. 58.
15. Ibid. pp. 38–39.
16. SG 17.3.1923 p. 2.
17. SG 20.3.1923 p. 4.
18. Ibid.
19. SG 18.2.1929 p. 4.
20. Ibid.
21. SG 21.3.1923 p. 4.
22. Ibid.
23. SG 23.3.1923 p. 4.
24. SG 14.2.1929 p. 4.
25. SG 15.2.1929 p. 5.
26. Similar issues were raised in Cardiff as an excuse to tighten controls

over the coloured population and to segregate Black people within Butetown. See Evans (1985), op.cit., pp. 93–5.

27. SG 7.2.1929 p. 2.
28. SG 2.1.1930 p. 6.
29. SG 9.2.1929 p. 4.
30. SG 8.2.1929 p. 6.
31. SG 2.5.1929 p. 2.
32. Ibid.
33. Ibid.
34. SG 6.6.1929 p. 2.
35. SG 9.1.1930 p. 4.
36. SG 22.1.1930 p. 4.
37. SG 3.4.1930 p. 5.
38. Ibid. p. 4.
39. Ibid.
40. SG 28.1.1935 p. 1.
41. SG 18.1.1935 p. 5.
42. SG 28.1.1935 p. 1.
43. SG 31.1.1935 p. 3.
44. Ibid. Salem Abuzed's claim that Arabs in Cardiff could live where they liked was incorrect. Evans has shown that Cardiff City Council imposed stringent controls to restrict the Arab population to Butetown. See Evans (1985), op.cit., p. 97. This is one of a number of examples where the Arabs in South Shields attempted to argue that the treatment of their fellow countrymen by the local authorities in Cardiff was better than that which they received in South Shields. In most cases the evidence does not support their argument.
45. SG 31.1.1935 p. 3.
46. Ibid.
47. Ibid.
48. SG 7.2.1935 p. 3.
49. Ibid.
50. Ibid.
51. SG 20.2.1935 p. 3.
52. SG 13.3.1935 p. 3.
53. Ibid.
54. Ibid.
55. SG 18.3.1935 p. 5.
56. SG 11.4.1935 p. 2.
57. SG 13.6.1935 p. 3.
58. SG 25.9.1935 p. 5.
59. SG 7.5.1936 p. 11.
60. SG 17.3.1937 p. 5.
61. SG 1.4.1937 p. 5.

62. SG 29.3.1937 p. 1.
63. SG 1.4.1937 p. 5.
64. SG 9.10.1937 p. 5.
65. Ibid.
66. Ibid.
67. SG 15.10.1937 p. 9.
68. Collins (1957), op.cit., p. 157.
69. Ibid. p. 156.

8 Religious Revival and Political Rivalries

1. SG 20.4.1936 p. 4.
2. SG 20.1.1931 p. 5.
3. SG 15.3.1935 p. 3.
4. SG 29.3.1936 p. 5.
5. Collins (1957), op.cit., p. 182.
6. SG 20.1.1931 p. 5.
7. It is also worth noting that in the South Shields courts a copy of the Qur'an was available for use by Arabs who were called to take the oath before giving evidence. An interesting case on this subject was reported in the *Shields Daily Gazette* in January 1925 entitled 'Taking the Oath—Trouble with Arabs at Shields County Court.' At the hearing, the solicitor Victor Grunhut, explained that in the police court a Muslim touched his forehead with the Bible and said he would speak the truth. The Judge commented that if he did that with the Bible it was an inducement to lie. After some observation was made to Mr Grunhut, he admitted that he was mistaken and stated that they did it with the Qur'an. A copy of the Qur'an was obtained and the witness was sworn in properly (SG 29.1.1925 p. 5).
8. SG 29.1.1916 p. 3.
9. SG 20.3.1917 p. 4.
10. SG 14.2.1935 p. 5 The Shemeri (Shamiri) and Shari referred to in the article are two of the 'seafaring tribes' of south-west Arabia (see Chapter Two, p. 40). 'Malaiki' does not appear to be the name of a tribe and the writer may have been referring to the Maliki *madhahib*, one of the four recognized rites of Sunni Islam. If so, there appears to have been some misunderstanding as the vast majority of Arab seamen from Yemen and the Aden Protectorate belonged to the Shafi'i *madhahib*. Line 12 should read '*La Ilah illa Allah* or '*llah(u) . . .*'.
11. Collins (1957), op.cit., pp. 188–9. Collins also describes in detail the preparation of the corpse for the funeral ritual. For other descriptions of funerals see SG 26.5.1919 p. 3 and 20.5.1936 p. 5.
12. Collins (1957), op.cit., p. 187.
13. This translation, made by the Colonial Office, is found in PRO CO

876/26 Letter from J.L. Keith to Mr Clauson dated 3.2.1942. The original document was in the possession of Sheikh Hasan Ismail.

14. SG 20.9.1926 p. 2.
15. Ibid.
16. Ibid.
17. SG 1.11.1930 p. 4.
18. Muhammad Mashuq Ally, *History of Muslims in Britain*, 1850–1980 unpublished MA thesis (University of Birmingham, 1981), p.77.
19. SG 11.3.1919 p. 2.
20. PRO HO 45/12314 476761/10 Letter from Dr Majid to the Under Secretary of State, India Office, dated 16 April 1925.
21. SG 21.8.1929 p. 5.
22. SG 18.3.1930 p. 5.
23. SG 8.9.1930 p. 5.
24. SG 25.9.1930 p. 5.
25. SG 24.9.1935 p. 5.
26. PRO CO 725/54/7 Report from Constable R.J. Hetherington to the Chief Constable, South Shields dated 8 October 1938.
27. PRO CO 725/66/17 Letter from the Chief Constable, South Shields to the Director, the British Broadcasting Corporation, Newcastle upon Tyne dated 28 November 1938. 'Allawouia' should probably be 'Allaouia' a combination of French and English for Alawiya.
28. PRO CO 876/26 Letter from Tualla Mahamad, Secretary, International Young Somali Society, Cardiff to J.L. Keith, Colonial Office, London dated 3 February 1942.
29. Collins (1957), op.cit., p. 176, note 1, stated incorrectly that these 'Alawi were a sub-sect of the Shi'a. The 'Alawi *tariqa* belongs to the majority Sunni sect of Islam.
30. For a discussion of the life and beliefs of Sheikh Ahmad ibn Mustafa al-'Alawi see Martin Lings, *A sufi saint of the twentieth century* (George Allen and Unwin Ltd, London, second edition 1971).
31. R.B. Serjeant, 'Yemeni Arabs in Britain', *The Geographical Magazine*, 1/3 (August 1944) p.143.
32. Collins (1957), op.cit., p.178, note 2.
33. Leigh Douglas, op.cit., p.69 and p.101. Sheikh Abdullah's two books are *Kitab din Allah wahid* (The Book of the One God's Religion) n.p., n.d. and *Kitab al-as'ila wa'l-ajwiba* (The Book of Questions and Answers) n.p., n.d.
34. SG 6.5.1938 p. 1.
35. Collins (1957), op.cit., p. 179.
36. Ibid. p. 180.
37. SG 10.4.1937 p. 3.
38. Lings, op.cit., p. 114.
39. SG 22.2.1937 p. 3.

40. SG 6.12.1937 p. 3.
41. SG 16.8.1937 p. 2.
42. Serjeant (1944), op.cit., p. 147.
43. Collins (1957), op.cit., pp. 206–07.
44. This is an argument put forward by Neil Evans with reference to the Arab community in Cardiff. See Evans (1985), op.cit., p. 102.
45. Lings, op.cit., p. 114.
46. SG 19.11.1936 p. 5.
47. SG 9.3.1937 p. 1.
48. Ibid.
49. SG 30.7.1937 p. 7.
50. For reports on the case see SG 30.7.1937 p. 7; 10.8.1937 p. 5; 1.9.1937 p. 3 and 21.9.1937 p. 5.
51. PRO CO 725/61/8 Colonial Office memorandum signed K.W. Blaxter and dated 1.12.1938. Collins states that some couples who had been married in accordance with English law went through a second form of marriage according to Islamic law after Sheikh Abdullah's arrival in South Shields. See Collins (1957), op.cit., p. 174.
52. SG 16.2.1938 p. 5.
53. Ibid.
54. Collins (1957), op.cit., p. 206.
55. SG 16.12.1936 p. 4 and 18.12.1936 p. 9.
56. For reports on these meetings see SG 30.4.1937 p. 9; 24.5.1937 p. 1; 31.5.1937 p. 7; 3.6.1937 p. 1 and 8.6.1937 p. 5.
57. SG 6.5.1938 p. 1.
58. SG 29.10.1938 p. 8.
59. PRO CO 725/61/8 Letter from Stewart Perowne to Blaxter, Colonial Office containing draft greeting from the Governor of Aden to the South Shields community dated 21.11.38 for Sir Bernard Reilly's signature.
60. PRO CO 725/66/17 Letter from the Chief Constable, South Shields to the Director, the British Broadcasting Corporation, Newcastle dated 28 November 1938 enclosing letter from Yussif Hersi Sulliman to Mr Perowne dated 26 November 1938.
61. PRO CO 725/66/17 Letter from the Chief Constable, South Shields to the Director, the British Broadcasting Corporation, Newcastle dated 28 November 1938.
62. PRO 725/66/17 Letter from Sir Bernard Reilly, Governor of Aden, to the Right Honourable Malcolm MacDonald, Principal Secretary of State for the Colonies dated 18 January 1939.
63. PRO CO 725/61/8 Memorandum addressed to Sir John Shuckburgh and dated 9.11.1938.
64. SG 29.6.1942 p. 4.
65. SG 19.2.1938 p. 3.

66. SG 20.8.1938 p. 1.
67. SG 13.11.1939 p. 4 and 6.1.1941 p. 2.
68. Serjeant (1944), op.cit., p. 147.
69. Collins (1957), op.cit., p. 180.
70. Ibid. pp. 180–1.
71. For a detailed analysis of the Free Yemeni Movement see Leigh Douglas, op.cit.
72. I am grateful to the late Professor R.B. Serjeant for this information.
73. Leigh Douglas, op.cit., p. 69.
74. Ibid. p. 101.
75. Ibid. p. 169.
76. The text of the letter is quoted in Collins (1957), op.cit., pp. 225–6.
77. SG 22.5.1937 p. 3.
78. *Western Mail* 28.5.1937 p. 13.
79. PRO CO 725/77/6 Relations with Yemen. See notes by Sir Bernard Reilly dated 23.11.1942 and 26.11.1942.
80. PRO FO 371/104543 EM1063/2 Letter from R. Sarell, Foreign Office to Sir Bernard Reilly, Colonial Office dated 19 September 1952.
81. The report can be found in PRO CO 537/3966 78009/1 Part III Letter from Champion to Sir Bernard Reilly dated 4 September 1948.
82. For a more detailed account of these rivalries see R.I. Lawless, 'Religion and politics among Arab seafarers in Britain in the early twentieth century', in *Islam and Christian–Muslim Relations* Vol. 5, No. 1 (1994) pp. 35–56.
83. Collins (1957), op.cit., p. 215.
84. Ibid. p. 177.
85. Ibid. p. 208.
86. IOR/R/20/B/2351 Aden Intelligence Summary period ending 30 September 1952, note 236.
87. PRO FO 371/98586 EM 1671/3 Letter from R. Sarell, Foreign Office to Sir Bernard Reilly, Colonial Office dated 19 September 1952.
88. PRO CO 1015/312 Letter from the Commissioner of Police, Aden to the Chief Constable, Cardiff City Police dated 4 February 1953.
89. Leigh-Douglas, op.cit., p. 170.
90. PRO CO 1015/312 Telegram from the Acting Governor, Aden to the Secretary of State for the Colonies, London dated 18 July 1953. A copy of the judgement of the Court of Appeal for Eastern Africa is found in PRO CO 1015/312 Telegram from Acting Governor, Aden to Secretary of State for the Colonies, London dated 30 July 1953.
91. PRO FO 371/104543 EM 1063/5 Letter from M.B. Jacomb, British Legation, Ta'izz, Yemen to Principal Secretary for Foreign Affairs, London dated 1 March 1953. The letter contains a detailed report on Sheikh Abdullah Ali al-Hakimi and the activites of the Yemeni Union together with a copy of the constitution of the union.

92. Leigh Douglas, op.cit., p. 180, note 80.
93. IOR/ R/20/B Report on the Yemeni Union by The Adviser and British Agent, W.A.P. Office, Aden (Ref:L/49/26) dated 20 June 1954.

9 The Post-War Years: Integration and Assimilation

1. Sean Carey, 'The Geordie Arabs', *New Society* (10 May 1984) p. 214.
2. Byrne (1992), op.cit.
3. SG 23.6.1942 p. 3.
4. Barry Carr, 'Black Geordies', in *Geordies; roots of regionalism*, edited by Robert Colls and Bill Lancaster (Edinburgh University Press, Edinburgh, 1992), p. 137.
5. Byrne (1992), op.cit.
6. Collins (1957), op.cit., p. 197.
7. Byrne (1977), op.cit., p. 275.
8. On the Yemenis who moved into industrial employment in the Midlands see Halliday, op.cit., especially Chapter Three.
9. Collins (1957), op.cit., pp. 170–1.
10. Ibid. p. 216.
11. Ibid. p. 212.
12. SG 14.7.1972 p. 3.
13. Halliday, op.cit., p. 118.
14. Zubayda Umar, 'Yemen to South Shields', *Inquiry* (May 1985) p. 63.

Index

jobs 77–112; disputes with boarding-house masters 50–52; illegal entry into Britain of 65–72, 100, 107–12; moral dangers of 174–94; police action against 80–83, 100, 105, 107, 110–112, 133, 135–52, 166, 168, 175–77; political rivalries among 237–44; popular hostility to 86–98; recruitment of 16–23; regulation and repatriation of 98–112; relations with tribal sheikhs 44–46; religious life of 207–36; and the rota system 126–60; service during World War One and Two of 11–15, 76–77, 245–46; tribal origins of 40–41; unemployment among 70–73, 115, 161–73
al-Baida 40
Board of Trade 48, 62, 64, 69, 78, 98, 99, 103, 104, 105, 114–17, 127, 171, 172
British Shipping (Assistance) Act, 1935 167–70

Cardiff 9, 19, 28, 41, 47, 63, 66, 68, 79, 105, 107, 112, 120, 126, 127, 131, 157, 161, 179, 180, 212, 217–18, 220, 230, 236, 237, 239–44
Colonial Office 34, 45, 79, 102, 103, 116, 156, 168, 171, 173, 234, 235
Communist Party 79, 123, 133, 135–7
    Tyneside District Party Committee of the 135–36

Dalali 40, 41, 249
Dhala, Amir of 44–45, 168–69
Dheli, Ali Hamed, 41, 68, 154, 156, 158, 160, 164

dhikr 224–25
Djibouti 39, 66, 67

Free Yemeni Movement 237–44

hajj (pilgrimage) 169, 209, 236
al-Hakimi, Sheikh Abdullah Ali and the education of Arab children 220, 236; and the Islamic revival in South Shields 200–236; political activities of 237–44
'half caste' children, problem of 77, 114, 119, 120, 174, 180–81
Hamid, Ali 187, 189–90, 246
Harrison, William 128, 132, 138–40, 146, 147, 149
Hassan, Ali 10, 13, 53, 61, 74, 174
Hassan, Said 50, 51, 61, 72, 192, 239–40
Hassan, Said Saleh 13, 19
Holborn 10, 11, 13, 49, 50, 51, 54, 72, 74, 81, 83, 133, 146, 153, 154, 164, 176, 177, 178, 187, 190, 192, 193, 194, 199, 201, 202, 203, 206, 208, 216, 247
Home Office, 15, 24, 26, 65, 69, 72, 73, 98, 99, 103–09, 111, 114, 115, 127, 160, 166, 168, 169, 171–73
Hujariya 33, 40
Hull 28, 64, 100, 106, 113, 120, 126, 127, 165, 202, 237
Hussein, Prince (of Yemen) 232 visit to South Shields of 239–40

Ibb 24, 40
'Id al-Adha 208, 221–22
'Id al-Fitr 208–09, 222–23, 233
al-Ihtifal, festival of 223, 231
Immigration Office 15, 70, 102, 107, 110, 112, 160

India
  Office 79, 84, 85, 98, 111, 115,
    154, 156, 158, 160, 215, 216.
  Office of the High
    Commissioner for 68, 79,
    108–9
International Class War Prisoners'
  Aid Committee 146
Islam
  in South Shields 207–232
  women converts to 214–15,
    220, 231, 236
Islamic
  festivals 208, 220–24
  law
    marriages according to
      228–30
  processions 220–24
  Society 84–86, 111, 215–16
Ismail, Sheikh Hasan 212–13,
  241–43

Jubani 40, 41, 249

Laygate 202, 205, 206, 232,
  247–49
Liverpool, 9, 28, 79, 104, 106,
  180, 237, 241

Ma'alla 31
Mabrouk, Said, 51–52, 63, 64,
  65, 131, 145, 162, 197
Majid, Dr Abdul 84–86, 111,
  215–16
marriages
  mixed 174–87
  popular feelings on 180–87
  according to Islamic law 228–30
Marseilles, 19, 26, 66, 67, 110,
  219, 236
Messageries Maritimes Steam
  Navigation Company 18,
  21–22, 31, 40, 44
Mill Dam 49, 53, 61, 74, 75, 80,
  82, 123, 131, 135–53, 205,
  232, 247

Mohamed, Hassan 50, 68,
  116, 132, 142, 156, 189,
  216–18
mosque
  campaign for 216, 231–36
Muckble, Muhammad, 11–12, 23,
  49, 54, 56, 63, 72, 133, 152,
  210
Muslim
  burials 209–11
  festivals 208, 220–24
  marriages 228–30
  processions 220–24

Nahdat al-Sufiya al-'Alawiya 212
National Union of Seamen
  and the Seamen's Minority
    Movement 124–35; campaign
    against the Arabs of 78,
    103–104, 113–121; and the
    rota system 126–35
naturalization
  Arab seamen apply for 169–70

O'Donnell, Peter 131, 132, 135,
  137–40, 144, 145, 147, 152,
  159, 163

police
  action against Arabs in South
    Shields 80–83, 100, 105,
    107, 110–112, 133, 135–52,
    166, 168, 175–77
P & O 18, 22, 31

racism 74–84, 86–98, 148–52
Radaa 40
religion see Islam
rota system
  introduction of 126–28;
    resistance to 128–60

Said, Ali 10, 23, 49, 50, 51, 53,
  58, 61, 62, 68, 75, 92, 128,
  130, 131–133, 138–40,
  145–47, 150–52, 156, 158,